EDWARD THE BLACK PRINCE

The Medieval World

Series editor: Julia Smith, University of St Andrews

EDWARD THE BLACK PRINCE

POWER IN MEDIEVAL EUROPE

DAVID GREEN

PEARSON

Longman

Harlow, England • London • New York • Boston • San Francisco • Toronto
Sydney • Tokyo • Singapore • Hong Kong • Seoul • Taipei • New Delhi
Cape Town • Madrid • Mexico City • Amsterdam • Munich • Paris • Milan

PEARSON EDUCATION LIMITED

Edinburgh Gate
Harlow CM20 2JE
United Kingdom
Tel: +44 (0)1279 623623
Fax: +44 (0)1279 431059
Website: www.pearsoned.co.uk

First edition published in Great Britain in 2007

© Pearson Education Limited 2007

The right of David Green to be identified as author
of this work has been asserted by him in accordance
with the Copyright, Designs and Patents Act 1988.

ISBN-13: 978-0-582-78481-9
ISBN-10: 0-582-78481-6

British Library Cataloguing in Publication Data
A CIP catalogue record for this book can be obtained from the British Library

Library of Congress Cataloging in Publication Data
A CIP catalog record for this book can be obtained from the Library of Congress

10 9 8 7 6 5 4 3 2 1
10   09   08   07   06

Set by 35 in 10.5/13pt Galliard
Printed in Malaysia

The Publisher's policy is to use paper manufactured from sustainable forests.

For WTS and ASAB-Musketeers

PLANTAGENET – CAPETIAN/VALOIS DYNASTIES

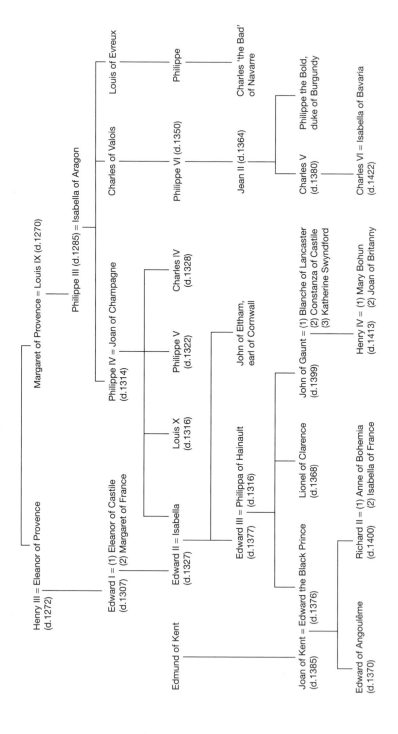

Henry III = Eleanor of Provence
(d.1272)

Margaret of Provence = Louis IX (d.1270)

Philippe III (d.1285) = Isabella of Aragon

Edward I = (1) Eleanor of Castile
(d.1307)   (2) Margaret of France

Edmund of Kent

Philippe IV = Joan of Champagne
(d.1314)

Charles of Valois

Louis of Evreux

Louis X
(d.1316)

Philippe V
(d.1322)

Charles IV
(d.1328)

Philippe VI (d.1350)

Philippe

Edward II = Isabella
(d.1327)

John of Eltham,
earl of Cornwall

Jean II (d.1364)

Charles 'the Bad'
of Navarre

Edward III = Philippa of Hainault
(d.1377)

Lionel of Clarence
(d.1368)

John of Gaunt = (1) Blanche of Lancaster
(d.1399)   (2) Constanza of Castile
                  (3) Katherine Swyndford

Charles V
(d.1380)

Philippe the Bold,
duke of Burgundy

Joan of Kent = Edward the Black Prince
(d.1385)   (d.1376)

Henry IV = (1) Mary Bohun
(d.1413)   (2) Joan of Britanny

Charles VI = Isabella of Bavaria
(d.1422)

Richard II = (1) Anne of Bohemia
(d.1400)   (2) Isabella of France

Edward of Angoulême
(d.1370)

CONTENTS

LIST OF MAPS AND PLATES

SERIES EDITOR'S PREFACE

Among the royalty of medieval England, Edward of Woodstock – known to history as the Black Prince – is one of the most famous but least understood. Black boar and flower of chivalry, generous master and tyrannical lord, the eldest son of Edward III was born to rule but died in his prime, leaving a reputation which was as glorious as it was dark in his own times. No one knows the sources for this enigmatic prince better than Dr David Green: Longman's Medieval World welcomes this fine study of the man and his age. But this is no narrow study of a would-be king. The Black Prince was earl of Chester, duke of Cornwall, prince of Wales and of Aquitaine, and David Green offers us a study of the realities of power in the late medieval world on a similarly broad canvas. Its geographical breadth is matched by the insights the Black Prince's career affords into all the central issues of the fourteenth century: the fluctuating course of the century-long struggle between England and France; the massive social and economic consequences of the Black Death; the rise of parliament but the strengthening ideas of royal sovereignty; chivalry as an inherited ideal at odds with the realities of new forms of warfare and new elite status groups; exuberant forms of religious piety and outbreaks of heresy.

In the pages which follow, we watch Edward III's eldest son asserting his power in the context of, and in response to, the tumultuous changes reordering the world around him. Whilst keeping the reader firmly focused on the Black Prince's interests, Dr Green also introduces us to the changing fourteenth-century fashions in everything from military technology to princely apparel and religious patronage. We also meet the Prince's family, friends, retainers, admirers – and critics. By end of the book, the Black Prince has emerged as a more human, less exceptional figure than his glamorous reputation would suggest. He becomes a man of his day, typifying its mindset and its values. Above all, David Green presents us with a prince caught within forces of change that no contemporary could ever have identified or understood. It takes a historian of Dr Green's ability to identify them for us – and to present the Black Prince not as an icon of his age, but as a window into it.

Julia M.H. Smith

PUBLISHER'S ACKNOWLEDGEMENTS

We are grateful to the following for permission to reproduce copyright material:

Plates 1, 4, 5, 6, 7, 8, 9 and 10 from the British Library, Plates 11 and 12 from Christ Church College with the kind permission of the Governing Body of Christ Church, Oxford, Plate 13 from The Bridgeman Art Library.

In some instances we have been unable to trace the owners of copyright material, and we would appreciate any information that would enable us to do so.

AUTHOR'S ACKNOWLEDGEMENTS

This book was conceived and written during time spent at the Universities of St Andrews, Sheffield and Dublin. Thanks are due to all friends and colleagues who have helped with suggestions, references and ideas. Various aspects of the research on which the book is based have been explored in conferences and seminars and I thank the conveners for the opportunities and insights these provided. In particular, mention must be made of the annual sessions organised by the Society of the White Hart (University of Western Michigan) and the Society for Fourteenth-Century Studies (University of Leeds). Both have ensured that the fourteenth century is a very happy time in which to work – certainly infinitely better than one in which to live.

My thanks to those at Pearson, especially Hetty Reid, Ben Roberts, Julie Knight and Christina Wipf Perry who have been patient and unfailingly helpful. Thanks also to Caroline Hamilton for her help with the index when time was short.

I am especially grateful to those who have read and commented on what follows. Michael Prestwich, Chris Given-Wilson, Gwilym Dodd and Niav Gallagher all gave me valuable advice on individual chapters. Patrick Healy and Freya Verstraten ('woestijnratten lopen op clompjes') helped greatly with particular sections.

Michael Jones, as of old, was kind enough to read a (nearly) complete first draft and put me right on a number of things. Not least he ensured that Edward III had a miraculous year in 1346 rather than something quite different.

Julia Smith first suggested I might like to write something for the Series and guided my, often faltering, steps throughout the process. I am deeply indebted to her for all her help.

ABBREVIATIONS

BIHR	*Bulletin of the Institute of Historical Research*
BL	British Library
BPR	*The Register of Edward the Black Prince Preserved in the Public Record Office*, ed. M.C.B. Dawes, 4 vols (London, 1930–33)
CCR	*Calendar of Close Rolls*
CPR	*Calendar of Patent Rolls*
EcHR	*Economic History Review*
EHR	*English Historical Review*
GEC	G.E. Cockayne, *The Complete Peerage*, 13 vols (London, 1910–59)
ODNB	*Oxford Dictionary of National Biography* (Oxford, 2004)
PRO	Public Record Office (National Archives)
Rymer	Thomas Rymer, *Feodera, conventiones, literæ, et cujuscunque generis acta publica, inter reges Angliæ* etc. (2 editions, 1704–35; 1816–69)
SCH	Studies in Church History
TRHS	*Transactions of the Royal Historical Society*
VCH	*Victoria County History*

A NOTE ON MONEY

In England the basic monetary units were: the silver penny ('d.'); the shilling ('s.', worth 12d.); and the pound ('£', worth 20s. or 240d.). A mark was a unit of account worth two-thirds of a pound (13s. 4d.).

In France the units were: a *livre* (*l*) worth 20 *sous*, each with the value of 12 *deniers*. The value of the *livre* varied a great deal depending on its place of origin (Tours, Paris, Bordeaux) and levels of devaluation. £1 sterling was usually valued as: 5–6 *livres tournois* (*l.t.*); 5–6 *livres bordelais* (*l.b.*); 4–5 *livres parisis* (*l.p.*).

Other coins in circulation included: the florin, which varied in value (36d. sterling in 1338); the French *écu* (depreciating value, worth 40d. sterling in 1360); and the French *mouton* (first minted in 1355 and worth 4s. 10d). In 1344 the English gold noble was introduced, valued at 6s. 8d. The Castilian *doblas* was worth about 4s.

GLOSSARY

Advowson – the right to present a clergyman to a bishop for appointment to an ecclesiastical benefice.

Affinity/Retinue – a characteristic feature of 'bastard feudalism', comprising a network of servants and supporters that assisted a magnate in local affairs, in his household, and on military campaign. Such men might be contracted to serve in a variety of ways including the payment of annuities, the grant of household privileges, and indentures (both for life service and more limited durations).

Appanage – arrangement for the support of children of a royal person, usually property set aside to be held by a younger son. The Capetian and Valois kings adopted an *'appanage* policy' by which the French royal domain was divided into a number of semi-independent territorial units of which Burgundy became the most powerful.

Black Prince's Register (abbrev. *BPR*) – records of the prince's household and estates, held in National Archives, PRO E36/144,278–280; calendared, edited and translated in *The Register of Edward the Black Prince Preserved in the Public Record Office*, ed. M.C.B. Dawes, 4 vols (London, 1930–33). Very little remains of the North Wales register and the material concerning Gascony has been lost.

Bouche de/en court – the right to eat at a lord's table; a household privilege often granted in return for service or as part of a contract with a member of a retinue/affinity, possibly in addition to wages or an annuity.

Chevauchées – military raiding expeditions conducted by English armies in France with the intention of destroying revenue and resources. They may have been deliberately provocative, aiming to force the French into a pitched battle.

Condotierri – a military leader who contracted (*condotta*) mercenaries under his command.

Fletcher – a maker of or dealer in bows and arrows.

Joachite – beliefs and attitudes influenced by the Cistercian abbot, Joachim of Flora (d. 1202), who wrote mystical treatises about the unfolding pattern of history, based on scriptural analysis. His works were regarded as prophetic.

Lollardy – insulting name applied, sometimes wrongly, to the heretical beliefs held by the followers of John Wyclif (d. 1384). Wyclif attacked the papacy, the secular authority of the Church, the doctrine of transubstantiation, masses for the dead, pilgrimages, and the veneration of images. The beliefs of the later Lollards were strongly influenced by unorthodox interpretations of the New Testament which became available to them as they translated the Bible into the vernacular.

Staple (wool) – a place designated by royal ordinance as a special centre of commerce.

Trailbaston – judicial commissions first instituted by Edward I in 1304 to deal with outlaws and those that benefited from criminality.

Wardship – the right to control the property of a deceased individual whose heir was a minor. Revenues might be used as the guardian saw fit, but the property was to be returned to the ward in good condition when he reached his majority. Wardships were often granted by or purchased from the king.

Map 1   Places mentioned in the text

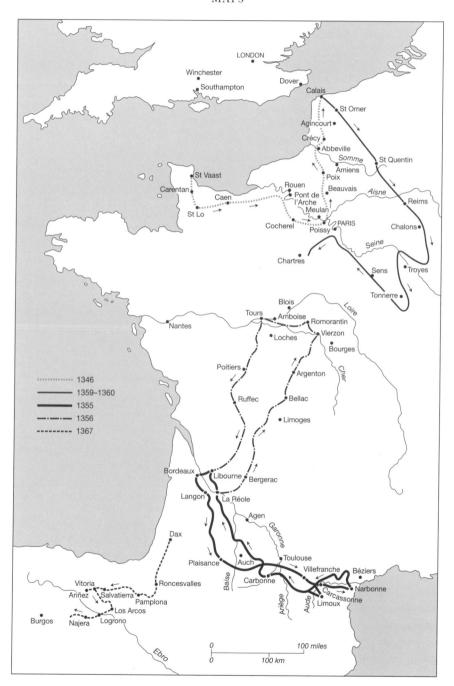

Map 2   The Black Prince's Military Campaigns

INTRODUCTION: THE KING'S SON

... the most valiant prince in all the world. The most valiant there has been since the time of Charlemagne, Julius Caesar or Arthur ... the flower of chivalry.[1]

There is a certain incongruity that the man whom history for reasons of her own has called the Black Prince was the brightest bloom in a field of chivalric flowers. But such an apparent contradiction is entirely appropriate, characterising as it does the career of Edward of Woodstock and the incongruities of the age in which he lived for a few brief years.

That age, the fourteenth century, was calamitous we are told; it saw the middle ages waning and a sad decline from the height of medieval culture.[2] It saw economic and social catastrophes in the Great Famine and the Black Death; it saw endemic warfare between England and France that entangled Scotland, Castile, Portugal, the Low Countries and the Empire. The basic fabric of society was rent and its hierarchies threatened in the tumult of the Jacquerie and the Peasants' Revolt. The very conception of Christendom shifted with the loss of the Holy Land, the dissolution of the Order of the Temple,[3] the enforced relocation of the bishop of Rome to Avignon, and the Great Schism.[4] The approach of the Ottoman Turks and the crushing defeat of the crusading army at Nicopolis in 1396 only compounded the discomfort. In England two kings were deposed and probably murdered, while kings of France and Scotland suffered the indignity of defeat in battle and imprisonment. There were outbreaks of heresy, anti-Jewish pogroms and visions of the apocalypse.

For the majority in Britain and France, the fourteenth century must have been appalling. If not facing the common struggle against hunger, most people were attempting to cope with the inexplicable horror of the Black Death and, if in France, having to deal with the depredations of English armies or the mercenary Free Companies. Yet even here we see incongruities, for the horror of plague weakened the shackles that bound the peasantry to its lords and reshaped the socio-economic relationship in their favour.

And this was also the century of Dante and Boccaccio, of Machaut and Chaucer, of the Gawain poet, of Froissart and the Limburg brothers, and of the Wilton Diptych. There was the growth of a form of representative government, of lay education and literacy. Less commendable perhaps, but no less noteworthy, was the development of gunpowder and artillery, of professional armies, and of the machinery of bureaucracy.

The Black Prince's career highlights the incongruities of the age in which he lived, a period when 'English society was in greater flux . . . than at any time between the eleventh and twentieth centuries'.[5] It also serves as a paradigm for the English experience in the Hundred Years War, albeit one with a number of interesting and significant distinctions. As the future king, a title he never inherited, the prince was central to a war effort that employed innovative and professional military techniques while simultaneously delighting in the ancient traditions of chivalry. Indeed, his example was the spur for one of the earliest chivalric verse biographies, written by the anonymous herald of Sir John Chandos, himself a close associate of the prince and a prominent military and political figure.[6] Similarly, Jean Froissart, the foremost chronicler of chivalry and the Hundred Years War, chose the Black Prince to be one of his leading protagonists and in so doing shaped the character of the chivalric image, an image often seemingly at odds with the new realities of the battlefield.

It is as a military leader that the Black Prince is remembered, and his victories in the battles of Crécy (1346), Poitiers (1356, where he captured King Jean II of France) and at Nájera (1367) in Castile are testimony to his abilities. But he was far more than just a martial captain. As earl of Chester (from 1333), duke of Cornwall (from 1337), and prince of Wales (from 1343) and Aquitaine (1362–72), he was a leading political figure, important domestically and on the international stage. He was closely involved with the English parliament, European diplomacy and issues of local government in which he often came into contact and conflict with important members of the local nobility, particularly in Wales and Aquitaine.

The life of the Black Prince not only demonstrates the incongruities of his time but also the changing nature of power in later medieval Europe. He was born at a time when royal power was subject to great strain and during his life he witnessed many other changes in the characterisation and implementation of authority. Indeed, in the course of his career he directly influenced changes in a variety of fields – social, cultural, political and religious.

This book explores changes in theories and structures of power and especially in its application and manifestation. By tracing some of the main events of the prince's life (and death) it aims to highlight and explain changing claims to power and the various ways by which it was shown and implemented in the later middle ages. Consequently, it examines changes on the battlefield and in the preparation of armies in a period of sustained military conflict. It considers the demonstration of aristocratic and royal power through the chivalric ethic, itself under great strain at this time. It examines the prince's household to discuss the restructuring of political society and changes in the role and status of the nobility and the emergent gentry. Bound up with such change was the lingering demise of 'feudal' means of social and political control and the emergence of new systems by which the aristocracy sought to enforce its will over the increasingly self-assured lower orders. One of the chief forces encouraging such changes was endemic plague – the mortality arising from its repeated outbreaks left few aspects of late medieval society unmoved.

Domestic power structures and the changing relationship between king, Lords and Commons will be examined through the example of parliament, especially the Good Parliament of 1376 in which the Black Prince is said to have played a prominent role. In that assembly the Commons was able for the first time to impose its will on the Crown with only marginal support from the Lords. Royal power, albeit briefly, was compromised by the new authority of parliament. This though was no simple exchange of power from king to Commons since the wealth and political mandate the support of parliament could ensure meant that the potential scope of royal policy was much extended.

The prince's death in 1376 coincided with substantial religious change: the emergence of England's first heresy, and deteriorating royal relations with the pope. Edward's support for John Wyclif is considered in this context and demonstrates major changes in ecclesiastical structures and religious belief. The changing nature of worship in England in the later middle ages, and both the 'Babylonish captivity' of the papacy at Avignon and the 'Premature Reformation' in England point toward the eventual superiority of secular over ecclesiastical power.

Although the book provides insights into the life of the Black Prince it is not a biography. Rather the prince's career provides a narrative thread to allow for the exploration of various themes. Due to the nature of evidence some of these themes are discussed with less direct reference to the prince than others. In particular, attention is given to the early stages of the Hundred Years War and to the effects of the Black Death even though the prince played no real role in the conflict until 1346 and little is known regarding his personal response to the plague. It cannot be said with certainty that war and plague were formative influences on the prince's life, but there can be little doubt that they were among the major forces galvanising change in the nature and demonstration of power and influence in the second half of the fourteenth century.

The disruption caused by plague may have contributed to the non-survival of certain forms of evidence and especially to difficulties determining the precise extent of the prince's financial resources. In this bastard feudal environment the ability to reward with annuities, gifts and grants was of great importance and the prince constructed a retinue appropriate to his status. Some consideration will be given to this in Chapter Four and examples will be drawn from the prince's servants and comrades-in-arms throughout the book.

Edward was born at Woodstock, Oxfordshire on 15 June 1330, the eldest child of Edward III and Philippa of Hainault. The king had only recently come to the throne following the overthrow of his father in 1327. His had been a tumultuous reign and the country had been wracked by disastrous wars with Scotland, extended periods of rebellion and domestic civil strife. Edward II's injudicious distribution of patronage and the overbearing influence of the king's favourites, Piers Gaveston and later the Despensers, encouraged the revolt first of Thomas, earl of Lancaster (1322), and subsequently of Queen Isabella herself (1326–7).[7]

Growing Anglo-French hostility, which coloured the Black Prince's life, provided the opportunity to depose Edward II. Isabella, who had become a figure of distrust and dislike in England, was sent to France to negotiate a peace treaty with her brother, the king of France. Isabella's role in government and her relationship with Edward prior to this is difficult to establish. She first came to England as the living representation of a very unpopular treaty with France and found few friends at court – her husband may not have been among them. The marriage was certainly problematic in the early years and complaints were heard in France about the amount of time the king was spending with Gaveston, the new earl of Cornwall. But it seems that after his execution (when Isabella was still very young) and prior to the rise of the Despensers she was a supportive queen, although keen to look after her own interests.[8] Until around 1321 she and Edward had a 'working rélationship', but with the burgeoning authority of Hugh Despenser, the younger, it collapsed: the queen's access to her husband was severely restricted as was her independent income.[9]

Isabella's treatment at the hands of the Despensers was a key factor behind her opposition to the king and she took full advantage of her absence from court on a diplomatic mission to Charles IV in France in 1325 to make her dissatisfaction known. The conclusion of the Anglo-French negotiations was an agreement that Edward II should do homage and fealty for the duchy of Gascony. The king refused to perform the demeaning ceremony in person, but sent his son, the future Edward III, in his place. Once out of the direct influence of the king and his supporters, and with control of the heir, Isabella refused, in December 1325, to return to England until and unless the Despensers were removed from power.[10]

Isabella was not the only person the king had offended and she found allies among the English exiles abroad. Of these, Roger Mortimer was the most notable, but the earls of Richmond and Kent and the bishops of Hereford, Winchester and Norwich were also powerful figures.[11] Additional support was gained by marrying the future king to Philippa, daughter of the count of Hainault, in exchange for a small band of soldiers who accompanied the rebels on their return to England.[12] Once Isabella landed, support for the king dissolved, most significantly in London. Edward II, abandoned by most of his officials and household, fled to Wales with the younger Despenser and was captured in Glamorgan by Henry of Lancaster. Despenser was executed after a trial at Hereford in which he was convicted of being a heretic, sodomite, traitor and enemy of the realm; his genitals were hacked off and burned in front of him.[13]

The king was summoned to parliament in January 1327, but refused to attend and opposition grew further and feeling hardened against him. The archbishop of Canterbury declared that as the magnates, clergy and people no longer regarded Edward as such, he was no longer king. Edward, greatly distressed, received the news at Kenilworth where he resigned the throne in favour of his son. It remains uncertain whether, technically, he abdicated or was deposed.[14]

There are two particular features of Edward II's reign that are of special significance with regard to the future of the Black Prince and his role as heir apparent. First, it demonstrated in the most powerful manner the importance of maintaining good relations with the nobility. Second, the deposition charges provided a checklist of the attributes of a 'bad' king and, by implication, of the expectations that a ruler would do well to fulfil. They are the clearest possible statements of how a king (and a king in waiting) should not behave.[15] Edward II was accused of being incompetent to govern in person; he had made himself subject to evil counsellors; he was given to unseemly works and occupations, such as swimming, ditching and hedging; he had lost territories in Scotland, Gascony and Ireland; he had destroyed the Church and mistreated members of the clergy, as well as putting 'many and noble men of [the] land to a shameful death'; he had not done justice to all nor fulfilled the conditions of his coronation oath.[16] He had, the charges concluded, 'dilapidated his realm, and done all that he could to ruin his realm and his people, and what is worse, by his cruelty and lack of character, he has shown himself incorrigible and without hope of amendment'.[17]

The deposition of 1327 therefore provided a statement of monarchical failure and imposed a new penalty for it, despite being of questionable legality and justified by its success rather than due process of law.[18] A royal deposition overturned both the political hierarchy and a divinely ordained structure of government. It is therefore not surprising that justification for the act soon became couched in terms of moral imperatives, rights and responsibilities. The proper extent and character of sovereign power became central to discussions of Edward II's reign and the explanations given for his deposition. The author of the *Vita Edwardi Secundi* stated: 'Since a king is so styled from the act of ruling as one who should rule his people with laws and defend them with his sword from their enemies, he is fittingly called king while he rules well, but when he despoils his people he is rather adjudged a tyrant.'[19] While kings were not to be overthrown, it was the responsibility of the people, led by the nobility, to depose a tyrant to ensure just and fair government. Edward was depicted as a useless king (*rex inutilis*) – politically, personally and morally inept, incompetent and bereft. In such circumstances the nobility of England was beholden to remove him from power, and this act was made all the easier since a son waited to replace him – the line of succession was not interrupted.

Poor government, especially when subject to the influence of unsuitable ministers, military failure, the breakdown of relations with the secular and ecclesiastical nobility, failure to do justice, and a general lack of bearing and dignity as expressed by his pastimes and the company he kept, were the central causes for the deposition of Edward II. Consequently, a future monarch would do well to act in as contrary a way as possible to these. Government was to be undertaken by a king who sought the counsel of the great men of the realm and they should be treated properly according to their station and their rank valued properly.[20] The clear implication is that the patronage shown to Gaveston and the Despensers was improper and highly divisive. Furthermore, excessive authority wielded by a few, poorly chosen individuals did not only divide the political community at large, it could encroach on royal power to the detriment of the office and authority of the king.[21] Military accomplishment was a further necessary component of royal success, especially against the traditional enemies of Scotland and France, and this should be underpinned by a court where justice was done according to law and tradition, and in which the king participated and oversaw suitable activities both martial and chivalrous. To fail to fulfil these basic expectations was to face the threat of the fate of Edward II, deposition certainly and probably death.

The manner of Edward's death is uncertain. It is most likely that he was murdered, perhaps with a red-hot iron thrust into his bowels, although the chronicler, Geoffrey Le Baker, is the only near-contemporary source for the ghastly tale. The account of the Genoese priest and papal notary, Manuel Fieschi, who claimed to have met Edward after he escaped from captivity and had travelled through Ireland, France and Germany, is fascinating but improbable and perhaps fits too neatly into a folklore tradition involving the survival of monarchs as holy men, one that includes King Harold, Frederick II, Frederick Barbarossa, Arthur and others – sleeping kings who one day would return to save a land in jeopardy.[22] Whatever the fate of Edward II, the role of an English king was re-established in 1327 and the office of the king weakened fundamentally: or rather, the hold of an individual monarch on his office became much more precarious.

The deposition did not result in immediate stability in England. Edward III was only 14 when he was crowned and, as a result of his minority, a regency council was established, centred initially on Henry, earl of Lancaster. It was not long, however, before the king's mother and Roger Mortimer made their 'pestilent' influence felt.[23] Mortimer was created earl of March, endowed with the estates of the elder Despenser and the earl of Arundel, and in his arrogance and avarice outdid Edward II's former favourites. The new administration was not a success either at home or abroad. Indeed, the 1327 campaign against the Scots was a disaster that resulted in the 'Shameful Peace' of Northampton (1328). By this, Edward III was forced to give up his and his heirs' claim to the overlordship of Scotland and return various items of Scottish regalia including the Black Rood, which had been seized by Edward I. Additionally, the king's sister, Joan, was given in marriage to the young David Bruce, then five years old.[24] As a result, opposition to Mortimer and Isabella grew under the leadership of Lancaster, Kent and Norfolk, but it was quickly and brutally repressed. The blind earl of Lancaster was forced to come to terms, and Kent, after abandoning his allies, suffered execution for his pains.[25] In the event, just as the final opposition to Edward II had come from within the palace so too did the most significant challenge to Mortimer and Isabella.

In October 1330, the Council was summoned to Nottingham. It was there that the young king decided to make his move. His fellow conspirators, including William Montague and Robert Ufford, the future earls of Salisbury and Suffolk respectively, made their way up through the labyrinth of tunnels that led into the castle, seized 'gentle' Mortimer despite the protestations of Isabella and with that the coup was effectively over. Mortimer was taken to London, tried for treason – usurping royal power, and ordering the murder of Edward II – and executed in a manner not unlike that accorded the younger Despenser.[26] Isabella retired from public life and Edward III began to rule in fact as well as name.

Military Apprenticeships: Scotland and France

The Black Prince was, of course, unaware of all this, but it may be that his birth on 15 June 1330, combined with Mortimer's increasingly antagonistic and threatening attitude, encouraged the Nottingham coup and thereby brought an element of security to the realm that had been lacking since the death of Edward I.[27] That security, however, was threatened by sporadic conflicts with Scotland and France which presaged the hostilities that would shape the prince's life and career.

But conflict abroad could fashion political stability at home by uniting England in the face of a common foreign enemy. In addition to shaping a political consensus, conflicts against the Scots in the 1330s brought unintended dividends and prepared the English militarily for the war in France. The long shadow of the defeat at Bannockburn (1314) exacerbated trends that had been evident in English armies since Edward I's wars in Wales and Scotland, namely the development of an increasingly professional army recruited to implement a range of particular strategic and tactical plans. Such plans would evolve further and the army prepared for the French wars when Edward III sought to undo the indignity of the 'Shameful Peace' in the early years of his personal rule.

If the mark of military defeat and the shadow of deposition stretched over the English monarchy for the remainder of the century and beyond, then in France too humiliations on the battlefield and a change in the kingship in the last years of the 1320s would colour the succeeding years for at least as long. While the position and reputation of the English monarchy suffered gravely in the reign of Edward II (1307–27) and its financial authority had been compromised by the military expenditure of his father, the status of the kings of France had also fallen from the elevated position held by Philippe IV ('the Fair') after his death in 1314. 'Under Philip[pe] IV fissures in the body politic had been disguised by authoritarian government; internal division, a change of dynasty (1328) and foreign war exposed them again.'[28] Indeed, it is possible that the authoritarianism of Philippe's reign, marked most notably by the expulsion of the Jews, the expropriation of the Lombards and the dissolution of the Order of the Temple, led to a reaction against some of the nascent institutions of the French royal 'State' and the growing power of the monarchy. French kingship would not return to a position of comparable authority until the reign of Charles V (1364–80).

The image of the monarch in France, elevated greatly by Philippe IV, built on developments made in the reigns of Philippe II ('Augustus') and (St) Louis IX. Philippe IV encouraged Louis' canonisation and used

the image of the Saint King to project a pervasive model of powerful Christian monarchy in France. This picture of the 'most Christian
king', buttressed by Roman legal doctrines, gained greater significance
in the context of the struggle with Pope Boniface VIII. The reign of
Philippe IV also contributed to the prejudice against female succession,
which became bound up with the outbreak of the Hundred Years
War. This was a consequence of the alleged adultery of all three of his
daughters-in-law. Certainly by 1328, when Charles IV the last Capetian
died, the idea of a woman succeeding to the throne or even of trans-
mitting a claim to that throne was sufficiently unpalatable for Philippe
of Valois to be able to defeat with ease the aspirations of the young
Edward III.

The change of dynasty gave a new edge to the endemic Anglo-French
rivalry. To combat this the Valois kings emphasised their lineage and
family legitimacy: the rituals and the symbolism of monarchy were used
to demonstrate that little had changed with the death of the last of
Hugues Capet's dynasty. The new Valois monarchs continued to carry
the royal sword, *Joyeuse*, the sceptre and the *main de justice*; they wore
the royal crowns of Charlemagne and Louis IX, and the *Oriflamme*, the
royal banner, was still carried before them on the battlefield. But for
all the work of the Capetian and Valois lawyers, and for all the powerful imagery of monarchy developed over long years by the monks of
St Denis, the change of dynasty could not occur without making an
impact. To a considerable degree it was that change of dynasty which
shaped the life and career of the Black Prince.

Infantia *and* Pueritia

The prince's childhood was not closely documented: Chandos Herald
tells us nothing about his early years, merely giving a list of the (many)
virtues that he acquired in childhood.[29] His birth in 1330 at Woodstock
was clearly an occasion for celebration and in those celebrations we can
see Edward III's relief at securing the future of his own dynasty and
the succession. The dangers of birth to both mother and child were very
considerable so it is hardly surprising that the king was delighted with
the news of the safe delivery of a son, although the dangers were by
no means over. It has been estimated that 30 per cent of all offspring
failed to reach the age of 20. Of Edward and Philippa's 12 children only
five boys and two girls reached adulthood. The queen was given a robe
of cloth of gold edged with miniver in 1330 at her churching to mark
her recovery from childbirth, and the yeoman who informed the king of
the prince's birth was granted a pension of 40 marks a year.[30]

Perhaps the high levels of infant mortality encouraged the king to lavish estates on his eldest son, but it may also have been because Philippa did not give birth to another son until William of Hatfield in 1336, the same year that the king's brother, John of Eltham, earl of Cornwall, died. Whatever the reasons for the king's disproportionate generosity, titles came to the heir apparent in quick succession: the earldom of Cheshire in 1333; the duchy of Cornwall in 1337 (on its creation); and, on only the second occasion that the title was granted, the principality of Wales in 1343.

The prince also held the office of *custos angliae* (keeper of the realm) when his father was campaigning abroad from 16 July 1338 to 21 February 1340, again from some point in the summer of the same year until 11 November, and once more from October 1342 to March 1343. It was a mainly ceremonial office, but not an unimportant one.[31] Much of this time was spent in his manor at Kennington, which was held of the duchy of Cornwall. Consequently, for a while, Kennington became the centre of government. Official letters were sealed there in the prince's name and countersigned by the treasurer, and parliament met at the manor on at least two occasions (January 1340 and July 1342). It was clearly a favoured residence of the prince in these early years and for the royal family at large – the king celebrated Christmas there in 1342.[32]

Outside these exceptional periods the prince's childhood was spent mainly with his mother, and he lived in her household with his sisters, Isabella (b. 1332) and Joanna (b. 1333). Joan Oxenford was his nurse as she would be to his brother, Edmund of Langley,[33] and Walter Burley may have been his tutor. Burley was a renowned scholar, but his relationship with the prince is conjectural and belief in the association only emerged strongly in the sixteenth century.[34] It is more likely that the prince's education was in care of the masters of his household, Nicholas de la Beche (*c*.1340) and Bartholomew Burghersh, the elder (*c*.1341–8). Both were important men. Beche had served as deputy-marshal of England, and Burghersh as the king's chamberlain – they fulfilled a range of household duties in addition to caring for the prince. In these duties de la Beche did not excel and it was partly for his failure in this capacity that he was imprisoned in late 1340 when Edward III returned in secret from the failed siege of Tournai to find the prince and his sisters unguarded in the Tower.[35]

One of the people closest to the young prince was probably Elizabeth St Omer, the 'mistress and guardian of the earl of Chester and his sister'. Her husband, William, was steward of Edward's household. Among the other officials in the early household were John Brunham, the elder, who was treasurer of Chester, and an almoner who made suitable charitable payments and offerings to religious institutions. William Stratton served as the prince's tailor, foreshadowing Edward's later interest in and considerable expenditure on clothing. John Skirbek acted as his butler, and in case of illness he was to be attended by a physician, John Gaddesden.[36]

The prince was an active child. By 1338 he owned a tent and a complete suit of armour with a spare helmet, possibly for tilting practice – he had been introduced to the sport and spectacle of the tournament two years previously. Aged ten he was provided with funds to play *ad bill'*, a game with a stick, and he also played dice or knucklebones (*ad talos*) with his mother, the boys of his household, and with John Chandos who would become one of his most famous military companions and, according to some, 'the most celebrated knight of that time'.[37] It also seems the prince kept pets since there was a page with responsibility for his hares.[38]

The prince was seven years of age when, as had happened on several previous occasions, the king of France seized the lands of his recalcitrant vassal, the duke of Gascony, who also happened to be the king of England. This time it resulted in the outbreak of what would become known as the Hundred Years War. According to conventional wisdom this was also a significant year in the prince's personal development. Theoretically, childhood was divided into blocks of seven years. This had been postulated by Isidore of Seville in the seventh century and reworked by Bartholomew Glanville in the thirteenth: *infantia* from birth to seven years of age; *pueritia* from seven to 14; and *adolenscia* from 14 until 21 or 28. Giles of Rome (*c.*1245–1316) concurred with the schema in broad terms although he offered a slightly more flexible time-frame for the divisions depending on the maturity of the individual.[39]

Therefore, in both hypothetical and very specific terms, the year 1337 was important for the prince and it was also when he received his most important title to date, that of duke of Cornwall. If his education followed a conventional pattern it would have been at about this age that the prince passed from the care of his mother to de la Beche and then Burghersh. Certainly Henry VI and Henry's son, Edward, were considered old enough to leave the nursery and go into the care of male tutors when six-and-a-half years of age. In addition to administering the prince's household, his tutors would have advised him on dress, behaviour and various courtly and martial accomplishments. Others, although not necessarily Burley, probably guided his academic studies. His political education would have developed also through practical experience and serving as keeper of the realm.[40] But apart from some small details regarding his household, little is known about the prince's childhood (*pueritia*) until 1346 when he undertook his first military expedition at the age of 16.

The initial phase of Edward III's war with France (1337–41) was founded on a policy of international coalitions mainly with the emperor and various princes from the Low Countries. This proved to be financially crippling and militarily disappointing. The only notable success was a naval victory at Sluys in 1340. The cost of the alliances and the limited political results brought about a major governmental crisis in 1340–1. When the king next led a campaign abroad the great majority of the army was recruited within his domain. It included a large contingent from Wales under the nominal command of its young prince.[41]

A Career in Arms

In 1346, the Black Prince landed with one of the largest English forces of the Hundred Years War at La Hougue in Normandy and there he was knighted by his father. The army marched to Ponthieu and encountered King Philippe VI at the battle of Crécy. There, the chroniclers tell us, the prince was placed in command of the vanguard although he was certainly advised by the experienced earls of Northampton and Warwick, and it is likely that they took the major command responsibilities. Northampton had led an English army to victory some years earlier at the battle of Morlaix using tactics that foreshadowed those employed in 1346. The battle, in which the English secured victory by the use of archers and infantry, resulted in the slaughter of at least 1,500 French men-at-arms. The army capitalised on its victory by marching on Calais, which fell after a long siege on 4 August 1347.

Crécy proved to be the foundation for the prince's career. The battle provided the basis for his military and chivalric reputation, it coloured the nature of his household and military retinue, it determined the manner by which English forces would prosecute the war in France, and most of all it marked a sea change in the political environment in which the prince lived. The crisis brought about by the failure of the king's earlier policy of continental alliances and its astronomical costs meant that another failure would have had grave repercussions. Instead, the king of France was defeated in person on the field of battle and the flower of French chivalry broken by the English army that had been tempered in the wars with Scotland. It used the infantry/archer tactics, the value of which had been demonstrated at Courtrai, Bannockburn, and Morgarten, and the credit for the victory was given to a 16-year-old whom everyone thought would in time take the throne of England and perhaps that of France as well as King Edward IV. As a consequence of such a victory, which could only have been divinely inspired, there was no major opposition to the king's policies for nearly 25 years.

From this point onwards the prince's career is well known. The victory at Crécy and seizure of Calais were commemorated in 1348 by the creation of the Order of the Garter, and the Black Prince was a founder member. The lull in the war brought about by truces and the shocking appearance of the Black Death was broken by the naval battle of Winchelsea against Castilian allies of the French on 29 August 1350 in which the prince fought. Unaccountably, the Black Prince's younger brother, John of Gaunt, the future duke of Lancaster, also participated in the engagement and was nearly lost. During the battle the prince's ship tried to ram another vessel but was holed. Henry of Grosmont boarded the prince's intended target from the other side and as the ship sank he pulled the prince and the ten-year-old Gaunt to safety.[42] English naval tactics were similar to those employed on land, and on this occasion it did them no harm. On the whole, however, while England was at the forefront of military innovations on land, at sea it lagged far behind.[43]

The impact of the plague and various diplomatic initiatives prevented further military activity until 1355 when the Black Prince received his first independent command as Edward III's lieutenant in Gascony. He led an Anglo-Gascon army numbering some 7,000 men on a *chevauchée* (raid) eastwards and southwards from Bordeaux as far as Narbonne. Aimed primarily at the estates of the count of Armagnac, it caused tremendous devastation. Over 500 towns and villages were pillaged or burned including the suburbs of Carcassonne. In the following year the prince raided north to Bourges before turning towards Tours and then Poitiers, near which he encountered and defeated a numerically superior French army commanded by the king himself.

The capture of Jean II radically altered the political climate and the balance of power. The ransom negotiations produced the treaties of London (8 May 1358 and 24 March 1359), but the terms of these were not implemented and another campaign followed in 1359. In this, Edward III led one of the most powerful armies of the war on a march to Reims intending to capture the city and there be crowned king of France. The Black Prince led a very large contingent in what proved to be an unsuccessful expedition. After failing to take the coronation city the army marched on Paris, but to no avail. The walls could not be breached and because of the experiences of Crécy and Poitiers the French would not be drawn into battle. A peace treaty, negotiated in part by the Black Prince and Henry of Lancaster, was agreed at Brétigny (8 May 1360).

Unfortunately the treaty was flawed and the concluding *cest assavoir* clauses, by which French sovereignty over Gascony and English claims to the throne of France should have been renounced, were never signed.

Had they been, Brétigny would have given Edward III a much-enlarged Gascony in full sovereignty. Nonetheless, this did not seem to be a problem at the time and the territories were granted to his eldest son as the Principality of Aquitaine on 19 July 1362. This combined with the earldom of Chester, duchy of Cornwall and principality of Wales to create a lordship for Edward of Woodstock that ran from the Mersey to the Rouergue.

Before sailing to Bordeaux to take command in Aquitaine, the prince married Joan, 'the Fair Maid' of Kent. Joan is renowned for her marital entanglements with Thomas Holland, William Montague and finally the Black Prince, who became her husband on 6 October 1361 at Lambeth in a ceremony conducted by the archbishop of Canterbury, Simon Islip. The pair had required a papal dispensation before the wedding could take place because they were related within the third and therefore prohibited degree.[44] It was not the match his father had wanted and it may not have been enjoyed greatly by a knight of the prince's household, Bernard Brocas, who had given great service to the prince in the war.[45] Brocas, it is said, had asked Edward to represent him in pressing his suit to the recently widowed countess of Kent, but the prince promptly married her himself. They established a very lavish and splendid court at Angoulême and Bordeaux. Two sons were born to the prince and princess: Edward, who was to die in 1370, and the future Richard II.

A truce with France did not mean there was peace for the prince. An Anglo-Castilian alliance drew Edward into the Castilian civil war on the side of Pedro 'the Cruel' – his half-brother, Enrique 'the Bastard' of Trastamara, had deposed him with the help of mercenaries and French troops led by Bertrand du Guesclin, the future constable of France. In temporary alliance with Charles 'the Bad' of Navarre, the prince gathered an army of mercenaries, Gascon lords, and troops from England led by his younger brother, John of Gaunt. By the terms of the treaty of Libourne (1366) the Black Prince agreed to finance the campaign until January 1367 after which Pedro would repay and reward those who had supported him with land and money. The campaign was a success and resulted in victory at the battle of Nájera (3 April 1367) where du Guesclin was captured but Enrique escaped. Relations soon soured between the allies and Pedro who was quite incapable of keeping his side of the bargain. All attempts to secure payment failed and the army was forced to return over the Pyrenees due to illness in the camp which also affected the Black Prince. Henry Knighton tells us that 'so many of the English died in Spain of dysentery and other diseases that scarce one man in five returned'.[46]

Matters soon became even more grave. The relationship between Edward and the Aquitainian nobility, which had often been troubled, worsened on the return to the principality. Economic pressure forced the prince to ask the Estates of Aquitaine to levy a *fouage*, a hearth tax. This was not a new imposition, but it both encouraged and gave an excuse for the revolt of significant members of the Aquitainian aristocracy. The revolt was also fomented by the efforts of King Charles V and his lieutenant, Louis of Anjou. A formal appeal regarding Edward's regime was made to Charles and the parlement of Paris, and the prince was summoned to the capital to answer the charges. He refused, and in 1369, in time-honoured fashion, after consulting learned opinion over the legality of his actions, Charles formally confiscated the principality and the war restarted.

The Black Prince was not prominent in the action that followed. His health had deteriorated and it was left to trusted commanders such as James Audley, John Chandos and Jean de Grailly, the captal de Buch, to try and hold back the French advances and retain the loyalty of towns and nobles both secular and ecclesiastic. Limoges, led by its bishop, was one of the towns to return to the French fold. This spurred the prince to take action and he directed the siege and sack of the city from a litter. It is unlikely that the scale of the slaughter was as great as Jean Froissart described, but it has been seen as a slur on the reputation of the 'flower of chivalry'. The event marked the end of the Black Prince's active military career – a later expedition from England was cancelled due to bad weather. With his health failing and following the death of his eldest son, Edward returned to England leaving Gaunt in command. He handed back the principality to his father in 1372.

The prince's final years marked a great contrast in the fortunes of war as English gains were completely overturned. He now took a greater interest in domestic affairs, participating in parliaments and great councils and seeking to ensure a smooth succession for his son, Richard. The faltering position in France made for problematic political conditions throughout the 1370s which may have led to divisions within the royal family. While the animosity between Gaunt and the prince in these last years has been much exaggerated, as has his role in the Good Parliament of 1376, there may have been a strained atmosphere among the political elite in and around the court.[47] However, evidence for this is shaky. Some chronicles have to be approached with considerable care due to the political leanings of the authors. Thomas Walsingham is one of the most notable of these. Walsingham's extraordinarily vituperative attacks on Gaunt, influenced by the duke's association with Wyclif and Katherine Swynford, distorted his narrative, at least in its early forms. But other sources, notably the king's entail written to confirm Richard's succession also suggest the possibility that Gaunt had his own royal ambitions not restricted to the throne of Castile. Perhaps he too had heard the prophecy of Bartholomew Burghersh, recorded by Froissart, that the Crown would come to the house of Lancaster, and neither the prince of Wales nor the duke of Clarence would become king.[48]

The Black Prince died during the Good Parliament, on Trinity Sunday (8 June), the feast day for which he had particular reverence, one week before his 46th birthday. But the impact of his career and the almost mythic reputation that he left would continue to influence and colour English political life for years to follow. He was not blamed for the collapse of the English position in France. Nor were the weakness of royal authority in the final years of Edward III's reign, the impending minority rule of Richard II, and opposition to the government, seen as his responsibility. But the victories of Edward III's reign were, at its conclusion, little more than pyrrhic and in such conditions the shadow of the deposition of Edward II returned. The fallibility of the monarchy had been made plain in 1327, or at least the fallibility of the king since the office itself remained inviolate – even the demand of the peasant rebels in 1381 to end all lordship was made with the exception of that of the king. By the 1370s, the political consensus that Edward III had striven so hard to establish, and which had operated effectively for much of his reign, was beginning to fracture. One by one the king's comrades-in-arms died. They were those who had served him since the Nottingham coup and the early campaigns in Scotland and France and many of them had formed the Order of the Garter. The next generation were left without a natural leader as the king wandered into senility and his eldest son was laid low with the illness that would eventually claim his life. The decline of the Black Prince from 1368, and his death in 1376, a year before his father's, mirrored the decline of the English position in France. Indeed, to some extent it was responsible for it.

The Power of Princes

The premature death of the Black Prince has produced a perennial 'what if' question. How might matters have unfolded if he had lived, even a little longer, to provide a degree of continuity between the reigns of his father and his son? Even more circumstantially we can ask whether he would have been a good king. Such counterfactual exercises are rarely profitable, but underpinning those questions are a range of themes that impinge on the career of the Black Prince and which shaped his life and the influence that he brought to bear over wider events. In this regard the prince's administration in Aquitaine in the 1360s is a central element since this was the time in which he acted with all but sovereign authority and therefore provides an indication of the sort of king he might have been. Such a question requires an understanding of the expectations which there were of a ruler in this period and of the changing nature of power relations between rulers and ruled. Kingship, sovereignty, and theories of power and authority were being developed, undergoing re-evaluation and becoming subject to a range of new pressures.

Reconsiderations of monarchical power and increasing claims regarding the extent and nature of royal power were a key feature of this debate. At their most extreme, ideas such as that the king should act 'as an emperor in his kingdom' proved extremely provocative. Not least they provided a theoretical underpinning to the Anglo-French hostilities in the later thirteenth and early fourteenth centuries that grew into the Hundred Years War. In England such theories were often at odds with political reality: 'imperial' authority did not prevent five royal depositions in the fourteenth and fifteenth centuries. These depositions contributed further to the debate and led to a closer definition of monarchical authority, to a more refined definition of kingship, and to a consideration of the rights associated with sovereignty. In this process the practical power of the English monarchy was limited, 'for to define is to curb'.[49]

Theoretical and practical restrictions on monarchical power were, of course, not new in the fourteenth century. The need to establish and maintain good relations with the nobility underpinned medieval monarchy, and the smooth running of the kingdom required a degree of compromise between various interest groups. Restrictions on the ability of the monarch to act independently had been spelled out in no uncertain terms in Magna Carta (1215) and the Provisions of Oxford and Westminster (produced by the baronial opposition to Henry III led by Simon de Montfort in 1258 and 1259). There had also been opposition to Edward I in 1294–8 brought about by the catastrophic costs and mixed successes of his military involvement in Wales, Scotland and France. Indeed, it might be argued it was the crippling financial legacy bequeathed to Edward II that explains his calamitous reign, ultimately his deposition and the further restrictions consequently placed on royal power, although this would be to neglect a large number of more obvious causes for his failures.

Nonetheless, the pressures brought to bear as a result of the military demands of Edward I and his successors forced the monarchy into a different sort of relationship with the English political community and this, compounded by various trends in political theory, is evident in Edward II's coronation oath of 25 February 1308. The oath is significant for several reasons. It is the earliest official record of a coronation;[50] it provides a clear statement of early fourteenth-century expectations of kingship; it provides a link to subsequent legislation, such as the Ordinances of 1311; and finally, Edward II's failure to fulfil the oath was a reason given for his deposition.[51]

Royal responsibilities were made clear in the coronation oath and these responsibilities were owed to the political community at large. Reference was made to the 'community of the realm' and since this did not refer solely to the magnates or council, the king was becoming answerable, in some way, to his people as a whole. While Edward II gave no more than the most general considerations to the political preferences of the English peasantry, the coronation oath does provide an indication of an awareness of the importance of a wider political community and a broader polity. It is noteworthy that in January 1327, prior to the coronation of Edward III, Archbishop Reynolds preached on the text *Vox populi, vox Dei* (the voice of the people (is) the voice of God) and the medal struck to commemorate the coronation bore the motto *Populi dat iura voluntas* (the will of the people gives right).[52] This social expansion of political authority is evident in the greater power which had and would be acquired by the Commons in parliament and would be demonstrated most graphically when the 'peasantry' of England brought the king to account in 1381.

The coronation oath bound the king to uphold and fulfil existing legislation as well as those laws that might be passed in the course of his reign. It is indicative of the shackles that the political community at large was attempting to place on the monarchy. This is also evident in the so-called 'Declaration' of 1308, which declared that homage was due to the office of the crown not the person of the king.[53]

This distinction between office and individual – the notion of the king's two bodies – represents an important change in the conception of English monarchy and it facilitated the rash of royal depositions that would follow. The regime of the Black Prince has to be evaluated in this context, in which lordship and power were subjects under intense discussion and being defined more closely. The theoretical authority of a sovereign was increasing, but the hold of an individual on the office which conveyed that authority was becoming more fragile.

The Black Prince was obviously not a king, but such considerations of sovereignty, authority and the right to wield power influenced his life and career. If kings could claim sovereignty, in this 'age of principalities' when the blood royal united the monarchical family, why should princes not do likewise? Indeed, princes began to appropriate various concepts of Roman law that had been used by kings and there was also a semantic shift from considerations of *dominum* (lordship) to *majestas* (sovereignty).[54] Certainly the Black Prince's regimes in Wales and Aquitaine bear many of the hallmarks of sovereignty. These territorial blocs were, in essence, *appanages*, after the Capetain/Valois model, and conveyed considerable authority on the prince.

The heir apparent was not alone among Edward III's sons in receiving such grants. The appointment to the principality of Aquitaine was part of a wider political strategy developed by Edward III in the later 1350s and early 1360s. There are imperial connotations evident in this scheme that involved the grant of substantial lands and offices to a number of the king's sons – the princes of the blood royal. It was a plan that encompassed territories in France and the Low Countries, Ireland, Italy, Scotland and later in Castile. The break in the war with France after 1360 allowed Edward III to develop a new foreign policy. It was one that had 'Angevin' connotations and invites comparison with Henry II's empire.

The provision of (semi-) independent territorial authority bolstered the prince's power and narrowed the gap in status between the English monarch and his heir apparent. But the position and power of the heir should not be exaggerated either in England or France or indeed throughout Europe where numerous civil wars and succession crises shows the fragility of assumptions concerning princely power and royal inheritance. The most dramatic example is probably the exclusion of the future Charles VII from the French succession after his, albeit incapacitated, father agreed to the treaty of Troyes in 1420. But even in England in calmer times legislation was considered necessary to ensure the smooth transition of the crown from Edward III to his grandson.[55]

Power in the Principalities

The position of Edward of Woodstock therefore was ambiguous. He was king in all but name in the principalities of Wales and Aquitaine at a time when theories of sovereignty could be seen as affording him greater authority, but when political realities could render those theories meaningless. The test of his power came when it was opposed and the forceful administration of his demesne lands brought him into conflict with a number of highly significant noblemen. His behaviour and the ways in which he exercised his authority over them were a hallmark of his career.[56]

While there were close comparisons between the authority and expectations of behaviour of the king and the heir apparent there were also important distinctions, which, if muddied, could lead to problems. The

apparently overbearing character of the prince himself and his administration brought him into dispute with the Welsh Marcher lords and
the nobility of the principality of Aquitaine. In part this was a simple
consequence of the imposition of a new regime in areas which had
become accustomed to a high degree of self-determination: new political
imperatives and financial impositions did not encourage easy relations.
But underpinning such disputes were different and changing conceptions
of the nature of power and authority, how it should be exercised, and of
the mutual rights and responsibilities of lord and vassal.

One of many problems faced by Edward in both his principalities
was his uncertain status. Was he to act or be treated as a king, a near-
sovereign lord or a great magnate; a royal, a noble or all or any of these?
Such determinations established what the relationship should have been
between the Black Prince and his nobles and therefore their expectations
of each other. At its simplest, as Christine de Pizan later emphasised,
the 'thing which is appropriate for the prince to do is not appropriate
for the simple knight or noble'.[57] These were important and problematic
considerations since not only was the conception of royal power shifting,
but so too was the structure and role of the aristocracy. The situation
was especially complicated in Wales and Aquitaine where the prince
encountered foreign political cultures.

Aristocratic and royal authority and the correct forms of social and political interaction between them were a matter of intense debate throughout
Europe in this period. Considerations regarding apparently trivial matters
such as forms of address and the niceties of court etiquette underlay
very real areas of friction and concern. Claims to power and demands for
submission were reflected in these forms of ceremonial activity and they
might therefore provide a forum for conflict.

The prince's personal and economic relations with certain members of
the nobility threw such theoretical issues into sharp relief. The situation
was further complicated since the areas of friction, Wales and Aquitaine,
were idiosyncratic in terms of their political culture and social conditions.
In general, the prince's estates were not regions in which many of the
English peerage held a great deal of influence, but in Wales the principality adjoined the territories of the Marcher lords and here there was
considerable tension and antagonism. In Aquitaine the situation was
not one of juxtaposition and the occasional overlap of authority and
jurisdiction, but the direct imposition of the prince's regime. Here the
result was open rebellion.

The expectation of political independence held by the aristocracy of
Wales and Aquitaine was threatened by a regime eager to explore the full
extent of its authority. The principality of Wales together with all the

other possessions of the Crown in the country and all rights there, including advowsons and wardships, were granted to Edward on 12 May 1343. The prince and his administration soon began to exert the power which went with this grant. He took control of secular lordships when they became vacant and the temporalities of bishoprics when they fell into abeyance. Such actions were compassed by the 1343 grant but indicated the imposition of a newly intrusive and vigorous policy. This later extended to demands for military service, which had previously been considered a royal prerogative in the region. Tension reached such a height that Edward III was forced to step in and state that Marcher lands were held directly of the king rather than the prince of Wales.[58]

The prince's administration has been characterised as grasping and avaricious, but his was a new presence in Wales. He was only the second Englishman to bear the title and Edward II, his predecessor, seems to have paid little attention to the principality. Therefore it is likely that any new administration would have 'stepped on the toes' of the Marcher lords who were accustomed to a fair degree of autonomy. They were likely to be particularly wary of any central authority after the threat which had been posed to them by the Despensers and, more latterly, Roger Mortimer. In Wales, as would prove to be the case in Aquitaine, the presence of a vigorous administration upset a delicate political equilibrium.

In Aquitaine those Frenchmen who had been given over to English sovereignty in 1360 were unlikely to be supportive of a prince who had led such devastating military campaigns against them in the past. The position of the Gascon nobility is more interesting. There had been a number of royal lieutenants in Gascony, perhaps most notoriously Simon de Montfort, but none had been granted the authority bestowed on the Black Prince. Neither had any governed a principality and territory of such an extent – it encompassed nearly a third of the kingdom of France. The prince held a number of royal prerogatives by the grant made in 1362, but he had to pay a token sum to Edward III in recognition of his suzerainty.[59] As a consequence it is uncertain quite how the indigenous aristocracy viewed him.

The Gascons were an independent people, looking more to London than Paris but seeking to remain free of interference from either capital. The Gascon aristocracy had long been staunch defenders of the duchy, certainly so long as they felt it was in their best interests to do so, but they expected to be treated appropriately in return. They asked specifically for the appointment of the Black Prince as lieutenant of Gascony in 1355 and delighted in the prestige which the king's son could bring. There was a strong feeling that the duchy should be governed only by men of the highest rank. Certainly in 1391, when there was the danger of Gaunt being foisted on them, they stated that they were accustomed to being governed by the English king or his heir and not by third parties.[60] But the unexpected degree of interference and the imposition of direct sovereignty were unwelcome. The main problems for the Black Prince developed primarily, although not exclusively, from the nobility of the greater Aquitaine who came under his authority as a result of the aggregation of territories ceded by France in the treaty of Brétigny. But the political culture of the Languedoc as a whole created a climate in which changing English conceptions of power and authority and the imposition of rule did not sit comfortably.

The Black Prince, then, was provided with a regal demesne. He was not a king although the distinction was not always clear in terms of his relations with his great magnates. It is possible that his actions in the period c.1362–8 were governed by the prince's desire to gain a throne and this may not have been at odds with the king's own ambitions. One hypothesis suggests Edward III intended the principality of Aquitaine to become a kingdom.[61] It has also been suggested that the prince's later involvement in Castile (after the victory at Nájera) may be explained by his wish to acquire a crown, which, due to his father's longevity, was too slow in coming to him. If so it was ironic indeed, since the prince fell victim to the disease (possibly a viral infection) that would eventually claim his life while campaigning in Spain. This robbed him of the chance of wearing the crown, dying, as he did, a year before his father.

While relations were in general cordial between the prince and his father, there is some evidence of tension in the 1360s. This was the product of two marriages, the less significant, which took place by 26 March 1366, was between Jean de Montfort, duke of Brittany, and Joan Holland, the prince's stepdaughter. It followed a treaty of alliance between de Montfort and the prince.[62] The marriage was problematic for Edward III because it took place without his consultation. This was not only a personal slight, but the king's own support for de Montfort during the Breton civil war had been conditional on such consultation. It may be an indication that the prince was starting to flex his diplomatic muscles independently on the European stage. If so it was an attitude also evident in his personal relations.

The prince's marriage to Joan of Kent was extraordinary: 31 was an unconscionable age for the heir apparent to marry. More exceptional still was marriage to a woman with such a colourful past. Even Henry Knighton's restrained account of her marital entanglements hinted at a certain dark lasciviousness. If nothing else the marriage was a lost political opportunity, although Joan proved herself an able politician after the prince's death. There is no doubt that her reputation proved to be a liability for Richard II 'concerning whose birth many unsavoury things were commonly said, namely that he was not born to a father of the royal line, but of a mother given to slippery ways – to say nothing of many other things I [Adam Usk] have heard'.[63] No king of England or his heir had married a widowed mother since the mid-twelfth century and such a match was bound to cause political or dynastic trouble.[64]

The prince's motivation in all such relations, with his father, with his nobles, and in the Castilian campaign, must remain uncertain. All impressions are based on a relatively small amount of evidence and much of that circumstantial and contextual. A clearer understanding of the character of the Black Prince would be necessary to understand exactly how he conceived of his position and his relationship with the political community at large and the nobility in particular.

In the main, this book is concerned with wider social and political influences, and with *mentalités* rather than an individual's mentality. But the influence of individuals should not be downplayed. The centrality of princely and monarchical power to national success is self-evident in this period. A man, such as the Black Prince, could and did make a difference. Therefore his motivations, interests and passions could determine the implementation and manifestation of power. His character shaped the ways by which power was expressed. It is, however, difficult to get close to the man since the sources do not allow for such a study – a limitation true of almost every medieval figure. Any attempt must first break through a patina of chivalric idealisation and then one usually finds only a blueprint of the epitome of knighthood and princely qualities. We are told that the subject of Chandos Herald's biography came from 'the perfect root of all honour and nobility' – indeed, from the day of his birth he thought of nothing but loyalty, noble deeds, valour and bounty.[65] Romances and epics as well as hagiography influenced Chandos Herald; this made the distinction between reality and fiction of little importance to him since the subject is presented as a didactic example worthy of emulation. To hope for glimpses of the character of the prince we have, somewhat perversely, to look at sources other than his biography. Some aspects of this become apparent from the prince's religious beliefs, his political activities and the character of his household. What emerges is a character and a career that cannot be extricated from its military context and from deeds on the battlefields of the Hundred Years War. It was a career that began at Crécy.

chapter one

ENGLAND AT WAR

. . . let the boy win his spurs, for if God has so ordained it, I wish the day to be his.[1]

O
n 26 August 1346, a young man, 16 years old, stood in the front line of the English vanguard on the battlefield of Crécy. The day would be a turning point for him and for English fortunes in the Hundred Years War. The legend and reputation of the Black Prince was created at Crécy and the battle recast the English military reputation in Europe. Crécy became the first in a litany of English victories and Edward III made it known that he wished his son to be given the credit for the triumph.

Although the battle proved to be a remarkable success for the king and his son, it is not certain if they sought a battle in 1346. What Edward intended and how Philippe VI proposed to counter him is not clear. Crécy was the first major confrontation of a war that had witnessed many minor skirmishes and encounters on land and sea, but had not pitched the kings of England and France directly against one another. While the hostilities fought out from 1337 were no 'phoney war', Crécy marked the beginning of a new and highly significant phase in the conflict.

Crécy also marked a further development in what has been described as a military revolution;[2] it indicated an increasingly professional attitude on the part of the English aristocracy towards the business of war. Indeed, war was becoming a business rather than an act of *noblesse oblige*. It also became a matter of growing concern to the English political community at large as the Hundred Years War gathered momentum.

The Hundred Years War – Origins and Causes

The Hundred Years War was merely the foremost in a series of Anglo-French hostilities that had been ongoing for generations before 1337.[3]

The reasons for the outbreak of the Hundred Years War are now generally agreed upon even if their relative importance remains a subject of debate. A number of those causes continued to impact on the political environment in the later years of the fourteenth century and on the career of the Black Prince and so are worthy of mention.

Since the Norman Conquest, relations between England and France had been problematic and often resulted in open war. The significance of the struggle grew with the creation of the Angevin Empire and the much greater threat Henry II (1154–89) posed the Capetian regime. However, the Empire did not endure and the 'English' position was gravely weakened by political and military setbacks in King John's reign. By the terms of the treaty of Le Goulet in 1200, John paid homage and 20,000 marks to Philippe II ('Augustus') in return for his right to hold Angevin lands in France. As an important precursor to later political relations, the treaty gave Philippe the right to interfere in the government of John's continental territories.[4] The subsequent loss of Normandy (1204) and the defeat of John's allies at the battle of Bouvines (1214) clearly showed the growing authority of Paris and her king over the greater nobles of France, be they the king of England or not.

Capetian influence continued to expand beyond the Île-de-France through military intervention, political skill and judicious marriages. The rebellion against John and the long minority of Henry III meant English/Angevin opposition was limited for much of the first half of the thirteenth century. When Henry finally attempted to re-establish the English position in France, he encountered problems not only in the form of King (and later Saint) Louis IX, but also domestic opposition from his nobles. Indeed, the rise to power of the baronial reform party led by Simon de Montfort may have forced Henry to guarantee a degree of security for what remained of his Angevin birthright by signing the treaty of Paris with Louis on 13 October 1259.

By the treaty, Henry became a peer of France and vassal of her king. He abandoned Plantagenet claims to Normandy, Anjou, Maine and Touraine in return for the duchy of Gascony and some additional parcels of land. Although the treaty ensured an extended period of peace it established a highly contentious feudal relationship that lay at the heart of the friction which erupted in 1337 – for one sovereign ruler to be the vassal of another flew in the face of both political realities and developing theories of kingship.[5]

The importance of the English claim to the French throne as a cause for the Hundred Years War has been a subject of much debate. The consensus now is that, apart from brief periods, and most of these in the fifteenth century, it was not a central issue.[6] However, *kingship* was central to the struggle. With the death of the last Capetian monarch, Charles IV, on 1 February 1328, there were three main contenders for the French throne. Edward III was the nearest male heir but his claim was transmitted through his mother. Philippe of Valois and Philippe of Evreux were related more distantly but in the male line. It was for political rather than legal reasons that an assembly of nobles, secular and ecclesiastic, determined the throne should pass to Philippe of Valois.

It was not a surprising choice. The new king had served as regent since Charles IV's death and had considerable support in the court and country. He was an experienced leader by comparison with the teenage Edward who in 1328 was not 'his own man' and governed England under the supervision of Mortimer and Isabella. Not able to contest the decision, Edward III was forced to accept the situation; on 6 June 1329 he paid homage to Philippe at Amiens.[7]

The issues of homage, fealty and sovereignty were at the heart of changing notions of power in late medieval relations between individuals, be they kings, nobles, knights or peasants.[8] Personal relations were redefined in this period in theory and practice as individual expectations of lord and vassal altered. It was in this context that the war was fought, and explains why it was fought for so long. These changes in the roles and responsibilities of lord and vassal that made and sustained wars also contributed to spectacular demonstrations of peasant unrest in France in 1358 and England in 1381. Issues of sovereignty and lordship thus dominated the Black Prince's political life. They lay at the heart of the Hundred Years War and were also central to his problematic relationships with the nobility of Aquitaine and the Welsh Marches. Just as the collapse in relations between Philippe VI and Edward III led to war in 1337 so too did the rebellion against the prince's lordship in Aquitaine in 1368/9.

There were therefore theoretical issues involving the nature of kingship, power and authority at play in the build-up to the Hundred Years War, but more prosaic matters also concerned both parties. As the overlord of the duke of Gascony, the king of France had a responsibility and numerous opportunities to involve himself in Gascon affairs. The role that he took most often was a judicial one, and because of the stipulations of the treaty of Paris the final arbiter of justice in the duchy resided in Paris not London. Appeals over legal judgments made by the king of England and his officials were made regularly to the king of France. This low-key but consistent emphasis of French royal authority was particularly irksome; appeals to Paris slowed down the business of government, imposed themselves over daily administration and interfered with fiscal activities. It was one of the main reasons for the outbreak of war in 1294 and in 1337.[9]

This was an especially fractious issue because such interference impinged directly on the authority of the king/duke. A defining quality of a king was his ability to make and enforce law. The capacity to oversee, guide and direct the legal process was a central component of medieval kingship: to have this circumscribed and his decisions overturned struck at the heart of the power of the English monarch. In 1368/9, when the nobility of the greater Aquitaine chose to appeal to Charles V and the parlement of Paris, the vice-regal power of the Black Prince was shattered by just such interference.

If this suggests French action precipitated conflict by a gratuitous show of strength then it should be noted that the Plantagenets were just as willing to flex their muscles. Their actions, particularly those of Edward I in Scotland, were intensely provocative.[10] Indeed, Edward I may have hoped to goad the Scots into a reaction so that he could take control of the kingdom with the full backing of the law. Philippe VI and Charles V perhaps acted in exactly the same way so as to prosecute their respective claims to sovereignty in Gascony/Aquitaine.

Scotland remained a source of friction and cause of concern for the Plantagenet monarchy and it also contributed to the growing tension between England and France. If Gascony was a thorn in the flesh of the French monarchy because it gave England a bulwark across the Channel, so too was Scotland a problem for England for analogous reasons. Scotland was the first target for military activity in Edward III's reign. Having been forced to seal the 'Shameful Peace' of Northampton, it is not surprising that the young king wished to overturn that particular indignity. In 1332, in a manner foreshadowing English and French policy in the Hundred Years War, King Edward helped revive the Scottish succession dispute and gave his covert support for a military expedition led by Edward Balliol to unseat the young Scottish king, David II.

Direct and indirect English involvement in Scotland had two main aims. Edward sought to reverse his military and political humiliation of 1328 and use a war with Scotland to strengthen his own relatively fragile kingship by uniting the aristocracy in a national cause. In these objectives he was successful and the various Scottish expeditions also had an unintended benefit. They proved extremely important in producing a cadre of experienced, hardened soldiers who were strategically aware and tactically astute. These men provided the backbone of the English army that fought at Crécy.[11]

The minority kingship of David Bruce of Scotland provided an opportunity for Edward III to make his mark, but to fight there himself would be a violation of the treaty of Northampton. The king, however, circumvented this restriction by insisting that it had been ratified against his will. Initially he acted through the 'Disinherited', those who had lost their estates under the Bruce regime, led by Edward, son of King John Balliol, and Henry Beaumont, earl of Buchan. Some of Edward III's household knights participated in the first campaign including Walter Mauny and Ralph Stafford, both future associates of the Black Prince.

Victory for the 'Disinherited' against a much larger army at Dupplin Moor on 12 August 1332 changed the balance of power in Scotland. Support for Bruce collapsed, albeit briefly, and loyalties were transferred to Balliol. He took the throne and paid homage to Edward. In December 1332, however, Balliol was surprised and defeated in a dawn raid at Galloway and forced to flee to England.[12] There, Edward III agreed to restore him to the throne in return for a number of major territorial concessions. The subsequent expedition, in which Edward III personally took part, culminated in the battle of Halidon Hill (19 July 1333). The 'English' forces were victorious despite being outnumbered by perhaps five to one although this was less of a deficit than at Dupplin Moor.[13] Following this defeat David Bruce fled to exile in France. His presence there amplified the tension between England and France since Philippe VI insisted that negotiations over Gascony would have to include consideration of the status of Scotland. As a result, negotiations stalled and positions were polarised further.

The Black Prince had few personal associations with Scotland, but his father's experiences there were crucial in providing a military and political training for many of the English aristocracy who he would fight alongside at Crécy. It was in Scotland that many of the key members of the prince's household and retinue first saw service and it was along the Border that some of these gained experience of government in frontier regions. This experience would be put to the test in the principalities of Wales and Aquitaine. They included such men as: Thomas Bradeston; Bartholomew Burghersh, the elder; John Chandos; Roger Cotesford; Nigel Loryng; William Montague, earl of Salisbury; John Sully; and John Vere, earl of Oxford.

Royal status and the status of dependent territories (or what the kings of France and England wished to see as dependent territories, Gascony and Scotland respectively) therefore lay at the heart of the struggle that broke out in 1337. But these were not the only causes. There was also an economic dimension to the Hundred Years War. First, there is no doubt that the money one could make in the form of booty and ransoms made war an attractive occupation for many.[14] The profits to be made on campaign could be considerable and the Black Prince's raids in 1355 and 1356 provided some of the most financially rewarding examples.

Secondly, Gascony had been extremely valuable to the English crown due to the profits of the wine trade and, although that value had diminished, the duchy still had great economic potential. Furthermore, it was home to a number of Atlantic ports which the Capetian/Valois monarchy coveted. The wine trade in the south balanced the wool trade in the north where relations with Flanders, the main processing region for English wool, were extremely significant for the outbreak of Anglo-French hostilities.[15] Flanders, like Castile later, was a satellite region, another theatre for the Hundred Years War. French relations with the region were rarely easy and had been especially problematic since the defeat of the French at Courtrai in 1302.[16] Courtrai, the battle of the Golden Spurs, also served as a tactical precursor to a number of encounters between England and France; it was significant as a demonstration of the potential superiority of well-trained infantry over cavalry. This was a lesson that the English learned at Bannockburn and put into practice at Halidon Hill, Morlaix and Crécy.[17]

The status of Gascony and of Scotland, the disputed throne of France, the problematic monarchical relationship established at the treaty of Paris, and various economic issues all provided motivation for conflict. But the spark that ignited the Hundred Years War in 1337 can be found in the actions of individuals, not the growing pressure of social, economic or political forces. The duchy of Gascony was declared confiscate on Philippe VI's orders because Edward III was harbouring a renegade French nobleman, Robert d'Artois, in direct contravention of his vows of homage and duty to his overlord.

Robert d'Artois was seen throughout Europe as directly responsible for encouraging the war, probably as the result of an effective French propaganda campaign.[18] As the French king's cousin he had been favoured at court, but relations soured when his aunt's claim to the county of Artois was preferred to his own. He was accused of murder and forgery in 1332, condemned but managed to escape and eventually came to England where Edward III received him favourably. The king refused to hand him over to French justice following a demand in December 1336 and, according to a near contemporary poem, the *Vow of the Heron* (*c.*1340), Robert soon exhorted and shamed the king into a war he was unwilling to fight.

According to the *Vow*, Edward, after being accused of cowardice for not defending his claim to France, responded that he would

> cross the sea, my subjects with me, and I will pass through the Cambresis . . . I will set the country ablaze and there I will await my mortal enemy, Philippe of Valois, who wears the fleur-de-lys . . . I will fight him . . . even if I have

only one man to his ten. Does he believe he can take my land from me? I once paid him homage, which confounds me now, I was young; that is not worth two ears of corn. I swear to him as king, by St George, and St Denis that . . . neither youth nor noble ever exacted such tribute in France as I intend to do.[19]

Robert then demanded the participation of the earls of Salisbury, Derby, and Suffolk, as well as John Beaumont, Walter Mauny, and John of Valkenberg (Jean de Fauquemont). The mission was also encouraged by a number of ladies present at the feast including the queen who swore that she would kill herself and her unborn child, Lionel of Antwerp, if the king did not attempt to fulfil his vow. The *Vow of the Heron* is one of numerous late medieval vowing-rituals involving birds, of which the heron was considered the most cowardly. While the incident itself is probably fictitious it provides a clear demonstration of contemporary attitudes and of the ethos prevalent at Edward III's court.[20]

It is important not to underestimate the significance of individuals in the outbreak of war. The political status of Gascony was the chief source of friction and had brought England and France into conflict on a number of occasions. Conditions though were different in 1337 mainly because of the expectations and fears of individuals and, as a consequence, war, even though punctuated by various truces, would last 116 years. War had broken out several times in the intervening years after the treaty of Paris; the key difference in 1337 was the issue of the crown. The claim to the French throne, whether or not it was ever the real objective of the English monarchy, coloured the Hundred Years War and made it a conflict that proved impossible to bring to a peaceful conclusion. Edward the Black Prince was the heir apparent to the throne of England and also, for much of his life, to that of France as well.

Opening Gambit

On 24 May 1337, Philippe VI commanded the confiscation of Gascony and Ponthieu and, although there were no major hostilities until 1339, England and France were at war. Although the main area under dispute was Gascony, Edward III focused his attention on lands on the northern French border. There is no surprise in this. Since 1259 the English had tried to re-establish their claim to the duchy of Normandy.[21] They might now prosecute this more vigorously as a consequence of various alliances including Edward's marriage to Philippa of Hainault.

In 1337, Edward concluded a treaty with his brother-in-law, Ludwig of Bavaria. Negotiations had begun in August 1335, some time before the outbreak of war with France but when the political climate was deteriorating swiftly. This suggests that the king was preparing for conflict well before the confiscation of Gascony.[22] When war was declared Edward continued to look to the northern French border for support. Treaties costing in excess of £160,000 were made with the count of Guelders, the marquis of Juliers, and duke of Brabant – Edward was forced to mortgage his Crown as well as borrow at high rates of interest.[23] The focus on northern France was also encouraged by developments in Flanders where Count Louis of Nevers, who was supported by the French government, was attacked and replaced by Jacob van Artevelde in 1337/8.[24]

Flanders, one of the first of a number of smaller states to become embroiled directly in the Hundred Years War, was important to the English military effort because of the wool trade which the king hoped would finance his campaign. This failed and Edward was forced to borrow very heavily, mainly from the Italian banks, the Bardi and Peruzzi. Edward's inability to repay their loans hastened the bankruptcy of these institutions.[25] By 1340, Edward owed more than £300,000 and the kingdom was effectively bankrupt since no one would lend him any more money. The failure of the financial administration resulted in a complete overhaul of systems and personnel.[26]

The financial collapse was the product of a catastrophically expensive and fruitless campaign. The king had sailed for Antwerp on 16 July 1338 and arrived there six days later to prepare for an expedition into the Cambrésis. His allies, however, were unwilling to commit any forces until they had been paid in full. With the interest on his loans increasing and political opposition growing in England as a result of the pressure from taxation and purveyance, Edward's situation became bleak. Philippe of Valois took the opportunity to raid the Channel Islands and the south coast of England, and in April 1339 he orchestrated the capture of the Gascon towns of Bourg and Blaye.

An English-led expedition finally left Brussels early in September 1339 and marched on Cambrai, which was assaulted soon after 20 September but to no effect. Domestic political conditions deteriorated and the king only acquired further funds in return for reforms demanded by parliament including the establishment of a committee to control government expenditure. This was hardly surprising as the campaign of 1339–40 cost some £386,465. By comparison, Edward I's first Welsh war cost about £23,000 and the second probably reached an enormous £150,000.[27] The price of Edward III's initial foray into the continent was therefore extreme. A naval victory at Sluys in 1340 was the only real success before political tension in England, brought about by the huge costs of the alliance and heightened by agricultural problems that generated a great deal of opposition to taxation, forced a truce at Esplechin.[28]

It is significant with regard to the career of the Black Prince that the failure of this system of alliances necessitated a change of military and political policy and meant that in subsequent campaigns Edward relied for the most part on English, Welsh and Gascon troops. The years 1340–1 marked one of the lowest points in Edward III's reign. Forced to rethink his military and political strategy, it made the king's next major campaign, which led to Crécy in 1346, of critical importance – another failure would not be tolerated.

In addition, 1340 marked a change in the declared aspirations of the king: Edward III made his first major public statement concerning the French throne. He claimed it explicitly and to demonstrate this he quartered the arms of the English royal house with the *fleur de lys* of France. Probably done to gain Flemish support, this can be seen as part of what John Le Patourel has dubbed Edward III's 'provincial strategy' by which Edward hoped to take advantage of 'French' regional feeling to gain support for his own aims.[29] Van Artevelde might support the English, but Flanders owed obedience to the king of France. If, however, Philippe VI was not the rightful king of France then those who rebelled against him did not commit treason.

Philippe VI had often used the charge of treason to bolster his monarchy's shaky foundations and, in particular, to prevent disloyalty in Flanders. This can in seen in the retribution exacted after the battle of Cassel; in the brutal interrogation, torture and execution of Guillaume de Deken, a leader of the Flemish revolt in 1328; and in the beheading of Sohier de Courtrai, who had tried to convince the citizens of Ghent to ally with the English, in March 1338.[30]

The so-called Manifesto of Edward III provided the Flemish with a degree of legal security in this context. It was signed at Ghent on 8 February 1340 and addressed to the people of France, 'in the first year of our reign over France and the fourteenth of our rule over England'. Edward claimed to be closer in blood to Charles IV than Philippe of Valois who had 'intruded himself by force into the kingdom while we were yet of tender years', and he argued that Philippe held the kingdom against divine will and earthly justice. Edward vowed as king he would rule according to the laws of France and do justice as his predecessor, Louis IX, had done. There would be no new financial impositions and he would act upon the advice of the French nobility. He spoke of the need for peace between Christians and the opportunities that would result to recover the Holy Land. Philippe was portrayed as unreasonable and Edward had been forced to resort to arms to defend himself and his rights. He called for his faithful 'subjects' to pay homage to him 'as our beloved and faithful men of Flanders have already done'.[31]

It is unlikely that Edward truly hoped to gain the French throne at this point. There was, in any case, little to suggest that he could seize it by force of arms. But the claim gave him a strong diplomatic position in future negotiations over Gascony and it also strengthened his hand in his problematic relations with the English parliament. Parliament would, he hoped, feel compelled to support the king and grant him taxes so that he could take what had been withheld from him by treachery. The dignity of the Crown and the country was at stake.[32]

The year 1341 was a major turning point in the war and thereafter it took on a different character. It heralded the beginning of a brief period of startling success for the English followed by a complete reversal. This period was characterised and shaped by the Black Prince: he fought in the vanguard at Crécy, commanded the Anglo-Gascon army at Poitiers, and he oversaw the collapse of the principality of Aquitaine which brought with it the loss of nearly everything that had been won after 1341. Despite this political reversal, the prince's reputation did not suffer over-much. Perhaps ill health at the end of his life diverted any blame, but it was more that the very limited successes the English had enjoyed prior to his involvement in the Hundred Years War made his contribution seem all the greater.

The year 1341 also marked the beginning of English intervention in a succession dispute in the duchy of Brittany between Jean de Montfort and Charles de Blois.[33] It was to be a struggle in which the Black Prince and many of his associates took a close interest. The initial military intervention led by the earl of Northampton was also important since at the battle of Morlaix he used tactics reminiscent of those learned in Scotland and which would be employed at Crécy to such devastating effect.[34]

Crécy: A Case Study

The Crécy campaign was the most important of a number of connected military expeditions launched by the English in the mid-1340s. Among these, the campaign led by Henry of Grosmont to Gascony in 1345 proved to be particularly successful. His Anglo-Gascon forces infiltrated and seized Aiguillon.[35] Although they were besieged in turn, this divided and diverted French forces from Normandy where the main assault would land. Further diversionary expeditions were led by Richard Totesham,[36] Hugh Hastings,[37] and Thomas Dagworth who defeated Charles de Blois on 9 June 1346 near Saint-Pol de Leon.[38] Such a policy of multiple expeditions was characteristic of English strategy in this phase of the war. It can be seen at work again in 1355 when the prince's raid from

Bordeaux was one of several *chevauchées*, and in 1359 when preparatory strikes were launched in advance of the Reims campaign.[39]

This strategy aimed to disrupt French defensive preparations and to keep English plans secret. It was clear from the preparations in 1346 that a major expedition was intended, but the French did not know the destination of the fleet until a very late date. This was altered on a number of occasions and probably not revealed to any except the king's closest confidants. Perhaps only on or about 20 June was the final decision taken to attack Normandy. As a result French defensive preparations were inadequate.[40] This contrasts sharply with the situation in 1359 when there was no attempt to maintain any sort of secrecy regarding the invasion. Then Edward made his intention clear; to march to Reims and there be crowned king of France. While necessary from a political standpoint, this policy allowed the French to strengthen the defences of the coronation city and lay in supplies of victuals and weapons.

This highlights a particularly significant aspect of the military 'revolution' – the ability to keep troops supplied in fortresses or the field for extended periods. Hunger often determined the success or failure of campaigns, both the hunger of the soldiers or their victims. For example, the Bruce invasion of Ireland (1315–17) failed because of starvation. By 1317, conditions were so bad throughout the country (in the midst of the Great Famine) and the soldiers were 'so destroyed with hunger that they raised the bodies of the dead from cemeteries' to eat them 'and women ate their children from hunger'.[41] In 1346, the English started out with ample supplies but the army soon ran into trouble. Although Edward and his son gave such matters a great deal of attention their preparations were not always sufficient. A sizeable raiding force had great difficulty living off the countryside. This problem affected the English army after it reached Caen perhaps as a result of a change of plan. It is probable that the king's initial intention had been to lead an expedition from Gascony. This then became a scheme to establish a bridgehead in Normandy. It was only late in the day that he decided to launch a *chevauchée*.[42]

For comparison, the Black Prince's campaign of 1355 was always intended as an extensive raiding expedition. It covered a great distance, which demonstrates the mobility of English raiding forces and shows that supply trains could ford major rivers. However, the army itself was not of unusual size, which lessened problems of supply that were associated with more substantial forces. Supply trains were vulnerable when they were extended over long distances. This meant that, as in 1359, large slow-moving supply trains – it took a month to cover 150 miles (Calais to Reims) – could only be used when resistance was limited.[43]

Whatever the situation, it was rarely possible for an army to carry sufficient supplies. This became increasingly problematic with the devastation of France by repeated English raids and as the French adopted a scorched-earth policy. In 1359, knowing Edward's intentions, the French made sure that all provisions along his route from Calais were either destroyed or held in strongly fortified areas. Conditions were particularly difficult since the route led through a region that Lancaster had pillaged recently. As a consequence, Edward was only able to maintain the siege of Reims for 38 days; the main problem he faced was finding fodder for the horses.[44] This meant that the English were ill prepared for a long siege, especially of a town whose defences had been much improved in recent years. Edward hoped that his friendship and family ties with the archbishop of Reims, Jean de Craon, would result in the easy capture of the city. However, when Edward and his army arrived they found strong defences, determined resistance and a city well stocked with soldiers and supplies.[45]

The Crécy campaign was the launch pad for the prince's military career. Its organisation, strategic concerns and tactical imperatives influenced the conduct of his subsequent expeditions. The army landed at La Hougue on the Cotentin peninsula on 12 July 1346, where the prince was knighted with a number of young noblemen. The army embarked on a *chevauchée*, split into three divisions to cause maximum damage, rode south and then east. With assistance from the fleet, they laid waste to Cherbourg, Harfleur and much of the coastal region. Caen also fell and a number of important French noblemen were taken captive before the army turned toward Paris. On 12 August they came within 20 miles of the capital. Edward, however, decided not to engage the enemy and retreated to the River Somme, which was crossed at the celebrated ford at Blanchetaque and he made his stand at Crécy. Philippe, who had pursued the English from Paris, attacked almost immediately.

Among the lessons the prince learned in 1346 was the tactical advantage to be gained from an army composed of mixed companies of infantrymen and archers. Fighting together in a prepared defensive position they were able to repulse a numerically superior opponent; this was particularly effective against cavalry. The archers reduced enemy numbers at a distance and disrupted their approach, giving the advantage to men-at-arms fighting in close formation. Such a combination of dismounted knights and archers was not new, for William the Conqueror had used such a blend at Hastings, but it was considered innovative by contemporaries such as Thomas Gray in his description of the battle of Courtrai (1302) and still held good nearly 50 years later.[46] Following the Crécy model, the prince's force in 1355–6 consisted of three types of troops, men-at-arms, horsed archers and footmen. This allowed for tactical flexibility in a variety of situations. Michael Prestwich has noted the difficulties involved in reconstructing the initial disposition of the English troops at Crécy,[47] although it is reasonably clear how the battle unfolded thereafter. Like the English, the French army was organised in three divisions set one behind the other. In front of these were Genoese mercenaries armed with crossbows. Philippe VI probably commanded 12,000 men-at-arms, 6,000 Genoese and several thousand infantry, creating a force of up to 25,000 soldiers. While numerically superior, the French had been involved in a long march – reinforcements continued to arrive throughout the afternoon and – consequently, command structures were weak and an overall strategic plan was lacking.

The English made their stand at the end of an expanse of gently rising ground, their backs to the forest of Crécy-Grange and the sun. The prince led the vanguard with a number of highly experienced soldiers including Warwick, Northampton, Kent, Godfroi d'Harcourt, and Chandos. The king commanded the centre, and the bishop of Durham with the earls of Arundel and Suffolk led the rearguard.[48] The archers were probably deployed on the wings of each division or 'battle' but may have begun the encounter in front of the dismounted infantry. Certain questions remain because of Froissart's use of the word *herce* to describe their formation.[49]

Troop dispositions and battlefield preparation were crucial to the English and Anglo-Gascon victories. The troops were dismounted behind trenches and other defences designed to impede enemy cavalry. This basic formation remained in use from Dupplin Moor to Agincourt. It is not surprising that at Poitiers the prince mimicked a plan that had been so successful ten years before. A new feature in 1346, and one that became of increasing importance in the years to come, was the appearance of gunpowder weapons. There were a number of cannon at Crécy, which were used primarily to frighten the French horses. It was one of the first uses of artillery on a battlefield, but they had almost no impact on the outcome. The guns 'were simple light weapons, almost as dangerous to those firing them as to those at whom they were fired'.[50]

The French attack at Crécy was disrupted by the weather – there was a sharp shower before battle was joined – and it soon became apparent that the crossbows of the Genoese were no match for the English longbows.[51] Nor did it help that they had been commanded to attack without their *pavises*, large shields behind which they could reload, which were still en route with the rest of the baggage. The crossbowmen soon retreated, only to be cut down by the furious French cavalry who, led by the count of Alençon, attacked the English vanguard. The archers disrupted the charge, but some French troops reached the English lines where a fierce fight ensued. The standard fell and was raised again by the prince's retainer, Thomas Daniel,[52] and the prince himself was struck down and rescued by his standard-bearer, Richard FitzSimon.[53] The French cavalry repeatedly wheeled, rallied and charged. During one of these attacks entreaties were probably made to the king to ensure his son's safety. But the king, after being reassured his son was not wounded and could continue fighting, commanded that he should be left to win his spurs.[54]

As the French attacks failed, the horses were brought up from behind the English lines and, as they were to do at Poitiers, the men-at-arms remounted and charged the surviving French troops. It may be that a small bank or escarpment at the foot of the slope facing the English, perhaps six feet in height, had disrupted the French assault and now impeded their retreat, turning the valley into a killing ground.[55] At this point the bulk of the army fled leaving Philippe with only a handful of companions, his personal bodyguard and some infantry levies from Orléans. After being injured, he was led away by John of Hainault, abandoning the *Oriflamme* and the royal standard.[56] On the following morning 2,000 infantry reserves still following from Abbéville arrived unaware of the battle. They were scattered in a single charge by Northampton, Suffolk, Warwick and perhaps the prince.[57]

After the battle, the heralds were despatched to identify the fallen. A total of 1,542 French knights and squires fell near the prince's lines alone,[58] among whom were John, the blind king of Bohemia, and his knights, said by Froissart to have been tethered together so he might strike a blow in the conflict. It may have been from John, possibly slain by the prince himself, that Edward adopted the ostrich feathers as his device as prince of Wales.[59] Another of the fallen was Jean d'Harcourt, Godfroi's brother.[60] The extreme number of French casualties can be attributed to Edward's orders that no quarter was to be offered; no one was to break ranks to take prisoners or to plunder the dead. This was a tactical necessity based on the need to maintain order in the ranks, but also followed from the French deployment of the *Oriflamme*, which was a sign of *guerre mortelle*. They did so again at Poitiers where 'Sire Geoffroi de Charny bore the scarlet standard, which is the token of Death, for the French king had issued an order that the life of no Englishman was to be spared except that of the prince himself.'[61] By comparison, English casualties were very low in these battles. In 1346, only 40 men-at-arms were reported as missing although presumably many more infantry and archers were killed.

This aspect of the 'military revolution', the much-increased casualty rates among the defeated and the paltry numbers of slain among the victors, had considerable implications for subsequent encounters in the Hundred Years War. At Nájera, according to the letter the prince sent his wife, later circulated in England, Sir John Ferrers was the only member of the English aristocracy to die.[62] Such success made recruitment easier in England, built an image of military superiority and further strengthened the proud identity of the military caste. By contrast, the consequences for the French aristocracy were grave indeed and for many years after 1356 they avoided all pitched battles with the longbowmen and infantry of England. The experience of Crécy shaped not only the Black Prince's career but also the expectations of a nation. After 1346, defeat in battle to the French became unthinkable. The battle in which the prince won his spurs and for which he was given credit was both a blessing and a curse.

Transitions of Military Power: Strategy and Tactics

The tactics that secured the victory at Crécy were shaped by experiences in Scotland and used in France in a number of minor skirmishes before proving effective at Morlaix in 1342. The increasing professionalism of the Anglo-Gascon troops allowed them to deploy quickly and efficiently to a tactical plan based on an effective combination of mounted, foot and missile troops; indeed Prestwich has described a 'tactical revolution' occurring in Edward III's reign.[63] The potential superiority of infantry over cavalry had been demonstrated repeatedly although the heavy cavalryman remained a formidable warrior when employed intelligently, especially as full plate armour developed for man and horse.[64]

The traditional view of the battle of Crécy attributes the victory to the English archers and their longbows. But the importance of the longbow is a contentious matter. A number of issues are open to argument and interpretation, ranging from the nature of the weapons themselves, their power and rate of accurate fire, to their impact on the enemy, and the disposition of the archers on the battlefield. There are various difficulties with establishing the importance of the longbow. First, there is little contemporary literature on the subject written before the fifteenth century that survives although various illustrations show different uses of the bow and the stances adopted while shooting. These include the Queen Mary's psalter (probably made for Edward II), the Holkham Bible Picture Book (c.1330) and the Luttrell psalter (c.1341). The second and more significant problem is that no longbows survive that predate those found on the *Mary Rose* (1545) and there are also questions about these. If, however, they are representative of battlefield weapons then they were formidable indeed with draw-weights between 98 lb and 185 lb.[65]

The increasing use of the longbow, a popular, not aristocratic weapon (on the battlefield – it was used in hunting), indicates the need to draw on the support of all levels of society during times of war. It was not easy to master and required training from a young age, which is hardly surprising if the extreme draw-weights indicated by the *Mary Rose* bows are accurate for the early stages of the Hundred Years War. The importance of archery to the national cause is clear in legislation of 1363 which made regular practice compulsory.[66]

Such training could leave its mark. Investigations of a mass grave from the battle of Towton (1461) and of the *Mary Rose* crew show a substantial number of soldiers with signs of abnormal muscular development and greater bone circumference on the left shoulder and upper arm. This probably suggests strenuous exercise perhaps with a bow or unimanual weapon from a young age.[67] It is possible that a dedicated and highly trained archery unit fought (and died) at Towton and sailed on the *Mary Rose*, but it cannot be inferred from this that one was present at Crécy.

Although questions remain, it appears that at Crécy the bowmen were very effective against the French cavalry, and at Poitiers against dismounted men-at-arms.[68] Those battles also showed the superiority of the longbow over the crossbow in terms of range and rate of fire. The *Mary Rose* bows were probably effective at 300 yards, by comparison with 200 yards for a wooden or composite crossbow. More importantly, for every three crossbow quarrels (bolts) a bowman might fire 20 arrows and this disparity could become even greater in rain and poor weather, which was the case at Crécy.

The success of the archers at Crécy altered the composition and tactics of future English armies. The importance of archers and their weapons is evident in the Black Prince's campaign of 1356, when desperate requests for supplies resulted in the requisition of all remaining arrows and archery equipment in Cheshire, and the arrest of all the fletchers in the county who were then forced to work for him. In addition, a further 1,000 bows, 2,000 sheaves of arrows and 400 gross of bowstrings were to be purveyed from elsewhere in England.[69] By the time of the Reims campaign the emergence of the mounted archer and establishment of mixed retinues (men-at-arms and archers) was complete. The proportion of longbowmen to other troops in armies was regularly 3, 4 or 5:1 and sometimes reached as high as 20:1. This in turn is indicative of a shift in the social composition of the military community.[70]

The significance of archery is evident in official records and in popular stories. In addition to the training legislation, in 1357 and 1369 the export of bows and arrows was forbidden, and in 1365 archers were forbidden to leave England without royal licence. The development of the Robin Hood legends may also have been encouraged by the 'emergence of a military machine in which bowmen were playing so prominent a part'.[71] Nonetheless, while the range and rate of disciplined archer fire could prove extremely disruptive and sometimes lethal, the effective defence of the forces under Charles de Blois and du Guesclin at the battle of Auray (1364) demonstrated that close formations of well-armoured soldiers could provide a less easy target.

The longbow was not the only English advantage in 1346. The military encounters prior to Crécy meant that Edward commanded a remarkably well-disciplined and experienced army.[72] This was married to an increasingly professional approach to warfare based on new methods of recruiting and supplying troops. Recruiting captains were commissioned to provide a certain number of troops, armed in a particular fashion. The orders often stated that the soldiers were to be 'tested and arrayed' ensuring that they had some skill with their weapons. This was necessary as evidence that these troops received training after recruitment is limited and there is no suggestion that medieval armies were drilled formally. It is likely that archers were well practiced and there are certainly various illustrations that depict longbowmen firing at targets. Individual skill though had to be applied to collective action – the bow was probably effective in a battle only if the archers fired *en masse*. This is shown in numerous manuscript illustrations in which archers are depicted arranged in ranks and shooting simultaneously. Similarly, while a knight received some taste of warfare in tournaments and much individual training, there is little to suggest he was well prepared for the realities of battle.[73]

It can therefore be assumed that most training was undertaken on the field itself and this may have been another advantage for the English forces. For Edward III's armies, military service in Scotland established a cadre of experienced and battle-hardened troops who became accustomed to fighting to certain strategic and tactical plans. They were also soldiers who received payment and were not subject to the limitations of service associated with the feudal array. Troops could be maintained in the field for extended periods of time. While of great strategic value this had implications with regard to supplies of food and arms. A proportion of the necessary supplies might be looted or purchased while on campaign, but more had to be acquired in England prior to departure. Often the supplies were purveyed, an extremely unpopular system of requisition that was nonetheless tolerated except during poor harvests and times of English military failure. If expeditions followed the coastline, as in the early stages of the 1346 operation, ships were used to resupply the army.

Such indentured armies (named after the contracts – indentures – used to secure military service) were not 'standing armies' or fully professional, but they indicate a transition along that road and certainly mark an important stage in the evolutionary path. Such an attitude also led to the development of uniforms – the prince's Cheshire soldiers were provided with green and white cloth for this purpose.

However, for this professional, disciplined and defensive strategy to work, chivalric impulses had to be avoided at all costs. Chivalric romances lauded individual deeds of prowess and reckless bravery – preferably performed on horseback. Crécy, Poitiers and Nájera were victories constructed by collective, disciplined infantry and archers. In this sense, the Black Prince, the 'flower of chivalry', contributed to the demise of chivalry on the battlefield.[74] In all of the prince's battles, the enemy assault failed in part because it was too chivalrous, because it relied on knightly individualism and lacked co-ordination.[75] In 1346, this problem was compounded by communication problems since the French army was multinational. By contrast, the only foreign troops in Edward's army were the Welsh who were organised in small groups with English-speaking commanders.

French commanders would have done well to give greater consideration to the maintenance of order in the ranks. In the past, Philippe had successfully avoided battle. The challenge in 1346 to his honour and to his kingship proved too great to evade. He, like Jean II at Poitiers and Enrique of Trastamara at Nájera, was forced into combat, more by personal and domestic political concerns than military necessity. Certainly in 1356, Jean had to fight at Poitiers, not because of the military conditions but because Geoffroi d'Harcourt and Robert le Coq were campaigning and conspiring against him and Etienne Marcel was gathering strength in Paris. The financial contributions to the war effort had been very great and he had nothing to show for them.[76] The king needed a victory, and with rather more luck, and rather more co-ordination within the ranks of the French hierarchy, he might have had one.

The situation was repeated in the prince's third great battle in Castile in 1367. At Nájera, Enrique of Trastamara would have done well to heed the advice of Bertrand du Guesclin and Charles V, who wrote urging him against engaging the prince in battle. The Trastamaran failure in 1367 was partly due to morale and numerical inferiority but, more importantly, it was a battle Enrique never needed to fight. The invaders could have been bottled up in Álava long before they reached Nájera. Even when they arrived there it would have been entirely possible to hold the bridge over the Najerilla river against them until the invaders' supplies gave out. Even so, once the decision to fight was made, the conservative

Castilian nobility did not make use of the knowledge their French allies had gleaned from earlier encounters with the English. Apart from the Order of the Band, the Castilian knights remained mounted, the troops and horses were lightly armoured and suffered greatly under the attacks of the English archers.

Lack of defensive equipment had also been a problem in 1346. Once committed to attack, Philippe should have waited until his troops and their supplies were all present. The Genoese crossbowmen might have been much more effective if they had their shields, which were *en route* from Abbeville even as the arrows were falling. The haste of the attack also contributed to the lack of tactical direction. Philippe had proved himself no mean general at the battle of Cassel in 1328, but his victory had been constructed from a cavalry charge and this may have influenced his tactics at Crécy.

More detrimental to the French cause was the impatience of, and disruption caused by, the French nobles, especially Alençon, although he had some success in his attack on the vanguard.[77] In defending against this, the role of the prince himself and his division was critical. For all the superiority of the archers, the victory at Crécy depended on the ability of the vanguard to hold against repeated charges of those knights who, before that day, had been numbered among the finest in Christendom.

There is no doubt about the great skill of the French cavalry. Despite the defensive preparations, the use of cannon to frighten the horses, the lack of central direction and control, and the threat of the archers, they managed to repeatedly charge, wheel and reform to attack again. Quite unfairly, blame was heaped upon them by contemporaries for attacking in disorder and allowing themselves to be defeated by dismounted men-at-arms and mere archers, 'gens de nulle value'.[78] These accusations were repeated ten years later after the French defeat at Poitiers. There, the lack of caution shown by the Marshal, Jean de Clermont, mirrored the presumption of Alençon at Crécy. The author of *La complainte sur la bataille de Poitiers* put the blame for the defeat squarely on the shoulders of the French nobility.[79]

In a sense then it was failures of French and Castilian co-ordination rather than especial skill that were responsible for one of the greatest periods of English military success in which the Black Prince played a central part.[80] After Crécy the French began to experiment tactically by deploying infantry in greater numbers at the battles of Lunalonge (1349), Taillebourg (1351), Ardres (1351) and Mauron (1352). This was an important development, but one that did not go far enough. Certainly, Jim Bradbury has maintained that the French failures were the result of not developing a type of infantry to match the pikemen and infantrymen of other nations.[81]

By the time of Poitiers, however, some infantry advances had been made and the battle was a close-run affair although there was again a lack of co-ordination, perhaps compounded by the difficult terrain. Once more the initial French charge was presumptuous, premature and poorly co-ordinated. The command of the French vanguard became divided between the Marshals, Audrehem and Clermont, who are reported to have argued over the best course of action, one recommended patience, at which the other made accusations of cowardice. After the failure of the French attacks, as at Crécy, part of the Anglo-Gascon response was the classic cavalry charge. The Captal de Buch led a flanking attack in which he may have been supported by mounted archers and possibly Gascon crossbowmen.[82]

By 1359 and the Reims campaign, this succession of crushing defeats suggested to the French that a fabian approach was the better part of valour and there were few pitched battles of note between England and France until Agincourt. Conflict, however, continued in other theatres and showed the English tactical approach was not invincible. At the battle of Auray, du Guesclin successfully countered the missile threat by advancing his troops behind *pavises*, although they were defeated in the subsequent hand-to-hand combat.[83] Du Guesclin's experience was ignored at Nájera where, simply by avoiding battle, Enrique could have defeated Pedro and his allies. Again, his enemies' lack of discipline and tactical direction were major elements that secured the prince's victory. These allowed him to attack the Trastamaran army as separate units rather than a single fighting force. The prince also took advantage of the terrain and was able to advance, hidden from Enrique by a hill, appearing on his enemy's left flank at daybreak.[84] Then, as at Crécy and Poitiers, the men-at-arms dismounted and the vanguard could await the enemy under the cover of archer fire.[85]

The prince's own military ability was demonstrated by his generalship at Poitiers and Nájera. In those battles the deployment of troops and tactics followed the model laid down at Crécy: victory was achieved through the use of (new) defensive tactics and a (traditional) chivalric *coup de grâce*. At Poitiers this allowed him to defeat a French army that was perhaps twice as large as his own Anglo-Gascon force. But it is important to remember that those numbers were not brought together at one time and in many of the phases of the battle the prince may have not been at any sort of numerical disadvantage. The battle again showed the effectiveness of longbowmen against cavalry, but they proved less devastating against infantry advancing in close formation, that is until the French were at close range when the longbows with their heavy draw-weights could punch through French armour. After the opening salvos, however, arrows were in short supply.

But these victories were not only the product of careful strategic planning – a good deal of luck was involved and plans often went awry. In 1356, the failure to link up and combine forces with Lancaster in accordance with the initial plan could have been disastrous, while the Castilian campaign as a whole was poorly organised and embarked upon with little thought of the consequences and cost. The prince's army arrived at Nájera exhausted, and the expedition could have ended without any sort of major engagement. Nonetheless, the movement of 10,000 soldiers with their horses and baggage through the pass of Ronsevalles, some 3,500 feet above sea level, in the cold of February, was a logistical triumph.

Vegetian Strategy: Avoiding Battles or Seeking Them?

It has become a truism to say that the Hundred Years War is remembered for its battles but was characterised by its sieges. Indeed, England and France fought remarkably few battles, and they were uncommon throughout the medieval period. It is open to question whether this should be attributed to fear of the consequences, a lack of strategic awareness or the inability to manage battles effectively at a tactical level. Perhaps battles did not always provide the answer to a particular strategic problem. Certainly they did not guarantee major political gains, although the chance of capturing or killing high-ranking members of the opposition meant the potential value could be very high.

Beyond these practical issues, military theory warned against joining battle unless the odds were stacked in one's favour. So said Flavius Vegetius Renatus in one of the most popular texts of the middle ages, the *Epitoma re militaris*. This survives (if only in parts) in more than 320 manuscripts, presumably a mere fraction of the total number produced.[86] Written in the late fourth century in an attempt to revivify the Imperial army, it was first translated into French in the thirteenth century and became one of the first classical works to be printed. Vegetius was hugely influential and his work is found in many royal and noble libraries. More interestingly, simple, compact versions of the manuscript were also produced, perhaps suggesting that commanders consulted it on campaign. Certainly his writings were used and adapted by authors such as Honoré Bonet and Christine de Pizan in the late fourteenth and early fifteenth century.[87]

The extent to which medieval commanders applied Vegetian principles remains a matter of debate and it is one that has been reinvigorated recently, mainly as the consequence of a detailed study of Edward III's campaigns.[88] Clifford Rogers has argued persuasively that rather than strategies that aimed to inflict damage while avoiding a pitched encounter the Crécy and Poitiers *chevauchées* were deliberately provocative. Rather than fleeing from Philippe and Jean, Edward III and the Black Prince aimed to bring them to battle. There were certainly good political reasons for seeking a decisive military encounter. Edward III had achieved very little in France before 1346. Philippe had effectively destroyed the great alliance by declining to confront it at Vironfosse in 1339 and a year later at Tournai. The expense of these failures may have been such that Edward decided that he could only achieve his objectives by victory in battle. If so then the devastation wrought during the march from La Hougue was designed to damage tax revenue, cause baronial discontent and induce pressure to attack.[89] In this interpretation the retreat over the Somme was no retreat and rather, as Villani suggested, Edward was seeking a suitable site for a battle. This may well be the case since 'in view of the speed with which he took up position after crossing the Somme, the battlefield must have been reconnoitred in advance'.[90]

In addition, various delays during the campaign and attacks made on sites of limited value do suggest Edward was trying to tempt the French to fight a battle which he was confident of winning. The king had faith in his cause, his army, and its commanders – five earls fought at Halidon Hill, and Bartholomew Burghersh, senior, had first seen military service in 1315. Morale was good and the army was perfecting a tactical system that had defeated odds of 10:1 at Dupplin Moor.[91] Although the English were exhausted after covering over 300 miles in the previous month they did have time to prepare themselves and the battlefield.[92] By marching towards Flanders there was also the chance of being reinforced or escaping in the event of defeat. There were also political imperatives. Parliament had advised the king to seek battle; the 1344 subsidy had been granted on that condition, and Edward had publicly and privately proclaimed this intention. By 1346 it was in his best financial interests to seek a swift resolution, as tax revenue was all but exhausted.[93]

The same financial and political imperatives did not apply to the Black Prince's campaign in 1356. Following the success of the *chevauchée* of the previous year, a second expedition set out from Bordeaux. The intention was to join forces with an army led by Henry, duke of Lancaster. Had this taken place the combined force could have sought a battle with some confidence. When, for logistical reasons, this failed, a battle still remained a possibility, but only a battle fought on the prince's terms. Certainly, like his father ten years previously, the prince made various delays and detours, apparently to allow the French to catch him. One of the advantages, as at Crécy, was the time this gave the English to prepare their position. They dug-in behind earthworks and used the protection of the terrain and certain natural features to their advantage.[94]

However, the concessions that the prince was willing to make prior to the battle, and some of his subsequent comments suggest he was not confident early on the morning of Monday 19 September. He later remarked: 'Because we were short of supplies and for other reasons, it was agreed that we should retreat in a flanking movement, so that if they wanted to attack or to approach us in a position which was not in any way greatly to our disadvantage we would give battle.'[95]

This does not indicate that the prince was determined to fight a battle, nor did he feel the need to hide the fact that retreat had been an option. Although he did not suggest the manoeuvre was a feint, it is a possibility and if so it was a brilliant success since '. . . there died . . . the full flower of French chivalry'.[96] Those that did not fall in the disorganised assault on English lines were taken captive alongside their king.[97] Whether or not Edward III and the Black Prince actively sought battles, there is no doubt that they were in a good position to prove victorious if battle was joined. Described as 'the incredible victory':[98] Poitiers reinforced the prince's reputation and changed the balance of power in the war.

The reward for English battlefield success in 1346, 1356 and 1367, however, was never as great as it might have been. After Crécy, weary though victorious, the English army was in no position to capitalise on its success in Paris or the heartlands of France. The English and Welsh were too few in number to besiege the French capital which, in any case, would take them far from necessary supplies and reinforcements. Edward decided on a less ambitious target – Calais. The decision to besiege the town was apparently not discussed in advance and there may have been other possible targets, including Boulogne, which was attacked by English ships on 4 September 1346, a day after Edward laid siege to Calais – he would not capture it until 4 August 1347.[99]

The siege was notable for a number of reasons: its length; the number of soldiers involved (between 26,000 and 32,000);[100] and the widespread, if relatively ineffective, use of artillery. Edward had at least ten cannon and materials for over 5,000 lb of gunpowder, but the weapons do not appear to have contributed a great deal in capturing the town.[101] The potential of artillery was, however, becoming clear and the prince also used cannon in 1356, particularly in the siege of Romorantin, as well as Greek fire.[102] From 1360 to 1370, many towns and almost all the great powers in western Europe came to possess their own arsenals.

In 1369, the receiver of Ponthieu purchased for Edward III: 20 copper cannon; five iron cannon; 215 lb of saltpetre; sulphur and amber for making powder; and 1,300 large quarrels (bolts).[103] But it was not until the late fourteenth century that these crude guns evolved into (semi-) formidable artillery. At this stage, they did not replace the trebuchet or mangonel as siege weapons, and on the battlefield they did not influence tactical thinking to any great extent.[104] However, the appearance of gunpowder weapons marks the beginning of a new epoch of warfare. It was an evolutionary rather than revolutionary change, but by the end of the fourteenth century cannon were breaching the walls of fortifications. It was in the fifteenth century that the revolution really took place: in the final act of the Hundred Years War the French guns destroyed the English armies at Castillon (1453), the same year that Constantinople fell to the artillery bombardment of Mehmed II.[105]

Philippe VI took steps to relieve the siege of Calais and the English naval embargo; when these were unsuccessful he encouraged David Bruce to divert the English by leading an attack from Scotland. David encountered an army at Neville's Cross near Durham in October 1346, but was captured himself and his army completely defeated, setting the seal on Edward's *annus mirabilis*. On 27 July 1347, Philippe finally rallied his forces and brought an army to relieve the siege. There was some skirmishing between the armies, but little of consequence. Negotiations opened and continued until 31 July: they came to nothing, and when Philippe struck camp, with the last hope of rescue gone, the town surrendered.

Calais may seem to be a minor acquisition after such a comprehensive victory and in some ways it was, but the port provided an excellent base for future military incursions and also became a major trade centre when the wool staple was transferred there. It may be that a further campaign would have been launched in 1348, but military action and much else besides was curtailed by the devastation and social dislocation wrought by the Black Death.

It is difficult to overestimate the importance of the campaign of 1346–7, the twin victories of Crécy and Calais, augmented by the success at Neville's Cross. Crécy was the first major English continental victory in more than 150 years and also a personal triumph for the Black Prince. Such a success, which built upon lesser victories such as Morlaix and the triumphs in Scotland, altered the political atmosphere radically and was a clear indication of a new power coming to the fore in Europe. As a consequence there would be no major domestic objections to English royal policy for almost 25 years. The new methods of fighting had been established and found to be devastatingly successful and the king had surrounded himself with a group of commanders and advisors on whom he could depend. Together, in 1346–7, they mobilised over 30,000 troops and kept them supplied in the field. Not least of the successes of the Crécy–Calais campaign was the military and political baptism of the prince of Wales who had showed himself a worthy successor to a king who was still young enough to secure many more such victories. But the 1346–7 campaign also showed that the conquest of France could not be achieved with a single victory, however great. The English did not have the resources to turn on Paris and had to settle for the lesser prize of Calais. While outside the walls of the town, the menace of Scotland re-emerged and although the battle of Neville's Cross was yet another victory, the threat on the English northern border remained.

The battle of Crécy and the siege of Calais and their associated campaigns provide clear examples of the changing nature of military power in fourteenth-century Europe. They were victories achieved through the use of strategies and tactics that had been used by commanders for centuries, but were given new focus by the ability of kings to keep troops in the field for extended periods – much longer than allowed by the traditional feudal array. They confirmed the superiority of trained infantry over cavalry and they established the importance of missile weapons, particularly the longbow, on the Continent. Most revolutionary, they pointed towards the role that would be played by gunpowder weapons in years to come.

More might have been achieved by the Black Prince and his father had they been able to return to France, but while they were still celebrating their victory news began to reach them of a terrible plague spreading throughout Europe. The first phase of the Hundred Years War had shown the changing nature of military power in Europe; the Black Death would change a good deal more.

chapter two

THE BLACK DEATH: 'A PLAGUE ON EMINENCE'

It [the plague] left hardly enough people alive to give the dead a decent burial . . . Ulcers broke out in the groin and the armpit, which tortured the dying for three days . . . And there was in those days death without sorrow, marriage without affection, self-imposed penance, want without poverty and flight without escape . . . In the end the plague devoured a multitude of people . . . Scarcely a tenth of the population survived.[1]

John of Reading's account is something of an exaggeration; it was probably a mere third and almost certainly no more than a half of the population of England that died during the plague of 1348–50. It has been ranked, if such events can really be graded, as the second worst catastrophe in history, falling behind the Second World War by two tenths of a point on the Foster scale of disaster magnitude.[2] The disease to which John of Reading was referring has long been diagnosed as bubonic plague, possibly with pneumonic or septicaemic variants encouraging the great speed of transmission. It did not become known as the Black Death until the sixteenth century and it only became a term common in English from the mid nineteenth.

More recently, various historians have challenged the identification of the Black Death with bubonic plague, and continuing medical research remains inconclusive as to the precise nature of the disease that swept through Europe regularly after 1347.[3] Similarly, historians continue to question and attempt to quantify the impact of the plague: again, due to the nature of the available evidence, conclusions must be speculative. There is no doubt, however, that the plague changed the balance of power and the character of medieval Europe. Its impact, however heavy, was widespread and few aspects of life were unaffected by its passing. Economic and social relations, agricultural practices, and land use all changed.

The plague also altered the way individuals conceived of their place in the world, in relation to their neighbours and their social 'superiors', both secular and ecclesiastic. Since, for the majority, the only conceivable explanation for the plague was that it manifested God's wrath, the Black Death changed perspectives regarding the divine and His Church as death became ever-present and brought with it the closer proximity of the Almighty. Since the plague influenced almost all aspects of later medieval society, reference to it will be made throughout the remainder of this book. In particular, the religious connotations were extensive. Some mention is made of these in this chapter where considered appropriate and others that sit within a broader trend of religious changes are examined in Chapter Six.

It is impossible to know how the Black Prince perceived the Black Death, but its impact was surely considerable. He lost his sister in the first outbreak of the plague and a number of his comrades-in-arms in the 1360s. The high levels of mortality put the administration of his estates under great pressure and the revenue he enjoyed from them was severely compromised. He may have been involved in formulating policy in response to these problems, but it is more likely that this was the responsibility of local officials since attitudes differed considerably between Wales, Cheshire and Cornwall. In some parts of his demesne the responses were both compassionate and effective economically; rents were remitted and attempts were made to alleviate the worst of the effects so as to keep tenants on their lands. But elsewhere, little notice was taken of the terrible impact of the plague and exactions continued to be made almost irrespective of the appalling death toll.

Administrative dislocation resulting from the impact of the plague may account for the unfortunate gap in the evidence of the prince's register between the first months of 1348 and 1350. This document, which provides details of household organisation and estate administration, is invaluable for a study of the milieu in which the prince lived, but tells us little about the consequences of the Black Death for Edward and his household. There is no doubt though that the plague changed the world in which the prince lived and it is impossible to imagine that he was unmoved by this most powerful demonstration of divine wrath. It would be unwise to suggest that his experiences of plague contributed to some of his more 'puritanical' religious attitudes, but the plague did lead to changes in the religious environment in which the prince lived. It also changed structures of power and authority as a consequence of the catastrophic levels of mortality among the peasantry. Indeed, no force was more significant in altering the balance of power between lord and vassal in the later middle ages.

Apocalypse

For some, when 'Plague' and 'Death' arrived in Europe in 1347, these two horsemen heralded the end of the world and the imminent approach of the Last Judgement. They were the last of the cavalcade: 'Famine' had struck in 1315 and 'War' was now a constant companion. It was not only authors such as the Rochester chronicler, Gabriel de Mussis, Louis Heyligen and John Clynn who saw the Black Death as a portent of the Apocalypse.[4] This is hardly surprising; the 'biblical' scale of the plague was such that the only comparisons to be drawn were with epidemics in the Old and New Testaments.

As in so many respects, this millenarianism was an instance in which the plague encouraged and catalysed existing trends. The exact time of the Apocalypse had been a subject of speculation throughout the Christian era and this had, since 1240, encouraged the production of a remarkable series of illustrated Apocalypse manuscripts in England, many for the royal courts. These works were perhaps encouraged by Joachite teachings and the relevance of the theme they expressed only increased with the tribulations of the fourteenth century.

Numerous works were concerned with the 'end times'. The final section of the Middle English *Cursor Mundi*, a universal history written at the beginning of the century, considers the last age of the world and the arrival of Antichrist. This age would, it was said, be heralded by war, famine and death. Further information on Doomsday was provided towards the middle of the century by the extremely popular poem, the *Pricke of Conscience* (*c.*1340) that, with a certain prescience, foretold a fracturing of the Church and the devastation of nations.[5]

With the arrival of the first pandemic, visual images of the Apocalypse also became increasingly common and many English parish churches were painted with a 'Doom' or scene of the Last Judgement, such as the fresco (dated to the 1430s) at the church of the Holy Trinity in Coventry. In these the dead are seen to rise from their graves, their souls are weighed and they are separated into the saved and the damned.[6]

Such images reinforced biblical and theological teachings. The plague did not only provide what appeared to be a clear demonstration of divine castigation, but it also, along with its accompanying signs and natural catastrophes, fitted an understanding of the world in millenarian or chiliastic terms in which the arrival of Antichrist would be preceded by disasters.[7] Indeed, the birth of Antichrist was widely reported in the mid-fourteenth century. In his aptly-titled *Companion in Tribulation*, John of Rupescissa foretold the arrival of Antichrist in 1365 and stated that in the five years prior to this there would be natural disasters and plagues which 'will kill the greater part of the present evil generation, so that the world may be renewed and led back to the unity of the Catholic faith'.[8]

A concern with spiritual salvation was, of course, not new. It lay at the heart of the Christian message – life was merely a preparation for the inevitability of divine judgement. The scale of mortality associated with the Black Death, however, gave a new emphasis to the necessity to secure salvation and an immediate need to put one's spiritual house in order. This may also have been associated with a greater awareness of the doctrine of purgatory, demonstrated most famously by Dante Alighieri in the second volume of his *Divine Comedy*. Lessening one's time on the 'mountain' of purgatory and providing oneself with a better chance of eventual salvation became all the more necessary in the face of the divine anger manifested by the Black Death.

The Great Famine – Economic Conditions before the Plague

Despite the very high levels of mortality associated with the Black Death it appears that the full socio-economic impact of the plague only began to be felt from about the middle years of the 1360s. This can be attributed to the demographic profile of the population and also the effects of the second major outbreak of the disease in 1361–2. It may also be indicative of the remarkable resistance of the European population which, since the start of the century, had been battered by a range of disasters and had suffered from a general downturn in economic conditions. Agricultural productivity fell because of climate change, the so-called 'Little Ice Age', which resulted in severe winters and wet summers. In addition, the growing population of the thirteenth century had relied increasingly on cereal crops. These reduced the fertility of the soil, a situation worsened by the inability to leave the land fallow. Consequently, yields per acre fell although the total area under cultivation continued to expand.[9]

The increasing fragility of the agricultural situation put the population at ever-greater risk of famine and this struck with a vengeance not long into the century. The Great Famine, the worst such event in recorded history, was the result of a poor harvest in 1314, followed by two years of wet weather. Although there was a much better crop in 1317, it was not sufficient to restore arable prices to pre-famine levels, meaning that poor families could not purchase grain. Another poor year in 1321–2 coincided with disease among sheep and cattle epidemics in 1319–21.

It has been estimated that in 1315 wheat production fell to 60 per cent of average levels and to 55 per cent in 1316, leaving very little spare for feeding animals or for sale. The north of England generally suffered more than the south, and there the harvest in some manors brought in a mere 11.5 per cent of former yields. In response, wheat prices trebled, rising from 5s./6s. to 16s. per quarter. To add insult to injury, salt production also failed and this adversely affected the preservation of meat, and a lack of hay was a further blow to animal health. Estimates of the mortality rate range from 10 to 17 per cent as a result of famine and accompanying disease, possibly typhus.[10]

The people of England and Wales showed great resilience. They suffered terribly during the Great Famine with a catastrophic loss of life, but it appears that population levels recovered somewhat in the years prior to the arrival of the Black Death. Certainly, a poor harvest in England in 1346–7 was enough to cause food riots in Bristol, King's Lynn and Boston. This implies that the population remained of such a size to be vulnerable to a single harvest failure although the situation was worsened by military conditions. The Crécy–Calais campaign demanded high levels of purveyance and the export of substantial amounts of grain to Gascony (15,950 quarters in 1347). This drove up food prices especially in the vicinity of the ports.[11]

The Impact and Extent of the Black Death

While the people of Europe struggled to recover from the Great Famine another greater threat was stirring and its approach and its terrible effects were reported while still far off. The sense of impending death must have contributed to the extreme reactions to the plague. News of its approach grew steadily. At first it was just a murmur: in the 1320s the plague had broken out in Mongolia and the Gobi desert (where it remains endemic); it passed overland to China, Azerbaijan and the Crimea, and then linked into the European trade routes.

The traditional story tells that Genoese merchants brought it to Europe. They had been besieged at Kaffa on the Black Sea by Yanibeg, the khan of the Golden Horde, who is said to have had the bodies of plague victims catapulted into the city. Whether or not this is true the Black Death reached the Mediterranean in 1347 and quickly spread inland in all directions. Working its way along the trade arteries, such as the rivers Rhône, Saône, Seine and Rhine, the plague quickly penetrated western Europe. In 1348 it came to the British Isles and by 1350 it had spread to the northern extremities of the Continent, Iceland, Orkney, Greenland and the Faroes.[12]

The impact of the plague was not uniform, not all areas were affected, and among those that were the mortality rates varied considerably. In

Britain, the plague spread northwards, probably from Melcombe Regis in Dorset. It continued to follow the trade routes and, if traditional diagnoses are to be believed, many of the fleas carrying the plague bacillus were transported in cloth and other goods. The Black Prince's estates in Britain suffered less than many other regions mainly because Wales, Chester and Cornwall did not have many towns and trade centres where the plague was most virulent. But, even on the fringes of the kingdom, the level of mortality was considerable. In Wales, the progress of the plague can be tracked from the southeast to Abergavenny and Carmarthenshire, which it reached by March 1349, and then northwards via Whittington and Chirk.[13] Flintshire was particularly hard hit and in June 1349 the plague arrived in Ruthin. In Dyffryn Clwyd, 193 people died in two weeks. In a fortnight, ten died in Llangollen, 13 in Llanerch and 25 in Dogfalen. These figures probably soon doubled. Denbigh was also affected grievously. The north of the country probably suffered most, but later outbreaks of the plague in 1361–2 and 1369 brought the highest mortality rates to the south and south-east, although Flint, Denbigh, Anglesey and Caernarfon were again ravaged. This compares, however, very favourably with the situation in London where there were losses of between 25 and 50 per cent (perhaps as many as 25,000 people). At its height perhaps 290 people were dying every day in the capital.[14] (In 1348 the population of England and Wales was approximately 4.2 million and by 1377 poll tax returns in England suggest a population of around 2.5 million. Perhaps 2 million people died in Britain during the plague.)

The consequences were extensive and, if only considered in financial terms, the concentration of the plague in urban areas was extremely damaging. The decline in income from market tolls was a main cause of the difficulties that confronted British towns in the later fourteenth century.[15] This caused particular problems for the Black Prince who received a life annuity of 1,000 marks from the customs of London. As a consequence of the severe dislocation of trade, the farmers of the customs, Walter Chiriton and his associates, had to default on a number of payments between October 1348 and March 1349.[16]

While the prince's lands in England and Wales were spared the worst of the effects, his future French estates were not so fortunate. The sheer size of the principality of Aquitaine, which he held from 1362, meant it was bound to suffer high casualty rates and it appears the plague was especially severe in the south of France with perhaps three times the mortality levels of the northern and central parts of the kingdom. In the north, children and poorer people were the most common victims. This may help to explain a number of issues, not least that England and

France were able, despite the impact of the plague, to muster armies and pay for military and governmental developments in the 1350s. The disproportionate impact of the plague on the young and the poor meant that those least affected were those most able to pay taxes and fight in armies. In France, the number of taxable hearths did not decline sharply until a dozen or so years later when the children of 1348 became heads of households.[17] By this time the prince was resident in Aquitaine and dealing with the real impact of the 1348–50 outbreak as well as the immediate consequences of the *malaise des enfants* of 1361–2.[18]

Economic Effects and the Impact on Land Use

The impact of the plague on the regime of the Black Prince in Aquitaine was considerable, and throughout Europe the consequences of such high levels of mortality were felt deeply. The financial effects were not restricted to the towns, and with financial change came social destabilisation. In England, Wales and France, the Black Death forced the aristocracy to change the way it used land and those who worked it. The grasp of the landed classes on their demesnes and peasants slackened as land became less valuable and labour much more costly. This did not just mean that new ways had to be found to finance aristocratic lifestyles and military campaigns, but that the very identity of the aristocracy altered.

The aristocracy was identified by and with its land. Its members drew their income and often their names from it. Land had given them wealth and lordship, but from the later years of the fourteenth century it simply did not sustain the aristocracy in the same fashion as in earlier years. This is not to say that the Black Death of itself broke the manorial system, still less did it signal the end of 'feudalism' in England or elsewhere in Europe, but it changed the relationship between lord and peasant through the impact it made on the use and value of land and labour.

The deaths of 30 to 50 per cent of the population of England and Wales left few socio-economic orthodoxies unshaken. The extreme levels of peasant mortality created immediate financial problems: incomes from rents fell, wage costs rose, and the peasantry was increasingly reluctant to perform labour services. Seigneurial reactions to the plague varied, but many landowners attempted to re-establish the socio-economic *status quo* and the lord-peasant relationship expressed in the control of land, labour and property. A shift in the character of the relationship between lord and vassal had been evident for some time, but the process was given greater impetus in the changing economic and social climate created by the Black Death.[19]

In order to deal with such disturbances and to try and restrict the consequences that were almost immediately apparent to central government, Edward III introduced the Ordinance of Labourers in 1349 and the Statute of Labourers, two years later. The legislation had three main aims. First, it regulated wages and the value of labour by pegging them to acceptable, usually pre-plague levels. Secondly, the movement of labour was restricted by reinforcing traditional impositions, tying peasants to their manors and preventing them from seeking higher wages elsewhere. Finally, it enforced terms of employment and contracts with favourable conditions for employers. As far as the government was concerned the legislation was necessary '[b]ecause a great part of the people, and especially workmen and servants, late died of the pestilence, [and] many [of those who remain] . . . will not serve unless they receive excessive wages, and some are willing to beg in idleness, than by labour to get their living'.[20] This continued to be a major aspect of parliamentary business and more than a third of the 77 parliaments that sat between 1351 and 1430 passed labour legislation in some form. As time passed the legislation gave increasing emphasis to the requirement of all persons to work, further restrictions were made to the work options of the peasantry, and greater penalties imposed for vagrancy, begging and vagabondage.[21]

The continuing concern with restricting social mobility and economic opportunities for the peasantry is a clear indication of the threat felt by the governing elite. It is also an indication that the legislation was less than successful. The responsibility for enforcing the labour legislation fell on the aristocracy: 'commissions were made to divers people in every shire to enquire and punish all those who offend'.[22] The members of the commissions were subject to diverse pressures: they wished to maintain the traditional economic balance between lord and peasant, but in order to maintain their income they were compelled to compete for labour, this valuable new commodity. The aristocracy was to some degree responsible for the failure of the legislation it imposed. Higher wages were not the only inducement – some landlords may have circumvented the labour legislation by offering the peasantry more comfortable living and working conditions, such as better board, food and drink.[23]

This was not the first attempt to regulate labour, economic conditions, and contractual and social obligations. A history of legislation stretched back to the Assize of Measures of 1189, and most recently there had been action in response to the famine in 1315.[24] The speed with which the Ordinance was passed reflects an awareness of earlier legal responses to problematic conditions and also an immediate consciousness of the dangers posed by the plague. Nonetheless, it appears that the later outbreaks and the continued pressure exerted by repeated incidents of plague led to the most significant socio-economic changes and these took some time to become fully apparent.[25] In the interim there were concerted efforts through the offices of local and central governmental to restrict or at least regulate the new freedoms afforded to the surviving peasantry. Through the labour legislation as well as the later sumptuary and game laws, traditional impositions were reinforced.[26] As a result of seigneurial action, the lot of the peasantry may not have improved greatly in the immediate aftermath of the first outbreak of the plague. Customary dues and fines continued to be raised and, while wages improved (by 15 to 30 per cent) despite the labour legislation, food prices rose as well, especially in 1369 when grain prices approached those of the famine years of 1315–17. Consequently, even though the socio-economic environment of the post-plague years favoured the peasantry, conditions only improved substantially in the 1370s when food prices fell.[27]

The image of the later middle ages as a golden period for the peasantry is a great exaggeration. But the conditions did allow for the emergence of a peasant elite, able to take advantage of the land glut and accumulate property for itself. Such people acquired livestock and engaged in effective agricultural practices balanced between pastoral and arable farming. Langland's description of the peasants of the later fourteenth century living a life of leisure as a result of higher wages was a caricature, but it does show that some were able to profit substantially in the post-plague economic climate. Clearly though this was not the case for all.[28]

The greater wages and demands of the peasantry and the lessening value of land were major problems for the aristocracy. Many of them also acquired new responsibilities as a result of post-plague legislation. There were also immediate and pressing concerns regarding the administration of estates which was heavily disrupted by the plague, not least because of the deaths of some of the key members of the secular and ecclesiastical communities. For example, in many parts of the principality of Wales, in the immediate aftermath of the plague, the essential offices of beadle, reeve, rhaglaw, rhingyll and woodward had to be farmed out for sums approaching half their customary fee and many such positions could not be filled at all.[29] In the prince's earldom of Chester, plague fatalities in 1348–9 included the abbot of Chester, prioress of St Mary's, prior of Norton and at least 24 parish clerks. Such disruption to administrative, governmental and religious life continued at irregular intervals throughout the prince's life because of the Black Death. For example, Thomas le Young, who held the offices of escheator, sheriff and steward of Cheshire and Flintshire, was a plague victim in 1361.[30]

The most serious consequences of the plague in the prince's estates resulted from the deaths of his tenants. In some regions he and his officials were able to mitigate these effects, but in others he was not so success-ful. In the manor of Drakelowe in Cheshire, 57 men died, as did at least 88 Macclesfield tenants. However, despite severe short-term administra-tive and socio-economic dislocation, by 1355 all but six of the holdings had been let to new tenants.[31] The local administration was resilient, and in Macclesfield Robert Legh, the deputy steward, was able to hold manorial courts throughout the plague period. Nonetheless, the financial realities of the situation could not be avoided. Rent arrears, despite an early tough policy towards revenue collection, had to be ignored in some cases as attempts were made to re-let now vacant holdings. Despite such measures, the value of the lordship of Macclesfield did not recover in the prince's lifetime, falling from £291 19s. 11d. in 1348–9 to £242 8s. 10d. in 1374–5, a loss of some 17 per cent.[32]

Progressive administrative policies could, however, mitigate the impact of the plague and this is particularly evident in the duchy of Cornwall. There, rents were reduced with the consequence that vacant holdings were filled on all but the least fertile manors and the profitability of the duchy, if not the stannaries (tin mines), was restored within a few years of the plague. By comparison, in the prince's manor of Berkhamsted (Herts) in 1360 there was still some land that had not been sown since 1349.[33] The impact of the plague in Cornwall can be seen from one small example. The annual value of Calstock weir fell from £10 to £6. In 1353, William Stacy, a prominent Tavistock burgess, purchased a seven-year lease for £8 a year. Nine months later the abbot of Tavistock offered £10 a year and was granted the lease. Stacy received £3 com-pensation for his expenditure on the weir.[34]

This seems to have been the general pattern in Cornwall – a steady recovery after the abrupt fall of income. The success can be attributed directly to the prince's administration: the 'policies initiated . . . to deal with the unprecedented crises caused by the Great Plague were remark-able in their wisdom and foresight'. It was because of these that the profits of the assessionable (Cornish demesne) manors were only 25 per cent lower in 1348–9 than during an average year earlier in the decade, and while the greatest loss of revenue was felt in 1350–1 (a 40 per cent drop) there was a progressive recovery thereafter.[35] The success of the post-plague policy in Cornwall seems to have been the work of the prince's council rather than Edward himself. He is said to have marvelled 'that his council was prepared to listen sympathetically to poor folk . . . importuning him and his council so much . . . and on such petty matters'.[36]

Attitudes were different in Wales, and the socio-economic complex-ion of the principality made it particularly vulnerable to the pressure imposed by the plague. Effects on revenue were immediate since the mortality rates were especially high among the bondsmen who carried the greatest burden of rents and dues. While policies were not as benign as in Cornwall, the Welsh administration was not entirely careless of its responsibilities to its subjects in such extraordinary circumstances. For example, the burgesses of Rhuddlan were granted a rebate of a quarter on their farm of £40 for certain mills. In Caernarfonshire, the authorities were also sympathetic in some small ways to the economic hardship although most rents continued to be levied. In Carmarthenshire, rents were not collected until 1351 at which point the 'Great Roll of Debts for South Wales' was begun. Income from mining was also affected. Pre-plague revenue from Englefield had been 100s. a year; by 1352 it was non-existent due to the death of the miners. The high mortality levels did, however, generate some compensatory income for the prince's coffers as escheats increased, as well as fees from the chancery seal.[37]

Over the longer term the plague contributed to changes in land use in the principality. More arable land could now lie fallow and some estates were not farmed at all. Some land, particularly in the mid-eastern marches of Wales, was turned over to pasture and sheep farming became a mainstay of the agricultural economy. Furthermore, many tenements were amalgamated as the rural population diminished. This process had been underway since the beginning of the century; it was encouraged by the plague and further galvanised by the revolt of Owain Glyn Dŵr (1401–c.1409). Some urban areas were also turned over to grazing and the bottom dropped out of the market for leases of escheat land.[38]

A consequence of such changes in Wales was the breakdown of the kin-based system of free land tenure and the virtual abandonment of demesne farming by the last quarter of the fourteenth century.[39] In part this was because considerable areas of marginal farmland were no longer needed now that the population had fallen so substantially. It was a process evident throughout Britain, although not a uniform one. The scaling down of demesne production further changed the relationship between lords and peasants especially after the fall in grain prices (most notably following a particularly fine harvest in 1375).[40] Since 1343, the prince's administration had worked hard, sometimes oppressively, to increase revenue from his Welsh estates and it was not prepared to allow income to fall without a struggle. The immediate response to the plague was to appoint local men to the various offices, especially that of sheriff, presumably in the hope that they would be able to compel payment where Englishmen had failed.[41] This did not, however, indicate a slackening in generally hostile attitudes to the Welsh and previous legislation was reinforced, such as Edward I's restrictions on Welshmen holding land in England and their acquisition of property elsewhere through purchase, marriage or inheritance. Trading was also limited as Welshmen were forced to sell their produce in the local borough market. As elsewhere, many were fined for taking wages above those prescribed by the Statute of Labourers. Not all legislation was unforgiving of the plague, however. In July 1352, a general order from the council to the chamberlain and deputy-justice of north Wales relieved the villeins and men of the advowry of each commote (unit of territory and lordship) from their obligation to contribute cattle for the munitioning of castles until such time as conditions improved.[42]

It is remarkable that despite further outbreaks in 1361–2, 1369 and 1375, and the reduction of the English and Welsh populations by approximately a third following the first onset of the plague, agriculture remained buoyant, and urban, industrial and commercial development continued. Revenue may not have recovered by the time of the prince's death, but it was not dramatically lower than in pre-plague years. In East Anglia, Denbigh, Monmouthshire, Somerset and Dorset income was only 10 per cent lower than in the 1340s. Cornish tin production, however, was devastated and had not completely recovered by the 1380s.

Assessing the precise effects of the plague on the prince's income is problematic. Indeed, a complete examination of the prince's finances is prevented by the lack of records from the receiver-general and losses in documentation from some estates. The rich evidence that survives from Chester and Cornwall is balanced by the very limited sources for the principalities of Wales and Aquitaine. Further, although the impact of plague was considerable in the short-term, the lack of efficiency in revenue collection and assessment in earlier years meant that pre-plague incomes were not of a high order. Hence a post-plague recovery to 1346 levels may well reflect improvements in financial administration as much as the broader economic climate.

It is clear that throughout his lifetime, the prince's administration extracted higher levels of finance than had been the case hitherto and the management of his estates became more rigorous and effective. Resources were centralised and profits circulated between the various estates. Consequently, inward investment was often negligible and resources from Chester and Cornwall were lavished on expenditure elsewhere, particularly Aquitaine. A consequence of this was friction and dissatisfaction and, if only by comparison with what went before, the prince's administration was exploitative and avaricious. Undoubtedly, it contributed to the revolt in Aquitaine and promoted disaffection in Wales.

The clearest statement of the prince's income is to be found at his death when the average value of his estates was calculated by reference to income over the previous three years (1372–5). The findings are noted on the table below.

Valor of the prince's estates[43]	
North Wales	£3,041 7s. 6d.
South Wales	£1,830 4s. 11d.
Cheshire, Flint & Macclesfield	£1,695 1s. 10d.
Cornwall	£2,219 7s. 9d.
Devon	£273 19s. 5d.
English estates	£922 11s. 2d.
Total	£9,982 12s. 8d.

Social and Religious Impact

The social consequences of economic dislocation following the long period of growth in the twelfth and thirteenth centuries were profound. First, the turmoil of the Great Famine threatened basic social structures and institutions throughout England and Wales. A lack of resources and the threat to the aristocracy – real or perceived – posed by the peasantry meant that the mutual responsibilities of lord to vassal were neglected. 'The famine strained the normal social bonds by which poverty was alleviated.'[44] Landowners, it seems, felt threatened by the poor and reduced contributions to charity and their attitudes hardened towards low-key crime.

Social disruption increased with the Black Death, which 'threatened to sever the bonds that held society together'.[45] The peasantry abrogated their 'responsibilities' by leaving their lords' estates and seeking higher wages elsewhere. This breakdown of the traditional social order was compounded by a huge rise in crime, especially the theft of foodstuffs. This was especially evident in Cheshire where the 1353 trailbaston sessions revealed a high incidence of casual violence at all levels of society.[46] Elsewhere there is evidence of growing tension, violence and disturbance in the 1350s and 1360s; in some areas caused by population movements, in others by the enforcement of government legislation and increasing demands for taxation.[47]

In Cheshire and throughout the prince's estates, the breakdown of law and order was partly attributable to administrative disruption caused by the deaths of his officials. Not all those who died in 1348–9 and 1361–2 were victims of plague, but there was a considerable turnover of personnel in the prince's administration and household at these times. At a national level comparable disruption served to weaken the unity of the Edwardian regime. The successful prosecution of the war and the effective government of the country were threatened by the deaths of several of those responsible for the accomplishments of the previous years.[48]

Even so, the mortality rate of tenants-in-chief and those making up the prince's personal circle was considerably lower than in other groups, perhaps 27 per cent as opposed to 45 per cent among monastic communities and parish priests, and up to 66 per cent for the peasantry. But there were some very significant individual casualties of the plague such as Thomas Bradwardine, archbishop of Canterbury, in 1349. A noted theologian and philosopher who influenced Wyclif, he served as a clerk in the royal household during the Crécy campaign and preached the victory sermon before the walls of Calais in November 1346. It may have been at this time that he came to the prince's attention. Certainly it was soon after, and not long before his death, that the Black Prince presented him with the benefice of Llanbadarn Fawr.[49]

Although plague mortality was lowest among the elite the Black Death contributed to the reshaping of the social fabric of the aristocracy as a whole. Every lineage was fragile. The necessity of producing a male heir, the high risk of childhood mortality, and the dangers inherent in military action all contributed to the threat to the continuance of a family line. Such dangers increased substantially with the arrival of the Black Death. Certainly by the 1370s, there was something of a crisis in the English aristocracy. Perhaps as many as 30 per cent of landowners died with no surviving child and, of these, female collateral relatives succeeded in 60 per cent of cases.[50] As a consequence it was often necessary to promote new men and families to aristocratic and noble status. This was also a process in which the economic implications of the plague were significant. The redistribution of wealth that the Black Death encouraged allowed certain members of the rising middle classes to adopt the style and, in time, the title of the gentility or even nobility. Clearly a matter of grave concern to established members of the elite, legislative measures were introduced such as the sumptuary laws that regulated what clothing individuals might wear according to their status and thereby controlled at least the appearance of nobility. Nonetheless, the forces of the plague were not so easily balked and there were substantial changes in the structure and complement of the late medieval aristocracy.

As well as concern with such changes in social order, a deep unrest with the behaviour of individuals followed the arrival of the Black Death. The response to such individual and collective deaths was very varied. Some commentators noted a general degeneration of manners and morality.

Traditional mores were thrown off, family responsibilities and loyalties were ignored, there was greater sexual promiscuity, a higher crime rate, gambling, swearing and, for some most troubling, the wearing of the new scandalous fashions.[51] Boccaccio's *Decameron* shows a full gamut of reactions to the Black Death – sobriety and abstinence, isolationism, singing, drunkenness, merrymaking and many who steered a middle course.

Of those who recorded such ideas, most had a social or religious agenda and an objective and personal view is difficult to find. One such source is the diplomatic letter Edward III sent to the Castilian court following the death of his daughter, Joan (d. 1348) in Bordeaux when *en route* to her marriage to the Infante Pedro, son of Pedro 'the Cruel'.[52]

Ostensibly, this communication was an attempt to maintain a political alliance, but it also reveals something of the king's personal loss. It shows an effort to explain the death of an innocent, and a father struggling to come to terms with the loss of his daughter. God (in his mercy) 'has deigned to snatch her away, pure and immaculate, in the years of her innocence'. But while her death was an upset of the 'proper order of mortality' she was at least free from the 'miseries of this deceitful world . . . [and] her intercessions on our behalf may unceasingly avail'. There was some cold comfort in that Joan, having been taken up to God, innocent and free from sin would have pride of place in Heaven.[53]

The indiscriminate nature of the plague confused contemporaries. God seemed willing to slay the good as often as the wicked. This haphazardness made preparation for death all the more important. It was vital from a spiritual perspective that one have a good death and come before God shriven and repentant. In this period of sudden mortality there might not be sufficient opportunity to prepare for the afterlife as one would wish and this could compromise one's chances of salvation. The contemplation of death was a valuable part of this process of preparation and helps explain, from a theological perspective, the constant emphasis on mortality evident in this period.[54]

One hoped, of course, to forestall death and assuage divine anger. In their attempts to do so most turned to conservative and entirely orthodox religious institutions. For these, probably the first port of call was to turn to the saints for intercession: St Sebastian, St Roch (d. 1327) and the Virgin were among the most popular. Such acts of veneration might have greater efficacy if performed in the course of a pilgrimage, which as Chaucer shows remained extremely popular in the later fourteenth century although not always for entirely spiritual reasons.[55]

For the wealthy, the prayers of clerics and the performance of good works could be gained through patronage of various monastic houses or conventional institutions. Such institutions could care for the souls of the departed as well as those of the living, which became of greater concern with a growing awareness of the doctrine of purgatory promulgated at the second council of Lyon (1274). Patronage in the post-plague period tended to focus on alternatives to the Benedictines and Cistercians whose prayers had failed to ward off the plague. Smaller orders, which were seen as more austere and contemplative and fostered a simple and uncorrupted religious environment, such as the Carthusians, received greater attention. There were also smaller orders and foundations that gained the patronage of some of the great men of the realm. William Edington (d. 1366), bishop of Winchester and treasurer of England, founded a college in 1351 at Edington (Wilts). In 1358, at the Black Prince's request, it became a house of a very small order known as the Bonhommes. There were good reasons for such an association: Ashridge, another Bonhommes' foundation, was close to the prince's manor of Berkhamsted and the house there had been founded by Edmund of Almain, Edward's predecessor as earl of Cornwall. There was little distinctive about the order apart from its unusual azure habit. The order followed the Rule of St Augustine or a close variant and normal monastic observance was conducted according to the Use of Sarum. The church at Edington was very austere in design and appearance, which was in keeping with the spiritual demands of the times, but can probably be attributed to the shortage of skilled craftsmen.[56]

Austerity did not preclude vivid depictions of divine power and the Black Death contributed to changes in the context and environment of worship. Images of death became prevalent in places of worship and extended outside those buildings. These were often pre-existing depictions or themes that were given a new emphasis with the arrival of the plague.[57] The Danse Macabre, the image of the Three Living and the Three Dead, and the cadaver tomb effigy were among the most important of these.[58]

As a clear statement of divine power the plague implied, for some at least, that the Church had failed in its mission. This encouraged the search for less orthodox remedies for the disease. These were not, in most cases, a rejection of the Church so much as an attempt to supplement it with various somewhat nonconformist or superstitious practices and built on a strong anti-clerical tradition stretching back to the late thirteenth century. The mystical tradition was among these. Not created by the Black Death, it nonetheless found fertile ground in post-plague Europe. Works such as the anonymous *Cloud of Unknowing*, Walter Hilton's *The Scale of Perfection*, and Julian of Norwich's *A Book of Showings*, were part of a European movement that incorporated such figures as Meister Eckhardt, Johannes Tauler, Heinrich Suso, Jan van Ruysbroeck, Margery Kempe, Angela of Foligno, St Catherine of Siena and St Bridget of Sweden. One of its leading lights, Richard Rolle, probably died of the plague in 1349. Mysticism involved a rejection of the material world and repeated acts of prayer until God revealed himself in all his glory in a mystical union with the supplicant. The mystical approach allowed the possibility of understanding the will of God which was of such importance in the context of the plague. Illness and suffering were often a part of the personal theology of mystics such as Julian of Norwich – those afflictions allowed the practitioner to feel closer to Christ and to share the merest hint of his Passion.[59]

The Flagellants manifested another less-than-orthodox religious response to the plague. The movement was not new; it had been popular at earlier times of millennial fervour. They were a highly disruptive social and political force and were repudiated by Clement VI on 20 October 1349. The Flagellants sought to exculpate the collective sin and guilt of mankind. If the plague was God's scourge on earth then the proper response was to scourge oneself in God's name. The movement started in Austria and Hungary in late 1348, spread into Germany and reached Flanders in June 1349. They were not received enthusiastically in England. The Flagellants identified their actions with the sufferings of Christ and the saints and can be seen as exemplifying an extreme form of confession and penance.[60]

Clerical Deaths and Clerical Responses

The Black Death was generally assumed to be the manifestation of divine anger. This produced a wide range of personal religious responses as individuals sought to assuage that anger or at least provide themselves with the best chance of salvation. There were also considerable ramifications for the religious institutions. A number of questions were raised by the arrival of the plague and many of these centred around the perceived failures of the Church and its ministers.

First, the Church had not warned its congregations of the impending plague. Secondly, it was failing in its mission since God had seen fit to visit mankind with such pestilential wrath. Thirdly, churchmen suffered disproportionately high mortality levels and so can have been no better in the eyes of God than their secular brethren. Among the ecclesiastics in the prince's retinue, John of Castle Goodrich, controller of Cardiganshire and collector of customs in South Wales who also served as deputy-constable of Cardigan castle, died of the plague in March 1349.[61] Robert Swynnerton, onetime dean of St Mary's, Stafford and rector of Barrow, Cheshire, may also have been a plague victim.[62] Fourthly, many churchmen were accused of failing in their parochial and spiritual duties by fleeing from areas which were visited by the plague. There were responses that the Church might make to all these accusations and there is no question that the sheer numbers of churchmen who died is a testimony to their dedication to their congregations, but there is also no doubt that the plague lessened the Church's reputation. Chaucer's Parson, a model of priestly behaviour, was seen as exceptional and against whom the majority compared poorly. Gower was scathing of the clergy in the *Mirror de l'Omme*, and Langland noted that the clergy tended 'to sing for simony' and the sweet jingling of silver.[63]

Some of the official responses to the problems caused by the plague exacerbated the situation. A lack of priests to administer to the dying encouraged some bishops to authorise parishioners to choose their own confessor in the hour of their deaths (later a hallmark of Protestantism). This situation did not arise only because of deaths in the ecclesiastical community; there were well-founded accusations that priests were leaving their parishes and abandoning their communities to serve richer patrons and perform private masses for them. Their replacements were often illiterate and little better than laymen (according to Henry Knighton).[64]

For those clerics who did not succumb, the plague also provided opportunities to improve their situation that did little for ecclesiastical reputations in general. The Church was forced to adopt prohibitions similar to the labour legislation and curb the trade in and exchange of benefices. Of course, not all such transactions were occasioned by avarice, there was an inevitable turnover of benefice holding in this period, but it was a disruptive process. For example, monthly institutions to benefices in the diocese of Norwich rose from five in December 1348 to a highpoint of 222 in July 1349 and then declined to six by May 1350.[65]

The general impact of the plague on the institutions and representatives of the Church can be seen in the diocese of Coventry and Lichfield. This was of significance to the Black Prince since he came to hold Cheylesmore manor in Coventry. The diocese also included parishes in Cheshire, Warwickshire, Staffordshire and Shropshire. The plague approached the midlands in the spring of 1349, and after six months 208 parish priests had died. Some of these must be discounted as plague victims on the basis of age or other cause of death, but in an average non-plague year only 13 beneficed clergy died. This leaves a probable mortality rate of 36 per cent, spread unevenly throughout the diocese – the archdeaconry of Chester lost only 29 per cent of its parish priests, while the figure was 57 per cent in the archdeaconry of Derby. In general, nearly two-thirds of the parish priests of Coventry and Lichfield survived the Black Death, although in some parishes not only did the priest fall victim, so too did his successor.

There is also considerable evidence of benefice exchange. In Coventry and Lichfield there were two parishes in which four different men held the benefice during a period of three months. The thirteenth-century Legatine Constitutions required a vicar to reside in his parish and consequently, when the plague struck, benefice holders should have stayed at their posts. It is significant that in Coventry and Lichfield the mortality rate was appreciably higher among vicars than rectors, for whom there was no residential obligation. It may have been for this reason that between July and December 1349 there were nearly 50 resignations in the diocese, although none of these took place in the first three-and-a-half months of the epidemic. It is likely these men were taking up attractive vacant benefices elsewhere.[66]

The transfer of benefices in the plague years does not, of course, need to have been due directly to the Black Death: in many cases it is not apparent from the available evidence what occasioned the move by one cleric from one parish or benefice to another. For example, among ecclesiastics in the prince's household, Robert Walsham, the prince's confessor and executor of his will, held a prebend of St John's, Chester, for a brief period in 1361, but whether this was influenced by plague fatalities is not clear.[67] The case of John Harewell is similar. Later a member of the prince's and Richard II's council, Harewell became archdeacon of Cornwall and acquired a prebend of Exeter in 1349.[68]

However individuals were motivated, there is no question that the authority of the Church and clergy was compromised by this most striking manifestation of God's anger. Dissatisfaction with particular religious orders and with the quality of parochial clerics, by no means new in the fourteenth century, was heightened in the context of this almost inexplicable and perhaps apocalyptic event. The broader context of the Avignon papacy, seen as so decadent, so avaricious and, in England, as so unquestionably 'French', added further to discontent. In addition, the slow development of literacy among the laity placed increasing expectations upon the clergy at just the time when parish priests were least qualified to respond. As a result, the spiritual power of the Church was brought further into question and encouraged individuals to seek alternatives to certain traditional means of assuaging divine wrath.

The Black Death was catastrophic and traumatic, but it is difficult to see it as a cause for immediate and calamitous change in most attitudes, practices or beliefs. There was, however, an immediate and conscious attempt to turn the clock back, to rely on tried and trusted methods, which is particularly evident in the remarkably swift response of the government in formulating the Ordinance of Labourers (1349). In the middle years of the fourteenth century as death became a constant companion, illustrations and personifications of Death did become more numerous and macabre, but not substantially so. It would be the last years of the century that would witness the great 'flowering' of the cult of death and this was not merely designed to shock and induce fear, but to warn and encourage preparation for the life to come.

Similarly, the effects of the plague were slow to appear in labour relations, changing standards of living and in the relationship between landlords and peasants.[69] It was in the 1360s and especially the 1370s that the major changes were felt and the social dislocation that resulted from the loss of perhaps half the population finally became apparent. It would change the economic and social balance of the country and the political balance also, something that can be seen in the tumultuous events of 1381. It is going too far to say that the Peasants' Revolt of 1381 was due to the Black Death, but without a plague a peasants' revolt seems much less likely.

The personal experience of the Black Prince is difficult to evaluate. The loss of his sister must have been traumatic, although she was only one of several of his siblings to die prematurely. Perhaps his father's letter to the Castilian court can be taken as some indication of the impact of the death of a member of what seems to have been a genuinely close-knit family. The loss of various members of the prince's household and a number of his comrades-in-arms must, similarly, have been deeply troubling. It may be that the plague also coloured some of his religious attitudes, but again there is little direct evidence to support this. More though can be said about the economic and political impact of the plague on the prince. In Wales and Cheshire the prince's administration struggled to maintain traditional economic structures and behaved in what might be seen as a characteristically grasping and uncaring fashion towards the people. However, the example of the duchy of Cornwall shows that this was not the only possible response to the plague. There, the administration behaved with understanding, kindness, and sought to mitigate the worst of the consequences of the Black Death. The result was that, with the exception of the tin mines, the prince restored and maintained both his authority and his financial affairs within a short period of time. Therefore the prince provides a fine example of a wide range of aristocratic responses to the Black Death. Like everyone else he did not know how long the plague would last and its return in 1361 must have come as a terrible shock. The consequences of this outbreak of plague were particularly great in Aquitaine. Indeed, the economic fragility of the principality and its ultimate failure can be attributed, if only in part, to the *malaise des enfants*.

The significance of the plague lies not only in the major epidemic of 1348–50, but in its recurring visits. The initial dislocation to social structures, administrative systems and religious attitudes seemed to have ended by the middle years of the 1350s, but this did not last. Social and economic forces were not to be restricted by legal measures, however stringently they were enforced. Although not only a legacy of the Black Death, the relationship between lord and vassal shifted in the second half of the fourteenth century. This, in turn, threatened the position of the aristocracy. Various means were instituted to prevent or at least restrict such changes, but few were successful. This is no cause for surprise since even chivalry, the identifying ethic of the aristocracy, was itself under threat.

chapter three

CHIVALRY AND NOBILITY

The same day of the battle at night the prince made a supper in his lodging for the French king and for the most part of the great lords that were prisoners . . . and always the prince served before the king as humbly as he could, and would not sit at the king's board for any desire the king could make, but he said he was not sufficient to sit at the table with so great a prince.[1]

Following his great victory at the battle of Poitiers, according to Froissart, the Black Prince treated his captive and guest, King Jean II of France, with all the courtesy and nobility expected of this flower of chivalry. Yet there is within this incident, if broadly considered, an apparent dichotomy. The expedition that led to Poitiers was a *chevauchée*, a deliberately destructive raid, which attacked the social and economic fabric of the enemy. It aimed to undermine the morale and productivity of the French peasantry, to reduce the authority of the monarch, and his ability to tax his subjects. It was warfare waged on non-combatants and some of the most vulnerable members of society whose homes were burned, crops destroyed and livelihoods crushed.

The year before, the Black Prince had orchestrated the *grande chevauchée*, perhaps the most devastating raid in the entire war and an unprecedented catastrophe for the people of southern France. Over 500 villages, towns and castles were burned on a march from Bordeaux on the Atlantic to Narbonne on the Mediterranean and back. The prince and his army fought nothing more than minor skirmishes and gained the long-standing reputation as being no better than brigands who pillaged a defenceless country in search of booty.[2] Whatever the strategic intention, whether or not he was seeking to lure the French to battle, the Black Prince instigated a programme of widespread and calculated devastation. He destroyed the lives and property of those least capable of defending themselves. By the time the prince reached Carcassonne his reputation was such that the citizens attempted to pay him off with 250,000 gold *écus* – it was not accepted and the suburbs were burned.

It was a substantial sum to refuse, but the *chevauchée* strategy was designed to exact a far higher cost to the French kingdom. In a letter of late 1355, Sir John Wingfield wrote to the bishop of Winchester outlining the sophistication of the English strategy:

> It seems certain that since the war against the French king began, there has never been such destruction in a region as in this raid. For the countryside and towns which have been destroyed . . . produced more revenue for the king of France in aid of his war than half his kingdom . . . as I could prove from authentic documents found in various towns in the tax-collectors' houses.[3]

Wingfield, a knight, was also Edward's business manager (governor of the prince's business). His value to the prince was not military, but lay in his financial and administrative abilities. In this particular instance he was carefully calculating the precise value of the taxes lost to the Valois in burned homesteads and trampled crops. The financial and social consequences of military action were being evaluated in purely monetary terms. It was a strategy that suggests a different approach to military conduct and shows a new role for the knight on campaign.

The expeditions of 1355–6 require us to re-evaluate what chivalry meant to those who claimed to practice it in the fourteenth century. Certainly there is little here that speaks of those aspects of chivalry which encouraged disdaining conflict with inferiors and looking to the care of women and clergymen. Indeed, it may make us question whether chivalry was more than a literary ideal, or whether it had declined in the autumn of the middle ages to become a cynical and hypocritical façade behind which men could loot, pillage and rape to their hearts' desire. Alternatively, it may simply be the case that we need to have a less idealised view of chivalry and of those who constituted the chivalrous classes. This is an unapologetically secular view of chivalry, but before it was anything else chivalry was a secular, military code, one that determined behaviour between members of the warrior caste. War was brutal and battles were few and far between, so '[w]ar as conducted by the chivalrous meant raiding and ravaging'.[4] Such qualities that mitigated the brutality of warfare, at least for the non-chivalrous classes, tended to be those valued by ecclesiastical writers, or which were demonstrated in a courtly environment. This was the courtesy demonstrated by the Black Prince, but only after he achieved victory at Poitiers.

The Black Prince's chivalrous reputation lay at the heart of his power since it reflected both his military and social status. Chivalry continues to be a lively area of scholarly debate, and its proper form and precise definition were also matters of concern to contemporaries. As the key identifying ethic of the secular aristocracy, chivalry is a lens through which the changing nature of lay power can be evaluated. For much of the first three centuries after the millennium there was a simple correlation, chivalry was the code of the nobility and the noble classes were chivalrous. This became uncertain in the later middle ages and, as the association weakened, so the role, conception and authority of chivalry and nobility altered. Two influences of particular importance that coloured the changing nature of aristocratic power were the implementation of new means of waging war, and socio-economic decline and the ramifications of the plague. These downplayed the value of the mounted knight on the battlefield, undermined the traditional position of the aristocracy, and changed contemporary expectations of the chivalrous classes.

This, however, was no simple transition. It is clear that the military strategy the Black Prince employed in France, one centred on burning and looting, was not contrary to the dictates of chivalry. Chivalry, at heart, was about war, and war was about burning, as Henry V knew so well when he said that war without fire was like sausages without mustard.[5] Similarly, the prince's chivalric reputation, established at Crécy and cemented at Poitiers, was created using tactics that appear contrary to the chivalric ethic in their use of infantry, archery, discipline and defence. This is not to say, however, that by the time of Crécy and Poitiers: 'All that remained of a once idealistic military and social system was its bastard child' – chivalry as a warrior code was more resilient than that. This is because chivalry maintained its essential integrity as an ethic that identified the 'chivalrous' and which codified behaviour between members of the chivalrous classes. Despite changes in army structures, the aristocracy continued to be identified with militarily activities in the fifteenth century and the term *chevelria* was used to indicate both chivalry and gentry.

The second influence said to encourage chivalric decline is bound up with the changing nature of 'feudal' relations in later medieval England. It is often implied that chivalry in England became somehow degenerate as a result of socio-political changes that altered the relationship between lord and vassal. But the Statute of *Quia Emptores* in 1290, which allowed cash to be used instead of land in feudal contracts, did not change the chivalric ethos fundamentally. The knightly aristocrat had never been totally dependent upon a tenurial arrangement with an overlord. Nor did the chivalric ethic wither as a result of livery and maintenance – it was not the victim of bastard feudalism.[6]

But chivalry did change in the later middle ages, as it had changed throughout its history and it was, to some extent, a victim, if not a casualty, of the military revolution. The traditional knightly qualities of skill at arms, prowess and bravery lessened in importance as battles in the later middle ages were dominated by long-range weapons and the disciplined deployment of infantry. This is not meant to imply that battlefields became more violent in the fourteenth century, although the capacity for causing death and injury at a distance certainly increased. Nor does it indicate that chivalry had inculcated a gentle approach to military conduct that was lost in the later middle ages. The battlefields of fourteenth- and fifteenth-century Europe did not mark the grave of chivalry because it remained a practical military ethic. This is ignored when, for example, it is argued: 'The injuries exhibited in the Towton mass grave suggest that chivalry was not a driving force in this War of the Roses battle.'[7] The Towton soldiers were cut down from behind with heavy blows from edged weapons, but there was nothing inherently unchivalric about this. Had the Towton soldiers been victims of injuries caused by longbows, crossbows or artillery then such a claim might be made. Presumably the suggestion is that those killed should have received mercy.

Mercy was certainly a literary ideal, although only due to those deemed worthy of mercy. For the most part, those who should be shown mercy were members of the chivalrous classes. This was given practical expression in the ransom system. In many ways ransoming was the key feature of chivalry in the years before the military revolution. It served to mitigate the perils of the battlefield for those to whom it applied, but it had only ever applied to those worth ransoming. The changes demanded by the new military strategy meant that knights became less numerous on the battlefield, there was a greater need to maintain discipline in the ranks, and there was an increasing proportion of infantry and missile troops in armies. With these changes in strategy, tactics and the social composition of armies, so the opportunity to ransom a defeated opponent lessened. As a consequence, the protective aspect of chivalry that the ransom system provided also lessened. Certainly, the Swiss rarely offered mercy to a defeated opponent and neither did the Flemish. Nonetheless, mercy was still an ideal and when Henry V slaughtered his prisoners at Agincourt, albeit for sound military reasons, it proved to be the one blemish on his reputation, his Limoges.[8]

To some extent this is an indication that battlefields were becoming less chivalrous, but it is not a clear indication. Essentially, later medieval warfare continued to be chivalrous because war remained the business of the chivalric classes. Those who commanded armies in the Hundred Years War or in the Wars of the Roses may have been more or less chivalrous than their ancestors but, for the most part, they were cut from the same cloth and they were of the same order, members of the chivalry of France and England.

Chivalry therefore defined a caste as well as behaviour appropriate to that caste. The origins of this caste distinction lay in the tripartite division of society, the Three Orders, which first emerged in an organised form in the ninth century. By this construct, those who fought (*bellatores*) were distinguished by their divinely ordained function from those who prayed (*oratores*), and those who worked (*laboratores*). Within these orders there were various ranks, often ill defined, but there was a common function that bound them together. In the case of the *bellatores* there came to be an association between military function and noble status by which the title of 'knight' became a prerequisite for inclusion into the caste.[9]

Disagreements concerning the nature of chivalry are and were dependent on the conflicting demands made of the chivalrous by contemporary authorities. A literary ideal tended to project a courtly image; religious writers encouraged knights to behave in a manner that supported the Church; secular writers, some of them career soldiers in this period, focused on the purely military responsibilities incumbent upon the knight. Conflicting analyses of the chivalric code have therefore been dependent on the differing emphasis given to these elements. Part of the reason for continuing confusion over the chivalric ethic also is attributable to the pervasive influence of Johan Huizinga (1872–1945).[10] His vision has cast a long shadow over the study of chivalry despite the work of Maurice Keen, Richard Kaeuper, Richard Barber, Malcolm Vale and others.[11] It is evident in the popular conception of chivalry, one viewed through some sort of Pre-Raphaelite filter by which the grim realities are extracted leaving an aesthetic, an ethical ideal, little more than a fantasy culture.[12]

Most British scholars in recent years have emphasised the secular and pragmatic aspects of chivalry. Another school, exemplified by the work of Stephen Jaeger, sees chivalry, especially courtly chivalry, as the product of clerical culture and promulgated in courtly environments from as early as the tenth century. Those who emphasise the religious component of chivalry, such as Jean Flori, see it as the product of an attempt by the Church to make secular violence more acceptable and to channel it for its own ends, particularly the defence of Christendom.[13]

Balance between these is difficult to achieve, but at least 'there is now a general acceptance that there never was a golden age when men behaved according to universally recognized ideals'.[14] Nonetheless, an overtly pacified definition of chivalry remains pervasive even in scholarly works.[15] Chivalry did not merely connote but was an extremely violent way of life. It meant the 'worship of prowess, and prowess (whatever gentler qualities idealists wanted to associate with it) meant beating an opponent with really good hacking and thrusting. Chivalry was a code of violence in defense of a prickly sense of honor (and the honorable acquisition of loot to be distributed in open-handed largesse) just as thoroughly as it was a code of restraint'.[16]

To emphasise the significance of the military core is not to ignore the various additional qualities – religious, social and cultural – that combined to form the chivalric ethic. Chivalry was a way of life, an ethic, a cult, perhaps a militant secular religion, and formed the defining characteristics of an order, a social cadre, credited with divine sanction. While centred on military qualities it expanded to become 'the practice and ideal code of the dominant strata of lay society for roughly half a millennium . . . it became the framework for debate about how the dominant laypeople should live, love, govern, fight and practice piety'.[17] Chivalry had deep roots and was steeped in traditions that retained a powerful influence over the beliefs and attitudes of the late medieval aristocracy. The interpretation of those traditions was, however, changing and the chivalric ethos itself was placed under strain as concepts of aristocratic behaviour and hierarchy altered. Such concepts were reshaped by factors including increasing military professionalism, the development of alternative aristocratic career paths in law and administration, and the greater influence of the lesser nobility in representative assemblies.

Such tensions were not new. There had always been strains and friction within the knightly order – it was inherent in the incongruous concept of the *miles Christi* (the knight of Christ). There had also always been high expectations from outside the aristocratic ranks, especially from the Church, which the chivalrous often failed to live up to.[18] As a result, from its inception, chivalry was always seen as being in a state of decay, perhaps entropy, and the order of knighthood always in need of reform. For Langland in the fourteenth century, as for Bernard of Clairvaux in the twelfth, chivalry was a fine ideal, but it had failed in practice, although for Bernard there was hope in the shape of the New Knighthood (the Order of the Temple). John Gower in the fifteenth century suggested: 'Chevalerie . . . in som partie is worthi forto be commendid, and in some part to ben ammendid.'[19]

Thus the conflict evident in the fourteenth century within the chivalric order and the attacks made upon it from outside were not new, but the context in which they were made was different and changing quickly. Contemporary chivalric exemplars seemed increasingly contradictory in their conduct and the values they espoused. Was true chivalry exemplified by a practitioner such as the mercenary leader Bertrand du Guesclin or the paladin Geoffroi de Charny? But then du Guesclin was laid to rest alongside the Valois kings in St Denis and became the subject of a chivalric biography, and Charny was not above stooping to bribery in his attempt to take Calais in 1350, an act for which he was reproached in the pages of Froissart's chronicle by no less a chivalric icon than Edward III. Was chivalry those actions glorified by Jean Froissart or those broadly condemned by Honoré Bonet whose *Tree of Battles* was a tree of mourning? Was this a chivalry that mitigated the worst of war or which encouraged it, which fed it with the lure of honour and prowess and watered it with the chance of winning booty and ransoms? Such changes and conflicting attitudes impinged directly on the life of the Black Prince and his career provides one of the best case studies by which to analyse those changes and contradictions.

Chivalry has three main elements requiring definition: it referred to a group – the 'chivalry' of England or France; it referred to the ethic by which this group was supposed to live; and that ethic was shaped into an idealised lifestyle by religious authorities and through literary examples. Some consideration has been given to the first of these, the caste distinction; the second element, the ethic, may be identified by the qualities considered appropriate to the chivalric warrior. To be truly chivalrous one needed to demonstrate a range of skills and virtues: prowess; loyalty or fealty; mercy or forbearance; hardiness; largesse and liberality; honour (and fear of shame). In addition, one should demonstrate good lordship or rulership by protecting the weak, defending the Church, opposing the unjust, dispensing justice, and keeping the peace. This last category was important since it justified, perhaps even legitimised, secular power.

Such a list shows that chivalry and nobility were defined by a range of interdependent qualities: chivalry was (often) a demonstration of noble estate; the noble man was (usually) chivalrous; the chivalrous man was honourable; and the actions of the honourable man were conditioned by chivalric and noble ethics and so on. They are qualities best defined by equally amorphous virtues. Although these three elements were undergoing change in the fourteenth century, some of the terminology used to refer to the upper echelons of aristocratic society remained as it had been since the Conquest: *nobilitare* continued to mean to ennoble or to act in a lordly way, and *nobilis* still designated a nobleman. It is worthy of note that even in the 1380s Chandos Herald could refer to an individual as *liber* (free/freeman/freeholder) and imply nobility, which is a definition redolent of an ancient bipartite division of society into the free and unfree. Similarly *haut* (high) recalls an earlier age when divisions between ranks and social status were more clear-cut.

It was, in part, because of changes in aristocratic structures that the association of knighthood, nobility and chivalry began to unravel in the later middle ages.[20] Although they remained intertwined, there was an increasing dichotomy between chivalry and nobility, certainly in the sense of chivalry as a military activity. To a degree this was due to the depreciating value of knighthood and, in England, the development of the gentry – a semi-distinct lesser nobility. This distinction was not so apparent in France where nobility acquired a legal definition, but even there tensions were becoming apparent. Chivalry, at least in its military senses, and nobility were becoming respectively distinctive as can be seen in a remarkable incident that took place in 1408 in the Dauphiné. Twenty-one persons including two ecclesiastics, 11 nobles and eight commoners were asked what it was to be noble. The case involved a trial concerning the claim to exemption from tax by an innkeeper on the grounds that he was a noble. The majority decided it was 'to live from one's revenues and property without doing manual labour, which is to say, not ploughing, reaping, digging, or doing other peasant work'.[21] Sixteen witnesses, with representatives from all groups, asserted this – all the ecclesiastics and commoners and six of the 11 nobles.

Nobility was therefore, for most, a way of life. Remarkably, of the Dauphiné witnesses, only two believed it to be dependent on birth and, equally significantly, only 11 saw nobility as being tied to a career in arms, including five of the 11 nobles. Strangely, nine of the witnesses, two fewer, stated a noble was supposed to go to war on behalf of his lord. Others suggested the noble had a duty to defend the Church, perhaps going on crusade, and five of the 21 said a noble should not engage in usury or trade. Another aspect emphasised by some of the deponents was the importance of dining and entertaining in a suitable fashion as well as being clothed elegantly. In this sense, to be noble was to appear noble, and so keeping company with others of similar standing and participating in 'noble' activities such as tournaments were also mentioned. Those who were or who considered themselves noble viewed the 'courtly' virtues of probity, goodness, mildness and good manners as significant.[22]

The chivalry of the later middle ages, which the Black Prince exemplified, was not so different from that which existed before. It was an unashamedly military code that bound the aristocracy together. However, the nature of the military aristocracy was changing in this period. Nobility and knighthood, once almost synonymous, were becoming disentangled from one another. With the development of a sub-knightly aristocracy in England in the form of the esquire and gentleman, chivalry was not a quality restricted to knights. Further, as traditional mounted knightly military activity lost its potency on the battlefield so the form changed by which chivalry was demonstrated. This also brought into question the means by which nobility, formerly the caste who were chivalric, should be defined. As a result, the authority of the nobility and of the wider military aristocracy was brought into question and had to be reinforced in new ways. It was partly because of this uncertain context that chivalry and nobility came under increased scrutiny and subject to greater criticism in this period.

Chivalric Commentaries

Chivalry, however it is and was defined, was an ethic of the powerful. The secular aristocracy was judged and measured by chivalric criteria, although these were not always criteria of its own choosing. Some of these criteria were those traditionally associated with the military aristocracy and included qualities such as prowess, loyalty and courage. According to medieval thought, some of these qualities might be inherited from one's forebears, so too might additional virtues associated with justice, nobility of spirit and pity. Such virtues were stated and reinforced in religious and secular works that might be read or performed publicly. The Arthurian stories of the fourteenth century, such as *Sir Gawain and the Green Knight*, emphasised many of these qualities, and ecclesiastical works performed a similar function although they tended to focus on less 'courtly' attributes. There is no doubt that knights read or listened to chivalric biographies, *chansons de geste* and manuals of chivalry. It is more difficult to be sure whether they also read romances, but their focus on deeds of arms, and often very bloody deeds at that, suggests that they were directed at knights just as much as at their ladies. Certainly a work such as the alliterative *Morte Arthure* presents a cool and realistic portrait of fourteenth-century warfare. Nonetheless, such works were, no doubt, idealised and they caricatured knightly behaviour. Richard Kaeuper suggests the chivalry of the romances was prescriptive rather than descriptive.[23]

In the case of the Black Prince, his chivalric status was fashioned in a military environment by which victory was achieved using discipline, order and long-range weaponry even if those same victories were proclaimed in traditional chivalric terms and by comparison to a mythic past and in a spirit of romance. He was a chivalric icon because he was depicted as such by Jean Froissart and his first biographer, Chandos Herald. The herald's 'Life' of the Black Prince was the first of a series of late medieval chivalric biographies, which also included Guillaume de Machaut's *La prise d'Alexandrie*; Cuvelier's *Chronique de Bertrand du Guesclin*; and Christine de Pizan's *Le livre des fais et bonnes meurs du sage roy Charles V*.[24] The purpose of the work that has become known as the *Vie du Prince Noir* was laudatory and probably didactic. It rejoiced in acts of chivalry and, like Froissart's *Chroniques*, delighted in the deeds of great men. An individual was judged great not just by his birth or position but by his deeds which revealed the virtues appropriate to

EDWARD THE BLACK PRINCE

the great. Accordingly, the prince 'from the day of his birth cherished no thought but loyalty, nobleness, valour and goodness and [he] was endowed with prowess'.[25] Such qualities had been the basis of knightly virtue for more than 200 years.

Loyalty, valour and prowess were at the heart of the warrior ethic that formed the main foundation of chivalry. Following these, nobility and goodness (broadly defined) provided a religious justification for the social and political authority that the knight won by his military power. There were also a host of additional, lesser, qualities that defined the noble and the chivalrous. *Largesse*, for example, had connotations associated with the traditional practice of gift-giving which in a new form still provided a means of social cohesion. Jean de Meun, in the *Roman de la Rose*, noted:

> *Fair gifts, without doubt,*
> *Bear witness to a good life.*
> *Everywhere gifts give strong support to a fair place,*
> *And he who gives them is a true nobleman* [preudon].[26]

The Black Prince followed this advice through his many generous gifts to members of his retinue and through the magnificence of his court and household. Appropriately, one of his most generous gifts was awarded following his great triumph at Poitiers when he granted Sir James Audley an annuity of £400 for the prowess he showed in the battle – he was said to be the bravest of the knights that fought for the prince. Even more appropriately, according to Froissart, Audley promptly offered this extremely handsome sum to his four esquires. Sadly we cannot be sure of the truth of this and there is no secure evidence regarding their identities.[27]

While there were certain flowers of chivalry that flourished in the fourteenth century, the bulk of the crop was far from satisfactory according to many commentators. Those, comparatively few, secular reformers such as Geoffroi de Charny aimed to revitalise the martial prowess of the chivalrous classes. Charny was concerned with gathering aristocratic support for the French king and marshalling military might in defence of the kingdom. But in the main, critics of chivalry had a clear religious or social agenda, and so tended to focus on those aspects of chivalry that served as some form of restraint on secular violence. John Gower in *Vox Clamantis* (*c*.1377–81) was outspoken in his criticism of the knightly order. It had, in his opinion, failed to live up to proper standards of behaviour especially in its role of protector of the other two orders. Its members had also failed militarily, in their role as peacemakers and as dispensers of justice. Now the knightly *ordo* bore arms only for fame, avarice and the love of women. By the time he wrote *Confessio Amantis* (*c*.1386–93) Gower's criticism had become even more outspoken and he had begun to question the morality of killing in any worldly cause and thereby the central purpose of the military aristocracy. He argued, by strict reference to the Augustinian concept of the just war, that national conflicts should be ended. Military action with its inevitable fatalities was the *raison d'être* of the chivalrous classes. To suspend that action, even if it meant greater involvement in crusading, would change the role of the aristocracy fundamentally. Gower stated that the war with France was being fought merely for the economic, political and social benefit of the knights, and although an exaggeration, it was not a completely unfair assessment. Chaucer, whose work often revealed a 'detachment from knightly values', showed similar sentiments in two short poems, *Lak of Stedfastnesse* and *The Former Age*, which were laments for a lost golden age destroyed by greed and war – a familiar refrain in political and romance literature.[28]

Chivalric criticism did not stem only from disillusionment with knightly activities; it was also encouraged by wider social change. It is possible, for example, that the Robin Hood tales, probably assembled in the first half of the fourteenth century, have elements of chivalric parody that were encouraged by the changing balance of economic power which narrowed the social boundaries between classes, especially the upper echelons of the peasantry and the lowest ranks of the aristocracy.[29] While the chivalric figure remained of immense literary importance, as can be seen in the popularity of Malory's *Morte d'Arthur*, the 'interval between 1350 and 1500, when for the only time before 1945 a non-gentleman was everyone's literary hero, must tell us something about the England and Englishmen whose hero [Robin Hood] was'.[30] The glamorisation and successful use of non-aristocratic violence in support of (sometimes) just aims in the Robin stories, reflects the changing military and social environment. In this new context, noble power became somewhat disassociated from individual knightly prowess and, in the post-plague world, the economic and, hence, social distinction between the lesser aristocracy and peasantry became increasingly narrow.

In this way the foundations of the hegemonial aristocracy began to be undermined. The prowess of the individual knight could achieve little in a battle against longbows, crossbows, infantry and eventually artillery. Meanwhile nobleness, the very concept of nobility, was changing as the broad body of the aristocracy began to be restructured, altering what it meant to be noble. It was no longer a truism to speak of the 'knightly' aristocracy – one could be a member of the aristocracy and not a knight. This refashioned the aristocratic order since chivalry identified not only a range of qualities but also a collective unit. Indeed, this had been central to the classification of the aristocracy. The chivalry and nobility of France and England were the terms by which they were described as groups and also implied the qualities they were supposed to posses.[31] As chivalry and nobility began to change their meanings so did the power, purpose and identity of the chivalrous and the noble.

Birth and Virtue

Concern with social mobility had encouraged the strict demarcation of the knightly and the noble from those below when the two had first merged. The barrier was a semipermeable membrane at best, but birth was a particularly important means by which eligibility for knighthood and therefore nobility (in those early years) was determined. Consequently, the lack of emphasis on birth as a criterion of nobility in the Dauphiné example is surprising and significant. However, the implication may have been not that birth should of itself confer status, but that a noble lineage conveyed noble qualities, which in turn made one suitable to rule, govern and have status as a member of the nobility. According to Christine de Pizan: 'Since the rank of nobility, that is, noblemen, have among the highest and most exalted honours in this world, it is reasonable that they be adorned with the virtues which are properly called noble as well.'[32] This was an area of consideration that had been much debated. Although certain writers, as early as the twelfth century, had noted that 'the claims of birth and of virtue [as the origins of nobility] were mutually incompatible', more were convinced of the power of lineage (as David Crouch has called it) and had 'sound' medical reasons for believing in the transmission of virtue down a bloodline.[33] Virtue might be bequeathed to subsequent generations so that a scion of a noble house could inherit the qualities of a distinguished ancestor. It is clearly expressed by Chandos Herald with regard to the Black Prince: 'son of the noble and valorous King Edward, and of Queen Philippa, the perfect root of all honour, nobility, wisdom, valour and bounty.'[34]

Such theories presupposed a point of origin for nobility and its qualities. For Philippe de Beaumanoir (c.1250–96), noble lineage was inextricably linked to virtue, those of gentle blood were descended from the men who had been marked out to rule after the Fall as the wisest, strongest and most handsome. Bartolus de Saxoferrato (1314–57), the Italian master of the dialectical school of jurists, provided a more sophisticated bipartite model which separated nobility into civil and natural sections. Civil nobility was a 'title' conferred by a prince and rested on recognition of the claim to ancient riches and fine manners. The second form, 'natural' nobility, was innate and marked by virtue, specifically the capacity to rule. Early in the fifteenth century, Christine de Pizan used classical and late antique authorities on nobility, such as Juvenal and Boethius, to emphasise the essential link between nobility and virtue.[35] Later medieval theory therefore sought to show that nobility was not simply the consequence of inherited titles or wealth or found in jurisdictions or riches, but rather that it resulted from personal virtues, although these might be inherited as in the case of the Black Prince.

These virtues, which provided the foundation for noble status, were to be demonstrated in a public environment and often in the service of the wider community. Nobility, according to this theory, was acquired and verified through service in aid of a prince, the people and/or the common good. It had been traditional to serve the nation and the *res publica* in battle, but the development of new institutions of government extended this field of service.[36]

The rise of the professional army compromised the military effectiveness of the military aristocracy in battle, and the use of chivalric tactics might now be overtly detrimental to the national cause. Instead there were opportunities to serve in the new administrations and bureaucracies. 'By the later fourteenth century the aristocracy in England as elsewhere, were no longer, if they ever had been, an exclusively military elite. They were valued by rulers for their administrative abilities as well as for their skill in arms.'[37] Hence, from *c.*1260 *miles literatus* denoted a knight with legal training, and with the summoning of knights of the shires to parliament we find *milites parliamenti*. Christine de Pizan also makes it clear that, in early fifteenth-century France, nobility was not restricted only to those engaged in martial pursuits. Indeed, there seems to be very little that she did not describe as noble or as having a quality of nobility. Philosophers could be noble, human pity was noble, as were diligence, eloquence and honouring age and experience. There was also ecclesiastical nobility: 'the clerical class is high, noble and worthy of honour amongst the others.'[38]

There was therefore a wider dissemination of the concept of nobility in France and England, but nobility in a 'class' sense was acquiring different and distinctive definitions in these respective countries. In both nations, however, these reflected a new social environment and also changes in the traditional function of the military aristocracy. In some ways it marks the end of a phase of aristocratic development that had begun with the chivalric unification of knighthood and nobility.

Knights, Mercenaries and Professional Soldiers

According to Marc Bloch, Georges Duby and Jean Flori, the separate concepts of knighthood and nobility fused partly through the common acceptance of the chivalric ethic so that by the end of the twelfth century, the terms *nobilis* and *miles* were interchangeable. Duby concluded from this that aristocratic society had become homogenous; the twin poles of the aristocracy – nobles and knights – had been brought together by various military, political and social influences.[39] These included chivalry and it was as a result of this melding that chivalry was further defined. In this manner, nobility became chivalric. Following this conclusion Duby proceeded to ask what was the identifying characteristic of this new aristocracy. Did 'the self-awareness of the aristocracy [relate] to the notion of nobility or to that of knighthood'?[40] As knights became noble and nobles embraced the title of knight, what was the essential characteristic of this new homogenised aristocracy, knighthood or nobility?

Duby's thesis has, of course, been subject to much criticism and few would maintain that the Mâconnais – the area that provided the main sources for his research – was representative of all France.[41] More also have questioned the reality of the so-called 'feudal mutation or revolution' said to have taken place *c*.1000, which provides a further element in the argument for the association of nobility and knighthood. Nonetheless, Duby's thesis remains highly influential and certainly provides a useful framework by which to examine the evolution of aristocratic structures in the high middle ages and the stresses those structures came under in the fourteenth century. Furthermore, with the increasing stratification of the aristocracy that becomes evident in England in the later medieval period, and the differentiation of the aristocracy once more into two groups – nobility and gentry – Duby's question regarding the nature of the once unifying ethic may be addressed in a new context.

It must be acknowledged that Duby's model does not sit happily throughout France and it certainly cannot be transplanted wholesale to England. There, in the twelfth century, it appears that the greater families – the old nobility – took various steps to differentiate themselves from the petty nobility who, as a consequence of their new status, were emulating their lifestyle. This suggests the fusion of chivalry and nobility was not complete. However, the common bond of military service to the English Crown does seem to have been of particular importance especially when this became closely associated with knighthood. Service was a significant element of knighthood – it extended the older concept of loyalty to a wider, national sphere. In addition, the religious significance of knighthood provided an important spiritual link between all those that bore the title. Therefore a strong elite mentality was forged through co-membership of the order of knighthood encompassing the old nobility and the arrivistes.[42]

This is significant for an understanding of the chivalric world inhabited by the Black Prince. While not a perfect union, there had been some sort of fusion between the twin poles of the English (Anglo-Norman) aristocracy in the twelfth and thirteenth centuries. In the later middle ages, major differences within the aristocracy re-emerged and an exclusive order of knighthood was pulled apart leaving a distinct gentry, a higher nobility, and a chivalric ethic that might be applied to the actions of men-at-arms of all sorts.[43] Knighthood, its purpose and its changing membership, was a central focus for debate regarding the aristocracy in the fourteenth century. Consideration was given to appropriate knightly behaviour that highlights the tensions and scrutiny under which chivalry and nobility were placed at this time. Knighthood clearly remained an overtly military concept and this can be seen in the knighting of the Black Prince. The ceremony was performed when he landed in Normandy for his first military campaign in 1346. The conferral of knighthood often preceded or followed a campaign or deed of arms. Christine de Pizan also maintained the association by writing of 'the rank of knighthood – that is, the worthy nobles who carry arms'. But there is no doubt that these worthy men should not be merely *milites in armis strenuis* (militarily active knights), they should be men of integrity, experienced in arms, noble in manners and condition, loyal in deed and in courage, and wise in government as well as diligent in chivalrous pursuits.[44] They should be men fit to serve the king and protect and govern his people. Such a view of knighthood was not new, for it exemplifies the ideal of the *preudhomme*, which resonated through the literature of the thirteenth century and before. But, with the lessening role of the knight in battle and the reconstruction of the aristocracy, especially in England, the purely military aspects of knighthood were devalued in practice if not in theory.

The France of the early fifteenth century in which Christine de Pizan wrote was sorely in need of good government and also protection from enemies within and without. It was, in part, to address this need that she also composed a military treatise, *The Book of Deeds of Arms and of Chivalry* for the dauphin. Although much of her work was written during the madness of Charles VI and the foment of the Armagnac-Burgundian civil war, de Pizan's idealised vision of society and her extremely practical military approach that advocated the use of 'wise tricks' and stratagems was not unrepresentative.[45] In this work we see a clear realisation that traditional chivalry with its acts of stupendous, independent bravery and sacrifice was no match for the disciplined deployment of infantry and missile troops.

To turn to another and more controversial example: Chaucer's knight loved chivalry, truth, honour, freedom and courtesy; he was worthy, wise, never spoke any villainy and he dressed soberly. He was not called noble, which is perhaps indicative that he was not among the highest ranks in the realm, but the many expeditions in which he participated were described as such.[46] Yet it has been suggested that this 'parfit, gentil knight' was nothing more than a brutal mercenary, a hypothesis that has resulted in strong and convincing counter-arguments.[47] Whatever the truth of the matter, the debate highlights the problems in defining chivalry and knighthood in this age of the Free Companies (*condotierri*, organised mercenary bands) when these *routiers* threatened the social and economic fabric of France in the middle years of the fourteenth century.

The Hundred Years War was fought for the most part by paid professional soldiers whether they were mercenaries or members of the aristocracy receiving wages for military service. Consequently, it becomes difficult to separate the actions of the traditional military aristocracy serving a king, from soldiers (*milites* in the older sense of the word) serving their own interests. The 'decline of chivalry', as Raymond Kilgour described it, can be understood in this context although this underestimates the purely military connotations of chivalry as a code that applied to the chivalrous, i.e. those who fought.

The activities of the Companies were of particular importance during extended periods of truce, such as after the treaty of Brétigny (1360) and particularly following the conclusion of the Breton civil war (1364). Then the opportunities for lucrative military service disappeared. Consequently, the Free Companies continued their activities in their own name and plundered much of France. Their military potency was evident at the battle of Brignais (1362) where they defeated a French royal army. It was an encounter that resembled Poitiers, perhaps because some of the leaders of the companies may have fought alongside the Black Prince. If chivalry and nobility had previously been concepts linked to military service, directed in a just cause, then this association was compromised in this period as a consequence of undirected and selfish military action. The fracturing of that association was a significant change in the character and hence the power and position of the nobility.

It was the destructive effect of the *condotierri* that encouraged Charles V and Bertrand du Guesclin to become involved in the Castilian civil war between the English-allied Pedro 'the Cruel' and Enrique of Trastamara. Not only would the establishment of an anti-English monarch on the throne of Castile prove of great political value, the removal of the Free Companies from France was a necessary step towards a French economic and social recovery after the disastrous years of Crécy and Poitiers.[48]

The role of the companies highlights the changing image and authority of the late medieval aristocracy. Service in arms, despite changes in military organisation, remained one of the most significant ways of achieving social advancement, and the potential economic gains that could be made either in a *chevauchée* or by serving in a private army were very considerable. The chivalric cult had imbued military service with an allure and a glamour that was further enhanced and reflected by chivalric chroniclers who, concerned with the 'deeds of great men', rarely noticed the depredations suffered by the peasantry. As Maurice Keen put it: 'The wars of princes brought together great companies of men at arms, and in their course cast a tinsel glamour of chivalry over their activities.' In truth, the activities of the companies were little different from those of the Black Prince's army in 1355 that 'had among its principal objects the wasting of the countryside with fire and sword and the acquisition of booty'.[49] For those instilled with the spirit of chivalric romances, there was no great distinction between those who fought for their lords and for glory, and the mercenaries who fought for loot and anyone who would pay them. Certainly it was not a distinction Froissart chose to make or one that troubled Chandos Herald when he wrote of the 1367 Castilian campaign. In this expedition Chandos recruited and the Black Prince led an army composed in no small part of mercenaries to restore Pedro 'the Cruel' to the throne of Castile – a throne from which he had been deposed by some of those who now fought to reinstate him. But criticism of the military aristocracy did emerge from different circles, as noted above, and the link was weakened between the nobility and 'righteous' violence that had been established firmly in the Crusades and other 'just wars'.

Prowess and Skill-at-Arms

The glamorisation of warfare was focused on the worship of prowess. As Froissart noted, 'as firewood cannot burn without flame, neither can a gentleman [*gentilz homs*] achieve perfect honour nor worldly renown without prowess'.[50] While longbows and artillery lessened the potency of chivalric skill-at-arms, and while a gentleman now might serve his king in places other than on campaign, the late-medieval aristocracy remained responsible for the defence of the kingdom: to shirk that responsibility meant that 'their nobility [was] nothing but a mockery'.[51] Above all, they should love deeds of arms, be bold, give heart and steadiness to one another, be truthful and fulfil their oaths, love and desire honour, and be wise and crafty against their enemies.[52] This last quality emphasises the importance of military success and indicates that, while warfare should be conducted in the correct, chivalric fashion, the behaviour of the man-at-arms was not restricted greatly.

In the course of the Crécy expedition, according to the *Vie du Prince Noir*, 'the noble and gentle prince . . . made a fine beginning as a knight.

He made a raid across the Cotentin, burning everything and laying waste'.[53] Fighting in a war that attacked those least able to defend themselves and which aimed to destroy livelihoods and tax revenues and the personal status of the opposing monarch did not make one less knightly, noble or gentle. But once in personal combat with someone of similar status there were certain proprieties to be observed. During the siege/sack of Limoges, John of Gaunt came to blows with a French knight, Sir Jean de Villemur. They fought a fierce duel observed by the prince from his wheeled litter. According to Froissart, the superb display calmed Edward's anger. Eventually Villemur and his companions were forced to submit to Gaunt with the words: ' "Sirs, we are yours, you have beaten us. Treat us according to the law of arms." "By God, Sir John," said the Duke of Lancaster, "we would never dream of doing anything else. We accept you as our prisoners." '[54]

This incident emphasises that chivalry was primarily a code of behaviour that applied to the chivalrous. It was self-sustaining and protective of the first of the Three Orders in both theoretical and practical senses – the ransom system being the clearest indication of this. Unless taken by a vindictive captor – the Spanish and Germans were often viewed as such – conditions for the aristocratic captive were not usually too onerous. Periods of captivity were not usually extensive, although this might be because a hostage took the place of the captured man-at-arms. Ransom demands might be excessive although, in theory, they were not supposed to be crippling financially.[55]

One of the most spectacular non-royal ransoms was that of Bertrand du Guesclin, captured by the Black Prince at Nájera in 1367. Du Guesclin accused the prince of being afraid to ransom him at which Edward stated he should name his own value. Du Guesclin placed this at a staggering 100,000 francs of which the prince immediately remitted half and sent him to back to France to find the remainder.[56]

Individual prowess, always at the heart of the chivalric ideal, was perhaps in the later medieval period extended to a broader concept of military success. Nonetheless, like Jean II, one might maintain one's honour even in defeat. There was still though a powerful allure to personal skill-at-arms, especially when viewed by an author such as Froissart for whom the battlefield was an intricate selection of *tableaux vivants* – a series of individual contests. Froissart noted that at Poitiers, the prince, 'like a raging lion under his battle-helmet', revelled both in the fighting and the rout of the enemy.[57]

For Charny, he who achieved more was the more worthy, and by extension he who did best was most worthy, and those achievements were military be they in the tournament, at war, or on crusade. One had to be careful though about the use of subterfuge. If one employed the cunning ruses advocated by Christine de Pizan it was as well not to get caught as happened to Charny, to his shame, at Calais in 1350.[58]

As noted above, however, military qualities, while paramount, were not the exclusive criterion of aristocratic status – nobility or gentility. Nor was it easy in this new world of infantry and weapons that killed at a distance to make a chivalric name for oneself on the battlefield. It may have been for this reason that service in law and administration were becoming more acceptable, especially for the newly constituted gentry. By serving in these areas they contributed to the war effort and the fulfilment of a national cause. The bureaucracy of government and the developing 'State' machine needed the services in the treasury and the courts of those who previously had ridden out to defend the nation's borders and do justice to her enemies.

However, as royal authority became more clearly expressed through the developing institutions of government it clashed with the chivalric ethos. Royal power, expressed in central and local government, in the actions of commissions and sheriffs, impinged on the rights of the aristocracy to lordship and justice and the right to uphold their honour. In France, this most commonly took the form of royal attempts to prevent private war.[59] These would not be successful for some time, and during the prince's tenure of office in Aquitaine the Foix-Armagnac feud was a destabilising backdrop to his regime. Indeed, it was not until the reign of Charles VII that such attempts began to take effect and the 'State' sought to acquire a 'Weberian' monopoly on violence.[60] In this new environment of enforced military and chivalric restraint, 'the autonomy and proud prowess of the chivalrous would be mastered by the emergent state'.[61] Such a blunt claim can be disputed, but there is no doubt that in countries that enjoyed increasingly strong and centralized systems of government, the independence of noble power and of knightly activities was constrained or at least reshaped in this period.

Loyalty and Treason

If prowess was the cardinal virtue then loyalty came a close second. It was, after all, Brutus and Cassius whom Dante placed alongside Judas in the lowest circle of hell.[62] This attitude to disloyalty and treason must be remembered when we consider the sack of Limoges (1370). On the prince's return from Castile and the battle of Nájera, it became clear that the political climate in Aquitaine was worsening and military reinforcements were sent from England. The appeal against the prince's regime led by Armagnac and Albret soon followed and resulted in the summons to Paris in January 1369 and, when he failed to respond, the reopening of the war. The territorial losses were immediate and extensive. Some regions returned willingly to Valois allegiance and others soon capitulated to French royal troops. Among the English casualties in the desperate rearguard action were two of the prince's closest friends, Chandos and Audley. By 1370, with du Guesclin back at the head of French royal forces, the attack turned towards Bordeaux.

The speed with which the principality fell was startling and shaming. It was one thing for one's vassals to retreat grudgingly in the face of superior numbers and eventually, when no other option was available, to surrender. But the immediate capitulation of a town such as Limoges, believed to be an English stronghold, was quite another matter. On 19 September 1370, accompanied by his brothers, Lancaster and Cambridge, the prince laid siege to the town that had surrendered so meekly to the duc de Berry. The operation was brief, lasting only six days. Froissart stated that after mining the town walls the prince's army entered the city 'in a mood to wreak havoc and do murder, killing indiscriminately, for those were their orders. There were pitiful scenes. Men, women and children flung themselves on their knees before the Prince, crying: "Have mercy on us gentle sir!" But he was so inflamed with anger that he would not listen. Neither man nor woman was heeded, but all who could be found were put to the sword'.[63] Froissart suggested that 3,000 were killed in the ensuing massacre, but the lack of evidence from local chroniclers suggest the sack was not so savage.[64]

But '[i]f one condemns the Black Prince, then one condemns virtually all medieval siege commanders'.[65] According to the laws of war, a city that resisted assault abrogated all rights to mercy should it finally succumb; a city that refused to submit to a prince insulted his majesty and should be punished accordingly.[66] In the case of Limoges there was also a more personal issue at play. The bishop of the town had been a close ally of the prince's administration who had reneged on his oath of loyalty. He was also godfather to the prince's son, Edward, and although not a blood relation, he might be accused of *disnaturesse* (disloyalty to a kinsman). This was a charge that 'went to the heart of the chivalric system of values by which the nobility of later medieval England judged themselves and their peers'.[67]

Froissart remarked of the massacre: 'I do not understand how they could have failed to take pity on people who were too unimportant to have committed treason. And paid for it more dearly than the leaders who had committed it.'[68] This may, incidentally, serve as a definition of 'noble' – one important enough, of the necessary status, to commit treason and of whom to make an example. The late thirteenth and fourteenth centuries witnessed the development and standardisation of brutal penalties for such offences. Certainly Edward I preferred to suppress rebellion (and treason) by combining a general amnesty with the single, symbolic and deliberately gruesome execution of a leader, usually involving hanging, drawing, quartering and the burning of the viscera of the condemned.

The prince at Limoges was accused of lacking pity, which was a chivalric virtue and one also appropriate to rulers. According to Gower, princes should show pity when it is due or they will be '[t]yrants whose hearts no pity bore'. However, he did not call for this in an unqualified fashion and noted the importance of strong rule, asking: 'What is a monarch governing, if he but rule a lawless land?'[69] Even if the scale of the slaughter of the citizens at Limoges was commensurate with Froissart's description it should, like the actions of Edward I against certain Scottish garrisons, 'be judged within the context of his perception of [them] as perjured rebels and traitors . . . Given this, it can be argued that Edward [both king and prince] operated firmly within the dictates of chivalric convention'.[70]

In the period between Edward I's Scottish wars and the siege of Limoges new concepts of treason developed. Edward II's reign saw a great increase in political violence and in the number of executions for treason. Such acts were the cause of great concern to the author of the *Vita Edwardi Secundi*, who highlighted the explosion of violence in 1322 following the defeat of Thomas of Lancaster and his allies at Boroughbridge. This was the response of a king who had contended with extreme opposition from the beginning of his reign and who was also subject to broader circumstantial forces that increased the severity of the penalty for treason at this time. Theories of kingship that emphasised the elevated status of the monarch and the nature of his office, as well as a developing if abstract idea of the 'State', contributed to the greater political fury with which treason was viewed. It is not surprising therefore that there were commensurate developments in the penalties enforced for betraying that office and the 'State'.[71]

This was also the case in France where the 'law of treason, nourished by the authority of Roman law, was very much the child of royal claims to sovereign rights'.[72] Rulers such as Philippe VI and Edward II, uncertain of their authority, were likely to use all the power at their disposal to prevent any diminution of their status since *lèse-majesté* was not only the 'sister of rebellion and . . . an act of disloyalty', it was 'tantamount to sacrilege'.[73]

The broad definition that Edward II (and later Richard II) applied to treason inhibited the upper aristocracy and the body politic as a whole since the opportunities for questioning or criticising the actions of the king were heavily restricted. In the past there had been, if only in theory, a distinction between an acceptable *diffidatio* (renunciation of homage) and unacceptable treason. This was becoming more problematic with the application of Roman legal principles and theocratic concepts of kingship. Such an environment made breaches of fealty easily equated with acts of treason.[74] It may be for this reason that, in certain situations, the only course of action open to a disgruntled aristocracy was to dispose of the monarch since they had no recourse to lesser means of complaint.

It is by no means surprising that Edward III, as part of his attempt to unify the English aristocracy, defined treason in a clear and restricted fashion. After the Statute of Treasons of 1352, the crime encompassed plotting the death of the king, queen or heir; the violation of the queen or the king's eldest daughter; waging war against the king in his realm; providing direct assistance to the king's enemies; counterfeiting the privy seal, great seal or the king's money; and the murder of the chancellor, treasurer or the king's justices. Other possible cases of treason were to be brought before parliament. There also remained a broader conception of treason that may be construed as treason against the correct social order. It was to come into effect 'when a servant slays his master, or a wife her husband or . . . a cleric . . . kills his prelate'.[75] Such a view may be associated with Giles of Rome's view expressed in *De Regimine Principum* in which political loyalty was associated with justice or doing what the law commands, treating individuals according to their status and merit.[76]

Richard II overturned this legislation and his attitude towards treason contributed directly to the accusations of tyranny made against him. In 1398 he declared, 'the mere allegation that a man's treason was notorious was proof of his guilt'. In addition, forsaking liege homage was to be considered treasonous, as was any attempt to have treason legislation overturned. The penalties for treason were also extended to the heirs of those found guilty who were to forfeit their rights and property. Once again, it was in order to shore up an uncertain position that Henry IV, on assuming the throne, clarified the legislation on treason and repealed all relevant acts passed since 1352.[77]

The Estate and Extent of Nobility

Treason, as we have seen, provides some boundary and definition for nobility. But a precise definition of what it meant to be noble was, as the Dauphiné example shows, difficult to establish, even in France, and this in turn had consequences for an understanding of chivalry. Chivalry and nobility were concepts and conditions that were twins, although not identical nor conjoined, for much of the middle ages: French sources speak of the 'state' or 'estate' of nobility by contrast with the 'order' of chivalry or knighthood (*ordo militaris*).[78] That state and membership of that order altered as there were changes in the structure of the aristocracy which in turn imposed different expectations on the noble and the chivalrous. Accordingly there were also numerous attempts to define rank and status within the aristocracy and to determine whether or not one was noble.

The nobility of the person, court and household of the Black Prince is not in question – it was an epithet extended to all aspects of his life and family. For Chandos Herald, his chief protagonist was the flower of nobility and his wife, Joan of Kent, was a noble princess. Even his enemies were noble, not only those such as the chivalrous King Jean 'the Good', but Don Tello, the noble count who led a raid against the prince in Castile at the behest of his brother, the Bastard Enrique to whom the prince wrote a letter opening with the words 'To the noble and honoured [Enrique], duke of Trastamara, at present calling himself king of Castile' – a bastard and a usurper could still be noble.

Of course, like Froissart and other chivalric writers, Chandos Herald was concerned with praising military deeds, and criticism of the aristocracy regardless of nationality was rare in works written for an aristocratic audience even during times of political friction or open war. As Chris Given-Wilson has pointed out, the purpose of the chivalric author in the later middle ages was to enhance reputations. They were concerned with renown and great deeds of arms. 'Lesser', more grubby and mundane issues such as politics only rarely intruded on the work of Jean Le Bel or Froissart or the Herald of Sir John Chandos.[79] As a result the prince's biographer is a somewhat indiscriminating source since he portrayed almost everything as noble. He writes, for example, of squires of noble degree – an interesting comment given the changing nature and status of certain members of the lesser aristocracy. If it is not enough that almost all the characters in the *Vie du Prince Noir* were noble, then events including feasts and welcoming ceremonies were also described as such.

It was not only chivalric chroniclers and biographers, however, who wrote in such glowing and encompassing terms. Christine de Pizan in the *Book of the Body Politic* wrote of burghers and merchants, noting: 'In some places, they call the more ancient families noble, when they have been people of worthy estate and reputation for a long time.' In *Le songe du Vergier* the author stated: 'It is not true that no one is noble except those descended from noble fathers, or that the son of a peasant or a plebeian cannot be noble – for nobility had to begin somewhere.'[80] Christine de Pizan continues to say, by contrast with the Dauphiné witnesses, that involvement in trade did not make one less noble and indeed that 'the office of craftsmen . . . is good, noble and necessary'. Indeed, of all those whom de Pizan addresses only simple labourers are not described as noble or do not have qualities of nobility attributed to them and even then she uses the example of Actilus who was raised up from being a labourer to become emperor of Rome and then re-established the Republic by his noble courage and many noble and great victories. After which he returned to the fields, leaving his imperial title behind.[81]

Perhaps this was considered the proper course of action since social mobility was the subject of grave concern in the post-plague years and attempts were made to create some borders to protect the noble. Over-hasty promotion to high rank upset proprieties as well as being a cause of jealousy, as the examples of Gaveston, Michael de la Pole and the *duketti* demonstrate only too clearly. These were exceptional cases but the threat was pervasive. Since nobility was partly dependent on appearance – to be noble was to look noble and to live nobly – social mobility was inevitable. As the landed wealth of the aristocracy was compromised in the years after the Black Death so it was necessary to restrict not only the reality of social mobility, but also its appearance through sumptuary and game laws and labour legislation.[82] Edward III often made grants to (comparatively) impoverished noblemen in order that each might 'maintain his estate'. This served to maintain the social and political integrity of the established aristocracy and especially those the king had himself established. It was essential for a noble to live in a noble fashion and in order to do this he required an appropriate income.[83]

The Structure of the Aristocracy

The functional partition of society into three orders had always been more a theory than a reality, but it was fractured further in the later middle ages. The *bellatores* became increasingly divided as there was greater stratification within the aristocracy and the introduction of new titles both great and lesser. The Black Prince was himself the first English duke, a rank created in 1337. By the end of the century, the title had found its way outside the royal family. The number of non-royal earls was also increasing and Richard II introduced the rank of marquis for his favourite, Robert de Vere. At the lower end of the aristocratic spectrum, the sumptuary regulation of 1363 laid out the status of some ranks below that of knight and marked an important step towards the acceptance of esquire as a worthy rank in its own right. By 1379, it had been defined further and the poll tax distinguished between three types of esquire. In 1413, with the Statute of Additions, the 'gentleman' arrived in a legal sense, distinct from the 'yeoman' below him.[84] The yeoman, who came to literary prominence in the Robin Hood tales, was a land-holder who might have pretensions to gentility, but who was not far from the common bulk of the population. The term might also have official connotations – it was often translated as *valetti* when specifying an individual serving in a noble or royal household. Robin himself was a radical figure who rejected the very concept of service.[85]

The labour laws, sumptuary legislation and social prohibitions on hunting reinforced these new ranks and aimed to restrict mobility between them. Such legislation reflected the new social structures and also helped to crystallise them. They were legal responses to the new opportunities afforded the peasantry and merchant classes by the economic conditions evident after the plague. Such attempts to regulate and restrict economic opportunities and basic freedoms were generally ineffective, but they became the focus of considerable resentment as seen in the Robin stories and the example of Chaucer's Franklin.[86] Collectively, they show the wish of the elite to reinforce traditional lord–vassal relations. This was to be achieved through the regulation of wages and the mobility of labour, restrictions on the demonstration of wealth according to social status, and restrictions on pastimes that had clear aristocratic connotations. Numerous complaints arose from them and they were a cause of major unrest. The Great Revolt of 1381, although first and foremost a response to taxation, also reflected the dissatisfaction of a peasantry that was aware of new social and economic possibilities and whose members were prevented by central legislation from realising those possibilities.

There was a major outbreak of peasant unrest throughout Europe in this period. Germany, Iberia, and Italy all suffered although not for all the same reasons. France was one of the first countries to experience such social upheaval. The Jacquerie of 1358, rather than being a direct response to restrictive central legislation, seems to have stemmed from a deep dissatisfaction with an aristocracy that had failed in its traditional roles of keepers of the peace and defenders of the realm. This had been demonstrated graphically by the defeat at Poitiers.

Such a distinction between the causes of peasant unrest also reflects the different evolutionary paths of the aristocracies of England and France. In England the reconfiguration of aristocratic society became a pro-cess most evident in parliament with the growing distinction between Commons (lesser aristocracy) and Lords (greater aristocracy). With the evolution of the parliamentary peerage – members of those families that by the middle years of the fourteenth century were receiving regular personal summonses to parliament – comes a functional, if not entirely satisfactory definition of nobility. It is problematic because membership of the parliamentary peerage was not static and, in the context of the Hundred Years War, many members of the aristocracy who were certainly not of the upper echelons of that group were called to assist the king, council and parliament with their deliberations due to their talents and personal experience. The problems in making a distinction between nobility and gentry are especially apparent in this context since, with the development of the authority of the Commons, the gentry acquired greater political aspirations and began to see themselves as the king's essential partners in government. From the second half of Edward II's reign the Commons became a serious force in English politics. In the 1320s and 1330s the Commons were starting to develop policy semi-independently of the Crown and magnates, and in 1376 the Commons stood against the Crown in the Good Parliament. The changing structure of the broad body of the aristocracy required changes in linguistic usage. The Middle English term *per* (peer) is attested at least as early as 1300 with the meaning equal or companion; by 1312 it had developed a parliamentary context, and from at least 1375 it indicated a 'nobleman'. Soon after, by 1387 at the latest, the Middle English *nobelte* (nobility) came into use.[87]

The restructuring of the aristocracy in England is a process that comes into clearer focus if compared with developments across the Channel. There, 'a sociologist observing the English nobility around the year 1300 . . . could be forgiven for thinking that it was evolving along the same lines as the French noblesse'.[88] However, a command of 1360 in France was sent to 'all nobles of whatever estate they are' [*tous nobles de quelque estat que ils soient*][89] and it is evident that in the later medieval period a nobility of lordship transformed into a territorial aristocracy with its rights, powers and privileges publicly established.[90] While this makes for a clear and legally defined distinction between noble and non-noble in France it was not necessarily a distinction that extended to the lifestyle or qualities appropriate to the nobility. For example, Christine de Pizan discussed an individual who was 'a very noble man but very poor'.[91] In England we can observe a 'shift in the line of demarcation separating the gentle from the non-gentle, expanding the ranks of the former to embrace a wider range of people whose way of living gave them something of the quality of a lesser knighthood or *petite noblesse*'.[92]

Gentry, petite noblesse, *and* nobilitas minor

K.B. McFarlane showed that the nobility (the higher ranks of the aristocracy) in England was not a closed group; there was constant recruitment into its ranks if for no other reason than to fill the gaps caused by extinctions in the male line. The group was a large one; he said that 'its members cannot be contrasted with the gentry because they include them; the baronage is merely the upper-layer'. He used the term 'petty-nobles' for those of lesser status. Perhaps though, some comparisons can be made between these indistinct sections of the body politic. Peter Coss has described gentility as a watered down version of nobility while noting that the distinction between upper and lower nobility had always been blurred. What particularly linked this broad grouping was a tradition of chivalrous fellowship that lingered between the armigerous and yet, or perhaps because of this, 'nobility was always for sale'.[93]

While the aristocracy always contained individuals of varying status and greater 'worth', in both a financial sense and that indicated in a military context by Geoffroi de Charny, the particular ranks by which they were evaluated had been few in number. This was changing as 'the gentry was formed in an accelerating process, from the mid-thirteenth century to the mid-fourteenth'.[94] It was this lower and middle ranking section of the aristocracy which was to play such a varied number of roles in politics – local, international, parliamentary and otherwise – on the battlefield and as religious patrons.[95]

By the later fourteenth century, nobility and gentry were no longer interchangeable terms and the differentiation between the two was becoming clear. Like 'noble', the term 'gentle' was most commonly used to indicate birth, high rank and a number of shared qualities. Land ownership remained a significant characteristic although this was complicated by the development of an urban aristocracy. The sumptuary laws of 1363 make clear the distinctions and differentiations which now characterised the aristocracy. Mention was made of knights, esquires and all manner of gentle men below the estate of knight. Around this same time the banneret (who ranked higher than a knight bachelor and so-called because of his square-shaped banner) became a military and social distinction, within the knightly ranks – it was a title that was awarded to John Chandos, 'the most celebrated knight of that time' by the Black Prince at the battle of Nájera.[96]

Peter Coss developed the following definition: gentry were lesser nobility; they were property owners and part of a territorial elite; they served the Crown usually in the localities; they exercised communal social control; and they had a collective identity and interests.[97] By the middle of the fifteenth century, aspects of gentility were extended not only to knights and esquires, but also to gentlemen, yeomen and husbandmen.[98] The apparent homogeneity of the aristocracy was fractured with the establishment of the gentry and the creation of intricate status gradations.

It is evident to some degree in the increasing use of the word 'estates' in its various Latin or vernacular forms from the end of the thirteenth century with its clear concern with status.[99]

Orders of Knighthood

Royal service remained a binding quality among the aristocracy, both nobility and gentry. As has been noted, it took a variety of forms, but military duty remained of particular importance. It was service on the battlefield that was celebrated, rewarded and commemorated by Edward III in 1348 when he founded the Order of the Garter. The Garter, in its earliest incarnation, was intended to encompass the whole aristocracy, binding together the whole community in the war with France. 'With its elite fellowship of twenty-six knights, comprising the most distinguished soldiers and peers in the realm . . . the brethren of the fraternity stood at the apex of the English chivalric hierarchy.'[100] A similar situation evolved soon after in France with the creation of the Company of Our Lady of the Noble House, more commonly known as the Company of the Star.

The secular chivalric orders that flourished throughout Europe in the later middle ages had clear political and social functions, some of which were indicated by conditions of membership, motifs and mottos. Certainly in the case of the Garter, *Honi soit qui mal y pense* (dishonour on he who thinks ill of it), seems to apply directly to Edward's French campaigns and there is no doubt that the founder knights were closely associated with those and particularly the victory at Crécy. Through the use of chivalry and demonstrations of military prowess in tournaments, monarchical orders such as the Garter were used to strengthen the bonds that linked the king to key members of the political and military elite.[101]

The Order of the Garter was designed to be a perpetual memorial to Edward III's continental aspirations and it created a chivalric elite within the ranks of the military aristocracy. It was to be a chivalric forum of the highest order, recruitment was international and membership was dependent not on political rank but chivalric achievement. Its founder members tended to be the king's comrades-in-arms and many also served as his household or chamber knights.[102] Consequently, the Garter reflects the continuing importance of military service to the king. This still served to bind the aristocracy together in a national mission. Edward III harnessed the glamour of military service, indeed the glamour of chivalry, in support of his political aspirations. Despite the increasing social differentiation between members of the aristocracy, chivalry could still serve as a unifying concept. However, the fact that it now had to be propounded in such an elite form also indicates the need to galvanise the chivalric ethic.

Wisdom, courage and martial prowess were the ideal qualities of the Garter knight. These were to be shown through service to the Crown, especially in the king's French campaigns. It is clear that those who were seen to have obstructed Edward in the early years of the war were not included in the Order.[103] The policy of Edward III in melding chivalric values to foreign policy was mimicked in France by Jean II and the Company of the Star, which was probably provided with a guide for conduct by one of the luminous chivalric figures of the age, Geoffroi de Charny in his *Livre de Chevalerie*.

The military orders served as vehicles for propaganda and a means for the dissemination of royal messages about the legitimacy of various royal projects. It was a scheme that Edward had been toying with for some time. Plans had been well underway in 1344 for the development of a more grandiose order, the Round Table. However, this gave way to an order in the keeping of St George after the miraculous year of 1346 with the victories at Neville's Cross and Crécy. All but four, or at most six, of the founder knights played no part in the battle or in the preceding campaign. After the king, the prince of Wales, who had won his spurs at the battle, was given pride of place and probably all those who first sat on his side in St George's chapel fought in the first division at Crécy.[104] As the Order gained status and stature over the years many more of the prince's followers, and those of his wife, found inclusion in this select group, and others of their households became members in Richard II's reign.[105]

Meetings of the Garter and of other chivalric orders, which multiplied over the fourteenth and fifteenth centuries, also reinforced the continuing importance of chivalry and of the military qualities of the aristocracy. While the knight no longer played as vital a role on the battlefield as he once had, he could demonstrate military skills in the tournaments and other meetings of the Garter (even if they were somewhat redundant). In this way, valour, bravery and prowess were displayed in the company of fellow members of the elite and so served to enforce the validity and necessity of the chivalric order.

Courtesy and the Lady

Garter celebrations also served to emphasise the courtly qualities that, while secondary in the pantheon of chivalric virtues, were essential in marking out the aristocracy from the rest. Those qualities and the appropriate aristocratic lifestyle came to be indicated most commonly by the term *gentilesse* which supplemented the older *courteoisie*.[106]

The court was not a new environment for the fourteenth-century knight; it had always been an intrinsic part of the milieu of the military aristocracy, and proper behaviour within the court had long been an important element in securing promotion or a good marriage. It was important therefore that a 'gentleman' knew how to behave in the company of his peers and there was no lack of information he might consult for advice. Latin courtesy-books appeared in the twelfth century and were written in vernacular languages from the thirteenth. The most substantial of these was Daniel of Beccles' *Urbanus Magnus* or *Liber Urbani* (*Book of the Civilised Man*). Written in the twelfth century, this informed the reader how to behave in church, when to bathe, when to exercise, and how often to have sex. He should, it advised, cultivate entertaining conversation and avoid subjects that could cause quarrels. Courtesy-books were often particularly concerned with appropriate behaviour during feasts – what one should eat and drink and how one should conduct oneself at table. In addition, they advised where, when and how to defecate, urinate, spit, belch and fart politely.[107] A feast provided the opportunity to display a fine appreciation of *courteoisie* and one's social rank. The significance of feasting is clear in many literary works and is particularly evident in *Sir Gawain and the Green Knight* and *Cleanness* which focus on the proper roles of guest and host and the correct rituals of eating and feasting.[108]

Like chivalry, courtesy was a demonstration of inner virtue through formal, ritualised behaviour and outward gestures, but unlike chivalry it urged restraint and control. Such moderation was to be exercised in a number of ways. In a personal sense control of the body was important. Of greater political importance was the injuncture not to say or do anything to cause offence.[109] This could impose a dichotomy as a consequence of the differing pressures and requirements of these sometimes contrary ethics.[110] Broadly speaking, chivalry was a code founded on and steeped in violence whereas courtesy demanded moderation and certain standards of restrained behaviour to which all who were courteous should conform. Restraint was not easily compatible with the requirement to defend one's honour by deeds of arms.

Honour may be defined as 'the value of a person in his own eyes, but also in the eyes of his society. It is his estimation of his own worth, his claim to pride, but it is also the acknowledgment of that claim, his excellence recognized by society, his right to pride'.[111] Such demonstrations and acknowledgments of status and value were made daily in courtly environments and, while status was to be recognised and its value demonstrated in courtly etiquette, the courtesy-books advised the urbane man to avoid the acknowledgement of any breaches of honour and etiquette, certainly in public. However, chivalry demanded any slight be returned with violence since to fail to do so would result in shame.

It is possible that the Black Prince may have been advised directly on such matters. A poem, *Edward*, the only extant manuscript of which was written in the middle years of the fourteenth century, has many features of a courtesy-book. It opens with the words *Instructio patris regis ad filium Edwardum*. It is impossible to tell if this was the Black Prince since there are a number of possibilities and it is likely that the poem was composed rather earlier than the 1330s. But it may well have been circulating in the royal family since it has a much more 'courtly' tone than many similar works and seems to assume an audience of high rank and power. It gives suggestions regarding the importance of having pride in one's lineage and the proper form of the giving of gifts to worthy knights.[112] Although there was a long tradition of urging courteous behaviour among the knightly aristocracy, according to some commentators the niceties of courtesy might be taken too far: Thomas Walsingham described the men of Richard II's household as knights of Venus rather than Mars, more suited to the bedchamber than the battlefield. Certainly courtesy books have little to say about war and a great deal to say about how a suitor or husband should deal with women.[113]

Dealing with women was at the heart of courtesy and therefore intrinsic to chivalry. The courteous should not kiss a gentlewoman without her permission. A lady should be protected – rape was unconscionable for a woman of noble birth. But a lady's fate was not of her own choosing, her wishes were rarely considered. She might be won through the demonstration of prowess; she might be little more than a prize in a tournament.[114] Women themselves of course could not be chivalrous; they were merely the inspiration for chivalric actions and lovers of prowess. Joan of Kent was said to have loved a knight (later exposed as the Black Prince) 'whose prowess knows no peer'.[115] Consequently, the qualities expected of noble ladies were different, for the most part, from those of men and were to be shown in different ways. In the case of a young woman, her nobility was partly aesthetic – as masculine nobility was revealed through virtuous action so feminine nobility was evident in beauty.[116]

That beauty was shown to best advantage in a courtly environment. Charny advised young, noble women to be beautifully dressed and 'adorned according to what is right and fitting' in order that they might attract a better husband or, if already married, so as to please their menfolk. Charny's reasoning was that women could not gain renown, recognition or a splendid reputation for themselves through deeds in the outside world, but could do so through their appearance. It is likely that this was also to encourage knights not to give too much attention to their dress and apparel, and so suggested that to do so was effeminate and the province of women.[117] This was significant since the French defeats at Crécy and Poitiers were, in part, blamed on moral laxity expressed through the adoption of foreign fashions.[118]

Since deeds of arms and military qualities were not demonstrable by women, their virtues could only be shown and displayed in the court and household – these included acts of largesse and almsgiving. There were therefore not the same incongruities as those concerned with male concepts of nobility and gentility. Additionally, it may be that 'noble' was used as a title more than as a quality with reference to women.[119] The knight of La Tour Landry advised his daughters that they should be courteous and humble, 'For there is no greater virtue to cause you to have the grace of God and the love of all people.' He did though also note they should dress appropriately, neither excessively nor poorly.[120] A noble lady should not be arrogant and although she should be at pains to act in such a way as to receive reverence from the people she should not take any personal delight in it. This was of great significance – the acquisition, without pride, of a good reputation. For women, sexual honour was of critical and growing importance and this might not be restricted to the premature loss of virginity, or infidelity, but included a poor choice of husband.[121] The knight of La Tour Landry advised his daughters against loving men of lower or higher estate than themselves: 'These whiche loven suche folke done ageynste theyre worship and honoure.' In particular, women should not love married men, priests and monks, servants and 'folk of nought'.[122]

Deviancy from social standards, especially when there were sexual connotations, resulted in shame for women. But the sexuality of men was also held responsible for various political and personal failures. Lust was responsible for the loss of martial powers. According to Thomas Bradwardine, the pursuit of military glory for the love of women was, at best, foolish and he attributed the military failures of the French and Scots to sexual immorality and their unrestrained pursuit of sexual pleasure, which was said to include adultery and incest.[123]

The key identifier of a noble lady was not nobility but honour: 'there is nothing', according to Christine de Pizan in the *Treasure of the City of Ladies*, 'that is so becoming to noble people as honour'. This was acquired through good manners and behaviour. If these were lacking and 'if she does not lead a life by which she acquires praise, honour and a good reputation by doing good, she entirely lacks honour'.[124] It was an accusation levied at Joan, princess of Wales and Aquitaine, when she and her husband took up residence in Bordeaux.

The contrasting requirements of courtesy and chivalry was just one of the pressures placed on the role, conception and authority of the secular aristocracy in this period. The changing nature of warfare, the socio-economic conditions of the post-plague period, and the changing relationship between lord and vassal contributed to an atmosphere of uncertainty. In this environment, some aspects of the chivalric ethic reverted to an earlier form. The military qualities that had provided the practical foundation for the pre-eminence of the knight remained of crucial importance although those qualities might not now be demonstrated on horseback and were to be part of a collective action undertaken in the service of the nation. It was for this same reason that the monarchical orders of chivalry were founded. The continuing allure of the chivalric ethic is evident in these orders and in contemporary literature. But this was a chivalry that had to exist in a new world, in which the distinctions between knighthood and nobility were greater than ever, and in which battles were won by the efforts of the base-born. With the disassociation of knighthood and nobility, the chivalric ethos was extended to all warriors. Even though chivalric action on the battlefield was often more detrimental than beneficial, it was crucially important that 'anyone who wanted any share of power and influence, any recognition of high status [should show] signs of a chivalrous life'.[125] Such signs could be seen all too clearly in the principality of Aquitaine.

chapter four

A PRINCE'S HOUSEHOLD: LORDSHIP AND STATUS

He reigned seven years in Gascony, in joy, in peace, and in pleasantness, for all the princes and barons of all the country round about came to him to do homage; for a good lord, loyal and sage, they held him with one accord, and rightly, if I dare say, for since the birth of God such fair state was never kept as his, nor more honourable, for ever he had at his table more than fourscore knights and full four times as many squires. There were held jousts and feasts in Angoulême and Bordeaux; there abode all nobleness, all joy and jollity, largesse, gentleness, and honour, and all his subjects and all his men loved him right dearly, for he dealt liberally with them.[1]

As the embodiment of royal and seigneurial authority, the household was the 'supreme expression of power, wealth, ritual and hospitality'.[2] Consequently, the changing character of aristocratic and princely power was reflected in the form, structure, membership and character of households and courts. Such changes are evident in the Black Prince's household where we also see the new trends in ceremonial and etiquette that princes were beginning to demand in various European courts. This is especially the case in the courts at Bordeaux and Angoulême, formed after the creation of the principality of Aquitaine. The territorial concessions made at Brétigny appeared to set the seal on Edward's glorious military career. The principality provided him with social and cultural status at a truly European level, a great deal of political power, and the opportunity to display it.

While Chandos Herald exaggerated the 'joy, peace and pleasantness' forged by Edward in the principality of Aquitaine, his observations emphasise the political importance of the court in uniting the aristocracy under the sovereign through the staging of feasts, tournaments and revels of all sorts. Liberality and largesse were the hallmarks of a fine household and few were as fine, as honourable, noble or gentle as that

· 107 ·

of the Black Prince. Like all royal and princely courts it was characterised by display and conspicuous consumption and proclaimed the wealth and quality of a lord. But in Aquitaine such display was associated also with deeper cultural trends and an Occitanian delight in excessive, perhaps vulgar, displays of expenditure. This was a courtly culture that praised the sowing of fields with gold, that lauded a prince who had a banquet cooked over costly wax candles, and which congratulated a lord who slaughtered oxen in their hundreds merely to show his affluence.[3] It was a milieu in which the prince and Joan flourished and allowed them to indulge their tastes for exuberant celebration. This was most evident in a tournament held to commemorate Joan's churching and to celebrate the birth of Edward of Angoulême. Accounts of the event vary; Froissart for once appears to be quite restrained, merely stating that 40 knights and 40 esquires comprised the princess's entourage. By comparison, the *Chronicle of the Grey Friars of Lynn* suggests Joan's retinue consisted of 24 knights and 24 lords and noted the presence of 154 further lords and 706 knights at the festivities. The prince is said to have stabled 18,000 horses at his own expense and the celebrations lasted for ten days. The cost of the candles alone was said to be over £400.[4]

No doubt such extravagance placed great strain on the prince's coffers, but it was an exceptional event. More regular payments had to be made to his retainers and those who received wages and annuities from him. The prince was a generous employer and, as befitted his status, he maintained a substantial household and broader retinue: power and authority was demonstrated by patronage and the ability to retain. It was also demonstrated by domestic luxury and the prince followed his father's example, making substantial refurbishments to many of his homes. In England he rarely ventured far from London and his favoured manors were within a day's ride of Westminster and within fairly easy reach of Windsor, which provided a model for princely and aristocratic domestic style as well as a home for the Order of the Garter.

The Garter was designed to embody the unity of the nation in the struggle against France and it was an image of which the prince would have done well to take note. His regime in Aquitaine, exemplified by his courts at Bordeaux and Angoulême, established an environment both loved and loathed by the Aquitainian nobility. It provided a forum for conspicuous consumption, the most modern fashion, and chivalric display of the highest order, and yet also emphasised status divisions and the new claims for lordship and sovereignty. These were proclaimed by kings and princes throughout Europe and they were proclaimed most loudly in their courts.

Display and Ceremony

Such tournaments as the prince held to celebrate the safe delivery of his first son emphasised his power and also demonstrated the collective authority of those who participated – the military aristocracy. The tournament had served an important and practical purpose in years past, but as the mêlée became outmoded it became less representative of conditions on the battlefield, especially for English knights who usually fought on foot. But, if the military relevance of the joust and indeed the military purpose of the aristocracy were called into question, the tournament still offered an important forum to emphasise the political and social exclusivity of those who participated. It provided an environment in which traditional chivalric skills were demonstrated and the *raison d'être* of the aristocracy was affirmed. There is no doubt either that such skills were hard earned. Geoffroi de Charny wrote of the 'physical hardship, crushing, wounding and sometimes danger of death' that a participant could face and noted the strength, skill and agility necessary to compete successfully. For Charny, while it ranked as the least of a man-at-arms' military achievements, it was still praiseworthy to fight in tournaments. It brought home to a young knight or man-at-arms some of the realities of combat and it offered him an opportunity to make a reputation for himself.[5] Others placed a higher value on the military experience to be gained in the tournament: Cuvelier, the biographer of Bertrand du Guesclin, attributed the Black Prince's military success to his being surrounded by knights hardened in the tourney.[6]

There is though no doubt that, while dangerous, tournaments were becoming more refined affairs as can be seen in another of Charny's works, *Questions Concerning the Joust, Tournaments and War* (*c*.1350). This posed a number of questions regarding the minutiae of the rules, various issues concerning prizes, recompense in the case of certain accidents, and unlikely situations in the midst of a contest. For example, he asked what should happen if '[t]wo knights joust . . . and at the striking of the lances both come out of the saddle. Will each take the horse of his companion, or each be content with his own?'[7] As to all his *Questions*, he provided no answers.

At least as important as the tournament's military purpose were its social and political functions as demonstrations of chivalric prowess and status to shore up the ranks of the aristocracy against those below and to encourage unity with one's fellows. This is especially evident in meetings of the Company of the Star (to which Charny's *Livre de Chevalerie* was addressed) and the Order of the Garter. Indeed, the Garter may have been deliberately structured with such activities in mind and the knights of the Order may have been chosen as members of two tournament teams headed by the king and his son.[8] Perhaps it was in this spirit or to demonstrate the prowess of the knights of Edward's household that for the tournament at Windsor in 1352, 60 buckles, 60 girdle-tips and 120 bars were purchased for 'knights of the prince's companionship'.[9] Similarly, at Smithfield in 1359, he purchased 11 ostrich feathers for the jousts and there are several other records of gifts of shields and other arms being 'powdered' with his device. As a more personal gift in 1354, he gave Chandos and Audley a pair of plates of tournament armour covered, interestingly enough, with black velvet. Unfortunately for those looking for a reason for his pseudonym, he purchased red velvet covered plates for himself.[10]

Participation in tournaments was right and proper for a ruler and the prince appears to have been a genuine devotee of the sport. The political virtue of creating a chivalrous atmosphere at court was evident through the negative example provided by Edward II; it served to foster a spirit of unity and both Edward III and his son also used the meetings to send a broader political message. Arthurian connections were emphasised, with knights fighting incognito or wearing fantastic outfits – both the king and the Black Prince are known to have participated in wearing disguises or costumes. The prince was only 13 in 1343 when he fought in the Pope and Cardinals Joust at Smithfield. It was a tournament organised by Robert Morley that coincided with English parliamentary protests against the practice of papal provisions to Church benefices.[11]

The spectacle of the tournament was often embellished with music which played an important role in a variety of court activities. At the Garter feast of 1358 the prince paid £100 to heralds and minstrels[12] and he brought at least six minstrels with him from England to Aquitaine. There were, at this time, profound developments in musical composition mainly thanks to Guillaume de Machaut (*c.*1300–77) and his advancement of polyphony. Machaut, the most important figure of the French *Ars Nova* and the most distinguished composer of the middle ages, was particularly renowned for his four-voice *Messe de Notre Dame*.[13] His influence was felt throughout Europe, but may have been particularly strong in southern France. After his patron, Jean de Luxembourg, died at Crécy he entered the service of Charles 'the Bad' of Navarre and then the prince's neighbour, Gaston Fébus. He seems to have made a great impact; certainly Froissart was very taken by the quality of music performed at Gaston's court at Orthez.[14]

This cultural environment may well have influenced the prince's household in Aquitaine, but music had been of interest to him throughout his life as can be seen in records of the purchase of instruments and pay-ments and gifts to minstrels.[15] Such men were important figures on the battlefield as well as at court. Gilbert Stakford, a trumpeter, may have been wounded on the Poitiers campaign, preventing him from taking part in the Reims expedition and an alternative living was found for him in the household of the prior of St Michael's Mount. Stakford recovered from his injuries and later served Richard II who gave him a pension of 6d. a day. But music was not only used to marshal the troops: famously, before the battle of Winchelsea, Edward III enjoyed hearing his minstrels play a German dance that Chandos had learned.[16]

Gaston Fébus may have had an ear for music, but it was as a hunts-man that the count was renowned and he committed his knowledge to posterity in the *Livre de Chasse*. The prince was also an enthusiastic huntsman, as were members of his household. In organising a meeting in which the prince hoped to secure Gaston's homage for Béarn, the count of Foix asked for Chandos' hounds to be brought so that he might see them.[17] Hunting and hawking were the favoured pastimes of the aristocracy. The prince had a number of hunting grounds through-out his estates in England, and Edward III was so enamoured of hawk-ing that he took falcons with him on his French campaigns. He also maintained and built several hunting lodges. Like tournaments and other courtly activities, hunting emphasised status divisions and would do so to a greater extent when Richard II issued the game laws. As described in works such as *Sir Gawain and the Green Knight*, hunting was a highly ceremonial activity. *Sir Gawain* may have been written for an English expatriate audience, such as that in Aquitaine, and it is possible that Bertilak's castle with its adjoining deer park was modelled on the prince's fortress at Beeston in Cheshire.[18]

Hunting also made a practical contribution to a chivalric and military education. It required a fine sense of observation, placed the warrior in a perilous situation, giving him a taste of battle, and it developed his stamina on horseback. Ramon Lull advocated hunting as training for a young knight to develop physical and tactical skills since it gave him an opportunity to organise men and hounds in the field.[19]

No doubt the prince often hunted in Aquitaine, but evidence for this is scanty. He had certainly maintained extensive facilities for doing so in England and Wales, despite never visiting the principality. The impact of the plague changed land use and contributed towards the abandon-ment of demesne farming in Wales, meaning that some property such as Kilford in the manor of Denbigh became a hunting park by 1362 – one the prince never used.[20]

Alongside hunting, the prince had a passion for horses. He had at least nine studs, some which must have been rather grand. Certainly, Somersham (Lincs) provided suitable accommodation for Jean II after his capture at Poitiers. In addition to breeding his own horses, the prince purchased animals from all the major domestic horse markets: Smithfield (London), Stamford (Lincs), Chester, and from abroad – Germany, France, Cologne, Brussels and possibly Lombardy. He also bought horses bred from animals imported from Spain and Sicily.[21] Responsibility for these animals was an important household office and, for much of his life, the Surveyor and Master of the Prince's Great Horses was Baldwin Botetourt who also served as the Keeper of the Parks and Chases of Buckden and Spaldwick (Hunts) and Rising (Norfolk).[22]

The gift of a horse from the prince and the right to hunt on his estates were valuable and much prized. It may have been as a consequence of his service during the Reims campaign that Sir John Sully, one of the Black Prince's few life retainers and among the most experienced soldiers of his generation, was granted the right to hunt once a year in the royal forests with his dog, Bercelette (a 'bercelet' was a hound used to track down deer wounded by archers in bow and stable hunting).[23]

There were three main types of hunting: casual – as the opportunity arose (either on foot, but more often on horseback); formal – carried out on horseback following a pack of hounds; and the stable hunt – shooting driven deer from butts and conducted on foot. Ideally this had three archers and three horsemen dressed in green to merge with the undergrowth. It was the most productive form of hunting for meat for the household and to supply military campaigns.[24] The prince may have participated in this form of hunting since he employed Mathew Becheston as keeper of his bow.[25] The prince and his father pursued hares regularly when they hunted with Abbot William Clowne of Leicester (1345–78),[26] but what the order of the day was in 1353 when the prince stopped to hunt at the castle and manor of Shotwick is uncertain. The importance of hunting is indicated by this occasion: the prince found time to hunt while involved in a major reorganisation of the Cheshire administration on one of only two visits he paid to the earldom.[27]

Hunting had always been primarily an aristocratic activity and enforced status distinctions. This was even more evident in hawking in which there was a hierarchy of birds appropriate to be flown by different ranks. It was also an activity broadly symbolic of lordly power since it involved the taking of life. The curtailment of hunting rights in the later middle ages further emphasised such social differentiation. In France, Charles IV had allowed everyone to hunt at least for rabbits and hares in areas other than warrens, but in 1396 Charles VI prohibited the non-nobleman from hunting any game unless he had specific permission. Meanwhile, Richard II in 1390, in the first of a series of game laws, decreed that hunting with hounds, ferrets and even snares was to be restricted to those laymen with an estate worth 40s. a year and clerks with an income of £10.[28] In this way hunting and tourneying became increasingly important demonstrations of the prince's authority. So too were the foods he ate and the clothes he wore. The restrictions placed on participation in tournaments and hunting were part of an attempt to reinforce those traditional hierarchies under pressure in this period. Sumptuary legislation played a similar role in the fluid social and economic environment of the post-plague years. Such concerns with precedent and power were of crucial significance in Aquitaine as the prince tried to enforce a new regime in a politically fractious setting.

As Chandos Herald made clear, one of the key means by which status and authority were demonstrated within the household was the feast. During this period domestic spaces became increasingly formal and so too did the etiquette appropriate for those areas, especially when eating. This process reflected the increasing intricacy of political society and the greater stratification of the aristocracy whose members might find their way to table.[29] This evolution can be seen in various guides and manuals. Household protocol developed considerably in the period between Bishop Grosseteste's 1240–2 regulations (drawn up for the countess of Lincoln) and the much more complex Harleian regulations of the late fifteenth century (prepared for a comital household).[30]

The precise nature of such ceremonials is, however, unclear for the fourteenth century. We cannot be sure that feasts in the prince's household were organised in a manner like that suggested by John Russel, usher of the chamber and master of the hall to Humphrey, duke of Gloucester, in his *Boke of Nurture* (*c*.1450). In this he noted the order of precedence between individuals of different rank and 'how they shall be served [and] in what place according to their dignity, how they ought to sit'. There were detailed instructions regarding the proper treatment of the various ranks, secular and ecclesiastic, and how they related to one another within an increasingly intricate social structure. The worth of those who held governmental, judicial, administrative and household offices was assessed in this peculiarly domestic yet political setting in which seating was determined in accordance with '[t]he rank of all the worshipful officers of the communities of this land, of shires, cities, boroughs according to their dignity'.[31]

Such socio-political rituals and ceremonies conveyed and attributed a sense of honour by establishing and demonstrating an individual's place in the order of precedence.[32] With the development of several of the institutions of the 'State', precedence came to be determined by office as well as hereditary status. Royal service, always valued, now brought with it, almost without exception, a defined social standing and a clear rank in one of many status gradations within the previously hegemonic knightly estate.

The proper organisation of meals both in terms of the standing (and sitting) of individuals and the manner in which they should conduct themselves was of great importance due to the practical and symbolic importance of food and feasting. Such events were often great ceremonial occasions: homage might be given or taken, oaths made and alliances formed. In literature, feasts were often important events that frequently provided the setting for the opening scene when reputations were established and characters displayed in a formal environment. They were often occasions for the public declaration of pledges such as the *Vow of the Heron*, at which, according to literary tradition, Edward III was goaded into launching the Hundred Years War.[33]

Feasts were also important since food and drink were fundamental expressions of largesse and played a primal role in the demonstration of good lordship. They were major aristocratic expenses because costly delicacies were served to the elite and because of the sheer numbers that had to be fed. When Elizabeth de Burgh entertained the Black Prince and the bishop of Llandaff for three days during Lent in 1358, the feast consisted of 81 'messes' (groups of two or four people who ate together). The time of year demanded that fish was served and the company demanded it was served in sufficient quantity and quality. Presumably those items noted in very small quantities were reserved for the guests of honour. The household records indicate the provision of: 568 herrings, ten stockfish, four saltfish, three cod, one-and-a-half salmon, eight pike, six lampreys, four sturgeon, six crayfish, 650 whelks, 42 codling, one conger eel, 12 mullet, 24 skate, 50 whiting, three eels, three sole, 400 oysters, and a slightly troubling quarter of a porpoise.[34] Elizabeth was a close friend of the prince and remembered him in her will with the gift of a golden tabernacle bearing an image of the virgin, two little gold angels, and a large silver and enamel cross.[35]

Because of its role and significance, those with the task of purchasing or acquiring food and drink had a heavy responsibility and it was one not restricted to peacetime. Although few formal records remain, an indication of the food requirements of the prince's household can be seen in orders to Thomas Dover, purveyor of the household (appointed 25 April 1352). In preparation for the Reims campaign he was ordered to buy 160 'great beasts' in Cheshire, and on the prince's return from Calais in 1360 he purchased a further 200 great beasts from Cheshire and north Wales. Dried and salted fish were also procured in large quantities – up to 1,200 in 1351 and the same number in 1352 from towns on the north Norfolk coast.[36]

The size of the operation necessary to feed the prince's household is also evident in the range of offices connected with food. There were numerous purveyors with responsibility either to a particular part of the household or for a particular type of food. There was a purveyor of poultry, of the scullery, the buttery, of fish and flesh for the household, of the kitchen, a purveyor in gross for the kitchen, a purveyor for the great kitchen, and a purveyor of wheat. Other offices included a saucer of the household, a spicer and apothecary, and numerous bakers. There were also yeomen of the buttery, ewery, spicery, scullery, poultry and pantry.

The food that these men acquired and prepared reflected the status and authority of those who consumed it. The typical daily diet for a household servant was based on a common standard in quantities of bread and ale – two to three lb of wheat bread and about a gallon of ale.[37] The upper class diet was based mainly on meat and fish (two to three lb per day); game was usually reserved for special occasions and then served to those at high table. This was also the case with swan, which from time to time the prince ordered to be brought to his household,[38] and with prized luxuries such as wine and spices (including dried fruits and condiments).[39] These were valued not only for their taste and exclusivity, but also because they provided a European cultural link and were indicative of a certain culinary and cultural sophistication. As a result, regular enjoyment of wines and spices was confined to the very wealthy and this indicates the value and generosity of the regular gifts of wine (and game) made by the Black Prince to his friends, acquaintances and members of his household.[40]

The aristocratic medieval diet lacked dairy products, fresh fruit and vegetables, and tended to be deficient in vitamins A and C. The choice of foods consumed was deliberate and again served to emphasise status and authority. Only a man such as Diogenes (recorded by John Gower in *Confessio Amantis*), who was completely unconcerned with the opinions of the world would grow and eat the produce of his garden:

> *When roots and herbs are wholesome, went*
> *Into his garden with intent*
> *To gather both legume and beet*
> *Which presently he meant to eat.*[41]

Diogenes was mocked for his consumption of peasant foods and involvement in manual labour. Fruit and vegetables were not always easily available in aristocratic households, at least for eating: seigneurial gardens were often used to grow flax and hemp, and apples and pears were grown but mainly for making cider or perry, although this was changing. Those vegetables that found their way into English kitchens mainly served as flavourings rather than major ingredients.[42] This is hardly surprising since, according to the cookbook written for Richard II's court, *The Forme of Cury*, food should be prepared in accordance with dietary science. The ideas of Galen, Hippocrates and Arabic medicine suggested that different foods should be mixed according to their Aristotelian properties – hot, cold, wet and dry.

Concerns regarding food are also evident in the composition of numerous literary works on the subject between the thirteenth and sixteenth centuries. The earliest extant English recipes date from the late thirteenth and early fourteenth centuries. They reveal that English recipes made much greater use of fruits and flowers than their French equivalents and they tended to be more specific and discriminating in suggesting the spicing of different dishes. By the later fourteenth century there seems to have been a greater consumption of fruit and a fruit course became common in France.[43] The Valois court was certainly a culinary centre and in Guillaume Tirel (*dit* Taillevent, *c.*1310–95), probably the author of the cookbook *Le viander*, it had one of the most celebrated cooks in history. The Black Prince was served by Thomas Beueschef from at least July 1357. He was clearly a trusted servant in receipt of generous grants and offices and he may have gone on to become mayor of Wallingford.[44]

The growing interest in food and food preparation can be seen in domestic architecture: kitchens and associated buildings were becoming increasingly important. At the prince's manor of Byfleet, a new kitchen and other buildings were erected in 1347 by the master mason, Richard of Wallingford.[45] William of Wickham, one of the executor's of the prince's will, had his kitchen at Bishop's Waltham remodelled in 1388–93 and an external larder added.[46]

During the feast there might be various sorts of entertainment. Minstrels usually played, often performing between courses. In addition, poems or stories might be read, as Froissart did for Gaston Fébus at Orthez in 1388. Or there might be performances by mummers, short plays or various other forms of entertainment, all of which contributed to the theatricality of the event. This was underpinned by the decoration of the banqueting hall with tapestries or murals.[47]

Food and feasts therefore served an important social function and a forum for the demonstration of power, largesse, taste and hierarchy, and Plantagenet and Valois monarchs and princes used such opportunities.

This was supported by the sumptuary regulations concerning food in France and England (passed in 1336, predating the clothing legislation – see below).[48] It is a further indication that monarchs wished 'to regulate the table as a political event' and a public drama and let it serve as an allegory of power. Indeed, the importance Charles V gave to food and feasting was such that he employed more kitchen personnel than Louis XV (1715–74).[49]

Just as food allowed for the regulation and demonstration of status so too did clothing. 'While much could be done to establish the magnificence of a lord through a day-long round of ceremony, the display embodied in clothing, particularly in its decoration and quality, and in the further adornments of jewellery and personal ornament, made a substantial contribution.'[50] The first of nine major sumptuary laws governing clothing (Acts of Apparel) was passed in England in 1337. It was motivated more by economic considerations than social control and aimed to restrict imports of luxury cloth and fur. Special provision was made for the royal family and the secular and ecclesiastic magnates as well as those members of the clergy with benefices worth £100 a year or more.[51] The next, of 1363, was much more detailed and dealt with 'the transgression of social hierarchy'.[52] It was a response to 'the outrageous and excessive apparel of divers people against their estate and degree, to the great destruction and impoverishment of all the land'.[53] Unlike earlier attempts to regulate clothing, which were motivated by trading or political concerns, the regulations of 1363 were a form of social control and reflection of an increasingly stratified and hierarchical society in which status could be expressed by the means of dress.[54] It would be a century before there was another equally elaborate piece of legislation concerning the regulation of clothing although minor changes were made in 1388 and 1420.

The sumptuary laws reflect concern with social mobility and a need to regulate displays of wealth, power and status through fashion which was undergoing major changes at this time and a cause of much consternation. The elegant person wore short, fitted, tailored garments that made extensive use of buttons, lacing and points. There were elaborate belts, and tunics were short. Chaucer's Squire seems to have been the epitome of fashion:

> Embrouded was he, as it were a meede
> Al ful of fresshe floures, whyte and reede.
> Syngynge he was, or floytynge, al the day;
> He was as fressh as is the month of may.
> Short was his gowne, with sleves longe and wyde.[55]

The toes of men's shoes became very elongated – no doubt this interfered with the correct performance of certain court ceremonies; how did one kneel in such shoes? Throughout Europe there was a sudden transformation in fashion and dress that focused attention on clothing as a reflection of social trauma and moral turpitude.[56]

Geoffroi de Charny, writing for a chivalric and military audience, noted the various hazards of the new fashions and of having too great an interest in clothing. He warned against excessive ornamentation and embellishment in dress and suggested that the money could be better spent on other more appropriate and spiritually enriching activities. He also noted that tunics had become shamefully short and that men revealed their backsides when they sat down. With this shameless dress they forgot their sense of honour. The new fashions were also impractical for the warrior because they restricted movement. Rather, young men should be dressed 'decently, neatly, elegantly, with due restraint and with attractive things of low cost'. Pride in dress drew a man away from God, Charny believed, although 'one should dress well when in company with other young people and fit in with them'.[57]

What though was the motivation for wearing the new styles? While new fashions were a way of delimiting the elite from the rest, was an awareness of fashion indicative of an emerging individualism, or merely an act of emulation and aspiration in this period of social redesignation?

A concern with clothing was not new, it had been a subject of continual anxiety for clerical authors throughout the medieval period, but it was given a new impetus in the fourteenth century as a result of changes in fashion and the spiritual and moral crisis brought about by socio-political instability and natural disasters. The urge to control clothing was usually couched in moral terms or in a non-specific manner which indicated that the 'health of the nation' would be better maintained if there were fewer fashionable excesses. Attempts by Edward III's government to legislate against 'excessive apparel' took up this message and reflect an urge to establish a greater degree of control over individuals and groups in an increasingly fluid economic and social environment.

The sumptuary laws reflect the concern of secular authorities with the changing structures of society and show that extravagant contemporary fashions were considered politically dangerous.[58] Such attempts to shackle the population are also evident in the labour legislation occasioned by the Black Death, the outbreak of which John of Reading attributed to the 'empty headedness of the English, who remained wedded to a crazy range of outlandish clothing without realising the evil which would come of it'.[59] Clothing was seen as an expression of sin

– pride, lechery and greed. Such extreme associations between clothing and divine disapproval tended to be made during times of strife and social upset and there is no surprise in it being a particular topic of discussion in the years following the plague.

Excessive or inappropriate apparel was seen as an indication of moral laxity bringing divine disapproval. One of the major targets for such criticism was the royal court where the new fashions tended to be seen first. Richard II was subjected to coruscating censure for his expenditure on clothing, and Hoccleve made complaints about male clothing in his *Regiment of Princes* directed at Henry V.[60] If this was a valid criticism of Richard it may have been a trait he inherited from his father and mother. The prince spent lavishly on clothes and jewels and it is signifi-cant that he seems to have moved more quickly to ensure the presence in Bordeaux of his goldsmith and two embroiderers than he did to ensure his administrators had enough money for their own expenses.[61] Further records note a payment of £715 to an embroiderer for work for the prince, Joan and her daughter, while in 1362, £200 was paid for jewelled buttons for Joan.

The princess seems to have become a sartorial icon and many followed her style of dressing in tight-fitting garments of silk and ermine with low-cut necklines and wearing pearls and precious stones in her hair.[62] Not unlike her husband's political and courtly regime, Joan's fashion-able excesses in Aquitaine delighted some and scandalised others. A Breton lord, Jean de Beaumanoir, noted he wanted his wife to dress as 'an honest women' and not to adopt the 'fashions of the mistresses of the English or the Free Companies'. He was 'disgusted by those women who follow such a bad example, particularly the princess of Wales'.[63] Whether this reflected her wearing the new fashions or was a broader comment influenced by Joan's sexual reputation is difficult to judge. It should be noted that the stolid Philippa of Hainault also spent very significant amounts on fashion and jewellery – £20,000 over the last ten years of her life. It was after all 'expected of a queen that she should . . . use her appearance for the purpose of enhancing the regal image'.[64] None-theless, there is no doubt that Joan developed a 'reputation as a sexual libertine' and references made by contemporaries to her as the 'virgin of Kent' may have been somewhat sarcastic.[65]

Location and Personnel

The prince's household was therefore a demonstration of power and status. His authority was demonstrated in the spectacle of the tourna-ment, the ceremony of the hunt, the sophistication of his table and the food he ate, and the distinctiveness and luxury of his clothing. The significance of all these forms of display was changing in this period and in turn altered the very nature of the household. The cue for such change was taken from his father's court and it was also indicative of broader European developments such as those evident in the Valois court. The attention given to domestic comfort in the prince's many homes, especially those in and around London, followed such royal examples and allowed for a studied demonstration of his power. As his household became less peripatetic and more formal so his authority was shown by increasingly strict forms of etiquette that emphasised his lordship. These were conditioned by various theories of sovereignty that were the subject of considerable discussion. Such ideas, influenced by monarchical struggles such as the Hundred Years War and the long-standing conflict between ecclesiastical and secular power, were based on traditional rivalries between kings, and between papal and royal/imperial authorities.

The power that underpinned such theories of lordship was also shown by the prince in the scale of his household and of his wider retinue. This catered not only for his domestic needs but also administered his estates and provided the core of his military expeditionary forces. Aristocratic households and royal courts changed with the establishment of new concepts of lordship, systems of patronage and recruitment. In particular, the creation of bastard feudal retinues, affinities and clienteles that provided military, political and legal support, altered the character of the household and the nature of aristocratic life.

Bastard feudalism has been held responsible for all and none of the political turbulence characteristic of late medieval England. Its origin and definition have been much debated and remain a subject of conjecture. This is because of varying studies into the nature of the phenomenon itself and as a result of re-evaluations of its more 'legitimate' parent – feudalism. Indeed, it may be foolish to discuss late medieval society in 'feudal' terms of any sort following the ferocious attacks on the archetypal conception of feudalism by Elizabeth Brown and Susan Reynolds;[66] and Colin Richmond has been similarly scathing of bastard feudalism – 'that old, indeed senile, adversary'.[67] All present extremely strong arguments, however, the work of Brown and Reynolds seems to indicate that bastard feudalism was no dissolute and dissonant variant, but a relatively common form of service relationship prior to its attributed illegitimate birth at a suitably uncertain time in the late medieval period.[68] Certainly, medieval society was pluralistic in its structures with many sources of power and a single paradigm cannot describe all its forms, but that is not to say that 'feudalism' does not retain some utility as a concept. This is particularly so in the later medieval period when legal concepts of fief and vassal were formalised and did approximate to institutions around which important sectors of society were organised.

Nonetheless, the strict legal definitions applied by Reynolds and others have for some anathematised the concept of a feudal society. There is no doubt that it had become an 'easy' term to apply to post-Carolingian, perhaps post-Roman, societies in medieval Europe because it was mutable and malleable. Consequently it was problematic since few agreed in their understanding of the model or maintained a consistent definition and application of that model. A consideration of the limitations of 'feudalism' is significant for the later medieval period because it provides not only an abstract concept by which to evaluate later developments, but also because the structures under consideration were bound up with the subsequent development of the modern 'State'.

Although not a medieval word, 'feudal' has been used to define many forms of medieval societies. It implies a political culture in which land was offered in return for service, especially military service. It also suggests, in the context of the post-Carolingian period, an environment in which central authority devolved to the upper nobility. The construct also acquired an economic dimension since it was felt that the disorder which lessened central control impeded economic development. Feudalism, by this theory, prevented the natural development of capitalism. It was also a concept, as David Crouch has shown, that was used by historians and others for clear contemporary objectives. It was only comparatively late in its history that feudalism began to be defined in legal terms, and considered as an aspect of property law. It is this legal aspect that has in recent years provided the main battleground for the debate over the existence of feudalism and especially with regard to the contractual relationship between fiefs and vassals.[69]

Reynolds found the feudal model to be fundamentally unsound. Her arguments are based on historiographical and terminological grounds. The entrenchment of the feudal model has been such that generations of medievalists have unwittingly interpreted their sources in 'feudal' terms without giving them sufficient independent consideration. Although it is an approach that can be taken to a postmodern extreme, whereby language ceases to be a vehicle for meaning, there is no doubt that a single piece of so-called feudal terminology, indicating land was 'held of' an individual has, too often, been used to imply a much wider social structure and system of obligations and relationships. In addition, the belief of the hegemony of the feudal model in Europe and beyond has been encouraged or at least taken for granted by those who wished to make easy comparisons between one region and another.

Reynolds argues that the law of fiefs was the creation of the thirteenth century and of bureaucratic, professionalised governments in northern Europe, and that 'feudalism', the feudal construct, was the creation of this process, and categorised as such by political theorists, historians and antiquarians from the sixteenth century onwards. As part of her assault, Reynolds also denounces the importance of interpersonal relations in power structures, especially those that have been characterised in terms of 'vassalage' and constructed by oaths of homage and fidelity. She argues that vassals, and indeed fiefs, were not common enough in Europe before the thirteenth century to provide the basis for an institutionalised social and political structure. There was therefore, according to Reynolds, no institutional fusion of fiefs and vassals from which a chain of power and personal relations can be established.

There is no doubt that the term 'feudal' has become unwieldy and imprecise, having been defined in so many ways.[70] Nonetheless, this is not to say that it is moribund as a historical model. For example, 'feudal' society in England is often judged as the period $c.1066-c.1300$ in which certain customs and demands regarding reciprocal military and other forms of service held sway. Despite Reynolds' influence such a definition can still be useful in this country in this period. The term retains some validity when applied to a specific geographical and political area, and when the terms of reference are defined closely.[71] 'Feudal' also remains an attractive concept since it is not necessarily helpful to replace it with another indistinct term such as 'lordship', a convenient expression for all forms of medieval interaction by which authority was demonstrated and power was exercised. Lordship too defies precise definition, especially in the later middle ages when its implications and connotations were evolving swiftly due to a variety of circumstances and influences, not least Roman law. As a consequence of such changes, lordship came to be understood in terms of both jurisdictional authority and property rights. Lordship (*dominum*) gave authority over men mainly through possession of ultimate legal rights in a property relationship – very broadly defined. It also carried religious connotations since such authority was divinely ordained and apportioned. In practice, absolute and exclusive rights of ownership and control were broken into smaller jurisdictional parcels. This *dominum utile* allowed an overlord to retain ultimate authority and yet devolve a degree of ownership and control to his tenants.[72]

As monarchs claimed ever-greater powers in this period and the development of various 'State' institutions gave them a greater chance of making real those claims, the status of lesser lords (accustomed to wielding lesser powers of lordship) was brought into question. The later medieval period witnessed the end of a structure of political authority that had come into being around the eleventh century. At that time, lordship and military power coalesced with the attribution of the quality of nobility to those who wielded arms. In the later middle ages the twin poles of the aristocracy (nobility and what had become the gentry) began to separate, with a restructuring of the political elite and the replacement of certain forms of local lordship by central institutions.

The great households in England and France remained of key significance despite such changes. They were the places to which individuals were drawn seeking advancement and employment. Changes in the distribution of patronage and the means by which individuals might seek to make their mark in society (feudal to bastard feudal?) altered the process by which political authority was distributed, but the great households remained storehouses of power within which concepts of lordship and authority were most clearly demonstrated. Lesser households took their example from greater ones and at the pinnacle, setting the fashion, was the royal court.

Medieval aristocratic life could be semi-nomadic. The career soldier in an age of *chevauchées* rarely slept in the same place for long when on campaign (with certain notable exceptions during sieges) and this had been reflected, albeit to a lesser extent, in the habits of the nobleman in peacetime. This changed in the fourteenth century and is most apparent in the activities of the king. The development and increasing sophistication of various institutions of government and executive bureaucracy meant the king did not have to travel constantly around his domain in order to maintain law and dispense justice.

Like his father, the Black Prince came to favour a progressively limited number of houses, particularly after his return from Aquitaine in 1371. Edward III had about 25 residences early in his reign, but in his later years he rarely moved outside the Thames Valley. This was part of an ongoing trend and by the reign of Edward IV the number of royal residences had fallen to about ten. At the same time the royal household was increasing in size; between 1360 and 1413 it ranged from 400 to 700 permanent staff.[73] This may not have been a pattern followed in lesser households, which possibly reached their apogee in terms of numbers in the pre-plague period and declined thereafter in accordance with diminishing landed wealth and the increasing social and economic independence of the gentry. Nonetheless, the nobility attempted to maintain the influence previously focused on membership of their households through other forms of association such as the bastard feudal retinue, and by different means of recruitment such as the offer of annuity payments.[74]

The growth of the royal household and the increasingly static nature of the court are indicative of a range of changes concerning the nature of government and the role of the king in the governing process. With the establishment of the court as a physical entity, rather than merely a grouping around the monarch, it became a location requiring development in terms of its features, luxury, status and the practices to be observed within its confines. Trends in domestic architecture show military considerations giving way to issues of domestic comfort, a process also reflected in the habits of the aristocracy in both England and France.[75]

Indeed, the French example was crucial in establishing the new mores of kingship and these in turn filtered down to influence the domestic habits and attitudes of the nobility and gentry. French monarchs were also restricting the number of residences they used regularly. In the first half of the 1350s, Jean II settled more permanently in and around Paris, and Charles V continued this residential pattern, moving the royal household from the Palais de Justice to the Hôtel Saint-Pol. The Parisian focus provided a degree of security in the face of regular English raids and ensured French kings were in close contact with the institutions of government. As the machinery of national administration became focused on the capital so it was necessary for the king to be nearby.[76] After 1360, once Edward III finished his campaigning career, he resided in houses in London or within a day's ride of the capital, especially Windsor, which also provided a home for the Order of the Garter.[77]

As the court made longer stays in fewer residences, developments and improvements were made to and in such areas as the kitchen, private accommodation, and the chapel.[78] This was a process reflected throughout aristocratic society. Despite the concerns of the Hundred Years War, except in vulnerable locations, a greater emphasis was placed on domestic comfort rather than military defence. Although licences to crenellate continued to be sought and granted, many of these were for decorative rather than military reasons.[79] This domestication was also reflected in a transformation of the terminology of household ranks in the middle third of the fourteenth century. Some of those that had been synonymous with a military function such as esquire and valet became ranks that were differentiated militarily, socially and economically. For example, esquire was no longer only a military position, the servant of a knight, but a rank solidly associated with territorial and economic status.[80]

Domestic aristocratic architecture emphasised the status of the owner and his family and the fabric of buildings was usually embellished with symbols of lordship. This is particularly evident at Windsor, which Edward III rebuilt between 1350 and 1377 at a cost of over £51,000. The Great Hall was reconstructed, but the greater expenditure was on the royal apartments. Status and hierarchy at Windsor was demonstrated by a horizontal sequence of chambers of increasing quality. This was also seen in a vertical sense in Charles V's donjon at Vincennes near Paris. Both allowed for the performance and imposition of increasingly complex court ceremonial.[81] At Windsor the king had seven chambers as well as a closet and private chapel. The queen had four, one of which had an adjoining chapel. Guest quarters and lodgings for senior members of the household were also constructed and these were furnished to the highest standards. Such developments involved a new use of space within great households. A greater number of rooms with a wider range of functions were assigned and designed for individual use.[82]

Edward also undertook impressive redevelopments at Sheen and Eltham to which Richard II and Henry IV added. These three properties were the chief focus of expenditure on royal domestic housing in the later fourteenth and early fifteenth centuries and became the primary residences of the king, but they were not the only ones: King's Langley, Woodstock, Henley-on-the Heath and Kennington were all improved and extended.[83]

Domestic chapels were also being redesigned as part of this process. Among the royal properties, the most impressive development in this field was St Stephen's chapel, Westminster – the Plantagenet Sainte Chapelle – which was completed under the patronage of Edward III and Philippa in 1363. Religious, dynastic, domestic and political considerations are evident in the design. On the altar-wall to the north, beneath a painting of the Adoration of the Magi, was an image of St George at the head of a royal male line consisting of the king leading his five sons – the Black Prince was shown wearing a coronet. To the south of the altar, Philippa and her daughters were depicted. This is an important early example of English dynastic portraiture and appears to be a genuine celebration of the family. It was also a political statement: the family were depicted in a French style, Philippa and her daughters were seen dressed in the French fashion, and the wall-painting may have been based on a French prototype at Poissy commissioned by Philippe IV. It has been suggested that, in the context of the failure of the Capetian line, it was an 'overt display of English fecundity'.[84] To emphasise the political intent the quartered arms of England and France were shown. The image implies that the family was rebranding itself in accordance with the king's political ambitions.

The claim to the French throne gave a further impetus to general trends in the English royal court and the king's household. Greater assertions were made regarding the proper extent of royal authority and the power appropriate to kingly sovereignty. These were mirrored by a commensurate development in the etiquette and ceremonial befitting the king in these

increasingly formal surroundings. As a by-product of this process, procedures were set in place to provide, theoretically, all the king's subjects
with some sort of access to him now that he tended to be resident in
and around the capital. Perhaps Joinville's image of Louis IX dispensing
justice from his informal court held under an oak tree was too powerful
to ignore.[85] The magnificence of royal accommodation and ceremonies
performed therein were necessary to add lustre to the monarchy and it
was a pattern followed by the Black Prince in Aquitaine.

As levels of household organisation and ceremonial became more
intricate, different qualities came to be required of those who had to or
wished to operate within such environments. Walter Milemete wrote a
treatise on good government along with a copy of the *Secretum Secretorum*
for Edward III in 1326–7, which included advice on proper domestic
habits.[86] For those in search of patronage, political and social advancement might be determined or at least influenced by an understanding
of courtly etiquette. More than a hundred years before Castiglione, a
courtier was 'no longer to be understood solely by feats of arms, but in
the representation of self, manifested by his mastery of social codes and
his belonging to the courtly elite'.[87] They are qualities evident in Chaucer's
description of the Squire:

> *Wel koude he sitte on hors and faire ryde.*
> *He koude songes make and wel endite,*
> *Juste and eek daunce, and weel purtreye and write.*
> *So hoote he lovede that by nyghtertale.*
> *He sleep namoore than dooth a nyghtyngale.*
> *Curteis he was, lowely, and servysable,*
> *And carf biforn his fader at the table.*[88]

The attention given to domestic living arrangements was not restricted
to the interiors of buildings, it extended to the grounds surrounding them.
Late medieval gardens tended to be built on a quadrangular plan. Some
were enclosed within walls, with orchards and vineyards outside them.
Edward III made improvements to the gardens at Sheen and Rotherhithe
where there were extensive grounds.[89] He also had a new vineyard planted
at Windsor in 1361. Vines were brought from La Rochelle, and John
Roche, a French master vintner who was hired to oversee the project,
was paid the remarkably generous wage of 7s. a week.[90] The prince had
extensive gardens at Kennington, tended by John Aleyn and Nicholas le
Gardener.[91] Gardens came to be seen as an important part of an ideal
courtly society and were illustrated in a variety of media, perhaps most
famously and beautifully in the illuminated Book of Hours (*Très Riche
Heures*) commissioned by the duc de Berry.

The Black Prince's extensive estates provided him with a large number of houses and castles in which to reside throughout England and Wales and in Calais, but much of his time was spent in and around London.[92] Many of these residences were in a poor state when he acquired them, as can be seen from the surveys made of the duchy of Cornwall in 1337 and principality of Wales in 1343. It was estimated that if all the Welsh castles were repaired properly the cost would be £4,317 13s. 4d.[93] Although the prince did concern himself with the fortifications of Wales, especially while on campaign, he appears to have spent more on the upkeep of his duchy of Cornwall properties both in the south west (he had castles at Launceston, Restormel, Tintagel and Trematon and a fortified manor house at Liskeard)[94] and the 'foreign manors' throughout the country, of which the most important were Kennington, Berkhamsted (which housed Jean II in 1360),[95] Wallingford, Byfleet and the Prince's Wardrobe in London. The last of these was used as a store for clothes, arms, tents and other gear, as well as an occasional residence.[96] In addition, the prince had chambers at Westminster in the precincts of the king's palace, which contained a chapel and probably housed the prince's exchequer.[97]

Some of the general changes seen in domestic architecture were evident in the prince's houses and castles. In military constructions the curtain-wall replaced the keep as the main form of defence. The projecting towers set within the wall might be used to provide accommodation surrounding a courtyard. Some of the finest examples of these can be found in the principality of Wales. A great hall remained as a central forum for the purposes of display and entertainment and continued to serve its most important function as a daily eating room. In general, however, the hall lost its significance as the focus of daily life for the nobility to be replaced by an increasingly formal and segregated series of chambers. Bishop Grosseteste in the 1240s advised the countess of Lincoln to eat in the hall in the presence of her household, but by the later fourteenth century the lord and lady tended to dine in private chambers. The hall became the preserve of the servants and the lord's great and subsidiary chambers became the most significant areas where his close confidants came together. Great feasts continued to be held in the hall, and for members of the royal family the hall had to be an extensive building – Gaunt's hall at Kenilworth measured 90 feet by 45 feet.[98] The importance of the transition of the centre of power from the hall to the chamber is seen in changing service terminology at the highest level. By about 1370, the title 'knights of the king's household' was replaced with that of 'knights of the chamber'.[99]

Archaeological surveys of some of the prince's houses provide an instructive picture of the different sorts of buildings in his possession, the uses to which they were put, and the developments and improvements he made to them. At Lostwithiel in Cornwall the great hall appears to have consisted of eight bays with a two-light Gothic window set in each gable, and a rose window set high in the northern gable. The hall ran parallel to and not far from the River Fowey, and stood amid a cluster of smaller buildings that serviced it in various ways, some of which were leased or farmed to servants of the duchy. The prince never stayed there, when in Cornwall he resided at Restormel. Lostwithiel's functions were largely administrative; it was the focus of the activities of the receiver, John Dabernon (one of the prince's chief officials in the duchy), the steward, John Skirbeck, and the auditors.[100] Lostwithiel was also the location of the stannary (tin mining) and county courts where legal matters were settled and the knights of the shire elected. Finally, the manor provided the location for the assaying, stamping and weighing of tin for export.[101]

Among the prince's favoured manors was Wallingford, to which he made extensive improvements. General repairs and alterations were made in 1343 and again in 1352 when Richard of Wallingford was appointed carpenter in the castle. In the following year the walls were repaired, and in 1359 a new hall, kitchen and prison were built as well as a hall for the hearing of pleas. Between 1363 and 1370, £500 was spent on improvements to the great tower, great chamber and other buildings.[102] In 1375, a further £200 was spent on the great chamber, great hall and chapel. The manor became a favourite of Princess Joan's after her husband's death and she died there.[103]

Kennington, held of the duchy of Cornwall, was the prince's chief residence near London and it was the manor where he spent much of his time. It was situated two miles south of London Bridge in the parish of Lambeth and largely rebuilt by the prince in the years 1346–62. The building work was undertaken first by Richard Ailyngton, who had previously worked at St Stephen's chapel, Westminster, then by John Leicester, whose workmanship proved to be unsatisfactory, and finally by the noted architect and builder, Henry Yevele.[104]

In 1353–4, the prince ordered a new vaulted hall with pantry, buttery, kitchen and other chambers to be constructed.[105] Then, in March 1358, Yevele was contracted to complete the hall with two spiral staircases, three chimneys and buttresses to the porch as well as a garden wall. Soon after, John Heywood was contracted to build a bakehouse and two chambers near the kitchen and to demolish the old chamber and gate chamber. Some of the older buildings at Kennington were refurbished in 1359, and in 1360–2 a new house was built for the pastry cook and tiling work was undertaken. Some features of the work, including the (perhaps ceremonial) staircases and chimneys with multiple fireplaces, have been compared with those later built by Jean, duc de Berry, at his great hall in his palace of Poitiers.[106]

Whether this was also the case with any of the features in the prince's palaces in Aquitaine is unknown. Their location, size and design have left no records. During his time as the king's lieutenant (1355–7), when not on campaign the prince resided in the archbishop's palace in Bordeaux. Tiderick van Dale, usher of the chamber, William the Chaplain, and two senior members of the household, Stephen Cosington and Bartholomew Burghersh, made preparations for his arrival in 1355.[107] No doubt he established what he expected to be a permanent home when appointed to the principality. This may have been at Blanquefort, north of Bordeaux; Lormont, near the episcopal palace; Libourne or elsewhere – there are a large number of houses and chateaux in the area called 'du prince noir'.[108]

Authority was demonstrated in the activities and splendour of the household and the ability of its prince to distribute patronage. The growing intricacy of court ceremonial and the sophistication of the household contributed to considerable increases in the size of such institutions in this period. Evidence for the size and expense of the Black Prince's household and retinue is problematic for much of his life. We have a reasonably clear idea of the key members of his household and the chief household officials, but there are no remaining household accounts that allow for an exact measurement of the size of the household at any one time. However, the prince's register and other documents allow us to piece together much of the household and give an insight into its main functions.

An exact identification of any household is problematic; membership tended to be amorphous and fluid. 'The formal membership of the household could encompass individuals who were present infrequently, the lord's advisers and council, besides military retainers and others more loosely connected to him.'[109] One indication of the composition of the household – perhaps defined in the broadest terms – at any single time is to be found at the prince's death when he requested Richard continue paying the annuities he had granted his servants. These consisted of 94 grants, 32 made on his deathbed (5 June 1376) that totalled some £2,927.[110] However, this should not be taken as indicative of the true size of the household, certainly not for much of the prince's life when it far exceeded this number.

The size of the establishment can be seen in the only remaining household list drawn up on departure for Aquitaine in 1363. It numbered well over 250 individuals[111] (although only a few of these are named) and around this time the prince's broader affinity was also developing.

Ten of his 21 life retainers were recruited between 1 March 1365 and 6 November 1367, and 57 annuities granted for military service were made between 1361 and 1369, although some of these were delayed payments for service at Poitiers.[112] Such a retinue contributed to the considerable expenses required of a magnate, prince or king.

It is usually estimated that the prince's household expenditure in Aquitaine averaged about £10,000 per annum.[113] However, it is difficult to be certain about this because of the nature of the composite account enrolled by Richard Fillongley, probably the treasurer of Gascony, in 1370–1, which is the only evidence for principality finances. The account notes household expenditure at approximately £41,800, which was equivalent to nearly half the total income of the principality in this period. However, the exact duration of the account is unclear since the figures may apply to the periods of office held by various treasurers. If the account deals with a period of approximately five years, then average annual household expenditure in Bordeaux is in line with the usual figure (nearly £8,400) but, judging by the tenure of the treasurers, it seems that the prince was only resident in Aquitaine for two of these years. It is possible, although unlikely, that the account only covers the period from c.1363–6 and if so annual household expenditure could have been somewhere in the region of £20,000.[114]

The prince's household was composed of individuals drawn from throughout his estates and beyond. Its composition was determined by his military role in the Hundred Years War, his status as heir-apparent to the throne of England (and France), and his position as a lord of a great demesne. Its military character can be seen in terms of its member-ship and the means by which those members were retained. Household service, however, was not restricted in terms of location, nor in the various fields in which an individual might serve.

Those household functions that catered for the prince's domestic requirements were divided into different departments such as the pantry (bread and table linen), buttery (wine and ale), and the kitchen, which in turn had its own sub-departments, such as the saucery, scullery, and poultry. Officials from these departments played multifarious roles. For example, Henry Berkhamsted, porter of Berkhamsted castle, purveyed goods for the prince at home and on campaign. He was promoted to the post of constable as a consequence of his military service at Poitiers and later became the prince's pantler and usher of his hall. He accompanied him to Aquitaine in 1363 and seems to have crossed back regularly to England to see to the prince's affairs.[115]

At a higher level, many of the prince's chief household servants played important administrative and/or military roles. These were men such as the Garter knights James Audley (governor of Aquitaine, lieutenant in Poitou and the Limousin),[116] and John Chandos (constable of Aquitaine and keeper of the forest of Macclesfield).[117] John Wingfield (governor of the prince's business) was another who performed a wide range of duties in the prince's employ. He was a household bachelor and chief councillor who saw military service on the 1355 *chevauchée* and at Poitiers. He was also a notable administrator and financial official who, prior to the Reims campaign, negotiated a loan of 20,000 marks for the prince from the London merchant community.[118]

Among the other main household officers were Edmund Wauncy who served as steward of the household (from at least 1352 until 1361/2), and Richard Stafford, steward of the prince's lands (1347–60). Various individuals held financial offices: among the most notable was Peter Gildesburgh, keeper/treasurer of the wardrobe (1 February 1341–31 July 1344), and keeper of the privy seal. John Henxteworth was controller of the household (who kept a counter-roll or duplicate record of finances) during the 1355 *chevauchée*. Henxteworth was also keeper of the seal (1361–3) and receiver of the chamber (1360–61/2). Peter Lacy, one of the most important of Edward's chief financial officials, served as keeper of the Great Wardrobe (where valuable items and stores were held) and receiver-general for much of the prince's adult life (1346–1371/2).[119]

There was therefore considerable overlap between service in the household, administration and financial offices, and distinctions between the household, military retinue and broader political affinity must remain, as they were, deliberately uncertain. The prince's household bachelors were among the most important members of his retinue and formed the core of the military retinue that was augmented by a large number of annuitants. Among the prince's bachelors were such notable figures as Thomas Felton, whose military service at Crécy and Poitiers laid the foundations for later high office; he became steward of the household and then seneschal of Aquitaine.[120] Richard Stafford, noted previously as steward, was also the most consistent lay member of the prince's council and an administrator of his estates in Wales and the Marches.[121] Nigel Loryng, a founder knight of the Garter, formerly a king's yeoman and one of a number who joined the prince after serving Edward III, became chamberlain (from at least 1351 to 1375) and keeper and steward of the forest and lordship of Macclesfield.[122]

Evidence from the Register suggests that at least 72 individuals held the title of bachelor in the prince's household, although not simultaneously. By comparison, Gaunt's register of 1372–6 notes only 21 bachelors and that of 1379–83 has 27 with the title. The large number of bachelors in the prince's household equates closely to the royal household where there were an average of 70 knights in the first half of the fourteenth century. This is hardly surprising since he was expected in time to become king.[123]

In terms of recruitment practices, unlike John of Gaunt, the prince made sparing use of life indentures and followed methods comparable to those used by his father as well as Henry of Grosmont, first duke of Lancaster, and his other brothers, such as Lionel of Clarence. The Black Prince had only 21 indentured retainers, compared with Gaunt's 173 in 1382 (and a household of 115).[124] But it should be noted that the example of the Lancastrian affinity is extraordinary and it was an institution created for extraordinary circumstances.

In addition, indentures themselves were relatively unusual means by which household service was retained. An indenture might or might not provide privileges in the household such as *bouche de court*, as offered by the prince to Geoffrey Warburton.[125] Indentures provide clear evidence of a close connection between lord and retainers, but they were by no means the only way a connection between men was constructed and they were probably one of the less important methods. It may be the case that the Black Prince was simply 'a good and favourable lord' to those of his men who were neither tenants nor 'feed' retainers. While providing less tangible evidence of personal associations, such 'good lordship' remained at the heart of the 'bastard feudal' relationship. It was a relationship that was becoming increasingly reverential in some ways and especially in terms of behaviour appropriate to the two parties.[126]

Sovereignty and the Tensions of Lordship

As courts and households became increasingly ornate, segregated and fixed in location, so the rituals and etiquette performed within them became more extravagant and intricate. Such ceremonial activities also evolved in accordance with developing ideas concerning kingship, sovereignty and lordship. These customs were a key way by which power and authority were demonstrated and imposed and, in time, they became one of the main ways by which power and authority were defined.[127] Such rituals took a variety of forms and were evident in a number of situations. They were at work in the chapel, which provided (or enforced) a timetable or (liturgical) calendar that governed activities in accordance with saints' days, fasts and religious festivals, and so regulated 'the rhythms of the court's year'.[128] Common worship also promoted order in the household and emphasised the lord's status.[129] Meals and feasting also provided an occasion when hierarchical seating and the provision of different qualities of food and drink contributed to the general ritual of the household or court.

However, a successful ruler would make sure he did not alienate his subjects. Part of Edward III's success stemmed from his inclusive attitude to the English aristocracy and the deliberate fashion in which he brought the political elite together in support of his domestic policies and his continental ambitions. This was a policy born of necessity and also the result of seeing the dangers of division at first hand in his father's court. It was also a policy recommended by authors concerned with theories of political governance such as Christine de Pizan who, through the image of the body politic popularised by John of Salisbury, stressed the need for harmony between the estates, the importance of balance in aristocratic relations, and the mutual obligations of ruler and ruled.[130]

Good relations between monarch and nobility were also a concern of Philippe de Mézières although these were advocated primarily with the intention of promoting a crusade. He used the image of a great ship and its sailors working together under the command of the captain (king) to represent an ideal unity of purpose among the French estates.[131] Social balance was required to achieve unity of purpose directed by the king. If, however, the estates overstepped their bounds strict action should be taken to maintain order not only because it was politically necessary, but also since it indicated an overturning of a divinely ordained society. Richard II saw the Peasants' Revolt as an attack on the king's royal state and an offence against God.[132]

Maintaining order or exacerbating tension among the noble elite was, in part, dependent on the judicious use of patronage and the proper treatment of individuals according to birthright and service. Upsetting the accepted order could lead to friction and this might be done through the imposition of certain household rituals and forms of etiquette, as in the Black Prince's court in Aquitaine. Among such rituals those that were potentially the most problematic involved the giving and receiving of homage since they required a public acknowledgment of social and political inferiority. John Russell Major observed that in the course of the later medieval period the ceremony of homage itself became very unpopular. The 'kiss' was a particular problem, and kneeling before a noble came to be considered ridiculous since one only knelt before a king.[133]

The Black Prince took the homages of many of his subjects in a great ceremony at St Andrew's cathedral in Bordeaux and on an extensive tour of the principality. There were certain problems with this process and many of the Aquitainian nobility had no wish to be handed over to the sovereignty of a new overlord. In particular, the prince came into conflict with those claiming near-sovereign status in their own territories, most notably Gaston Fébus who was seeking to extend his own power within his vicomté of Béarn. As head of a small Pyrenean principality the count could not use royal (especially Valois) methods of establishing authority through thaumaturgical and religious rituals such as the coronation ceremony with its unction and sanctifying oil. Nor did he have enormous economic resources, but he did exploit various forms of iconography to imprint his rule and he developed institutional and governmental organs that modernised fiscal systems and allowed for the imposition of permanent taxation. This served to increase his own authority and lessened that of his own nobles. It was the development of an individual and publicised conception of power that compared closely, if on a smaller scale, with the actions of Edward of Woodstock in trying to establish his own rule over a generally unsympathetic principality.[134]

The Black Prince's use of iconography to bolster his position in Aquitaine is most evident in his issue of coinage both as lieutenant of Gascony and prince of Aquitaine. In 1355, the *léopard d'or* was issued, perhaps to deliberately supersede the French *mouton d'or* – the English leopards replaced the Paschal Lamb on one side and the *fleur de lys* on the back. The silver gros and half-gros coins showed a half-length figure of the prince, bearded and holding a sword. The significance of sceptre, throne and sword is clear enough; the beard may have indicated maturity and/or masculinity.[135] At some point after the arrival of Edward as prince of Aquitaine the *chaise d'or* appeared. It was the only gold coin to show him bearded and without a sword. He held a sceptre and was seated on a throne and leopards were quartered with *fleur de lys*. It bore the inscription 'God is a righteous judge, strong and patient'. The *pavilion d'or* (*c.*1364) showed two leopards at the prince's feet and the coin was personalised with the addition of two ostrich feathers. It carried the words 'The Lord is my strength and my shield, and my heart trusted in him'. On it the prince is depicted beneath a gothic canopy perhaps comparable to the *lit de justice*,[136] which was gaining significance just at this time. When the king of France sat in majesty in parlement he was surrounded by drapery (the *lit*) which cordoned off royal space. Later in the fourteenth century the *lit* came to symbolise royal justice and it was an image used accordingly by Froissart and Eustace Deschamps.[137]

Opposition among certain members of the Aquitainian nobility to the prince's rule was initially due to disquiet at being handed over to the man who had inflicted one of the most devastating examples of the *chevauchée* strategy in the war and had exacted the humiliation at Poitiers. Some of the Gascons had, of course, fought alongside him on those campaigns, but for both Gascons and the nobility of the wider principality, aspects of the etiquette demanded at the prince's court may well have encouraged opposition. It is recorded in the *Anonimalle Chronicle* that the prince sometimes forced his nobles to wait days for an audience with him and then, when he deigned to admit them, they were required to kneel before him, perhaps for hours.[138] This has drawn comparison with Richard II's court and the requirement that subjects should kneel if the king so much as glanced at them.[139] True or not, and both incidents are only recorded in a single source,[140] there was a strong Anglo-Gascon influence at court during the minority of Richard II. Guichard d'Angle, Baldwin Raddington, John Devereux, David Craddock and Simon Burley had all experienced the regime in Aquitaine. Burley, Richard's tutor, may have been particularly influential in guiding the young king and directing the atmosphere of his court. Writers such as Giles of Rome (Aegidius Romanus) may also have influenced Burley. Giles' *De Regimine Principum*, written for the future Philippe IV of France,[141] emphasised a subject's obligation of obedience, claimed the greatest possible authority for a monarch (under the Pope), and stated that all privilege and nobility came from the king and that, as the supreme lawgiver, he was above the law.[142]

Certainly both Burley and Michael de la Pole, Richard's chancellor, owned copies of Giles' work. But so too did Edward III, whose copy was a wedding present from Philippa of Hainault.[143] This was later given to Henry of Grosmont and subsequently Louis d'Orléans. Thomas of Woodstock and Thomas Lord Berkeley also owned copies.[144] Richard's style of rule, especially in the later 1390s, clearly was problematic for many of the upper nobility and may be judged tyrannical. But the extent to which it was directed by the example of his father's regime in Aquitaine is difficult to judge. Perhaps those who had been part of the princely court in Bordeaux and Angoulême poorly advised the young king.[145] If, however, the collapse of the principality of Aquitaine was attributable to the appalling manner in which Edward treated his subjects then it does not seem likely that Burley or anyone else would have encouraged the young king to follow a pattern of behaviour that had such disastrous consequences.

It is more likely that both Richard and his father were merely adopting a range of contemporary European practices and their styles of rule can be set among general trends by which greater claims were being made for the extent of sovereign authority and the deference due to those who wielded it. The later years of the thirteenth century had seen in France the propagation of theories claiming ever-greater status and authority for a king. The Capetian lawyers formulated ideas concerning

French royal rule that stated the king was as an emperor (without superior) in his own kingdom (*rex in regno suo est imperator*), which were later adopted in the English court.[146] The friction this created between the kings of France and England, as a consequence of the treaty of Paris, often boiled over into hostilities and indeed it contributed to the outbreak of the Hundred Years War.

During the same period, similar claims were being developed in England. The imperial connotations of monarchy are especially clear in Edward I's reign in his relations with Wales, Scotland and Ireland. The building of Caernarfon castle with its implicit echoes of Constantinople is one of the clearest and most impressive statements of Edward's wish to dominate the British Isles in an imperial fashion. It was, in a sense, a 'hegemonial' concept of empire, by which a king who ruled over more than one kingdom, and was acclaimed as such, was an emperor.[147]

Political struggles between competing monarchies, secular and papal, led to biblical, Greek and Roman sources being plundered to justify individual positions. Of these, Aristotle was especially important.[148] Nicole d'Oresme translated the *Ethics* and *Politics* for Charles V along with a commentary. He stated that royal power was limited by no superior organ of government although, like Christine de Pizan and Philippe de Mézières, he realised it should be shaped and balanced by the laws of the community and the interests of the estates. In Edward III's court, various governmental theories were proposed in the *Speculum Regis*, written for him as a young man by either Simon Islip or William of Pagula, and by Thomas Bradwardine who composed *De Causa Dei* using Aristotle's *Metaphysics* to argue in favour of autocratic kingship: 'Things do not wish to be ill-ordered and a plurality of commanders is no good thing.' Bradwardine also emphasised the thaumaturgical powers of the English king.[149]

The influence of Roman law was even more potent and clearly expressed by authors such as Giles of Rome and John Wyclif in *De Civili Domino* and *De Officio Regis*.[150] Giles referred to the prince or the king as a demi-god (*semideus*), and writers at the court of Charles V used even more extravagant language in their exaltation of royal power.[151] Such influences and trends can be seen in Richard's insistence in the 1390s on new ceremonial and the use of 'majesty' as a term of address.

So, while Richard's rule was 'arbitrary, uncustomary and bore heavily on certain individuals', this 'formed the normal small change of English [and European] medieval kingship' and it is unlikely that it was 'widely resented or so unpopular as seriously to undermine Richard's government.'[152] Although there was little to distinguish Richard's court from the other main courts of the day the English royal position was not as strong as some of his continental counterparts.[153] The Valois kings were buttressed in their authority by long years of thaumaturgical ritual and propaganda not evident to the same degree in England.[154] It is significant that in France the madness of Charles VI was not seen as a cause for deposition, although he was clearly *rex inutilis* (a useless king).

The development of Capetian and Valois monarchical claims had developed over a long period and evolved still further in the later middle ages. John of Salisbury's notion of the king as the image of God (*rex imago Dei*)[155] developed so that by the end of the second decade of the fifteenth century writers were avowing little less than a divine right of royal succession.[156] By comparison, the kings of England, notably Richard II, while at the apex of the political community were an intrinsic part of it and subject to its contractual principles. In addition, the English monarchy was haunted by the spectre of Edward II.[157] It is somewhat ironic that Richard precipitated his own downfall in attempting to avoid the fate of his great-grandfather. The consequences of losing a proper sense of balance and co-operation between king and nobility did not require him to look back as far as 1327; it should have been evident in the rebellion against the Black Prince in Aquitaine.

The rebellion against the prince, occasioned if not necessarily caused by taxation policies, can be understood in the light of the character of the prince's new 'Anglicised' administration, his personal relations with members of the Aquitainian nobility, and the nature of Languedocian society.[158] But it is important to question whether the principality could ever have maintained its integrity as a political entity in any circumstances.

The catalyst for the rebellion was the *fouage* granted by the Estates of Aquitaine following the Castilian campaign. Peacetime taxation in England and the rest of France was a cause of deep dislike, but Plantagenet and Valois alike had imposed the *fouage* throughout Languedoc on a regular basis for several years before 1368.[159] In that year it was granted by the Estates at a lower rate than had been levied in the past, 10 *sous* per hearth, for five years, and only then in return for substantial concessions.[160] Taxation therefore does not explain the revolt entirely.

Another reason lies in the Anglicisation of the administration. But while this was certainly a cause for discontent, attempts were made to gain the support of various interest groups for the new regime. For example, Jean d'Armagnac, the leader of the rebellion, had received substantial support from the prince to pay his ransom to Gaston Fébus accruing from the battle of Launac (1362). There was also a programme that aimed to establish concentrations of politically supportive families in various towns and cities such as Périgord;[161] charters and privileges were also issued to Cahors and many other towns. In La Rochelle several of the French chief officials of Saintonge were appointed to high office.[162]

The revolt was also brought about by outside influences. It was a rebellion encouraged by Charles V and Louis of Anjou and couched in nationalistic terms. Letters from them emphasised the illegitimacy of Edward's rule, both in real terms (the true overlord was Charles V since the renunciation clauses of the treaty of Brétigny had never been signed) and as a consequence of his wilful style of government.[163] Of course there were other incentives and when Armagnac, Albret and the rest turned to the Valois and Paris their allegiance was well rewarded.

Just as the nature of the prince's regime can be understood in the context of an evolving theory of lordship, so the rebellion against him was part of a developing concept of the limitations of power and the proper course of action should an overlord act outside the bounds of his authority. The extent of that authority and how it might and should be implemented were matters of intense debate throughout Europe at this time and were given an idiosyncratic dimension by social and political conditions in the principality of Aquitaine.

Although not a direct accusation of Edward or his regime there is an implicit implication of tyranny surrounding the Aquitainian administration. The image of a tyrant became a powerful one throughout Europe in the fourteenth century and especially so in England as a consequence of the reigns of Edward II and Richard II. The debate over the proper exercise of royal and lordly power had been encouraged in the early years of the century by the struggle between the papacy and several of the European monarchies, most notably France. The correct implementation of power and the balance between secular and ecclesiastical authority remained a major topic of contention as it had been in struggles between the papacy and empire over many generations. Ptolemy of Lucca, for example, made extreme criticisms of kingship during the early years of the Avignon papacy. For different reasons similar ideas became current and significant in England in the restrictions on royal power made in the Ordinances of 1311 against Edward II.[164] Such theories had direct and practical applications and they posed fundamental questions about the nature of kingship and lordship.

This debate was intensified in England by the deposition of Edward II and, while it cooled during the 'golden years' of Edward III's reign, it became topical once more when military failure scarred the king's reputation in the 1370s. Comment in the later fourteenth century on theories of social order and power came from several quarters.[165] The Peasants' Revolt expressed the clearest condemnation of aristocratic lordship when Wat Tyler demanded its abolition in 1381. Although this was the most extreme example of anti-aristocratic feeling it was by no means the only complaint.

When Richard II suffered the same political fate as his great-grand-father, he was portrayed as being found wanting in both his personae (or bodies) as king, the body politic and the body natural. The king was separated from the people by virtue of his status, but he was also the head of the body politic.[166] Like Edward II he was described as *rex inutilis* and his personal limitations and failures were emphasised. He was accused of perjury of his personal and coronation oaths, of sacrilege and of sodomy. His mismanagement of the government was said to have led to a loss of royal dignity, and he had failed to uphold the law and liberty of the realm. This included, most damningly, chapter 39 of Magna Carta: 'No free man shall be taken or imprisoned, or dispossessed or outlawed or exiled or in any way ruined, nor will we go or send against him except by the lawful judgement of his peers or by the law of the land.' The greater claims being made for the immutable power of the law and individual freedom from despotism are evident in legislation of 1369 when Edward III replaced the phrase 'no free man' with 'no man, of whatever estate or condition he may be'. He promised no one was to be dispossessed, imprisoned, or put to death without 'due proc-ess of law', which was the first use of that phrase in the statutes.[167]

Richard had attempted to be the source of the law rather than its mouthpiece (*rex loquens* as opposed to *lex loquens*). His actions were in accordance with certain Roman legal concepts: *princeps legibus solutus est* (the king is not bound by the law) and *quod principi placuit legis habet vigorem* (what the prince decides has the force of law),[168] but in the political context of 1399 he was adjudged a tyrant. The rule of law, the status of the monarch, his ability to govern, implement justice, and defend the country were, of course, founded on military power. King-ship in order to be effective had to be strong, but that strength could be used with evil intent and should it be so the aristocracy were beholden to defend the proper laws and customs of the realm against tyranny just as they were required to support a just ruler – by force of arms.

Concepts of lordship and authority then were undergoing a reappraisal in the late medieval period. Its extent, its proper use and even its origins were being considered. According to Diego de Valera, the Castilian knight whose writings found fame in the Burgundian court in the 1440s and 1450s, after the confusion at Babel the most able men were elected to rule. They were the most virtuous and best suited to defend society from both without and within. This model of lordship laid a great deal of emphasis on justice, defined as the measure which gave each man his due, and in order to dispense justice adequately there was a need to be magnificent and powerful, which certainly chimes with accounts of the Black Prince's court in Aquitaine.[169]

The means by which lordship was to be successfully imposed remained an issue of importance for a long time. By the end of the fourteenth century it was influenced in different directions by developing humanistic thought[170] and it came to be distilled in Machiavelli's *Prince* where the author asked if 'it is better for a prince to be loved or feared'. The resolution of the argument is that since love is out of a prince's control, and fear is something he can instil, the latter is the preferable option for governing effectively. Over a hundred years previously Christine de Pizan had reached the same conclusion[171] as did Jean Froissart, although predictably he expected rather more of his aristocratic heroes: 'a lord was to be loved, trusted, feared, served and held in honour by his subjects.'[172]

The Gascon/Aquitainian rebellion brought the principality of Aquitaine to an end. It was the product of many different forces. Over some of them the prince could exercise some influence and discretion, and he was less successful in these areas than he might have been; over others he was the victim of a number of trends. The changing nature of noble and royal lordship was one of these. In both England and France from the second half of the fourteenth century we can see the evolution of a new group of 'landed magnates of an entirely new type, with entirely new political ambitions'.[173] As a result of all these influences some aspects of his regime delighted the indigenous aristocracy while others were a cause of friction and dissent. With the loss of the principality and the disastrous resumption of the war with France, dissent also returned to domestic politics: the authority of the king and his ministers was shaken by the Commons in parliament.

chapter five

PARLIAMENT, REPRESENTATION AND THE BODY POLITIC

Lords . . . and magnates . . . I will by no means try to conceal from your wisdom how weighed down the common people have been by the burden of taxes . . . All of which they would bear cheerfully if the king or the kingdom seemed to get any advantage or profit from it . . . But it is obvious that the king has neither received advantage nor the kingdom any return from it. And so . . . the common people are demanding a statement of accounts from those who received the money, for it is not credible that the king should need such an infinitely large sum if his ministers were loyal.[1]

It was in the Good Parliament of 1376 that the Commons first launched a major programme of opposition to the Crown and its ministers. There had, of course, been conflicts in the past between king and parliament, most recently in the early 1370s, and there had been a major crisis in 1340–1. The 1376 parliament took such opposition to a new level, however, and it was, if not exclusively, the result of action initiated in the Commons, represented by the first Speaker, Peter de la Mare. Previous opposition to the king or his policies had been sponsored, to a far greater extent, by the Lords and reflected their concerns. The baronial opposition of the 1250s and 1260s led by Simon de Montfort had been primarily, like that which led to Magna Carta, the result of dissatisfaction and disaffection among the higher nobility. This is not to suggest that the 1376 parliament saw a nascent democracy at work, but the Commons by this time had become representative of a wider body politic, of a political society that had or felt it should have a greater stake and say in the government of the realm. It was in this political context that the Crown came under attack from the lesser aristocracy (the Commons) in 1376, from the 'peasantry' in 1381, and from the nobility (the Appellants) in 1386. It therefore suffered major assaults from representatives of all the chief secular power groups within a ten-year period.

Such attacks were reflective of a redistribution of political authority in the fourteenth century, but this did not necessarily entail a lessening of royal power in the face of burgeoning parliamentary influence. On the contrary, a skilful monarch could use the new-found authority of the Commons and political society as a whole to support his policies and augment his power. Edward III managed to do this for a good proportion of his reign, most notably from $c.1345$ to $c.1365$. In so doing, however, he shaped and strengthened a conception of the 'State' in which the community of the realm, reflected in the membership of parliament, began to play a more significant role in determining the fate of the nation. The idea of the 'State', which had never been static, was refashioned substantially in the later middle ages. It was seen in the changing relationship between king and parliament that altered as a consequence of the various Edwardian wars in Wales, Scotland and France, and by the vicissitudes of the reigns of Edward II and Richard II.

The relationship and balance between political power and financial muscle was at the heart of such changes. It was a relationship that began to alter with the need to pay for the conquest of Wales, the attempted conquest of Scotland and, in the reign of Edward III, by the cost of the Hundred Years War. The king could not establish grand foreign alliances or launch large scale, increasingly professional military expeditions to France out of his own pocket. But the new-found authority of the 'State' could be marshalled to provide the king with immense resources and these permitted him to conceive and implement policies of far greater scope and scale than his predecessors. 'Very much the king's instrument in a violent world, the *status regis et regni* was tempered to a new strength in the Anglo-French war, but it was more than simply the power to tax and deploy armies. Rather, the monarchical state was what made taxing and military adventures possible.'[2] With this development the members of the body politic became, in a sense, investors in royal policy and they demanded a return on their investment. Should that policy, those military adventures, fail or the king not fulfil his responsibilities satisfactorily as far as the key figures in political society were concerned then his position could be weakened dramatically and the glamour of kingship might not be sufficient to save him.

The extent of the power that came with the ability to influence grants of taxation should not be exaggerated however, and it was only occasionally an effective weapon in a power struggle between monarch and subject. It is also the case that many of the Commons' complaints concerned the misuse and misappropriation of taxation rather than opposition to the basic grant of funds.[3] While the king was popular, especially when he provided military success, political opposition was all but nullified,

Plate 1   The Three Living and the Three Dead – Robert de Lisle psalter (*c*.1310)

Plate 2   The battle of Crécy (1346) – *Grandes Chroniques de France* (*c*.1415)

Plate 3　The tomb of Edward the Black Prince – Trinity chapel, Canterbury cathedral

Plate 4　The transi tomb of Archbishop Henry Chichele, Canterbury cathedral (*c*.1424)

Plate 5   Use of the longbow: archers practising at the butts – Luttrell psalter (*c.*1330)

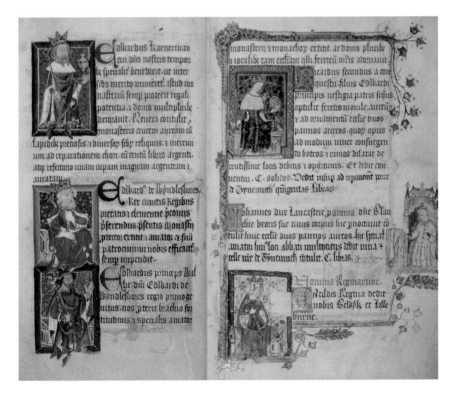

Plate 6   Royal benefactors of St Albans abbey (Black Prince, lower left corner) – Golden Book of St Albans (1380)

Plate 7   The Black Prince as a knight of the Order of the Garter – William
Bruges' Garter Book (1440/50)

Plate 8   Edward III granting the principality of Aquitaine to the Black Prince
(1362), Illuminated initial (*c*.1390)

Plate 9   The battle of Poitiers (1356) – *Grandes Chroniques de France* (*c.*1415)

Plate 10   Hunting with a bow – Queen Mary's psalter (*c.*1315)

Plate 11   Edward III bestowed with the arms of England by St George –
Milemete treatise (*c*.1326)

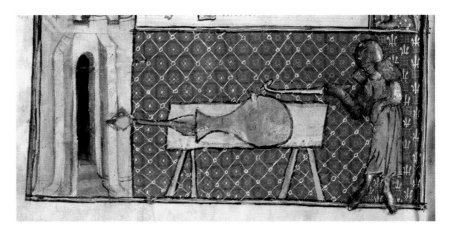

Plate 12   The 'Milemete Gun' – the earliest known picture of a cannon (*c*.1326)

Plate 13   Edward III and his sons depicted as demons – Angers Apocalypse tapestry, commissioned by Louis d'Anjou, woven by Nicholas Bataille (*c*.1380)

but when there was no longer a return on their political and financial investment the people and their representatives could take action of an increasingly decisive nature.

Taxation and the uses to which it was put were the main vehicles for the political realignment of the later fourteenth century and a cause of argument in parliament and in the country as a whole. Such concerns are evident in the *De Speculo Regis* (*c*.1331), which was written as a complaint against the levying of prises (compulsory purchase of foodstuffs), and in the *Song of the Husbandman*, written in English (*c*.1340), which protested at the oppressiveness of taxation. Significantly perhaps, with regard to many of those later involved in the Peasants' Revolt, it was a protest made by a moderately prosperous man. The *Song against the King's Taxes* (*c*.1340), written in Latin and French, suggests that the poor were so oppressed that they would soon rise in rebellion.[4]

The development of parliamentary authority and the resources that it gave his father therefore coloured the Black Prince's life and career. It allowed for the increasing professionalism of the armies which he led and in which he fought, and in that sense it allowed for the Hundred Years War. More particularly, the prince was born not long after the deposition of his grandfather, a parliamentary event that shaped the political climate of his life,[5] and he died in the midst of the Good Parliament when military failure (much of it his own) and governmental mismanagement resulted in focused opposition to royal policy, opposition which he was said to have encouraged.

Parliament, then, gained a new identity, definition and authority in the course of the fourteenth century, but its authority had been growing with gathering speed for some time prior to this. The earliest official use of the term 'parliament' was in 1236 and it soon acquired a technical meaning. Parliament was 'a special meeting, an afforced meeting, of the king's council to which the justices of the King's Bench knew they could refer for consideration one of the cases before them in which the king had expressed an interest'.[6] Such limited scope was broadened later in the reign of Henry III. Shire knights may have been summoned to earlier meetings, but the parliament of February 1254 has been considered significant in the evolution of parliamentary authority. While the king was in financial difficulties in Gascony, the sheriffs were instructed that two knights from every county should be chosen to go to parliament to assent to grants of taxation – perhaps significantly the grant was refused. The baronial wars gave parliament greater powers, at least hypothetically, and these grew further with the reign of Edward I and his reliance on parliament to finance his campaigns.[7]

Monarchical frailty in Edward II's reign encouraged the development of still greater parliamentary authority and the institution began to acquire an accepted part in theories of government. The role and function of parliament was sketched out in or around 1321 in the *Modus Tenendi Parliamentum*. This document described the main content of parliamentary business and the issues that were to be discussed: war and the king's affairs; the business of the realm; and the answering of petitions. This reflected an order of importance and not necessarily the formal process or agenda of a meeting. These issues reveal the chief way by which parliamentary authority increased. They emphasised the reciprocal nature of grants of taxation, indicating that parliament would provide financial support for the king's policies, but only in return for the answering of petitions and redress of grievances.

Throughout this period, monarchs fought a rearguard action to try to ensure no direct correlation was made between a grant of taxation and the redress of parliamentary grievances – broadly speaking they failed. The *Modus* makes it clear that parliament had become 'the focal point of the political relationship between Crown and subjects, the place where the mutual obligations of ruler and ruled were performed for the profit of the realm'.[8] The *Modus* may not reflect parliamentary practice or procedure exactly, but it marks an important development in the formal role of the institution and reveals the increasing importance of parliament in the construction of national policy and in governing the affairs of the realm. This importance was recognised by various governmental theorists such as Walter Burley who in *c*.1340 wrote a commentary on Aristotle's *Politics* which, although heavily based on Aquinas and Peter of Auvergne, provides a number of instructive contemporary references to the political process and includes the first comment on the English parliament in a work of political theory.[9] The role of parliament therefore was changing as a consequence of its developing financial muscle and the need for the Crown to direct that muscle. It was also changing in accordance with legal practice and theory, and its increasing authority developed alongside what had become, since the beginning of the fourteenth century, the binding force of statute law.[10]

The growing authority of parliament reflected broader changes in political society. Parliament began to include or at least take account of the interests of groups outside the traditional aristocracy – the burgesses, merchants, and the lawyers. Of course, urban elites might well be aristocratic, but they were not cut from quite the same cloth. In 1343, the county knights and the burgesses met together in the painted chamber at Westminster for the first time. In a later parliamentary assembly the Commons claimed to represent the mercantile community, and by 1373 the merchants asserted that parliament and not mercantile assemblies represented their wishes.[11] The increasing authority given to statute law also encouraged the greater significance of lawyers in the process of policy-making in parliament. In addition, this process was helped because many MPs had some sort of legal background or experience of the law through serving as sheriffs, stewards, coroners, and justices of various sorts.[12] There also came to be a close correlation and connection between membership of the Commons and appointments to various commissions. In 1338 the Commons first gained a say in nominations to the peace commissions, and ten years later the justices began to be chosen and sworn in parliament.[13]

This chapter examines the growth of parliamentary authority in England with particular emphasis on the increasingly assertive role of the Commons in the 1370s. The ability of the Commons to formulate a coherent and independent policy will be examined in the context of developing theories of political representation. The need for some sort of dialogue between Crown and parliament grew as taxation became all but permanent. Like many of the upper aristocracy, the Black Prince took an increasing interest in parliament, especially after his return from Aquitaine. There was a new awareness of the need to direct and control its burgeoning power and it may well be that the prince was involved in such an attempt in the Good Parliament of 1376, but the evidence for this is slight and contradictory. Nonetheless, his close association with a number of MPs in this most fractious meeting, and the wish of certain commentators to emphasise that association is indicative of the political importance of the prince and the weight that his support was thought to bring to parliamentary proceedings.

The growing influence of parliament, particularly the Commons, the shifting complexion of aristocratic society, and the greater authority of statute law, all of which took place in an uncertain political climate, resulted in a new balance of power being established in medieval England. In that new construct, law-making, which had been a key, indeed perhaps the defining royal prerogative, became partly dependent on the consideration and consent of parliament. This new political balance has been seen as part of a broader transition, namely from the Angevin 'law-state' to the Plantagenet 'war-state', but that fails to emphasise sufficiently the changing nature of power and authority, of lordship, kingship, and political power, which was taking place in this period.[14] It was a change that permitted royal power to be expressed on a far greater scale than hitherto and yet it also contributed directly to the degradation and depositions of half the ruling monarchs of the fourteenth century.

Kings and Parliaments: A Changing Balance

The Plantagenets were aware of this transition in the balance of political power and attempted to ensure that parliament did not gain too much authority at the expense of the Crown. Such developments in the authority of representative institutions can be seen throughout Europe. In France, for example, the authority of the Estates-General could be extensive during periods of monarchical weakness, but for various reasons the Estates did not develop into an institution of comparable power. By contrast, the English parliament grew to become the main forum for political debate. As such it became important for a ruler to ensure the compliance of parliament and its financial support for his policies, especially in this period of protracted warfare. Edward III managed to do this effectively for the bulk of his reign, but it is clear that such support was dependent on the success of the wars with France and Scotland, and on the king fulfilling the expectations of a nation that was increasingly politicised and politically aware.

In order to maintain his authority in the face of the potential threat from parliament, Edward III tried to disassociate redress of grievances from grants of taxation and used various alternative revenue streams which he could collect without parliamentary assent. The difficulties associated with these, however, illustrate the growth of a public opinion increasingly critical of any taxes levied without the approval of parliament.[15] Taxation was becoming the province of the Commons, although it should be noted that until 1395 Lords and Commons granted taxes equally and throughout this period the financial agendas of Lords and Commons were not dissimilar. While the Commons did tend to have greater concerns over the misuse and misappropriation of taxation, the Lords themselves paid very significant sums in tax and it was an issue that affected the whole aristocracy throughout the majority of the fourteenth century.[16] Nonetheless, the increasing authority of the Commons was bound up with its ability to provide the king with money, and the growth of that authority is evident in the difference between 1340, when political remedies for misgovernment were first sought, and 1376, when the Commons were in a position to launch a full-scale attack on the king's ministers with comparatively little (overt) support from the magnates.[17]

As far as the monarch was concerned there was a potentially deleterious association between taxation, government policy and the growth of parliamentary power. This first became apparent in Edward III's reign in the political crisis of 1340–1. The expense and limited success of the European alliance of the late 1330s resulted in major opposition to the king in parliament. The parliaments that met in October 1339 and

January–February and March–May 1340 made extensive and widespread demands. Some of these involved the reiteration of previous legislation and various rights and privileges, such as confirmation of the Great Charter, the Forest Charter and the liberties of the Church.

More radical was the demand that tax collectors and others who had received money since the start of the war were to be called to account before a committee of magnates and remedies made for various, mainly judicial, grievances. Particularly striking though were the demands that all the revenue of the realm was to be applied to war expenses under the supervision of a committee of magnates. Furthermore, all gifts of Crown lands since the time of Edward I were to be reassessed at the discretion of parliament and, as a final 'catch-all', the affairs of the kingdom were to be committed to a council of magnates with responsibility for settling difficult or delayed cases and exercising control over royal officials.[18] In the event, Edward was able to deal with the crisis of 1340–1 without succumbing to all these demands, but it is likely that it was only the triumph at Crécy which ensured longer-term parliamentary support for the war against France and the king's domestic policies.

The importance of military success in ensuring political compliance is clear in the contrast between an assembly of 1348 with those held at the start of the decade. The Commons were asked to consider what was to happen when the truce with France expired and how peace and order should be better maintained in the realm. In essence they were asked to consider the key matters of foreign and domestic policy. After four days' discussion they responded: 'Very dread lord, as for your war and the array of it, we are so ignorant and simple that we do not know, nor are we able to counsel on these matters.' They asked that the king act as he saw best following the advice of the 'great and wise men' of his council and said they would readily agree to whatever the king and magnates decided.[19] Such a comment was perhaps little more than feigned modesty or it may indicate that the Commons still 'knew their place', but in either case, basking in the aftermath of Crécy this was an easy decision to make. Once the English position in France had all but collapsed parliament again became less amenable. In the 1370s, the Commons were taking a direct and active role as the source and focus of opposition to the Crown. This is not to suggest that the Commons had become dominant in parliament, which was far from the case, but its authority had developed very considerably and become a force to be reckoned with.[20]

In this period, similar forces were at work in France and for many of the same reasons. There was a drive for reform in the Estates-General in 1347, following the defeat at Crécy, and when they were summoned in 1356, after the disaster at Poitiers, they again demanded changes of personnel and brought complaints about the actions of local officials. There were also complaints regarding judicial practices, matters of coinage and the proper expenditure of taxation[21] – 20 years later the same grievances came to the fore in England in the Good Parliament. However, the Estates-General did not evolve in the same fashion as the English parliament. Especially after the revolt of the Jacquerie, French kings never trusted the general assemblies and rarely called them unless absolutely necessary. During periods of crisis and monarchical weakness the Estates might wield considerable authority, although this was circumscribed because its members rarely had plenipotentiary power to make major decisions on behalf of those they represented.

The divergence in the evolutionary paths taken by the representative assemblies in England and France was the consequence of a wide range of influences. Of these the relative authority of the respective monarchs was of particular importance. It is instructive that despite moments of deep crisis in the later middle ages there was no attempt within France to depose the king. Even during the civil war engendered by the madness of Charles VI, the struggle was characterised by an attempt to control the monarch rather than replace him.

Various elements combined to place the French monarch on a higher level than his English counterpart, most especially the theocratic character of his office and its antiquity, both of which were emphasised by the Crown's associations with Clovis, Charlemagne and St Louis. It is noteworthy that when Edward III claimed the throne and quartered the arms of France with those of England he placed the *fleur de lys* in the superior position. He also tried to acquire some of the spiritual lustre of the French monarchy by touching for the king's evil (the belief that the royal touch could cure scrofula) and took particular pains to emphasise his own descent from France's most celebrated kings.[22] In part it was the solemnity, honour and spiritual qualities associated with the French Crown which meant that although the king was given a great deal of advice about how to rule he could resist the demands of the assemblies of Estates when they tried to prescribe how he governed.[23]

The independent authority wielded by the French monarch and the glamour of his kingship therefore exceeded that enjoyed by the king of England. The ability to implement that authority was, however, circumscribed by a variety of factors: geography (the sheer size of France) and regional independence being two of the most significant. As a consequence, and by comparison with England, France was an 'undergoverned' country and the institutions of government were, if not less sophisticated, then less able to enforce central authority over the realm. While the potential resources available to the king of France were much greater than those in England, his ability to marshal them in support of his aims and aspirations was, at this point, much more restricted.

The comparative financial weakness of the Valois monarchy is particularly evident in the first decade of the Hundred Years War when limited revenue, collected irregularly, made any detailed military planning extremely difficult. Subsidies were granted, but only grudgingly and royal officials were forced to use extortionate fiscal expedients. In addition, regional loyalties often proved stronger than those to the Crown so that only those areas directly affected by the war could be relied upon to support the military effort. For example, many towns in Languedoc resisted tax demands until the realities of the war were brought home to them by Henry of Grosmont's raid in 1345. Indeed, throughout much of France, it was only the English victory at Crécy which brought about a realisation that emergency measures were necessary.[24]

In England such problems were not so pressing, but there was clearly a need to emphasise the validity and value of the king's Scottish and French enterprises. Mainly due to the example provided by his father's political and personal demise, Edward III attempted to build a consensus and body of (political and personal) support. These men and the groups they represented were to support him on the battlefield and in parliament. In the 1350s and 1360s, a community of interest was established in what has been described as a 'golden age of cooperation'.[25] At the top of those groups was the royal family and the most important member of the royal family was the Black Prince who, as he did at Crécy and Poitiers, was also expected to play his role in parliament. While attention has often, and rightly, been drawn to the burgeoning authority of the Commons this is not to say that the magnates were distanced from parliament or from political debate. Politics was the business of the high nobility and the Black Prince was not, indeed could not, be divorced from the major political issues of his time and he played important roles in a variety of political arenas.

The Black Prince was a part of the new nobility raised to prominence by Edward III in 1337. This was not only in a literal sense of being the first English duke created at the same time as six new earls, whose promotion took place in the shadow of war, but also in that he formed the most important element in the new cadre of nobles who supported the king in his aggressive foreign policy. The deliberate expansion of the peerage by Edward III ensured the support of the Lords in parliament for the king since many of the peers were dependent on royal favour for their status and the means to sustain their positions. Absences from parliament during campaigns abroad lessened the overt support the king hoped to demonstrate, and while such absences were said to imply consent for royal demands the king was keen to ensure his peers attended. The expansion of the peerage was an ongoing process – in 1341 there were 53 secular peers, by 1377 there were 60 – and the king also drew additional advisors from a wider cross-section of military and political society.[26]

Edward III summoned a large number of 'new men' to parliament in the course of his reign. They were also dependent on the king for their newfound position. Many had distinguished war records or continental experience of which the king wished to make use and of these many were closely associated with the Black Prince.[27] Men such as Bartholomew Burghersh and Walter Mauny, both mere knights at the time, were raised to be members of the Council.[28] This policy was evident also in the decision to include representatives of all members of the aristocratic military community within the ranks of the Order of the Garter.

The continuing influence of the magnates in parliament remained clear during the reign of Richard II where it was the forum in which the balance of political authority swung between the king and the Appellants. First, Richard was forced to devolve monarchical authority following the 1386 crisis, and subsequently he attempted to claim hitherto unknown powers, in many ways following the Valois model. In the later years of his reign, parliament was the forum for major demonstrations of royal authority. In 1397, the chancellor, the bishop of Exeter, preached to parliament on the theme of Ezekiel 35:22, 'There shall be one king over all'. He asserted the need for the king to be powerful, that the laws by which he governed were to be executed justly, and that subjects should obey their king. Monarchs were obliged to maintain their prerogatives and parliament was to ensure that royal authority and rights were maintained.[29] It was an attempt to turn back the tide, but unlike Cnut, Richard did not wish to emphasise the limitations of royal authority – the results, however, were just the same.

Political Representation

The growing authority of the shire knights and the increasing importance of borough representation were encouraged by a range of social, economic and political forces. By the middle years of the fourteenth century the changing structure of the aristocracy and the evolution of the gentry contributed to the increasing influence of the Commons and the interest that the shire knights took in matters of central policy. This is not to say that local interests were becoming unimportant, or that regional associations and allegiances became weak, but the later middle ages did witness a change of political emphasis and awareness among the lesser aristocracy. The emergence of the gentry as a significant political class was encouraged by and depended on the growth of parliamentary power, but the authority of individual members, indeed, the basis of their political and personal identity, remained grounded in their estates in the counties. As Peter Coss has noted, the 'real focus for the political aspirations of the gentry ... was ... parliament. A full-blown political forum was vital to the realisation of the gentry, but that realisation was predicated on the county ... [T]he collective identity of the emergent gentry found its ultimate expression in parliament, but its penultimate expression in the county'.[30]

As a result of such developments the representative role of MPs and links between the centre and the localities were made stronger and gained greater importance from the middle and later years of Edward II's reign. This rested on the idea that the realm had a common identity with communal interests and certain shared duties and responsibilities. It was an idea expressed through the concept of the common good or the public weal and reflected in the use of collective petitions and the articulation of corporate interests. That common identity and those communal interests were represented in parliament, and in order for parliament to act in those interests it needed authority. This was achieved through the ability to grant or withhold taxation, but that ability was predicated on the right to bind the communities represented to its will. In practice this meant that an MP needed plenipotentiary power to make his community pay whatever tax parliament granted the king.[31]

The rise of parliamentary power, the redesignation of the lesser aristocracy, and an increasing awareness of common and national interests fed upon and gave rise to various theories of political representation, many of which were founded on ecclesiastical practices that came to their fullest realisation in the conciliar movement of the early fifteenth century. Concerns over representation had been evident in virtually all examples of friction between the king and parliament. In earlier years what had often been under dispute was the right of the magnates to be represented, or rather that the magnates, the king's natural counsellors, should have their opinions represented in the decisions and policies of the king. With that in mind, it is important to note that the continuing purpose of parliament was to give counsel to the king.

Good counsel was seen as vital for the health of the body politic and was emphasised in numerous literary forms, most notably the numerous 'mirrors for princes'. Many of these were influenced to some degree by the *Secretum Secretorum*, believed to be a genuine work of Aristotle written for the guidance of Alexander.[32] It was certainly used by: Gerald of Wales in *De instructione principis*; Vincent of Beauvais in *De Regimine Principum*; Giles of Rome in his work of the same title; Gower in *Confessio Amantis* (Book VII); and Hoccleve in *Regiment of Princes*.[33]

Such works argued that a king had to learn how to identify good counsel; he had to listen to it and act upon it. The machinery of 'State' and the government of the realm were dependent on the personal leadership of the monarch, and royal will was the force by which policy was driven. It was therefore necessary that royal policy was the product of good counsel. In this sense the main aim of political society, as represented in parliament, was to direct the king, not reduce his power. This was a clear motivation of the opposition to the government expressed in the Good Parliament.

During the fourteenth century, parliament became a funnel for complaints from town and country to the capital, and as these developed so too did various theories of representation whose roots lay in the reforms made in Henry III's reign.[34] The power of the Commons did not grow only for economic reasons, but also because MPs spoke for the people in their communities even if they were not chosen by them. Parliament was seen and described as a corporate body (*universitas regni*) representing the peoples of the realm in their entirety.[35] The broader intellectual environment was also important for the development of such theories of representation. Ideas were circulating throughout Europe which suggested that all subjects had some stake in the political community, in shaping the governing system, and in protecting their liberties. For example, in 1324, Marsilius of Padua wrote that the people were the true source of political authority.

Such ideas were reflected in England and are evident as society became increasingly politicised. Certainly there was widespread dissemination of information in the fourteenth century about the activities of parliament, and by the last quarter of the century broadsides began to be posted and circulated as part of political debates. This increasing politicisation is particularly evident in the reign of Richard II. The Peasants' Revolt of 1381 reveals a high level of political awareness among the lower echelons of society and produced one of the most radical political and social programmes until the civil war in the seventeenth century – the demand for the end of all lordship save that of the king. In 1381, the peasantry were aware of mismanagement in government and in the prosecution of the war. They knew who to blame and they exacted full retribution. The king was not held responsible, and due to his age he could not be said to have listened wilfully to evil counsel, but the rebels showed a clear understanding of the governmental hierarchy and those who had squandered the profits of the poll taxes.

Richard did not find so much popular favour later in his reign. Opposition to him and complaints about his regime often emphasised his tyrannical approach to government and rejection or ignorance of the good counsel of his people and parliament. His opponents stressed their more liberal and inclusive credentials in the crisis of 1386, when the Appellants wrote to the citizens of London defending their actions,[36] and following the deposition in 1399.[37] In the same year parliament heard a sermon preached before the new king, Henry IV, based on 1 Maccabees 6:57, 'It behoves us to ordain for the kingdom'. This was said to demonstrate the king's wish that he should be properly counselled by the 'honourable, wise and discreet persons of his realm . . . not wishing to be governed by his own whim . . . but by common advice, counsel and assent'.[38]

If the Good Parliament provides a clear indication of the new extent of parliamentary power, then the 1381 rising shows that political awareness and political power was not restricted to parliament. The Peasants' Revolt was one of the clearest demonstrations of local and national politics coming together. Although at heart a tax rebellion, the 1381 revolt was another indication of a shifting balance of power in the English polity and the increasing breadth and depth of the body politic. These were the people represented in however theoretical a fashion in parliament and it was their money that made royal government possible. As the Commons took a lead in parliament, at least in a fiscal sense, so the Crown was forced into a political dialogue with its subjects.[39]

The Black Prince, the Council and the Good Parliament

The Black Prince had an important political role to play, but this was not often reflected by his participation in parliaments or great councils until his return from the principality of Aquitaine. He was not a political animal. This is not to say that he was politically uninvolved but politically unskilled and not naturally inclined towards some of the more delicate and diplomatic aspects of political life.[40] However, almost every action he took had political implications. His relations with the nobility, with the church, and his deeds on the battlefield were inherently political. For much of his life though, parliament does not seem to have impinged a great deal on him. It was generally a compliant institution that provided him and his father with the resources necessary for their military expeditions. It was when those expeditions became less successful that it became necessary to engage more closely with parliament and the Council. There the support of the greatest of the polity could be ensured and policy determined. This concerned not only the prosecution of the war, but broader issues including the government of the realm, relations with foreign powers and between Church and 'State'.

The prince was first summoned to parliament in 1351 and it is probable that he attended only nine such assemblies (parliaments and great councils) throughout his life.[41] He probably did not attend the Good Parliament, at least not after its opening, as his illness was too far advanced. This relatively small number is explained by his campaigning activities and the time he spent in Aquitaine. His return from the principality coincided with the renewed growth of parliamentary opposition: it was in this period that he took a much closer personal interest in parliamentary affairs and matters of domestic politics. After his return from Aquitaine he presided over meetings of the royal council and was present in the parliament of 1373 that showed the ill feeling towards the government which would be manifested more strongly three years later. As in that gathering a number of those with associations with the prince were pitted against members of the government.

Not all these meetings and arguments concerned secular politics. One of the most notable such events in this period is recounted in the *Eulogium Historiarum* and describes a great council at Westminster in 1373 or 1374 when an argument took place in the presence of the prince and the archbishop of Canterbury concerning the validity of demands of papal taxation. It remains a subject of some speculation whether the account is authentic or simply a piece of propaganda. It is, however, indicative of the redefinition of the roles and relative authority of Church and State. This was another aspect of conflict and tension that placed new strains on the structures of the political status quo and became significant in the years prior to the Great Schism.

The meeting divided over the demands of the pope who, claiming the feudal overlordship of England, a position held by the papacy since King John's day, as well as spiritual and temporal lordship over all Christians, commanded Edward III to raise funds for him in his campaign against the Florentines. This engendered a dispute concerning the reality and legality of those claims that swiftly became focused on the traditional question concerning the superiority of spiritual or secular power. Royal and papal supporters debated the rival claims of the 'Two Swords', which signified the twin sources of earthly authority, with the arguments of the king's supporters winning out. The story may have derived from a Franciscan source since it credits a Franciscan with swaying the company against the papal party including the famous Uthred of Boldon who had spoken in support of the temporal dominion of the papacy. The weight of opinion against him, however, was such that he withdrew his remarks. 'When the Black Prince inquired what had become of the two swords, he replied meekly that he was now better informed.'[42]

It is clear that, like many of his fellows, the Black Prince was strenuously opposed to any demands from the Avignonese papacy. There had been numerous altercations between the pope and the king of England throughout Edward III's reign; bad feeling had risen to a peak in the 1360s following the refusal to grant his son, Edmund of Langley, duke of York, a dispensation to marry. It would not be surprising if the prince also believed that at least some of the proceeds from a papal tithe would find their way into Charles V's coffers. If the prince did indeed think along such lines then it may go some way to explain his muted support for John Wyclif who argued strenuously for the supremacy of temporal over ecclesiastical power. The association of the prince with such a dispute may be indicative of the increasing importance and time he dedicated to political matters (broadly defined) in this period. It may also be the case that the author recounting the dispute wished to make it clear that the prince was a fervent advocate of the Franciscan position. If so it is indicative of the prince's growing political stature. This may also go some way to explain the importance attributed to the prince in the Good Parliament.

It was not long after the 'Two Swords' dispute that the prince played his most famous political role, in the Good Parliament of 1376. His part has probably been overstated. He was very ill by this time and if his support for the Commons was implied by a number of the shire knights, it was not given expressly. The Commons reacted unfavourably to a request for taxation: on behalf of the king, Sir John Knyvet, the chancellor, had demanded a subsidy (a tenth from the clergy and a fifteenth from the laity) to support the kingdom and its overseas possessions that were on the point of being lost to enemies from France, Spain, Flanders and Scotland. Following this, he asked if there was any matter that needed to be amended in the kingdom. In response the Commons complained of poor government by the king's ministers and the misuse of taxation by his counsellors (and his mistress, Alice Perrers) who had misled the king. The allegations included misgovernment of the wool staple at Calais, misappropriation of funds, and the demand of high levels of interest made on loans taken out unnecessarily in the king's name that were then shared between the accused.

The Commons in 1376 were the prime source of opposition to the king's ministers, but they received support from certain peers.[43] Most significantly, six of the Commons' knights claimed the backing of the prince of Wales. The unreliable Thomas Walsingham is the main source for this, but there is no doubt that these men – Edmund Appleby, Thomas Blount, Thomas Gissing, John Kentwode (the accuser of Alice Perrers), John Ludlow and John Wood – had fought with the prince in the *grande chevauchée* and at Poitiers.[44] As a consequence of the complaints, the London merchants, Richard Lyons and John Peche, were impeached following accusations of extortion and misuse of taxation and royal revenues, as was William Lord Latimer for mismanagement during his service in Brittany and as the king's chamberlain and chancellor. John Lord Neville, Adam Bury, William Elys (farmer of customs in Great Yarmouth) and Alice Perrers were also impeached.[45]

The prince's supposed support for the Commons is based on the hostility, proclaimed chiefly by Thomas Walsingham, said to have existed between the prince and his younger brother after Gaunt had succeeded Edward in Aquitaine.[46] It is more likely, however, that the prince, who certainly mishandled his Gascon/Aquitainian subjects, was in no condition to deal with the situation which developed after his return from Spain and handed over the reins of power to Gaunt out of necessity, if not relief. In truth it is difficult to find any clear evidence of hostility between the king's eldest sons,[47] but it is possible that there was a 'clerical' party, nominally led by the prince, and a 'court' party, led by Gaunt, and that their differing aims led to conflict.[48]

The Black Prince has long been considered a champion of parliament and of the knights who spoke against the regime in the assembly of 1376.[49] However, the evidence for this is slight and mainly contained in the *Chronica Maiora* of Thomas Walsingham. According to Walsingham one of Gaunt's squires reported to his master, 'your Grace cannot be unaware of the powerful support being received by these knights . . . and in particular of the lord, Prince Edward, your brother, who is giving them useful advice and help'.[50] Walsingham had an undisguised loathing for Gaunt, and since the Good Parliament was a genuine protest against those close to the king, Gaunt in particular, his testimony should not be relied upon.

Furthermore, the evidence for politically sponsored action in any parliament by the prince is limited. There is certainly nothing to suggest that he was attempting to pack the Commons with his 'creatures' in 1376. Throughout the prince's life a number of his household and retinue sat as MPs. He was best represented in three sessions in 1358, 1365 and 1369 when seven members of his retinue sat in the Commons. There do not appear to have been any sessions from *c.*1344 until his death that did not contain at least one member of the retinue, although a few of these men, perhaps four, sat in parliament before they had a firm association with the prince. There is no indication, however, that they were brought into the prince's service because of their parliamentary experience. Few of those MPs associated with the prince were highly ranked in his household and administration, nor did many of them sit in parliament regularly. In the period between 1344 and 1376 only William Banastre (a sergeant-at-law, the prince's yeoman and a member of his council) was returned to the Commons on more than six occasions – he attended nine parliaments.

Those sessions when the prince was best represented were tax-granting parliaments, but beyond this, there is no evidence of an attempt to pack parliament and influence it from within.[51] The prince recruited widely and among men of high calibre, it is of no surprise that a number of these sat in parliament. These men were drawn from throughout the country with the largest number of MPs representing Cornwall and its boroughs, Herefordshire and Shropshire, with Norfolk a little way behind. Apart from Cornwall, the prince held relatively little land in any of these areas although some counties were close to his principality of Wales. It is important to note that Wales and Cheshire, where the prince's influence was especially strong, did not return MPs to the Commons. This makes any comparison with Gaunt and the suggested actions of the Lancastrian affinity problematic.

The majority of the appointments to parliament from among members of the retinue are dated to the last decade of the prince's life. This may indicate an increasing interest on the prince's part in the machinations of parliament, but more probably these years marked a period in which the members in question were older, more respected in county society, less militarily active and so more likely to take up seats in the Commons. However, if the prince was trying to develop parliamentary influence it is likely that this would have happened after his return from Aquitaine: prior to this 'neither king nor particular magnates tried to have their own men returned to parliament with any regularity . . . [and] evidence of politically motivated meddling in elections . . . begins to appear only in the 1370s'.[52] Even then, such influence as could be brought to bear was limited. A figure such as John of Gaunt, who established perhaps the most potent political affinity of the late middle ages, rarely had a great deal of influence over the choice of parliamentary representatives even in his duchy of Lancashire. County communities were difficult to manipulate and wanted a say in the appointment of local officials especially MPs, JPs and justices of labourers.[53] Whether or not Gaunt attempted to pack parliament for his own purposes the size of the Lancastrian affinity made it inevitable that a large number of members of parliament had links to the duke. During his brother's lifetime, however, that influence was not extensive, at least in simple numerical terms. In the Good Parliament there appear to have been no more than five members of the Lancastrian affinity, and there were only six in the 'packed parliament' of 1377, although Gaunt's influence may have kept some individuals out.[54]

Such numerical and comparative evidence suggests it was unlikely that the prince made a great effort to manipulate the activities of parliament or to take advantage of the greater authority of the Commons. If considered only in numerical terms, it is difficult to see how he could since, according to the *Anonimalle Chronicle*, there were 280 knights, esquires, citizens and burgesses in the Good Parliament.[55] More conclusive proof might be found in petitions, used by various individuals to press claims for lands, franchises and money. There is no evidence of petitions being made directly on the prince's behalf, but conclusions drawn from this must be tentative since there are no parliamentary rolls for the later part of Edward III's reign and petitions might be made orally and so leave no records. Furthermore, the practice of individual petitioning declined over the period as common petitions became more usual.

The common petitions focused on war burdens, both purveyance and military obligations, trade regulations and disgruntlement with local government, particularly concerning matters of law and order. They often took the form of complaints of maintaining and retaining royal justices, the partiality of *oyer* and *terminer* commissions and the ready issue of pardons to criminals.[56] In all these the Black Prince was a leading example of bad practice.[57] He was unlikely to be censured however, since he was closely linked with several of those appointed to try the petitions.[58]

Military purveyance had become a major bone of contention in England since at least the end of the thirteenth century and there was vitriolic criticism of the practice in the first decade of Edward III's reign that by 1362 had extended to the royal household. In that year the Statute of Purveyors, which became the subsequent benchmark for parliamentary criticism, bracketed the prince's household with those of the king and queen as the only three official bodies for which purveyance was to be permitted.[59]

Despite its radical character the 1376 assembly was not a 'major attempt at political change' and many of its acts were reversed in the following year. In truth 'no parliament . . . in the middle ages, however substantial its achievements, could impress its will on a reluctant government for long',[60] but contemporaries did consider it significant and it was the best recorded of any medieval parliament.[61] It witnessed the first use of impeachment, saw the evolution of the role of the Speaker, and its proceedings may have been conducted partially in English. To a new extent the Commons appeared to be acting as a single, unified body, and to be holding the political initiative, but it certainly acted in conjunction with the Lords.[62] In the main it was an attack on individuals rather than on policy.

The opportunity to make their complaints came about through the Commons' ability to control royal finances. The demand for a subsidy was dependent on redress of grievances. These appear to have been distinct concerns of the shire knights although they sought advice on how to proceed from representatives of the episcopacy, the baronage and the peerage, a process known as 'intercommuning'. It is intriguing that again, like his association with the Commons, among all these three groups were friends and close associates of the Black Prince, but again his direct support or involvement cannot be proven.[63] It is also noteworthy that the Commons, although clearly developing an independent political identity and greater authority were not able or sufficiently confident to act without reference to the higher estates. This practice of deferential intercommuning with the Lords continued into the sixteenth century. The Commons, however, did swear an oath to be loyal to one another, which indicates a collective purpose and attitude, and de la Mare demanded that they should all be present when he returned the first response to the king.[64]

The evidence then for the prince's support of the Good Parliament is circumstantial and there is little to suggest that he had a political agenda of his own beyond assuming the Crown himself and later ensuring that it would pass to his son. This, it appears, was an agenda much in keeping with Edward III's own. However, the recent discovery of the king's entail for Richard to inherit the throne may reveal concerns about Gaunt's ambitions. The fact that Edward felt it necessary to take the remarkable step of making a legal bequest of the kingdom to Richard may imply that he did not believe the succession was secure. The death of the Black Prince certainly left a power vacuum into which Gaunt could step. Certainly Walsingham suggests Gaunt was aiming to seize the throne, but Walsingham is by no means a secure authority on matters relating to the duke of Lancaster. Additionally, however, Froissart describes an intriguing ceremony performed on Christmas Day 1376 in which the young Prince Richard was presented to the lords and knights of the realm and proclaimed by Edward III as his heir. This may have been an attempt by the king to ensure the smooth succession of his grandson and make his feelings plain on the matter. But there is no substantive evidence to support an accusation against Gaunt that he was planning a premature Lancastrian revolution. The king was dying, the war had taken a disastrous turn, and the fate of the kingdom was to be placed in the hands of an 11-year-old boy. The last thing that was needed was any doubt regarding the heir. Seen in this context it is much more likely that Gaunt's bitter opposition to parliament reflected a hope to maintain the prerogatives of the Crown while his father grew ever more senile and his brother lay on his deathbed.[65]

The parliament of England and the community of the realm came to greater power during the fourteenth century, but it must be remembered that this was still the king's parliament and it was the community of *his* realm. Parliament responded to the wishes of the king even if it did not always accede to those wishes. The growth of the authority of the Commons did not mean that it was naturally employed in opposition to the Crown; indeed it was far more common for the reverse to be the case. While the Commons did not always approve of royal policy or those who implemented it, its members were concerned with the security and honour of the realm and they did not shirk their responsibilities to provide the necessary resources.[66]

The Good Parliament was an extraordinary meeting and must be viewed as such, but it does, however, hint at a different political balance that emerged in this period. The parliament of 1376 began in a power vacuum – the imminent death of the Black Prince, the encroaching senility of Edward III, and the impending minority rule of Richard II – and that vacuum was filled by the Commons and the community of a realm that was starting to exhibit some of the characteristics of a 'State'.

Claims for the birth date of the English State can be made for any time from Alfred's Wessex onwards. It is the word itself that is so troubling for many and perhaps we would do better to agree that it does not matter if we use the term State, or Crown, or Monarchy. Perhaps we would do much better to break off the teleological search for the origins of medieval States that existed of themselves and not merely as the progenitors of modern constructions.

Despite such caveats, there is much to commend the case for the later middle ages giving birth to this amorphous institution in England. It had bureaucracy and the common law, it had a professional army, if not a standing one. The realm was united, in some fashion, in a military endeavour, and it contributed in many ways to the realisation of that objective. As national concerns grew, so regional identities lessened: parliament became the focus of the political aspirations of the gentry; and, bound up with this, a national identity started to be fashioned. Such a belief was constructed over many years in conflict with Scots, Welsh and Irish; it became more closely defined in later medieval attacks on Jews, especially the expulsion in 1290, and in the endemic war with France. Later medieval England therefore shows indications of forming the kernel of a Weberian 'State' or something not so very different. Violence and coercive power was becoming monopolised and standardised, in military forms as well as government. Society was becoming regimented in terms of class divisions, culture and language.[67]

Consequently, this was a different political construction with which kings and princes had to cope. It was a construction that did not necessarily imply a loss of authority on the part of traditional power brokers, but it did mean that they would have to be more skilful in their use and manipulation of power in future. It was a skill that Richard II did not possess – nor did his father – and it would not be until the Lancastrian revolution that English kings would be able again, albeit briefly, to exploit the burgeoning authority of the State for their own interests. It is tempting to see the first indications of this in 1376 and the silky machinations of John of Gaunt, but the likeliest interpretation of the role of the duke of Lancaster is supportive, not oppositional, to the king or the Black Prince. The entail for Richard's inheritance must give us some cause for wariness, but nor should we forget that Gaunt was the first named of the executors of Edward III's will. For all the new-found authority of parliament and the 'lower orders', dynastic politics and dynastic loyalty remained at the heart of the body politic.

chapter six

RELIGION:
PIETY AND PATRONAGE

But now a caitiff poor am I,
Deep in the ground lo here I lie.
My beauty great is all quite gone,
My flesh is wasted to the bone.[1]

The Black Prince's religious preferences have been a matter of some conjecture due, in part, to his association with Wyclif and because of his funerary epitaph, part of which is quoted above. This is an expression, chosen by the prince, of contempt with the material world and a condemnation of the flesh that is strikingly at odds with the tomb on which it is engraved, the form of which was also specified by Edward.

The tomb was to be set ten feet from the altar and facing it in the chantry chapel he had built at Canterbury. The tomb-chest was to be fashioned of marble and around it were to be 12 shields, each one foot in breadth, six bearing the prince's arms and six with the three ostrich plumes he had adopted as the arms of the princes of Wales. On each of the ostrich plumes was to be written his motto, *houmout* (high spirits). On top of the tomb was to be a copper-gilt relief of the recumbent prince. It is a defiantly military image: he requested it to show him 'fully armed in plate of war'. Accordingly he is shown in full armour, which bears the quartered arms of England and France, and girt with a sword. His helm, bearing the image of a leopard, is set beneath his head. And yet, around the upper edge of the tomb-chest, incongruous in its humility against the potency of the political and military imagery, is the epitaph which speaks of the inevitable corruption of all earthly things.

With its inherent contradictions the prince's tomb is indicative of the widening range of aristocratic religious attitudes in the late medieval period.[2] The splendour of the memorial, its rigorously formal and militaristic image, contrasts with the disgust and pity for the human condition explicit in the epitaph. The text upon which the epitaph was based was not new, nor was the theme – *sic transit gloria mundi* – but such ideas and images grew in strength and number throughout the later medieval period. They were galvanised by the religious and political climate and by the constant awareness of war and plague. Similar attitudes concerning the denigration of the body are evident in various other images and funeral memorials. For example, the Danse Macabre showed or described the personification of Death dancing with a number of partners drawn from the whole social hierarchy. The earliest known use of the term is in a poem of 1376 and its popularity was such that the Danse became a theatrical performance – the first reference to which is in Normandy in 1393.[3] Similarly, there was the image of the Three Living and Three Dead, a theme from which the Danse may have borrowed. These paintings show figures, usually princes and often representatives of the three ages of man, out hunting or hawking, meeting three cadavers in various stages of decomposition. The living are admonished and encouraged to improve their ways since they too will soon be dead and rotten and face divine judgement. The theme, emphasising the role of death as the great social leveller, was probably introduced to England in the thirteenth century through the poems of Baudoin de Conde. But with the arrival of the plague there was a change of emphasis; treatments of the subject became more plentiful and more shocking.[4]

In a similar fashion perhaps are those memorials that depict a knight recumbent on a bed of stones, with bodies slightly twisted and contorted, such as the effigies of Oliver Ingham (d. 1344), former seneschal of Gascony, at Ingham in Norfolk, and William Kerdeston (d. 1361), a banneret of the prince's household, at Reepham in the same county. The intention of the image is uncertain and it may have been deliberately ambivalent. The motif may suggest self-mortification or it could convey a more secular message regarding the travails of life (and death) in the pursuit of a military/chivalrous career.[5]

The final interpretation of the motif, if correct, would reflect other changes in the form and fabric of worship in this period. Through the proliferation of memorials and other images and edifices, including the increasingly popular monumental brasses, laymen invaded the churches of later medieval England figuratively and symbolically, and some became little more than aristocratic family mausoleums replete with heraldic insignia. Churches became demonstrations of secular power commemorating past and present patrons and celebrating the deeds of the deceased and the status of their family and friends, while at the same time requesting the prayers of the congregation.[6]

Such requests were of vital necessity, and a striking image, such as a funerary memorial, may have encouraged prayer and personal reflection. The apparent discomfort of Ingham, Kerdeston and their ilk, and the revulsion with the body evident in the prince's epitaph were themes combined and developed in the *transi* memorials. These tombs bore the image of the deceased on two layers, the topmost showing a calm, recumbent and dignified form usually wearing official garments, while below the same figure was shown, skeletal and decaying, sometimes with frogs, worms or snakes writhing through the cadaver.[7] They are jarring, startling and arresting images, juxtaposing life and death, pride and humiliation, wholesomeness and corruption. Such contrasts are emblematic of conflicting attitudes evident throughout religious life in the later middle ages. In this period the orthodox came face to face with the heterodox for the first time in England. Old certainties became fragile as divine wrath was manifested in the Black Death, and the papacy, first through its relocation to Avignon in 1305 and then in the Great Schism (1378–1417), became evermore subject to political vicissitudes and stained with secular corruption. For many though, little changed – churches were built, prayers were said and mass attended as required. But for others a tension was introduced into English religious life and pressure was brought to bear on traditional belief and orthodox practice.

Such a tension can be seen not only in the tomb of the Black Prince, but also in his career and in the membership of his and his wife's household. It was there, and perhaps especially in Joan's household after the prince's death in 1376, that there is clear evidence of the growing influence of, if not heretical, then distinctly unorthodox religious sympathies. These were new to English society and were conditioned by many influences, some political as well as religious. At heart, however, they reflected the traditional and continual search for a means to secure salvation, but this now took on a new immediacy in a time of conflict and death.

Salvation and Judgement

The approach of the Last Judgement and the drive to achieve personal salvation was the key feature of religious life and motivation for patronage throughout the Christian middle ages. These were, however, given greater urgency by the constant companionship of plague and war and the not-so-distant memory of famine. A sense of the impending apocalypse was palpable in the later fourteenth century and it was into this context that the *transi* memorials arrived. They formed another element in preparing for the Last Judgement and lay within a tradition of humiliating the body in the service of God, something also evident in mystical literature.[8]

The decay or torment of the body might be a sign of inner sinfulness, mortal and moral corruption, but the *transi* tombs also provided a balanced image of mortification and glorification that were central to the concepts of death and resurrection.

The *transi* were the product of a range of influences in the post-plague period: moralistic writings, *momento mori* imagery, funeral custom, and individual wishes to demonstrate the contradictory states of wealth and humility. Most significantly, and like any tomb, a *transi* was an attempt to commemorate the deceased and to request prayers for their salvation. The tombs also played a didactic and contemplative function. The *transi* tomb of Henry Chichele, completed by 1426, bears two epitaphs, the upper proudly describing his earthly achievements, the lower emphasising his pitiful mortality. The tomb was commissioned and erected during Chichele's lifetime and it was positioned in full view of his archiepiscopal seat in Canterbury cathedral so he could ponder his own death image.[9]

Such tombs encouraged the composition of literary works such as the *Disputacion betwyx the Body and Worms* (c.1450). This reflected the broader preoccupation with human mortality and the decay of the body characteristic of much later fourteenth- and fifteenth-century art. They reveal not only fear at the inevitability of divine judgement, but also an urge to accept death and mortality as natural and a pale reflection of Christ's suffering. Like the tomb epitaph of the Black Prince, the *Disputacion* dramatises the stark contrast between temporal beauty and glory and the inevitable decay of the body. The poem concerns a young woman of high social rank:

> *Take hede vn to my fygure here abowne*
> *And se how sumtyme I was fresche and gay,*
> *Now turned to wormes mete and corrupcoun,*
> *Bot fowle erth and stynkyng slyme and clay.*[10]

A comparable allusion was employed by John Lydgate in *The Daunce of Death* (c.1430):

> *Seeth what ye bene and what is youre nature,*
> *Mete vnto wormes, not elles in substaunce,*
> *And haue this mirror euere in remembraunce*
> *How I lie here somtyme crownyd king,*
> *To all estates a trewe resemblaunce,*
> *That womes food is fine of oure lyuyng.*[11]

Such works emphasise the inevitability of death through the antithesis of the *quod eram, quod sum* topos (indicating that the deceased was once as vigorous as the viewer and the viewer will soon be deceased), but like the *transi* they emphasise that material decay is a necessary prelude to spiritual bliss. They aim to encourage humility and show the vanity of worldly power, but also to diminish the fear of mortality in a world captivated with and surrounded by death.[12]

Guarding against pride, vanity and the desires of the flesh was a central component in maintaining spiritual health. It may have been Henry of Grosmont's confessor who set him the task of describing his weaknesses – his pride, lust and gluttony – resulting in his *Livre de Seyntz Medicines* (1354). It was remarkable for such a work to be written by a layman, but in such a period of tumult and spiritual uncertainty it is perhaps less surprising that the highest in the realm should seek particular and unusual routes in the hope of achieving salvation. Such attempts are also evident in the household of the Black Prince and his wife in which some of these dissonant feelings regarding matters of belief, worship, and attitudes to the Church can be seen.

The extent of such changes should not be exaggerated and, in general, forms of worship and belief remained thoroughly orthodox even if not entirely traditional. Saints' cults continued to be a central feature of worship even though the popularity of some waxed and waned. Although not technically a saint, the cult of Trinity was one focus of devotion that regained considerable influence in this period. The prince's tomb effigy gazed up at a tester showing the Trinity to whom, with the Virgin, the prince bequeathed his soul. His personal dedication to the Trinity is well known and evident in a number of grants and pieces of material and literary evidence. This may have been occasioned by certain coincidental peculiarities – he was born within the quindene of Trinity Sunday and died on the feast-day itself at three o'clock in the afternoon, having been prince of Wales for 33 years, and Joan had been 33 years of age when he married her.

The cult of the Trinity, by no means a product of the later middle ages, gained new momentum at this time, perhaps because of the support shown for it by certain eminent individuals. Certainly there were several among the prince's retinue and household who founded institutions dedicated to the Trinity or were patrons to foundations with which it was associated.[13] Indeed the Order of the Garter was under the patronage of the Holy Trinity, the Virgin, and Edward the Confessor as well as St George, although these others were soon relegated to a minor role. The Order met at Windsor in a chapel that was partially rebuilt and rededicated to St George, who was well on his way to usurping Edward the Confessor as the royal and national patron.

The establishment of St George as a national saint was another significant development and serves to emphasise the changing political aspects of religion and worship in England. The association of the king of England and his country with St George, made throughout the later middle ages, came to the fore in the reign of Edward III. The Milemete treatise (1326/7) describes the young Edward III being armed by St George and the work encouraged the young monarch to emulate the saint in his values and virtues. The king also owned a vial of the saint's blood, and wall paintings from St Stephen's chapel, Westminster, showed George as the royal family's patron saint. The popularity of George was not restricted to the aristocratic elite – throughout the country there are almost 100 wall paintings featuring the saint, mostly dating from the late fourteenth and early fifteenth centuries,[14] and Chandos Herald recounts the battle cry of the Gascon armies of the Black Prince as 'Guyenne! St George!'[15]

If the prince's tomb highlights a range of changing religious attitudes so too does its location. Canterbury provided a focus for many of his religious interests and he left a personal mark on the cathedral with his patronage of two chantries, given in return for a papal dispensation to marry Joan. Those interests were, no doubt, associated with the presence of Becket's tomb and the importance of Canterbury as a centre of pilgrimage. Additionally, the cult of the Trinity had been founded at Canterbury by Becket on his consecration in 1162.[16]

The popularity of pilgrimage and the wish to seek the intercession of the saints was encouraged by premature death on a scale that had never previously been witnessed. As Margaret Aston has said: 'A great part of popular piety amounted to an endeavour to live with the inexplicable and intolerable.'[17] In addition, various orthodox theological principles were influencing the popular consciousness in a new way. Changing attitudes to death were shaped by the formal acceptance of the doctrine of purgatory at the Council of Lyons in 1274. This in turn allowed or offered the possibility to 'buy' one's way out of purgatory, shortening one's stay there before ascending to paradise. As a consequence there was a great increase in the practice of purchasing masses to be said for the souls of departed friends and family and oneself.[18] There was also a growth in the numbers of confraternities, chantry chapels and similar forms of association, and greater patronage for institutions which provided more dedicated care for the religious and spiritual well-being of those involved.[19]

Chantries were independent chapels endowed for one priest or more to sing masses for the soul of the patrons, and their popularity was such that they accounted for most of the new benefices in later medieval

England. Disaffection with many old monastic orders was one reason for this, and another was the greater awareness of purgatory. Thirdly, canon law forbade priests from saying more than one mass on most days, which reduced the chance of individuals receiving daily spiritual benefit. Chantries could also be observed and closely regulated by patrons and they formed a permanent memorial to an identifiable individual. Such a benefaction also served as a declaration of social position and wealth. In the century after the Black Death, parish churches, where most chantries were located, became the main focus of religious patronage for the aristocracy as well as a forum for social display. Since late medieval piety responded to visual images, churches could be exploited not only for spiritual but also social purposes. Self-promotion was achieved through the gift of devotional furniture, stained glass, altars, images, lights, vessels, vestments and books. Many of these were provided by individual or group benefactors and, in addition to proclaiming wealth and status, they encouraged the prayers of the congregation for the donor. It was such convictions that encouraged the rebuilding and refurbishing of so many late medieval parish churches. Furthermore, the organisation of the building itself was conscious of rank and also changing religious ideas. As well as demarking elite space, the introduction of private pews indicates a privatisation or at least a personalisation of worship.[20]

In the post-plague period there may have been a growing distinction between religion and religiosity. There was certainly greater ritual and perhaps greater superstition. Such ritual piety, evident in the reverence for the sacraments, especially the Eucharist, was given form and structure through the cycle of the liturgy, feasts of the saints and the ecclesiastical year. As with so many other aspects, those rituals were much concerned with death and easing the path through purgatory. Indeed, for the majority of people this was the key role of the church. If necessary, the laity could baptise their own children; they did not have to marry in church; not all went to mass regularly; and nor did all receive the last rites 'because they knew their salvation was not contingent upon doing so; but everybody recognized that the church alone could pray them out of purgatory'.[21]

Another reason for changes in religious attitudes and patronage lay in a lessening of respect felt for many members of the lower clergy. In the same way that aristocratic military service was devalued by inclusion into the military ranks of the lower orders, so too was the authority and reputation of the clerical estate compromised by the inclusion of men who entered religious life without seeming to abandon secular ways and who appeared to have no particular insight or spiritual calling. Such anti-clericalism is partly attributable to better literacy and education that increased expectations of parish priests at a time when the quality of the clergy was falling. Those, very many, ecclesiastics who died in the plague were not all replaced by men of high calibre.

Concerns about the failings of the Church at its highest levels as well as in the parishes also encouraged certain individuals and social groups to seek changes in forms of worship and the institutions to which they turned for salvation. Some, of course, remained entirely orthodox and traditional. For example, in 1352, John Dabernon, one of the prince's chief ministers in Cornwall, purchased Week manor and gave it to Tavistock abbey in exchange for free quarters in the abbey precinct during his lifetime and a chantry in the parish church after his death. Dabernon left nothing to chance regarding his salvation. He made bequests in his will to 26 religious houses in Devon and Cornwall, male and female, Augustinian, Benedictine, Cistercian, Carmelite, Dominican, Franciscan and Premonstratensian. Hospitals at Exeter, Lamford and Bodmin, parish churches and parish priests as well as Exeter cathedral also received sums of money.[22]

The Black Prince himself was also closely connected with a range of different foundations including the abbeys of St Albans (Benedictine) and Vale Royal (Cistercian). At Vale Royal he supported the building of 12 chapels designed and constructed by William Helpston. These are said to have Spanish influences, perhaps from Toledo cathedral. They were destroyed in a storm on 19 October 1360, but the prince must have been well pleased with Helpston's work, as he became Master Mason of Cheshire, North Wales and Flintshire in 1361.[23] The prince was also the patron of a much lower profile order, the Bonhommes at Ashridge and Edington, an association which emphasises the greater interest evident in this period with small, rather serious orders that were seen as uncorrupted by wealth and power and whose prayers were likely to be more efficacious.[24] Among the most popular of such orders was the Carthusians, at least partly because of their interest in and respect for the contemplative life. They were one of the few orders to remain free of criticism from such commentators as Langland and Wyclif. It was said that among the other orders the Rule was disregarded – personal possessions were permitted, and monks and nuns went out regularly into lay society. Although there was much malicious gossip regarding the old monastic orders, there is no doubt that non-resident abbots were appointed with increasing regularity, and monks and nuns decreased in number. By contrast, the Carthusians maintained their austere standards. The prince's family and household were patrons of the order. Edward himself made grants to the Selwood charterhouse (five marks a year), the prior and order of Hinton, near Bath (10 marks a year), and the prior of

Witham, which was the site of the first charterhouse in England (five marks a year).[25] Some of these grants were maintained by the prince's son and wife, and Richard II and Princess Joan were also independent donors. The king was associated with the foundation of the Coventry charterhouse and gave the London charterhouse a tun of Gascon wine each year. In 1383, Joan made grants to Michael de la Pole, a former retainer of the prince and by that time Lord Chancellor, for the Maison Dieu in Myton (the Carthusian hospital at Kingston-upon-Hull), which he had founded.[26] There were numerous others of the prince's acquaintance who were also patrons of the order which suggests a group mentality towards patronage. In the prince's household this may be attributable to the influence of Prior John Luscote who had links to the charterhouses at Hinton, Coventry and Smithfield.[27] This group included men such as Walter Mauny, founder of the Smithfield charterhouse, Robert Knolles and Hugh Calveley.[28] Knolles founded the 'P' cell of the London charterhouse and was also associated with a number of hospitals.[29] Calveley began re-modelling Bunbury church as a college of priests.[30] Career soldiers who profited in the wars and hoped to use their financial security to acquire spiritual security often set new devotional trends in this period.

Such changes in patronage and a new approach to the divine were reflective of a distinctive and perhaps deliberately divisive development in terms of worship amongst the aristocracy. Colin Richmond has used the example of the Pastons as a model to discuss the religious attitudes of the petty-nobility. He argues convincingly that the fifteenth century saw, for the gentry, a 'privatisation of religion'. Worship was becoming non-communal and even anti-populist with the introduction of private pews and chapels that were symptomatic of an 'interiorization of religion'. In part this is attributed to increasing literacy and scripture reading, allied to class and occupational differences. As a consequence of such influences, religion, formerly a great leveller, became two-layered; there was the religion of the people and the religion of the aristocracy, which was withdrawn, introspective and anti-communal and saw certain aspects of popular Catholicism as irreverent, indecorous, and in poor taste.[31]

This is not to say, however, that the Church in its more traditional guises had become moribund. There was a spirited response from the traditional ecclesiastical institutions to these dynamic challenges. Monastic houses developed a range of strategies to revive their pre-eminence including the composition of polemical works in the period c.1370–c.1440, which emphasised their importance and antiquity. Works by such figures as Uthred of Boldon, Thomas Walsingham, William Gillingham and John Wheathamstede emphasised the scriptural basis for the monastic life and responded to contemporary anti-monastic theologians such as

Wyclif and William Woodford, a Franciscan. Some such works were transferred to tabulae – large wooden display-boards placed in prominent positions in churches as a means of guiding worshippers. Other attempts to rebuild relationships with the laity at a local level included adapting the form of worship and fabric of buildings in order to attract devotional support as well as benefactions. New statues and images of patronal saints and founders were incorporated into monasteries as were local saints. And new altars were established with dedications designed to appeal to secular patrons. Efforts were also made to revive interest in shrines, by processions, religious dramas and by the establishment of conventual confraternities – Joan of Kent and members of the Black Prince's household were admitted to such an association at St Albans around 1376.[32]

Such steps did help to revive somewhat the position of the monasteries as the spiritual centres of later medieval England. However, they found themselves in a different and more eclectic environment in which various new forms of patronage, art and religious activities were driven by fear, dissatisfaction and an urge for individuals to secure a more 'personal' relationship with God. This was not only the result of the shock of the plague, growing lay religious understanding and greater expectations being made of the clergy: the conflict of the papacy first with the Hohenstaufen emperors (ending in 1268) and then with the Capetian kings (c.1296– c.1303) brought the papal monarchy more directly into the secular arena and compromised its spiritual authority in the process.[33]

The enforced transfer of the papacy from Rome to Avignon (1305– 78) was seen as a confirmation of this decreased stature. Petrarch spoke of Avignon as:

> Unholy Babylon, thou Hell on earth, thou sink of iniquity, thou cesspool of the world. There is neither faith, not charity, not religion, nor fear of God, no shame, no truth, no holiness, albeit the residence within its walls of the supreme pontiff should have made of it a shrine and the very stronghold of religion . . . of all cities that I know its stench is the worst.[34]

The Avignon exile did not only lessen the spiritual authority of the pope, it also contributed to a belief in his lack of political objectivity. Certainly, many who opposed France believed that they also opposed the papacy since 'while God was wont to be English, his earthly vicar was decidedly French'.[35] This encouraged a new sense of an English 'national' church, or at least a church in which domestic matters became as important as those which were introduced from outside. This developed in the fourteenth century as a result of political circumstances and developments in vernacular languages. It also reflected the debased status of the papacy. The authority of the pope had fallen a very long way from the heady days under Innocent III (1198–1216) when he might claim sovereign rule over Christendom.

The comparative authority of the 'Two Swords' of Church and State, spiritual and temporal, by which the world should be ruled had coloured political relations between the papacy and secular rulers from the Investiture Contest through to the conflict between Philippe IV and Boniface VIII. It continued to be a subject that shaped conceptions of power and authority in the later middle ages and although advocates of papal supremacy remained influential, they lost ground to writers who argued for the supremacy of temporal authority.[36]

The struggle between spiritual and secular power is evident in the works of a number of writers. In 1302, John of Paris wrote *On Royal and Papal Power* (*De Potestate Regia e Papali*) and, by applying Thomist principles to the political context, he emphasised their separate natures, stated that kings and popes should not interfere in each other's affairs, and thereby denied the Church any primacy in temporal matters. It was a position that, for different reasons, Marsilius of Padua supported in *Defensor Pacis* (1324), which was declared heretical in 1327, in part because it advocated the autonomy of the citizen and the State from ecclesiastical influence.

However, the papacy had its own advocates such as William of Pagula (d. *c.*1332) who endorsed theories of papal sovereignty including the power to appoint secular rulers in *Summa Summarum* (written 1320–3) and John Ayton, writing in the 1330s and 1340s, who defended the 'papal monarchy' and described the pope as a quasi-divine being.[37] A particular subject of debate, which fed directly into such arguments, centred on the role of poverty and mendicancy in the Church. Richard Fitzralph (d. 1360), who spoke against false mendicant poverty in a sermon, *Defensorum Curatorum*, also proposed a radical doctrine on the nature of lordship and its relationship to salvation. In *De Pauperie Salvatoris* (1356) he argued that all *dominum*, civil and ecclesiastical, was divinely sanctioned and founded in Grace. This inspired Wyclif who believed that all property was held of God and in turn his appointed secular rulers. The upshot of this theory was that all lordship, ownership and jurisdiction were founded in God's grace and over which the Church had no authority.[38]

These discussions were not mere theological or academic musings. They were inspired by and bled into political conflicts about the nature of power at the highest levels. The applications of such ideas can be seen in Edward III's struggles with the papacy that led to the statutes of Provisors (prohibiting the granting of papal benefices and legal appeals to the Papal Curia in 1351) and Praemunire (prohibiting an Englishman suing another Englishman in a foreign court in 1353) as well as the evident hostility in the negotiations for a dispensation for Edmund of Langley's proposed marriage in the 1360s.

The relative power of church and state in England came under close scrutiny again in the 1370s and, due to the political climate, even such an advocate of papal power as Uthred of Boldon was forced to modify his views, at least publicly, in the famous encounter with the Black Prince in 1373 or 1374. Nonetheless, Uthred and others such as Adam Easton retained their beliefs in the superiority of spiritual over temporal power even if they did not invest the same significance in the papal office as many earlier commentators. Easton was probably responsible for having Wyclif's *De Civili Domino* (1376) condemned by Gregory XI in 1377 – the pope described it as a work of 'execrable and abominable folly'.[39] Easton asserted that lay rulers were duty-bound to be subservient to the vicar of Christ and emphasised the superiority of priestly over royal government. Despite this he made a number of nationalist anti-papal comments.

The authority of the papacy was brought into question and it would be further compromised in the Great Schism and the conciliar movement. The role and authority of the papacy also was changing with a more insular approach to worship being developed on both a personal and national level. As a result, '[i]t is difficult to find wholehearted support for the papacy being expressed in late fourteenth-century England'.[40]

The authority of the Church was therefore threatened in the fourteenth century. The power of the pope was severely compromised in the transfer to Avignon and it was fractured literally and figuratively with the Schism of 1378. Direct spiritual opposition also existed. Heresy was an affront to the power of the Church, one which would soon appear in England for the first time and would tear apart Bohemia. But even in France, not so far from the papal seat, the embers of Catharism (a dualist heresy first securely attested in 1143 and the subject of the Albigensian crusade, 1209–29) still glowed in the early fourteenth century in areas that would become part of the principality of Aquitaine. It was, by this time, a rural phenomenon, but those embers flared a little once again as a result of anti-clericalism brought on by the demands for church taxation (tithes) and through the increased use of written Occitan. There was a clear concern throughout Europe with the possibilities of heresy being incubated through uncontrolled literature, whether those books were read or their contents transmitted orally.[41]

The attitudes of the papacy also drove groups into heresy or created heretics where previously there had been orthodoxy. The issue of clerical poverty was central to the clash between the Church and the Spiritual

Franciscans. These radical mendicants, who came to prominence in the early fourteenth century, aimed to adhere to St Francis' ideal of absolute poverty and also took an extreme position regarding apostolic poverty. This drove Pope John XXII to condemn their views as heretical. The ideal of poverty and the spiritual benefits to be gained by a life of material impoverishment maintained a strong hold over the religious imagination. It was to be a particularly potent force in Langland's *Piers Ploughman*.

The spiritual benefits of austerity, the attempt to develop a more 'personal relationship' with God, the privatisation of religion among the gentry, disappointment with the lesser clergy, and political strife with the Church hierarchy all served to encourage certain individuals into less orthodox forms of worship and belief. The most extreme form that this took in England resulted in support for Wyclif and Lollardy although there were many more who took steps towards the borders of orthodoxy but did not cross into heresy.

Lollardy

England had been a country untouched by heresy until the later years of the fourteenth century. The author of dissent and first English heresiarch was John Wyclif (d. 1384), an academic theologian at the University of Oxford who attacked various abuses in the Church. His teachings, however, extended beyond traditional condemnations of pluralism and non-residence to encompass established practices such as pilgrimage and the invocation of saints. Most radical were his criticisms of papal authority and condemnation of transubstantiation.

Wyclif's heretical ideas and the mutation of his ideas, which developed into what, for better or worse, has been described as 'Lollardy', gave rise to a vast corpus of comment by contemporaries and has continued to fascinate subsequent commentators. Disagreements abound regarding many aspects of the 'Premature Reformation', not least the extent to which the Lollards formed an identifiable 'sect' with a closely prescribed set of values or beliefs. The association between Wyclif and the later Lollards is by no means exact and to speak of Lollardy can suggest a unity of belief and the construction of a movement which simply did not exist. The popular Lollardy that existed down to the Reformation probably bore little resemblance to Wyclif's fiercely academic musings, but he was significant in his articulation of a theological programme of ecclesiastical reform supported by closely argued philosophical principles that chimed with political ideas about the proper balance of power between Church and State. Wyclif, albeit unintentionally, ensured that 'from about 1380 to the Reformation there was a continuous thread of heresy in England'.[42]

One reason for this development lay in the role Wyclif's ideas could play in the power struggle between Church and State. Although eventually shunned by the Establishment he found early favour with a number of the royal family and several members of the aristocracy. Wyclif's demand for a general *reformatio Ecclesiae* to be overseen by the lay powers fitted with general dissatisfaction with the clergy – this focused mainly on pluralism and non-residence. His anti-papalism was also popular in the context of a Francophile papacy in the Hundred Years War. In this way, Lollardy fits into a general context of nationalism and national churches – it was an archetypically English heresy. Furthermore, his call for the disendowment of the Church was also popular among the aristocracy in this time of declining landed incomes.[43] It was probably because of such political and financial influences that Wyclif received support and favour from significant members of the court and royal family including the Black Prince, John of Gaunt, Princess Joan and perhaps Thomas of Woodstock, duke of Gloucester.[44]

This support took various forms. In 1378, Joan was instrumental in halting proceedings against Wyclif. Similarly, Gaunt's patronage of Wyclif, as well as the Lollard preacher, William Swinderby, kept both out of prison. There seems little doubt the duke of Lancaster had, 'as [Henry] Knighton despairingly admitted, something of a weakness for Lollards'.[45] Meanwhile, Gloucester owned a fine copy of the first Wyclifite translation of the Bible and Lollards may have looked to him as a patron as they had to his brother, Gaunt.[46] Wyclif's royal links were such that he has been seen as a spokesman and propagandist for the court. As a result, he was duly protected by the royal family with whom many of the so-called Lollard Knights also found service.[47]

Wyclif, however, was not content only to attack clerical abuses and urge a reform within the Church; he also questioned established practices and matters of doctrine. He criticised pilgrimage and the invocation of saints, he questioned the very basis of papal power and, while professing a belief in the Real Presence of Christ in the Eucharist, he opposed central aspects of transubstantiation. As stated in his *De Veritate Sacra Scripturae* (1378), Wyclif's theology was dependent on a 'devout' philosophical realism and a belief in the Bible, which as a clear expression of divine will, contained a pure guide for faith and morality. The development of an increasingly literate laity provided a receptive audience for some of these views. However, in terms of much secular support, this marked the beginning of the end – the expression of certain theologically extreme attitudes lost Wyclif aristocratic and royal patronage in the late 1370s.

The failure of Lollardy was due to 'two acts of indescribable folly and . . . one piece of appalling bad luck'[48] in the years after 1379. Trouble arose over his advocation of the use of the vernacular in preaching on the sacrament, but much more significant were his comments on the Eucharist. Having resolved his doubts over transubstantiation, Wyclif published *De Eucharistica* and in so doing lost many allies who were eager for the reform of the clergy but would not follow him into outright heresy. Many of these fair-weather friends were members of the Mendicant Orders and Wyclif soon responded with a damning condemnation of the friars. Wyclif's views were condemned as heretical and he was suspended from teaching at Oxford (1381–2). Any residual support he might have received from the secular authorities was stillborn as a result of the Peasants' Revolt – in such a context none but the most foolhardy would support a man accused of sedition and Wyclif and his followers were soon blamed with inciting the revolt.[49] Thomas Walsingham accused John Ball in the most strident terms of being a disciple of Wyclif although there is no evidence to support this, especially since the Lollard 'movement' at this point was largely confined to the University of Oxford. Indeed, Henry Knighton suggested that the influence was the reverse and that Ball's ideas shaped Wyclif's thought: neither theory is likely and it is significant that Wyclif later condemned the Great Revolt.[50]

Wyclif's ideas, detailed, academic, learned, and occasionally impenetrable, were filtered and diluted as they were disseminated by such men as Philip Repingdon, Nicholas Hereford and John Aston. Their activities were made possible, at least in part, by the support, both financial and political, given by a number of courtiers who had been in the service of the Black Prince, the Princess of Wales, and/or John of Gaunt – the Lollard Knights noted by Walsingham and Knighton. The fact that two of these men recanted is indicative of the reforming rather than heretical appeal of Wyclif's work and perhaps also representative of the interests of these preachers' patrons. Repingdon abjured his heresy as early as November 1382 and later had a successful orthodox career. Hereford did likewise some time after and by the early 1390s was involved in proceedings against Lollards in Herefordshire. Perhaps significantly he joined the Carthusian order.[51]

The religious context in which Lollardy flourished is indicative of the changing nature of ecclesiastical influence in England and in certain other parts of Europe at this time. The support offered to Wyclif and various of his followers (whether or not they should be called 'Lollards') by certain members of the English political elite may be attributed to the political capital that could be gained from a sustained attacked on the Church and particularly on the papacy. Nonetheless, the urge to seek a reform of certain religious practices was not unusual among the aristocracy and certainly contributed to sympathy for a number of Wyclif's proposals even if they were not those considered heretical. This can be seen as part of a general movement in which individuals living in the period of the plague and the Avignon papacy started to examine a number of less orthodox means of seeking salvation. It is possible that they may have included Joan of Kent and those members of her household that have been identified as the Lollard Knights.

Joan of Kent and the Lollard Knights

Nigel Saul has called the Black Prince a man of vaguely puritanical religious preferences.[52] The evidence for this is circumstantial, but the composition of his household and that of his wife does suggest associations with Lollardy. It is a peculiar association with regard to Joan who remains better known for her personal extravagance, especially in the principality of Aquitaine, and as the most beautiful and amorous woman in the realm. This makes for an abrupt and awkward juxtaposition with her supposed Wyclifite tendencies and undoubted connection with Lollard Knights.

These men formed an important 'court circle' in the reign of Richard II, but they first came to prominence in the households of the king's father and mother. They included John Pecche, John Trussell, Richard Stury, Lewis Clifford, Thomas Latimer, William Neville, John Clanvowe and John Montague. They were identified by Knighton and Walsingham, who was rabidly anti-Ricardian as well as anti-Lollard and may have been attempting to discredit Richard's court. It is clear though that Neville was accused of iconoclasm, Latimer possessed heretical books and, according to Walsingham, Clifford recanted his heresy in 1402, although the executors of his will, made soon after, included the Wyclifite John Cheyne, the equally suspect Richard Colefax and the notorious John Oldcastle.[53] Similarly, four of the 16 executors of Princess Joan's will were supposed Lollard sympathisers, namely Clanvowe, Clifford, Neville and Stury, while another, William Beauchamp, may well have held unorthodox beliefs.[54] However, the executors also included the entirely respectable Robert Braybroke and William of Wickham, bishops of London and Winchester respectively.[55]

Clanvowe, one of the most interesting of the Wyclifite circle, wrote a clear statement of his views in his treatise, *The Two Ways*, which may have been representative of the beliefs of many of his fellows.[56] It was puritanical certainly, heretical possibly, but not necessarily a direct statement of Lollard belief. In this he shared with a number of others attitudes that were on or a little beyond the boundaries of orthodoxy in some 'no man's land' before Lollardy. Other knights of the group have been identified through the language of their wills although there are problems with such an analysis and many strictly orthodox individuals made wills that might be described as Lollard in tone or character.

Among the characteristics of so-called 'Lollard wills' were distinctive requests regarding their funerals. However, such requests were not restricted to England; there was a contemporary European 'fashion' for austere funerals or burials that were contemptuous of the body of the deceased. One of the most extreme examples of this can be found in the will of Philippe de Mézières (d. 1405), who asked to have an iron chain placed around his neck at the hour of his death, that he should be dragged by his feet naked into church, tied by ropes to a plank, and then thrown like carrion into a grave.[57] The Frenchman, de Mézières, was clearly not a Lollard but he did have associations with the Lollard knight, Lewis Clifford, who was a member of his crusading Order of the Passion, as well as a knight of the Garter. Despite Wyclif's contempt for pilgrimages and crusading, a number of his supporters indulged in such activities including Clanvowe and William Neville. Indeed, the Lollard knights have been described as 'essentially conservatives, looking back to the ideals of a court supposedly dedicated to the pursuit of Christian chivalry'.[58] Knighthood carried spiritual responsibilities and if one was so inclined then ecclesiastical reform along Wyclifite lines might be considered among such obligations.

There is evidence for Lollard associations among several of the prince's associates, not only those who were executors of his wife's will. Reginald Hilton, named as a Lollard by Knighton, was one of these. Probably not a knight but a priest in the prince's service in the diocese of Lichfield, he became controller of Richard's wardrobe.[59] John Montague, who maintained the Wyclifite preacher, Nicholas Hereford, in his house at Shenley was a knight of the prince's household from 1354, and Richard's steward, 1381–6.[60] Thomas Latimer also had some connections to the prince, serving in the 1355 expedition and in Spain, but this may have been in a freelance capacity. He married Anne, the widow of John Beysin who attended Joan during Richard's birth and brought news of it to the prince for which she was later granted an annuity of £20.[61] Before Wyclif's ideas became public, Latimer had acquired a grant from the pope to have a portative altar, a personal confessor and permission to have mass celebrated before daylight. While such attitudes clearly do not sit easily with Lollard anti-papalism they may show a search for a means of salvation not entirely within the commonplace structure of the Church.[62]

Latimer was associated with one Robert Lychlade, who was expelled from Oxford in 1395 for holding heretical opinions. He became rector of Kemerton (Gloucs.), of which William Beauchamp, another of Joan's executors, the probably Wyclifite knight was patron, and in the following year he and Lewis Clifford were among the executors of the will of Anne Latimer, widow of Thomas Braybroke, a noted Lollard sympathiser. Beauchamp, another Lollard crusader, later became a member of Gaunt's retinue and a knight of the Garter and he was chamberlain in the minority household of Richard II.[63] Another of the prince's close associates, Gerard Braybroke, also had close links to the Lollard circle, but was never named as one himself.[64]

Many members of the Lollard circle were or can be associated with the households of Joan and the Black Prince. Indeed, Michael Wilks suggested Wyclif himself was a spokesman and propagandist for a royalist 'party' comprised of the retinues of the Black Prince and John of Gaunt, which arguably, came together in the household of Joan of Kent.[65] This is probably stretching the evidence, but it does highlight the significance of the political aspect of Lollardy and the opportunities for the Lollard knights to pursue political and moral objectives through their membership of Joan's household. Whether these men were staunch believers in the richly detailed, painstakingly argued compound of theology and philosophy advanced by John Wyclif is difficult to judge but seems unlikely. To call these men Lollards is also to use a title that was deliberately abusive and misleading.

For these men and probably for Joan herself there was a considerable 'grey area' on the margins between orthodoxy and Lollardy. Anti-papalism and what has been described as 'a certain brand of alehouse anticlericalism'[66] were not necessarily indicative of heretical attitudes to transubstantiation or other aspects of Wyclifite belief. Rather, such people may have been 'attracted to the pietistic and moralistic attitudes of the early Lollards rather than to their more specifically anti-sacramental, anti-hierarchical and [in some cases their] pacifist teachings'.[67] Nonetheless, even if viewed solely in political terms, almost all the Lollard knights were connected with either the short-lived 'dynasty' of the prince of Wales, Edward himself, Joan of Kent, and Richard II or John of Gaunt and they provided financial and political support for Wyclifite preachers.[68]

Even if the Lollard knights were truly Wyclifite, it does not follow that Joan's household was the focus for a closely defined heretical sect. Just prior to her death and encouraged by increasingly hostile relations with France in 1385, Richard designated a number of knights to attend his mother. It is likely that these were men already close to her and probably members of her household. There are familiar names here – Lewis Clifford, Richard Stury, Thomas Latimer – but also those that were never accused of Lollardy – in total 11 others including William Harpele, Henry Norton, John Worth and John la Warre. Worth, Joan's steward and executor, however, may have been a Lollard sympathiser[69] and coincidentally or not John la Warre's stepmother, Eleanor Mowbray, later married Lewis Clifford.[70]

It is clear that one need not have been a Lollard to have such acquaintances and those tarred with the title 'Lollard' may not have been close or devout followers of Wyclif. For many, an interest in Lollardy 'was merely an interest in, not an active participation in or support of the Lollards' more radical tenets . . . [they] were merely curious about this reforming movement that embodied some ideas and assumptions that they already shared'.[71] Certainly, Joan acted in some ways in an entirely, perhaps overly, orthodox fashion. In 1372 she received an '[i]ndult . . . to enter once a month, monasteries of enclosed nuns with six honest and aged men and fourteen honest women and to eat and drink but not spend the night therein'.[72] She also maintained some of her late husband's religious allegiances, for example by acquiring a pardon for the abbot and convent of Rewley by Oxford – founded by Edmund, earl of Cornwall – for acquiring lands in mortmain without licence.[73]

Indeed, Joan's requests to the papacy for various grants reveal a wide range of typical late medieval religious concerns for herself, her friends and members of her household. Among these, she asked to choose her own confessor, she requested that one Marion Louches be permitted to have a portable altar, that Johanetta Peverel and Walter Bary, her butler, receive plenary remission of their sins, and for three other servants she asked for various ecclesiastical offices and benefices.[74] On another occasion she requested a portable altar for herself, that her damsel, Margery Mere, be permitted to eat milk, cheese and eggs in Lent, and that her friends Andrew and Elizabeth Lutterel might have a portable altar and the right to choose their own confessor.[75]

It is probable that Joan, like many of her household knights, had conventional religious beliefs, if broadly defined. Either Lollardy was a broad church or, more likely, the borders of heresy and 'acceptable' belief were blurred at the edges. In this period, as a consequence of a variety of social, economic and political influences, those borders were becoming wider and less clearly delineated. Joan exhibited elements of both strictly conventional and also nearly heretical religious behaviour that were not unrepresentative of the broader aristocracy and certainly not of those within her own social circle. She also had interests in broader pseudo-spiritual matters and owned an astrological calendar.[76] Attitudes to such interests were also changing in this period. The rise of 'learned' magics such as astrology and alchemy in the late thirteenth century had become linked to a new concern about sorcery and demonic worship. This developed particularly in the 1320s during the pontificate of John XXII when a number of bulls and edicts were issued and it was also reflected in Bernard Gui's inquisitorial handbook. Sorcery remained an issue for the papacy throughout the century and in the 1370s a further inquisitorial manual, written by the Dominican Nicholas Eyeric, concluded that some of the actions of sorcerers and diviners were heretical and 'his arguments form an important foundation for the later notion of witchcraft'. While chiromancy (palm reading) and astrology might be sinful they were not, unless tainted with demonic invocation, considered heretical. It was at this time though that the fear of witches and witchcraft began to grow. The form that this fear took is also indicative of changes in how power, albeit supernatural power, was understood. After 1350, in trials for *maleficium* (the ability to do harm through witchcraft or magic), women became the majority of the accused for the first time and the proportion continued to rise to over 60 per cent in the fifteenth century before reaching the great witch-hunts of the sixteenth and seventeenth centuries in which over 80 per cent of the victims were female.[77]

The religious attitudes held by the Black Prince, his wife and members of their households were then indicative of broader changes in belief and also serve to reflect the vicissitudes of the later medieval Church. While these should not be exaggerated – the papacy, though diminished, had become a model of bureaucratic and governmental efficiency – certainties were shaken and the basic conception of power, of authority at its most fundamental, shifted in the fourteenth and fifteenth centuries. The balance of power between pope and king, between Church and what we might start to tentatively call the 'State', altered. There was also a greater independence of thought and of attitudes to the hereafter and, consequently, a reconsideration of the best ways to achieve salvation. This led some to heresy and left many more teetering on the brink of orthodoxy. Like so many aspects of the life and career of Edward the Black Prince, it was an indication of things to come.

CONCLUSION

. . . the Black Prince, that young Mars of men.[1]

In England, between 1330 and 1376, everything and nothing changed. As Edward III approached the end of his reign, royal power was threatened once again and a minority kingship loomed near. A fearsome military reputation had been made and lost. Foreign territories had been conquered and squandered; those that remained were under threat. There were tensions among the population and the polity, factions at court, high levels of taxation and distrust of the papacy.

What was new was a difficult legacy, one of hope and of expectation, of a new role for England as a power in Christendom. This, in part, was due to the Black Prince although it was said with suitable hyperbole that with his demise 'the hopes of the English utterly perished'. The glories of Crécy and Poitiers were imprinted on the collective memory and so too was the image of the heir apparent. Walsingham compared Edward to Alexander in his military strength and recorded that his death brought tears to his people and joy to his enemies.[2]

There is something modern about the celebrity of Edward of Woodstock. Despite his slow, lingering death he is always seen as young and vigorous, snatched away too soon, 'to be mourned by the whole kingdom of England!'[3] His reputation, forged at Crécy, served him well for the rest of his life; because of it men were drawn to his service and to his banner. In England he became a symbol of 'truth, honour, freedom and courtesy'. Such a reputation was a power in itself and, because of that, a burden for Richard II who did not have the same qualities.[4]

Reputation was at the heart of chivalry: it gave a right to pride and status within the elite.[5] The prince's reputation was founded on a traditional code of conduct that determined behaviour within the chivalrous classes. But this was a time of military evolution, perhaps even revolution, when those same classes were being reconstructed and their role re-evaluated. Within the context of the Hundred Years War, the prince's reputation was truly that of a *miles* – knight and soldier – who sought military success at almost any cost. Hence he employed not only the *chevauchée* strategy, but also tactics at the battles of Crécy, Poitiers and Nájera that emasculated the traditional military aristocracy.

Before Courtrai, Bannockburn, Morgarten and Crécy changed the balance of military power, Ramon Lull emphasised the association of the knight with cavalry service and the equestrian ideal. For Lull, a knight received a horse to signify nobility of courage that he should have above all other people.[6] By 1346, English victories and those of other nations depended on the skills of the infantryman, the archer, and would soon rely on the support of gunpowder artillery.[7] Those people, the yeomen archers and their fellows straddling the new social margins, rather than the mounted knights, were the backbone of English armies in the Hundred Years War. As the yeoman of England became part of the military community so, to some extent, the battles in which he fought did 'gentle his condition'. The social exclusivity of the *bellatores* was shattered and the political authority and social standing that had been associated with military prowess was fractured by victories founded on discipline, collective action, infantry and longbowmen. But this is not to say that the higher aristocracy lost its martial associations, for violence remained 'part of a nobleman's upbringing. He was destined to fight . . . Even though courage, recklessness and skill at arms were of little use now'.[8]

Such changes in military affairs, revolutionary or not, coloured the Black Prince's life and shaped his reputation. Indeed, this may be in a literal sense in that military brutality and its glamorisation perhaps lay behind the title 'Black Prince'. Not recorded until Leland's *Itinerary* in the sixteenth century, the name is often said to have been given on account of his black armour. There is little to support this, but the prince's ostrich feather badge, his arms of peace, had a black background and it is possible that he may have had his armour painted to match. If so, he was in good company: Philippe the Good of Burgundy, in his later years, and René d'Anjou both favoured black for state garments and other trappings.[9] But the association between black and the prince was not such that a link would automatically be assumed by contemporaries: Chaucer could employ the image of the mourning Black Knight in the *Book of the Duchess* to (probably) represent John of Gaunt and not his brother.

It is more likely that the title has its origins in France, since the shade had few, if any, positive connotations, and where there is no doubt that the prince's reputation was dark indeed. For Philippe de Mézières he was the greatest of the 'black boars' – those aggressors who had done so much to destroy relations within Christendom and put it in danger of attack by the forces of Islam. It is not an inappropriate name. The boar was known to be powerful, courageous, vindictive, angry and proud, with great stamina and a palpable physical (and sexual) menace. The boar had no clear allegiance. In Arthurian tales it might be associated with either the hero or the villain. In hunting texts the boar was one of *les noires bestes,* one of the five black beasts, perhaps because some saw a link with the devil as a result of Biblical connections to the Gaderene swine.[10] It was an association that Louis of Anjou also made with the prince and his family. In the Apocalypse tapestries he commissioned for his palace, the Black Prince rode as a demon in the company of his equally fiendish father and brothers in a riotous devastation of France. As it was said, 'the English to disport themselves put everything to fire and flame . . . they made many a widowed lady and many a poor orphaned child'. It is entirely in keeping with the reputation of the Black Prince and the nature of late medieval chivalry that Chandos Herald tells us this and does so with a sense of pride.[11]

The association of the prince with the boar extends beyond de Mézières' derisive remarks. In various works of political prophecy, and there were several of these which invested great hope in the prince and his father, both were described as 'the Boar'. Notably, due to its Arthurian connotations, Geoffrey le Baker identified the prince as 'the Boar of Cornwall'.[12] But the boar association was not consistent. In the 'Bridlington' prophecy, the prince is the *gallus,* the cockerel, during whose reign England will be victorious in all things. The prince will be the new Arthur who ensures the integrity of the English Crown and who will take the throne of France from a grateful French people. Indeed, a royal title was insufficient – the prince was worthy to be an emperor. It is an indication of the great hope that the Black Prince inspired in the author and perhaps among the population at large in the early 1350s.[13]

As a consequence and despite his long illness, there is little surprise that the country was shocked and dispirited by the prince's premature death. This is evident in the numerous encomia and sermons that were written and preached.[14] For the most part these were conventional accounts that focused on military exploits. However, as he does with such regularity, Thomas Walsingham strikes a discordant note – not with regard to the prince's achievements, but in the manner of his death.

Walsingham's account of the prince's death is intriguing. God was said to have given Edward a long time to repent of his sins and he had suffered greatly for them. For more than five years 'almost every month he suffered a discharge of both semen and blood' which 'rendered him so weak on many an occasion that his attendants very often thought he had died'.[15] The precise nature of the sins for which the prince suffered is not specified. It is peculiar, however, that although the prince's wickedness is emphasised prior to death, after he has passed on the author makes the most effusive eulogy in which he praises Edward's great military deeds, which one would assume were those same sins for which he had to suffer and repent.

The meaning of the symptoms with which Walsingham credits the prince is difficult to interpret. The emission of both blood and semen were thought to remove impurities from the body and this may perhaps be a means of emphasising the prince's repentance – his body was rejecting evil, as was his soul. Such a view is perhaps strengthened later in Walsingham's account when John Gilbert, the prince's confessor and bishop of Hereford, was forced to sprinkle holy water before the prince could confess fully and ask God for forgiveness. This was 'because it is evident that [he had] offended God and many fellow men'.[16]

In this context, semen may well have been used as a general term to indicate a variety of bodily matter, and if the prince did succumb to a virulent strain of dysentery during the Nájera campaign it may be these symptoms to which Walsingham referred. One wonders, however, how the chronicler would know of the prince's medical condition, and questions are raised by the peculiarities of the monthly (almost menstrual) cycle of the emissions.

To improve one's chances of salvation, a 'good death' was important, but often a problem for the career soldier. Some comparisons of the prince's last days can be made with the biographical account of the death of William Marshal (earl of Pembroke and regent of England, 1147–1219).[17] Both were aware for a long time of the approach of death, the need to put their affairs in order, and ensure that their heirs and successors would care properly for their dependents and servants. Foreknowledge of the exact time of death was taken as evidence of sanctity although neither the Marshal nor, certainly, the Black Prince, were in this category. Nonetheless, the Marshal's slow death was presented by his biographer as a model for the Christian knight although William bridled at the suggestion that he was about to die. It seems that even the finest found it difficult to confront their mortality; the final confession and the last rites were often delayed until the last possible moment.[18]

It seemed as if the last rites were also needed for the English military machine and for the mission to France. Nearly 40 years of war had witnessed successes and catastrophes on both sides. By 1376, the long struggle had begun to take on the character of a national mission, encouraged by the development of some sense of national identity. While not the nationalism of the nation-state, a sense of *patria* and a collective identity was created in those years.

This took a variety of forms and was shaped by various influences. The development of parliamentary authority was a significant element since it brought with it a new sense of the will of the body politic. There was also an effective propaganda programme instigated in support of royal demands for taxation. The perfidy of the French, the justice of the

Edwardian mission, the threat to the English, their language and their way of life were all emphasised. Heraldry, coinage, sermons and processions were used to unite the people in opposition to France and her allies. Letters sent back from the front proclaimed divine approval for England when her armies were victorious and demanded greater support from her people when they were defeated by some fox trick of the French.

The development of this process can be seen throughout the early stages of the war in the works of Lawrence Minot, Thomas Bradwardine and John of Bridlington. In these there are various common themes – the English are often depicted as underdogs and Christ is proclaimed as protector of the nation. There is a strong moral tone and slurs were made on the French and Scottish kings: the traditional consecration oil (believed to date from the time of Clovis, first Christian king of the Franks) was not used at Philippe of Valois' coronation thus calling its validity into question; the Capetians were descended from a butcher; David II was an adulterer and soiled the font at baptism and so on.[19] In a poem written about Crécy, the author, probably a northern priest, wrote of the effeminate French comparing them to the lynx, the viper, the wolf – cunning, cruel and proud under their 'duke', Philippe of Valois. By comparison, Edward III was the true king, the leopard, who would prove his worth by deeds of arms, tearing at the French with his teeth.[20]

There was also a wider context to the construction of a national identity in both England and France. The nature of Christendom changed with the loss of the Holy Land and the growing realisation that the crusade movement had failed. A pan-European mission, even one sanctified by God, was thought to have little chance of success despite the calls of Philippe de Mézières and his fellows. The disaster at Nicopolis (1396) would only confirm the futility of the exercise. Furthermore, the pro-French attitude of the Avignon Papacy meant most Englishmen adopted a sceptical attitude to the pope and to Europe as a whole.[21] In place of the crusade though there was now a national mission and the emergence of what has been described as sanctified patriotism.[22]

Such attitudes contributed to the separation of England from Europe. The ejection of the Black Prince from Aquitaine is an eloquent metaphor for the process. This political and cultural division was also hastened by the development and increasing use of English as a language of law and government. By the late fourteenth century, linguistic changes meant manuals had to be written to teach the French language to Englishmen for conversational and commercial purposes.[23] Therefore Anglo-French hostilities divided England from Europe and, apart from a brief period in the 1420s, English interests on the Continent diminished. Attention was focused at home on the development of various institutions of government, on the marshalling of the resources of the kingdom in support of the national mission. As a result this was a 'key stage in the transformation of a feudal, better a seigneurial, polity into a rudimentary early modern state'.[24]

As part of that transformation, political expectations and the nature of the body politic changed a great deal. Understanding of the character of power and how it should be wielded shifted too. In part this was because of the changes in economy and society wrought by the Black Death as well as momentous political events, and the tribulations of the Church.[25] For the Black Prince, as for all the late medieval kings and nobles, power was exercised through control of land and, by extension, control of men and military strength. That power was bolstered by and enshrined in theological and legal principles. These elements were under stress and fluctuating as a consequence of changing social and economic forces.

Some of these forces were negative, some positive for the authority of rulers. As the power that came with control of land lessened in post-plague Europe, so the position of the nobility and of kings and princes was compromised. By contrast, the authority of kings and princes grew as Roman law and the teachings of increasingly 'national' churches were employed in their favour. It grew also as the resources of the nascent 'State' were brought to bear in support of royal policy. This authority had a price though, and in some ways it lessened the real power of kings of England. Monarchs were forced, albeit to a limited extent, to account for their actions to their people as parliament gained an awareness and recognition of its representative obligations as the mouthpiece of the community of the realm.

Despite such theoretical and structural changes in the construction of the body politic, the real threat to a king or a prince still came not from a true community of the realm, but from the highest levels of the nobility, indeed from that older community of the realm as it had been under-stood and defined for generations. But the Good Parliament showed, as the Peasants' Revolt would show more clearly, that the body politic was broadening and its members were willing to take action in support of their own political objectives, even if these were not focused on specific-ally royal failures. Governmental failure and corruption would be found out and those responsible would be removed, violently if necessary.

For the Black Prince, the threat to royal and noble power was evident in his relations with the Welsh Marcher lords and brought into sharp relief in the rebellion in Aquitaine. This highlights one of the key differences in the evolution of royal authority and power in England and France and also is central to an understanding the prince's legacy and reputation. The appeal of 1368 was to the king of France, to one of the greatest of the Valois line, to one who ensured that despite his son's incapacity he was never removed from the throne. Because of the spiritual, historical and legal power invested in the French Crown, Charles VI would not face the indignity suffered by Edward II or Richard II or so many of their fifteenth-century successors.

The 1368 rebellion followed an appeal against tyranny. As with so many aspects of the prince's life and career it is a charge that is difficult to evaluate, the evidence is contradictory. For example, there is no doubt that there was a wide-scale 'Anglicisation' of the Aquitainian administration, but there were also attempts to secure support for the new regime even if few Frenchmen found their way to high office. This was also the case in Wales, where much of the most oppressive anti-Welsh legislation was imposed by Welshmen who might rise to the apex of local government, but found more exalted office very difficult to attain.

In both principalities the most destabilising factor was the abrupt imposition of outside authority after years of absentee lordship. Indeed, in Aquitaine it is questionable whether the treaty of Brétigny could have ever provided the foundations for a political entity with any real cohesion. The events of 1346–7 and 1355–6 and the slow development of a French national identity did not provide an ideal environment for the establishment of an English regime in France. An inherent political antipathy was compounded by the demonstration of power in the prince's court. There, the formal etiquette was demanding and demeaning even if no different from that expected in London or Paris. But the prince was not a king and perhaps in craving a throne he called for more deference than his status required. This was, no doubt, a misjudgement, but it was not surprising. By this time he could have expected to acquire some true sovereign power. But the longevity of Edward III prevented this; indeed, had he lived to inherit the throne, the prince would have been 47 years of age, older by far than most English kings on their accession.

Despite all such demonstrations of political power, demands for deference, and the partial imposition of a new ruling class, the catalyst for rebellion in Aquitaine, as so often elsewhere, was taxation. Throughout Europe, extraordinary taxation imposed during a period of peace was a major cause of opposition. But while it may have been unwise of the prince to levy the tax, it was not an unusual imposition in the principality or elsewhere. Jean de Montfort, the prince's associate and brother-in-law, acted in a similar fashion in Brittany at just the same time. After 1365 the Breton Estates were summoned to consent to *fouages* and other taxes; by 1420 these grants became a formality.[26]

While this is suggestive of another turning point in governmental practice and perhaps of 'State' development, there is no doubt that the prince's financial policy (or that of his ministers) was vigorous and abrasive. It certainly resulted in substantial increases in income throughout his estates despite the impact of the plague. By the end of his life his English and Welsh estates had an annual value of nearly £10,000: if power can be measured in financial terms then the Black Prince was one of the most powerful men in the country. The price of that power though was high in Cheshire and especially in Wales. Both suffered financially under the prince's rule since the requirements to fund his military expeditions and extravagant lifestyle coincided with the ongoing depredations of the Black Death. In Cornwall, by contrast, while administrative efficiency increased, the impact of the plague was lessened for many of the prince's tenants through remarkably benevolent government.

Such contrasting policies are emblematic of the prince's life and career. Are we dealing with a man responsible for 'systematic financial rape'[27] or one whose policies 'were remarkable in their wisdom and foresight?'[28] Of course, governing the Welsh was different to governing the Cornish – xenophobia was enshrined in law – but many of those responsible for implementing draconian policies in Wales were Welsh themselves. Indeed, there were several important members of the household and retinue who originated in the principality. Similarly, Guichard d'Angle, who had fought with Jean II at Poitiers, was welcomed into the prince's court and became tutor to Richard II and, in time, earl of Huntingdon.

These apparent contradictions extend to what little we can infer of the prince's character. Are we dealing with the flower of chivalry or the butcher of Limoges? Are we dealing with the puritan or the spendthrift; the enraged warrior or the religious philanthropist? He delighted in a lavish court and household and married for love, or at least for infatuation, and yet wished to be remembered through an epitaph that spoke of corruption and decay and the fleeting foolishness of the material world. Are we dealing with a political incompetent or a man who, in his latter years, recognised and sought to manipulate the burgeoning power of parliament?

The answer is that in this period of transition, when structures of power and conceptions of proper behaviour were fluctuating, such apparent distinctions are not so incongruous. The Black Prince was a product of his age, an archetypal figure in a period of tumult. He did not become king, but he contributed much to the royal legacy and it is appropriate that the Black Prince ruby is set in the English crown. In the England of the later middle ages with her disparate monarchs and rulers of such contrasting reputations and quality it is easy to agree with Henry Knighton that Edward the Black Prince is 'one deserving to be remembered among kings'.[29]

NOTES

All manuscript references are to the National Archives (PRO) unless stated otherwise.

Introduction

1. 'De le plus vaillant prince du mounde. Si come il est tourney a le rounde. Ne qui fuist puis le tamps Claruz, Jule Cesaire ne Artuz.' Chandos Herald, *The Life of the Black Prince*, ed. and trans. E. Lodge and M.K. Pope (Oxford, 1910), 2, ll. 49–52. Both remaining manuscripts of the *Vie du Prince Noir* read 'Claruz', which is emended to Claris (Charlemagne) by Pope and Richard Barber, *The Life and Campaigns of the Black Prince* (London, 1979), 85; Diana Tyson suggests that instead it was a reference to Clarus, 'roi des Indes', one of the main characters in the *Voeux du paon*, one of the most popular of the Alexander poems. *La Vie du Prince Noir by Chandos Herald* (Tübingen, 1975), 50, 167, ll. 49–52.

2. Barbara Tuchman, *A Distant Mirror: The Calamitous Fourteenth Century* (London, 1979); Johan Huizinga, *Herfsttij der Middeleeuwen* (Haarlem, 1919), translated as *The Waning of the Middle Ages: A Study of the Forms of Life, Thought and Art in France and the Netherlands in the XIVth and XVth Centuries*, trans. F. Hopman (London, 1924); *The Autumn of the Middle Ages*, trans. Rodney J. Payton and Ulrich Mammitzsch (Chicago, 1996). The first English translation involved a considerable reworking of the text and the change of title lacks an ambiguity present in the original. The French edition was called, bluntly, *Le déclin du moyen âge*, J. Bastin (Paris, 1932). Raymond Kilgour, *The Decline of Chivalry as Shown in the French Literature of the Late Middle Ages* (Cambridge, 1937). See further Maurice Keen, 'Huizinga, Kilgour and the Decline of Chivalry', *Medievalia et Humanistica*, 8 (1977), 1–20; Margaret Aston, 'Huizinga's Harvest: England and the *Waning of the Middle Ages*', *Medievalia et Humanistica*, 9 (1979), 1–24.

3. The order was suppressed although not condemned by Apostolic Decree on 22 Mar. 1312 and the influence of Philippe IV in the matter is indicative of the changing balance between ecclesiastical and secular power.

4. David L. d'Avray, however, argues that sermons exalting the papal office in the fourteenth and fifteenth centuries were widely preached, probably influential and found a receptive lay audience: 'Papal Authority and Religious Sentiment in the Late Middle Ages', *The Church and Sovereignty, c.590–1918* [SCH Subsidia 9], ed. Diana Wood (Oxford, 1991), 393–408.

5. Colin Richmond, 'An Outlaw and Some Peasants: The Possible Significance of Robin Hood', *Nottingham Medieval Studies*, xxxvii (1993), 98; J.R. Maddicott, 'The Birth and Setting of the Ballads of Robin Hood', *EHR*, 93 (1978), 278, 298–9; J.C. Holt, *Robin Hood*, 2nd ed. (London, 1989), 115. The first mention of Robin is by Sloth in Langland's *Piers Plowman*, 'I can noughte perfitly my pater-noster as the prest it syngeth/But I can rymes of Robyn hood and

Randolf erle of Chestre.' Maddicott attributes the Robin stories to the oppressive conditions of the 1330s.

6. Diana Tyson, 'Authors, Patrons and Soldiers – Some Thoughts on Some Old French Soldiers' *Lives*', *Nottingham Medieval Studies*, xlii (1998), 105–20.

7. It should be noted, however, that Gaveston had little interest in political affairs at least from the evidence of charter witness lists. J.S. Hamilton, 'Charter Witness Lists for the Reign of Edward II', *Fourteenth Century England I*, ed. Nigel Saul (Woodbridge, 2000), 5–6. See also Michael Prestwich, 'The Charges against the Despensers, 1321', *BIHR*, lviii (1985), 95–9; J.R. Maddicott, *Thomas of Lancaster, 1307–22* (Oxford, 1970), 279–87.

8. Pierre Chaplais, *Piers Gaveston: Edward II's Adoptive Brother* (Oxford, 1994), 9, 44–5; J.S. Hamilton, *Piers Gaveston, Earl of Cornwall 1307–1312: Politics and Patronage in the Reign of Edward II* (Detroit, 1988), 47, 109–10; S. Menache, 'Isabelle of France, Queen of England: A Reconsideration', *Journal of Medieval History*, x (1984), 107–24.

9. John Carmi Parsons, 'The Intercessory Patronage of Queens Margaret and Isabella of France', *Thirteenth Century England VI*, ed. Richard Britnell, Robin Frame and Michael Prestwich (Woodbridge, 1997), 155–6 and n. 30. See also PRO SC1/49/188 (letter to the bishop of Exeter, 8 Dec. 1325) regarding Isabella's dislike of the Despensers.

10. *Vita Edwardi Secundi*, ed. N. Denholm-Young (London, 1957), 145. For discussion of Isabella's activities in France from 1325 see Carla Lord, 'Queen Isabella at the Court of France', *Fourteenth Century England II*, ed. Chris Given-Wilson (Woodbridge, 2002), 45–52.

11. For barbed comments on Isabella's relationship with Mortimer see *Chronicon Galfridi le Baker de Swynebroke*, ed. Edward Maunde Thompson (Oxford, 1889), 45.

12. On the courtship process see Veronica Sekules, 'Dynasty and Patrimony in the Self-Construction of an English Queen: Philippa of Hainault and her Images', *England and the Continent in the Middle Ages. Studies in Memory of Andrew Martindale*, ed. John Mitchell (Stamford, 2000), 158–60.

13. G.A. Holmes, 'Judgement on the Younger Despenser, 1326', *EHR*, 70 (1955), 261–7.

14. The most recent account is Roy M. Haines, *King Edward II: Edward of Caernarfon, His Life Reign and its Aftermath, 1284–1330* (Montreal, 2003), 188–94.

15. For what may have been a contrasting and positive contemporary image of the king see Claire Valente, 'The *Lament of Edward II*: Religious Lyric, Political Propaganda', *Speculum*, 77 (2002), 432, 434, 436–7.

16. A new clause was introduced in the 1308 coronation oath for Edward II – the ceremony was the first for which a record survives. Not only was the king to swear to confirm the laws made by his predecessors but also 'to maintain and keep the laws and rightful customs which the community of your realm shall choose, and defend and enforce them to the honour of God, to the best of your ability'. Alan Harding, *Medieval Law and the Foundations of the State* (Oxford, 2002), 256; Robert S. Hoyt, 'The Coronation Oath of 1308', *EHR*, 71 (1956), 353–83.

17. B. Wilkinson, *Constitutional History of Medieval England, 1216–1399, II: Politics and the Constitution, 1307–1399* (London, 1952), 170–1. The *Historia Roffensis* describes 'multos et magnos defectus et intollerabiles', Haines, *Edward II*, 344.

18. William Huse Dunham Jr and Charles T. Wood, 'The Right to Rule in England: Depositions and the Kingdom's Authority, 1327–1485', *American Historical Review*, 81 (1976), 741.

19. Cited by Wendy Childs, 'Treason in the *Vita Edwardi Secundi*', *Thirteenth Century England VI*, 181.

20. This may have been informed by Aristotelian concepts that 'created part of the mental atmosphere in which it became increasingly possible and respectable to justify and even to prefer consultative, constitutional, and representative rule.' Antony Black, 'Political Languages in Late Medieval Europe', *The Church and Sovereignty*, ed. Wood, 319.

21. The Despensers were accused of encroaching on royal power and restricting access to royal justice: Prestwich, 'Charges against the Despensers', 96.

22. Michael Evans, *The Death of Kings: Royal Deaths in Medieval England* (London, 2003), 121–31, 156–7. For the Fieschi letter see Roy M. Haines, *Death of a King* (Scotforth, 2002), 100–2.

23. 'Lanercost Chronicle', ed. and trans. H. Maxwell, *Scottish Historical Review*, 9 (1913), 168.

24. Rymer, II, iii, 6.

25. Le Baker, *Chronicon*, 43; *English Historical Documents, IV, 1327–1485*, ed. A.R. Myers (London, 1969), 50–1.

26. *Rotuli Parliamentorum II*, ed. J Strachey *et al.* (London, 1783), 52; Le Baker, *Chronicon*, 45–6 stated that 'by his death he [Mortimer] ended the civil wars which he had often stirred up through his life'.

27. Mortimer may have also had greater ambitions. Geoffrey le Baker in *c.*1350 suggested: 'It was being said in secret that Mortimer, the queen's lover and master of the king, yearned to extinguish the royal blood and to usurp regal majesty'. Cited by Haines, *Death of a King*, 63.

28. Michael Jones, 'The Last Capetians and Early Valois Kings, 1314–1364', *New Cambridge Medieval History, VI*, ed. Michael Jones (Cambridge, 2000), 389.

29. *Vie du Prince Noir*, ed. Tyson, 50–1.

30. Nicholas Orme, *Medieval Children* (New Haven and London, 2001), 32; *idem, From Childhood to Chivalry: The Education of the English Kings and Aristocracy, 1066–1530* (London, 1984), 2–3.

31. Rymer, II, ii, 880, 1049, 1125, 1212; May McKisack, *The Fourteenth Century: 1307–1399* (Oxford, 1959), 159–60; M. Packe, *King Edward III*, ed. L.C.B. Seaman (London, 1983), 91; Margaret Sharpe, 'The Administrative Chancery of the Black Prince Before 1362', *Essays in Medieval History Presented to T.F. Tout*, eds A.G. Little and F.M. Powicke (Manchester, 1925), 321.

32. Graham J. Dawson, 'The Black Prince's Palace at Kennington, Surrey', *British Archaeological Reports*, 26 (1976), 172, 174.

33. *CCR, 1349–54*, 299.

34. T.F. Tout, *Chapters in the Administrative History of Mediaeval England: The Wardrobe, the Chamber and the Small Seal* (Manchester, 1920–33), V, 319–20; Orme, *From Childhood to Chivalry*, 20–1.

35. 'Lanercost Chronicle', ed. Maxwell, 323, 324 n. 18; Tout, *Chapters*, V, 319; David Green, 'The Household and Military Retinue of Edward the Black Prince', unpub. PhD thesis, 2 vols (University of Nottingham, 1999), II, 14, 24; Anthony Verduyn, 'Burghersh, Bartholomew, the elder, second Lord Burghersh (d. 1355)', *ODNB*, VIII, 798–9.

36. BL Cotton Galba E III f. 190; Richard Barber, *Edward Prince of Wales and Aquitaine* (Woodbridge, 1978), 19, 21–2.

37. 'nominatissimus miles': *Knighton's Chronicle 1337–1396*, ed. G. Martin (Oxford, 1995), 170.

38. Orme, *Medieval Children*, 178.

39. Orme, *Childhood to Chivalry*, 6. Isidore of Seville, *Etymologiarum sive originum libri XX Isidori Hispalensis episcopi* (The Etymologies of Words), ed. W.M. Lindsay (Oxford, 1985); Bartholomew Glanville, *De Proprietatibus Rerum* (On the Properties of Things, *c*.1250); Giles of Rome, *De Regimine Principum* (On the Rule of Princes, *c*.1270).

40. Orme, *Childhood to Chivalry*, 17–18, 20–1.

41. On the prince's youth and his military role at Crécy see Kelly DeVries, 'Teenagers at War during the Middle Ages', *The Premodern Teenager: Youth in Society, 1150–1650*, ed. Konrad Eisenbichler (Toronto, 2002), 207, 214–17.

42. Packe, *Edward III*, 200–1.

43. N.A.M. Rodger, *The Safeguard of the Sea: A Naval History of Britain, I, 660–1649* (London, 2004), 91.

44. SC7/22/17. Her earlier marriage to William Montague, earl of Salisbury, was also dissolved. SC7/22/16 includes an order dated 1 July 1354 to the archbishops of Bordeaux and Nazareth and to the bishop of London to have Montague accept the annulment and Joan to solemnize publicly the marriage she contracted with Thomas Holland. See also Karl P. Wentersdorf, 'The Clandestine Marriages of the Fair Maid of Kent', *Journal of Medieval History*, 5 (1979), 203–31.

45. 'tres bon chevalier qui moult grandement avoit servi le prince et pour lui tant en ses guerres que autrement avoit moult travaillié.' *Chronique des quatre premiers Valois, 1327–1393*, ed. S. Luce (Paris, 1862), 123; Montagu Burrows, *The Family of Brocas of Beaurepaire and Roche Court* (London, 1886), 53, 55. Burrows' account of Bernard's life, repeated in *DNB*, II, 1273, is questioned with regard to his relationship with the Black Prince in J.S. Roskell, L. Clarke and C. Rawcliffe, eds, *History of Parliament, 1386–1421* (Stroud, 1993), II, 359–62. Although it is suggested that he may have fought at Poitiers, no mention is made of a request that the prince should approach Joan on his behalf in the most recent biographical account of his life. Henry Summerson, 'Brocas, Sir Bernard (c.1330–1395)', *ODNB*, VII, 740–1.

46. *Knighton's Chronicle*, 195.

47. David Green, *The Black Prince* (Stroud, 2001), 136; Mark Arvanigian, 'A Lancastrian Polity? John of Gaunt, John Neville and the War with France, 1368–88', *Fourteenth Century England III*, ed. W.M. Ormrod (Woodbridge, 2004), 138.

48. Jean Froissart, *Oeuvres*, ed. Kervyn de Lettenhove (Brussels, 1867–77).

49. Dunham and Wood, 'Right to Rule', 738.

50. Hoyt, 'The Coronation Oath of 1308', 353ff.

51. Michael Prestwich, 'The Ordinances of 1311 and the Politics of the Early Fourteenth Century', *Politics and Crisis in Fourteenth-Century England*, ed. W.R. Childs and J. Taylor (Gloucester, 1990), 10.

52. Michael Wilks, *The Problem of Sovereignty in the Later Middle Ages* (Cambridge, 1963), 190 n. 2; Claire Valente, 'The Deposition and Abdication of Edward II', *EHR*, 113 (1998), 859.

53. Robert S. Hoyt, 'The Coronation Oath of 1308: The Background of "les leys et les custumes"', *Traditio*, 11 (1955), 235–57; H.G. Richardson, 'The English Coronation Oath', *Speculum*, 24 (1949), 44–75.

54. Jones, 'Last Capetians', 421; *idem*, 'The Late Medieval State and Social Change: A View from the Duchy of Brittany', *L'État ou le Roi: Les foundations de la modernité monarchique en France (xive–xviie siècles)*, eds Neithard Bulst, Robert Descimon et Alain Guerreau (Paris, 1996), 121; Robert J. Knecht, *The Valois: Kings of France, 1328–1589* (London and New York, 2004), 8–9.

55. See below pp. XX.

56. A comparison can be drawn with the Lord Edward (I) whose actions were the cause of despair among contemporary writers such as Matthew Paris. Michael Prestwich, *Edward I* (New Haven and London, 1997), 3.

57. Christine de Pizan, *The Book of the Body Politic*, ed. and trans. Kate L. Forhan (Cambridge, 1994), 58.

58. R.R. Davies, *Lordship and Society in the March of Wales, 1282–1400* (Oxford, 1978), 269–73.

59. He could receive homages in his own name; he had certain feudal rights; could mint gold and silver; give favours and exemptions; consent to redemptions and the abridgments of fiefs; and raise commons to the peerage. Rymer, III, ii, 667.

60. *Westminster Chronicle, 1381–1394*, ed. and trans. L.C. Hector and B. Harvey (Oxford, 1982), 484.

61. Roland Delachenal, *Histoire de Charles V*, 5 vols (Paris, 1909–31), IV, 3.

62. For the ratification of the treaty (20 June 1365) see E30/21. See also Michael Jones, *Ducal Brittany, 1364–1399: Relations with England and France During the Reign of Duke John IV* (Oxford, 1970), 18–19, 45–6 and 45 nn. 2, 4.

63. *Knighton's Chronicle*, 184; *ex matre lubrice vite dedita: The Chronicle of Adam Usk, 1377–1421*, ed. and trans. Chris Given-Wilson (Oxford, 1997), 62–3. Gower provided a different tone, describing the supposed meeting between Joan and the peasant rebels in 1381 as if it were a rape: their intrusion into political society was a violation of the body politic. Joan as a victimised woman represented the victimised realm. Sylvia Federico, 'The Imaginary Society: Women in 1381', *Journal of British Studies*, 40 (2001), 179–80;

64. R.A. Griffiths, 'The Crown and the Royal Family in Later Medieval England', *King and Country. England and Wales in the Fifteenth Century* (London, 1991), 2 n. 7.

65. *Vie du Prince Noir*, ed. Tyson, ll. 60–2, 64–7.

Chapter One

1. Edward III, according to Jean Froissart, on the battlefield of Crécy. The reading in the Amiens redaction is merely 'laissiés l'enfant gaegnier ses esperons':

Jean Froissart, *Chroniques. Le Manuscript d'Amiens*, III, ed. Georges T. Diller (Geneva, 1992), 20.

2. The origins of the military revolution as discussed by Roberts, Parker and others have been relocated by some historians to the later medieval period. For further discussion see: Michael Roberts, *The Military Revolution, 1560–1660: An Inaugural Lecture Delivered Before the Queen's University of Belfast* (Belfast, 1956); Jeremy Black, *A Military Revolution? Military Change and European Society 1550–1800* (Basingstoke, 1991); Andrew Ayton and J.L. Price, 'Introduction: The Military Revolution from a Medieval Perspective', *The Medieval Military Revolution: State, Society and Military Change in Medieval and Early Modern Europe*, eds Andrew Ayton and J.L. Price (London, 1995), 1–22; Clifford J. Rogers, ed., *The Military Revolution Debate: Readings on the Military Transformation of Early Modern Europe* (Boulder, 1995); Geoffrey Parker, *The Military Revolution: Military Innovation and the Rise of the West, 1500–1800*, 2nd ed. (Cambridge, 1996); Michael Prestwich, 'Was There a Military Revolution in Medieval England?', *Recognitions: Essays Presented to Edmund Fryde*, eds Colin Richmond and Isobel M.W. Harvey (Aberystwyth, 1996), 19–38.

3. M.G.A. Vale, *The Angevin Legacy and the Hundred Years War, 1250–1340* (Oxford, 1990).

4. Anne Curry, *The Hundred Years War* (Houndsmill, 1993), 33.

5. *English Historical Documents, III*, ed. Harry Rothwell (London, 1975), 376–9; W.M. Ormrod, 'England, Normandy and the Beginnings of the Hundred Years War, 1259–1360', *England and Normandy in the Middle Ages*, eds David Bates and Anne Curry (London, 1994), 198; Pierre Chaplais, 'The Making of the Treaty of Paris (1259) and the Royal Style', *EHR*, 67 (1952), 235–53. Chaplais noted that the treaty 'was essentially an agreement between two equal and anointed kings . . . It was common practice . . . for a king never to take an oath in person before an inferior, with the exception of the coronation oath'. *Ibid.*, 237. The very act of making the treaty indicated the problems regarding superiority and sovereignty that would result from it.

6. See for example, Edouard Perroy, *The Hundred Years War*, trans. W.B. Wells (London, 1951), 69 and for a contrary view John le Patourel, 'Edward III and the Kingdom of France', *History*, 43 (1958), repr. in Rogers, *Wars of Edward III*, 247–64. For further comment see C.T. Allmand, *The Hundred Years War: England and France at War, c.1300–c.1450* (Cambridge, 1988), 7–12; Curry, *Hundred Years War*, 44–58.

7. Knecht, *Valois*, 1–2, 24; Craig Taylor, 'The Salic Law and the Valois succession to the French Crown', *French History*, 15 (2001), 358–77; *idem*, 'Edward III and the Plantagenet Claim to the French Throne', *The Age of Edward III*, ed. J.S. Bothwell (York, 2001), 156–7.

8. Various 'political theorists' commented on these questions. In general, both 'hierocratic and Thomist writers agreed that the ruler had an absolute authority over other members of the community, but they held to two very different interpretations of its extent'. This led to arguments as to whether the ruler had an absolute plentitude of power or if the subject had certain guaranteed rights. Wilks, *Problem of Sovereignty*, 207–8.

9. Vale, *Angevin Legacy*, 175–85.

10. As Fiona Watson has said: 'Few kings in the later thirteenth century were more touchy about royal rights than Edward I.' Nor does he seem to have understood the irony involved in 'extending his overlordship into Scotland using the same techniques employed by Philip IV of France to strengthen his position in Edward's duchy of Gascony': 'Edward I's Peace in Scotland, 1303–1305', *Thirteenth Century England VI*, 128; Prestwich, *Edward I*, 275.

11. Andrew Ayton, 'The English Army at Crécy', *The Battle of Crécy, 1346*, eds Andrew Ayton and Philip Preston (Woodbridge, 2005), 200–29. For a fine example of a military career that stretched from Bannockburn to the Reims campaign see Andrew Ayton, 'Sir Thomas Ughtred and the Edwardian Military Revolution', *Age of Edward III*, 107–32.

12. Michael Brown, *The Black Douglases: War and Lordship in Late Medieval Scotland, 1300–1455* (East Linton, 1998), 34–5.

13. On the military aspects of the 1332–3 Scottish campaigns see Clifford J. Rogers, *War Cruel and Sharp: English Strategy Under Edward III, 1327–1360* (Woodbridge, 2000), 27–76, esp. 28–33, 36, 54–5, 58–9, 63, 73–4. For the French Brut description of Halidon Hill, which emphasizes the importance of the longbow and the importance of discipline see Clifford J. Rogers, ed., *The Wars of Edward III: Sources and Interpretations* (Woodbridge, 1999), 38.

14. Michael Prestwich, 'Why did Englishmen Fight in the Hundred Years War?', *Medieval History*, 2 (1992), 63–4. For a summary of the economic interpretations of the war see Philippe Contamine, 'La guerre de cent ans en France: Une approche économique', *BIHR*, 47 (1974), 125–49.

15. E.B. Fryde, 'Financial Resources of Edward III in the Netherlands, 1337–40, Pt. 2', *Revue belge de philologie et d'histoire*, 45 (1967), 1142–216; J.E. Ziegler, 'Edward III and Low Country Finances: 1338–1340, with Particular Emphasis on the Dominant Position of Brabant', *Revue belge de philologie et d'histoire*, 61 (1983), 802–17.

16. For a survey of Franco-Flemish military antagonism see J.F. Verbruggen, 'Flemish Urban Militias Against the French Cavalry Armies in the Fourteenth and Fifteenth Centuries', trans. Kelly DeVries, *Journal of Medieval Military History I*, ed. Bernard S. Bachrach (Woodbridge, 2002), 145–69; *idem, The Battle of the Golden Spurs: Courtrai, 11 July 1302*, ed. Kelly de Vries, trans. David Richard Ferguson (Woodbridge, 2002).

17. Kelly DeVries, *Infantry Warfare in the Early Fourteenth Century: Discipline, Tactics and Technology* (Woodbridge, 1996), 66–85, 112–28, 137–44, 155–75.

18. Jean Le Bel, *Chronique*, eds J. Viard et E. Déprez (Paris, 1904), I, 119–20; Jonathan Sumption, *The Hundred Years War, I: Trial by Battle* (London, 1990), 292.

19. T. Wright, ed., *Political Poems and Songs Relating to English History*, 2 vols (London, 1859–61), I, 1–25, at 6–7.

20. M.G.A. Vale, *The Princely Court: Medieval Courts and Culture in North-West Europe* (Oxford, 2001), 213–18. He suggests that the poem has some associations with the Order of the Garter because Queen Philippa's vow bears a close resemblance to the Garter motto.

21. Ormrod, 'England, Normandy and the Beginnings of the Hundred Years War', 198–9 and n. 9.
22. On Edward's agreement with Ludwig of Bavaria see H.S. Offler, 'England and Germany at the Beginning of the Hundred Years War', *EHR*, 54 (1939), 608–31. Edward received the vicariate of the empire in return for his substantial payments but the title was rescinded in 1341 after the failure of the 1338–9 campaign and Lewis' subsequent alliance with King Philippe (24 Jan. 1341). This *volte face* seems to have been encouraged by the papacy, as well as Lewis' Italian concerns and Edward's inability to make the agreed payments.
23. Rogers, *The Wars of Edward III*, 59–62; Sumption, *Trial by Battle*, 241–2.
24. For events in Flanders see David Nicholas, *Medieval Flanders* (London, 1992), 219–20. Louis of Nevers was killed fighting for the French at Crécy and succeeded by his 16-year-old son, Louis of Male (1346–84).
25. The Peruzzi collapsed in 1343 and Bardi in 1346 with losses of 600,000 and 900,000 gold florins respectively; cf Edwin S. Hunt, 'A New Look at the Dealings of the Bardi and Peruzzi with Edward III', *Journal of Economic History*, 50 (1990), 149–62, esp. 157.
26. E.B. Fryde, 'The Dismissal of Robert de Wodehouse from the Office of Treasurer, December 1338', *EHR*, 67 (1952), 74–5.
27. Michael Prestwich, *The Three Edwards: War and State in England, 1272–1377*, 2nd ed. (London, 2003), 15.
28. Christopher Dyer, *Making a Living in the Middle Ages: The People of Britain, 850–1520* (New Haven and London, 2002), 236–7.
29. Le Patourel, 'Edward III and the Kingdom of France', *Wars of Edward III*, 247–64, esp. 254, 258, 260–3.
30. S.H. Cuttler, *The Law of Treason and Treason Trials in Later Medieval France* (Cambridge, 1981), 145–6.
31. Robert of Avesbury, *De gestis mirabilibus regis Edwardi Tertii*, ed. E.M. Thompson. [Rolls Ser.] (London, 1889), 309.
32. *Rotuli Parliamentorum*, 112–13; Rogers, *Wars of Edward III*, 82–3.
33. Michael Jones, 'Some Documents Relating to the Disputed Succession to the Duchy of Brittany, 1341', *Camden Miscellany*, xxiv (1972), 1, 4.
34. T.F. Tout, 'The Tactics of the Battles of Boroughbridge and Morlaix' *EHR*, 19 (1904), 711–15; Mathew Bennett, 'The Development of Battle Tactics in the Hundred Years War', *Arms, Armies and Fortifications in the Hundred Years War*, eds Anne Curry and M. Hughes (Woodbridge, 1994), 5; Michael Jones, 'Edward III's Captains in Brittany', *England in the Fourteenth Century. Proceedings of 1985 Harlaxton Symposium*, ed. W.M. Ormrod (Woodbridge, 1986), 104.
35. J. Viard, 'La campagne de juillet-août et la bataille de Crécy', *Le Moyen Age*, 2nd ser. xxvii (1926), 11–12; G. Wrottesley, ed. *Crécy and Calais from the Public Records* (Collections for a History of Staffordshire edited by the William Salt Archaeological Society, xviii), 92.
36. Jonathan Sumption, *The Hundred Years War, II: Trial by Fire* (London, 1999), 495.
37. E371/191/49 (Pay accounts); *Knighton's Chronicle*, ed. Martin, 58; Sumption, *Trial by Fire*, 498–9.

38. E101/25/17, 18, 19; Michael Jones, 'Sir Thomas Dagworth et la guerre civile en Bretagne au xive siècle: quelques documents inédits', *Annales de Bretagne*, lxxxviii (1980), 627–30; A.E. Prince, 'The Strength of English Armies in the Reign of Edward III', *EHR*, 46 (1931), 364–5.

39. Delachenal, *Charles V*, II, 144; Barber, *Edward*, 159.

40. Sumption, *Trial by Fire*, 494, 497; Barber, *Edward*, 47; Viard, 'La campagne de juillet-août', 3–4.

41. See James Lydon, 'The Impact of the Bruce Invasion, 1315–27', *A New History of Ireland II: Medieval Ireland 1169–1534*, ed. Art Cosgrove (Oxford, 1976), 275–302 at 285, citing *Chartularies of St. Mary's Abbey. Dublin and the Register of its House at Dunbrody; and Annals of Ireland*, ed. J.T. Gilbert, 2 vols (London, 1884–6). See also *Vita Edwardi Secundi*, 90; Julia Marvin, 'Cannibalism as an Aspect of Famine in Two English Chronicles', *Food and Eating in Medieval Europe*, eds Martha Carlin and Joel T. Rosenthal (London and Rio Grande, 1998), 73–9.

42. Sumption, *Trial by Fire*, 497–8, 532. Godfroi d'Harcourt may have been influential in encouraging Edward to invade Normandy. For his career see Leopold Delisle, *Histoire du château et de sires de Saint-Saveur-le-Vicomte* (Valognes, 1867), 50–108.

43. Yuval Noah Harari, 'Strategy and Supply in Fourteenth-Century Western European Invasion Campaigns', *Journal of Military History*, 64 (2000), 309, 316. Harari suggests that a supply train would have a ratio of 1:20 between carts and men, *ibid.*, 318.

44. For indication of military diets see Michael Prestwich, 'Victualing Estimates for English Garrisons in Scotland During the Early Fourteenth Century', *EHR*, 82 (1967), 536–43; *idem*, 'Was there a Military Revolution?', 27–9.

45. *Archives administratives de la ville de Reims*, ed. Pierre Varin (Paris, 1848), III, 81–2, 93, 96–7, 119, 136–41, 150–1; Pierre Desportes, *Reims et les Remois aux xiiie et xive siècles* (Paris, 1979), 550–3, 560–1.

46. Andrew Ayton, 'English Armies in the Fourteenth Century', *Arms, Armies and Fortifications*, 33–4; *idem, Knights and Warhorses: Military Service and the English Aristocracy under Edward III* (Woodbridge, 1994), 19.

47. Michael Prestwich, *Armies and Warfare in the Middle Ages: The English Experience* (New Haven and London, 1996), 320–1.

48. For accounts of the battle see Le Baker, *Chronicon*, 82–5; *Knighton's Chronicle*, 63; Adam Murimuth, *Continuatio Chronicarum*, ed. E.M. Thompson (London, 1889), 246; Jean Froissart, *Oeuvres*, ed. Kervyn de Lettenhove (Brussels, 1867–77), V, 33–8; Jean Froissart, *Chroniques*, eds S. Luce, G. Raynaud et L. Mirot, 15 vols (Paris, 1869–1975), III, 169, 405, 407, 409; Le Bel, *Chronique*, II, 99ff. For various interpretations see Viard, 'Le campagne de juillet-août', 67, 70–1; Barber, *Edward*, 65; Rogers, *War Cruel and Sharp*, 266–70.

49. For the possible formations used at Crécy see Prestwich, *Armies and Warfare*, 319–21. According to Oman and Burne a *herce* (translated as 'harrow') was a triangular formation with the apex facing the enemy. These formations of archers were either placed between divisions of dismounted men-at-arms or on the flanks. Jim Bradbury provides a number of other possibilities based on different translations: a candelabrum; a horn-shaped projection on the wings

of the army; a hedgehog or something with spikes possibly using stakes or pikemen for protection: *The Medieval Archer* (New York, 1985), 99. A 'hearse' is a triangular shaped candelabrum used in churches and therefore an item with which a clerk such as Froissart was likely to have been familiar. Whatever the strict definition of the term it is most likely that Froissart was referring to a triangular formation. My thanks to Michael Prestwich for his advice on this matter. See further, Prestwich, 'The Battle of Crécy', *Batttle of Crécy*, eds Ayton and Preston, 144–5.

50. Prestwich, *Armies and Warfare*, 293; T.F. Tout, 'Firearms in England in the Fourteenth Century', *EHR*, 26 (1911), 670–4, 676.

51. Note however, that according to Le Baker, French crossbows at Poitiers did considerable damage: *Chronicon*, 151.

52. *BPR*, I, 45; Philip Morgan, *War and Society in Medieval Cheshire, 1277–1403* (Manchester, 1987), 182, 186.

53. It was probably for this that he was granted a £20 annuity from Wallingford manor on 1 Sept. 1346, *BPR*, I, 14. There is an alternative tradition that the standard-bearer was Richard Beaumont. Le Baker, *Chronicon*, 261. He was said to have covered the prince with the great banner of Wales and defended him when he fell, Bibliothèque Nationale (Paris), Tramecourt MS, cited by Barbara Emerson, *The Black Prince* (London, 1976), 45.

54. Despite Edward's comments as reported by Froissart, reinforcements may have been sent by the bishop of Durham and the earls of Huntingdon and Suffolk: *Anonimalle Chronicle, 1333–1381*, ed. V.H. Galbraith (Manchester, 1927), 22.

55. Thanks to Michael Prestwich for pointing this out to me.

56. Le Bel, *Chronique*, II, 99ff.; Le Baker, *Chronicon*, 82–5; Froissart, *Oeuvres*, ed. Lettenhove, V, 37–8. On the French banner see Philippe Contamine, *L'oriflamme de Saint-Denis aux xive et xve siècles* (Nancy, 1975).

57. Barber, *Edward*, 68. The prince is not mentioned as participating in the morning attack by Knighton, Le Baker or the Anonimalle Chronicler: Sumption, *Trial by Fire*, 530.

58. According to Knighton, the prince himself slew the kings of Bohemia and Mallorca although it is certain the latter did not die at Crécy: *Knighton's Chronicle*, 198. For slightly varying lists of the fallen see: *ibid.*, 62; *Lanercost Chronicle*, 329; *Anonimalle Chronicle*, 23, 160.

59. It has been suggested that a reference in 'Winner and Waster' may be to the prince's arms of peace (tournament arms): 'Thre wynges inwith wroghte in the kynde/Vybygon with a gold wyre' (117–18): *Wynnere and Wastoure*, ed. Stephanie Trigg [EETS] (Oxford, 1990), 6; Lois Roney, 'Winner and Waster's 'Wyse Wordes': Teaching Economics and Nationalism in Fourteenth-Century England', *Speculum*, 69 (1994), 1087 n. 69. For a different (punning) identification with the Wingfield family, which was closely associated with the prince, see Elizabeth Salter, 'The Timeliness of Wynnere and Wastoure', *Medium Aevum*, 47 (1978), 40–65. Roger of Clarendon (the prince's illegitimate son), Thomas of Woodstock and John of Gaunt also bore ostrich feathers: Juliet Barker, *The Tournament in England, 1100–1400* (Woodbridge, 1986), 184.

60. Harcourt returned to French allegiance at the end of 1346, Delisle, *Saint-Sauveur*, 66–8.

61. Murimuth, *Chronicarum*, 247; *Knighton's Chronicle*, 143. The Hundred Years War was generally fought as a *bellum hostile*, i.e. declared under the authority of a prince and allowing the ransom of prisoners. E. Porter, 'Chaucer's Knight, the Alliterative *Morte Arthure* and the Medieval Laws of War: A Reconsideration', *Nottingham Medieval Studies*, xxvii (1983), 67.

62. He was referring only to the battle itself, as William Felton, seneschal of Poitou and the Limousin, died in an earlier engagement at Ariñez (19 March 1367). Eugene Déprez, 'La bataille de Nájera: le communiqué du Prince Noir', *Revue Historique*, cxxxvi (1921), 37–52; A.E. Prince, 'A Letter of Edward the Black Prince Describing the Battle of Nájera in 1367', *EHR*, 41 (1926), 415–18; *Life and Campaigns* ed. Barber, 83.

63. Bennett, 'Development of Battle Tactics', 2; Prestwich, 'Was there a Military Revolution', 22. Trumpets were used to pass orders regarding troop movements, *ibid.*, 3; 'la musique militaire était indispensable au bon fonctionnement des armées et au comportement des troupes': Philippe Contamine, 'La musique militaire dans le fonctionnement des armées: l'example française (v.1330–v.1550)', *From Crécy to Mohacs: Warfare in the Late Middle Ages (1346–1526), XXIInd Colloquium of the International Commission of Military History* (Vienna, 1997), 94.

64. For example, Irfon Bridge (1282), Maes Moydog (1295), Courtrai (1302) and Morgarten (1315). On the role of infantry see R.C. Smail, *Crusading Warfare, 1097–1193* (Cambridge, 1956), 116–30; DeVries, *Infantry Warfare*; J.F. Verbruggen, *The Art of Warfare in Western Europe During the Middle Ages: From the Eighth Century to 1340*, trans. Sumner Willard and Mrs R.W. Southern, 2nd ed. (Woodbridge, 1997), 111ff. For discussion of the role and importance of cavalry see Matthew Bennett, 'The Myth of Military Supremacy of Knightly Cavalry', *Armies, Chivalry and Warfare in Medieval Britain and France: Proceedings of the 1995 Harlaxton Symposium*, ed. Matthew Strickland (Stamford, 1998), 304–16; *idem*, 'The Medieval Warhorse Reconsidered', *Medieval Knighthood V*, eds Stephen Church and Ruth Harvey (Woodbridge, 1995), 19–40; Sean McGlynn, 'The Myths of Medieval Warfare', *History Today*, 44 (1994), 28–34. For a summary of technological innovations with special mention of cavalry see Andrew Ayton, 'Arms, Armour and Horses', *Medieval Warfare: A History*, ed. Maurice Keen (Oxford, 1999), 203–7.

65. P. Valentine Harris, 'Archery in the First Half of the Fourteenth Century', *Journal of the Society of Archer-Antiquaries*, 13 (1970), 19–21; Clifford J. Rogers, 'The Military Revolutions of the Hundred Years War', *Journal of Military History*, 57 (1993), 249–51 and nn. 36–41; Shannon A. Novak, 'Battle-Related Trauma', *Blood Red Roses. The Archaeology of a Mass Grave From the Battle of Towton AD 1461*, eds Veronica Fiorato, Anthea Boylston and Christopher Knüsel (Oxford, 2000), 109; Ann Stirland, *Raising the Dead: The Skeleton Crew of Henry VIII's Great Ship, the Mary Rose* (Chichester, 2000), 122–6; Peter Marsden, *Sealed by Time: The Loss and Recovery of the Mary Rose* (Portsmouth, 2003), 121, 124–5.

66. Bradbury, *Medieval Archer*, 93.

67. Novak, 'Battle-Related Trauma', 116. See *ibid.*, 104, 107–9 for a survey of the skeletons of archers, which shows that the Towton soldiers were not especially tall or robust.

68. It has been proposed that rather than causing a great number of casualties, archer fire disorganised an enemy assault making them easy prey for the infantry, Claude Gaier, 'L'invincibilité anglaise et le grande arc après la guerre de cent ans: un mythe tenace', *Tijdschrift voor gescheidenis*, 91 (1978), 378–85; John Keegan, *Face of Battle: A Study of Agincourt, Waterloo and the Somme* (Harmondsworth, 1978), 78–116. By contrast see Clifford J. Rogers, 'The Efficacy of the English Longbow: A Reply to Kelly DeVries, *War in History*, 5 (1998), 233–42. At Towton most of the victims died of blade wounds to the front or back of the head. Projectile injuries are the least represented wound type despite the fact that the initial conflict involved an archery exchange. Novak, 'Battle-Related Trauma', 97–8, 101.

69. *BPR*, III, 223–4. Prestwich notes that there does not appear to be any change in the use of bows or their design but suggests the armies of Edward III were simply much better supplied with arrows: 'Was there a Military Revolution?', 24–5.

70. Ayton, 'English Armies', 34; Robert Hardy, 'Longbow', *Arms, Armies and Fortifications*, 161–3, 180.

71. Andrew Ayton, 'Military Service and the Development of the Robin Hood Legend in the Fourteenth Century', *Nottingham Medieval Studies*, xxxvi (1992), 135.

72. A. Plaisse, *À travers le Cotentin: la grande chevauchée guerrière d'Edouard III en 1346* (Cherbourg, 1994), 31.

73. Prestwich, *Armies and Warfare*, 137–9, 227.

74. Helen Nicholson discusses a number of instances where the 'adherence to knightly ideals' brought about military failure, including Agincourt, Bannock-burn, and the Hussite wars: *Medieval Warfare: Theory and Practice of War in Europe 300–1500* (Houndsmill, 2004), 35–8.

75. For a wide-ranging discussion of military organisation see Dennis E. Showalter, 'Caste, Skill and Training: The Evolution of Cohesion in European Armies from the Middle Ages to the Sixteenth Century', *Journal of Military History*, 57 (1993), 407–30.

76. Jean Favier, *La Guerre de Cent Ans* (Paris, 1980), 212.

77. Bennett, 'Development of Battle Tactics', 9–10.

78. *Knighton's Chronicle*, 62. Le Baker, *Chronicon*, 85, refers to 16 attacks; Bradbury, *Medieval Archer*, 108, states there were 15.

79. Philippe Contamine, *Guerre, état et société a la fin du Moyen Âge. Etudes sur les armies des rois de France, 1337–1494* (Paris, 1972), 45, 175. French defeats were attributed 'à l'impéritie de la classe militaire par excellence, c'est-à-dire de la noblesse'. *Idem*, 'De la puissance aux privilèges: doléances de la noblesse française envers la monarchie aux XIVe et XVe siècles', *La noblesse au moyen âge, XIe–XVe siècles. Essais à la mémoire de Robert Boutruche*, ed. Philippe Contamine (Paris, 1976), 250. It was not the only such attack on the French aristocracy: BL Cotton Caligula D III f. 33 (report of Poitiers by Robert Prite, clerk); Froissart, *Oeuvres*, ed. Lettenhove, XVIII, 388; Françoise Autrand, 'La déconfiture. La bataille de Poitiers (1356) à travers quelques texts française des XIVe et XVe siècles', *Guerre et société en France, en Angleterre et en Bourgogne XIVe–XVe siècles*, eds Philippe Contamine, Charles Giry-Deloison et Maurice Keen (Lille, 1991), 93–121.

80. Rogers also highlights the peculiarities of terrain: 'Military Revolutions', 247–8.
81. Bradbury, *Medieval Archer*, 91.
82. David Green, *The Battle of Poitiers, 1356* (Stroud, 2002), 53, 62.
83. Bennett, 'Development of Battle Tactics', 13.
84. P. Russell, *The English Intervention in Spain and Portugal in the Reigns of Edward III and Richard II* (Oxford, 1955), 101.
85. Chandos Herald provides unique details of the battle: *Vie du Prince Noir*, ed. Tyson, ll. 3225–424.
86. There are 54 extant manuscripts written before 1300; Caesar's writings are found only in 41. Charles R. Schrader, 'The Influence of Vegetius' *De re militari*', *Military Affairs*, 45 (1981), 167–9, 171 n. 10; *idem*, 'A Handlist of the Extant Manuscripts containing the *De re militari* of Flavius Vegetius Renatus', *Scriptorium*, 33 (1979), 280–305. See also C.T. Allmand, 'Fifteenth-Century Versions of Vegetius', *De Re Militari*', *Armies, Chivalry and Warfare*, ed. Strickland, 30–45.
87. *The Tree of Battles of Honoré Bonet*, trans. G.W. Coopland (Liverpool, 1949); Christine de Pizan, *The Book of Arms and Deeds of Chivalry*, trans. Sumner Willard, ed. Charity Cannon Willard (Pennsylvania, 1999).
88. Clifford J. Rogers, 'The Vegetian "Science of Warfare"', *Journal of Medieval Military History I*, ed. Bernard S. Bachrach (Woodbridge, 2002), 1–19, and by contrast: Stephen Morillo, 'Battle-Seeking: The Contexts and Limits of Vegetian Strategy', *ibid.*, 21–41; John Gillingham, ' "Up with Orthodoxy!": In Defense of Vegetian Warfare', *Journal of Medieval Military History II*, eds Bernard S. Bachrach, Kelly DeVries and Clifford J. Rogers (Woodbridge, 2004), 149–58. There is no doubt that the 'orthodoxy', to use Rogers' word, shaped by Verbruggen, Smail, Gillingham and Strickland has influenced a wide range of historians in their belief that military strategy must have focused on the avoidance of direct conflict.
89. Clifford J. Rogers, 'Edward III and the Dialectics of Strategy', *TRHS*, 6th ser. iv (1994), 83–102.
90. K. Fowler, 'Letters and Dispatches of the Fourteenth Century', *Guerre et société en France en Angleterre et en Bourgogne XIVᵉ–XVᵉ siècles*, 79. Villani cited by Bennett, 'Development of Battle Tactics', 6–7.
91. In addition to the king, Warwick, Arundel and Suffolk had seen service in Scotland, Flanders and Brittany. Northampton had fought in Flanders and Brittany. They led a number of established military retinues which were important for the development and implementation of a tactical system. Rogers, 'Edward III and the Dialectics of Strategy', 93.
92. *Knighton's Chronicle*, 61, 63.
93. Rogers, 'Edward III and the Dialectics of Strategy', 95, 99. See also G.L. Harriss, *King, Parliament and Public Finance in Medieval England to 1369* (Oxford, 1975), 320–1.
94. Delachenal, *Charles V*, I, 220.
95. *Life and Campaigns*, ed. Barber, 58.
96. Froissart, *Chroniques*, ed. Luce, V, 60; Green, *Poitiers*, 50, 62–3.
97. Françoise Beriac-Lainé and Chris Given-Wilson, 'Edward III's Prisoners of War: The Battle of Poitiers and its Context', *EHR*, 116 (2001), 802–33; *idem, Les prisonniers de la bataille de Poitiers* (Paris, 2002).

98. Giovanni Villani, *Historia Universalis*, ed. L.A. Muratori (*Rerum Italicarum scriptores*, xiii, 1728), 419.

99. Kelly DeVries, 'Hunger, Flemish Participation and the Flight of Philip VI: Contemporary Accounts of the Siege of Calais, 1346–47', *Studies in Medieval and Renaissance History*, 12 (1991), 131–81.

100. *A History of Carmarthenshire*, ed. John E. Lloyd (Cardiff, 1935), I, 249. See also D.L. Evans, 'Some Notes on the History of the Principality of Wales in the Time of the Black Prince, 1343–1376', *Transactions of the Honourable Society of Cymrodorion* (1925–6), 80. Around 4,500 Welsh troops were recruited. Andrew Ayton has highlighted problems associated with previous estimates of the 1346–7 armies: 'The English Army and the Normandy Campaign of 1346', *England and Normandy*, eds Bates and Curry, 253–68.

101. Philippe Contamine, *War in the Middle Ages*, trans. M. Jones (Oxford, 1984), 140.

102. Froissart, *Chroniques*, ed. Luce, IV, 11; Jim Bradbury, *The Medieval Siege* (Woodbridge, 1992), 159.

103. S. Storey-Challenger, *L'administration anglaise du Ponthieu apres le traité de Brétigny, 1361–1369* (Abbeville, 1975), 286.

104. Robert D. Smith, 'Artillery and the Hundred Years War: Myth and Interpretation', *Arms, Armies and Fortifications*, 153–5; Richard L.C. Jones, 'Fortifications and Sieges in Western Europe c.800–1450', *Medieval Warfare*, ed. Keen, 180–3. Gunpowder was first used as an explosive in Britain in 1304 at the siege of Stirling but probably not in guns until the 1330s. The first artistic impression of a gunpowder weapon is in the Walter de Milemete treatise (*c.*1326): Prestwich, 'Was there a Military Revolution?', 25.

105. Kelly DeVries, 'The Impact of Gunpowder Weaponry on Siege Warfare in the Hundred Years War', *The Medieval City under Siege*, eds Ivy A. Corfis and Michael Wolfe (Woodbridge, 1995), 229. The French successfully used gunpowder weapons for the first time to bring down the town walls of Saint-Sauveur-le Vicomte in 1374. Maurice Keen, 'The Changing Scene: Guns, Gunpowder and Permanent Armies', *Medieval Warfare*, ed. Keen, 272–3, notes that the English defeat at Castillon was partly the result of strategic ineptitude and that the French guns had been intended for the walls of the town not the battlefield. Similarly, Constantinople fell only after an extended siege.

Chapter Two

1. Rosemary Horrox, *The Black Death* (Manchester, 1994), 74–5.

2. World War II (11.1), Black Death (10.9), World War I (10.5). Harold D. Foster, 'Assessing Disaster Magnitude', *Professional Geographer*, 28 (1976), 241–7, cited by Robert E. Lerner, 'The Black Death and Western Eschatological Mentalities', *American Historical Review*, 86 (1981), 533.

3. Samuel K. Cohn, Jr argues that the epidemics of 1348 and subsequently was 'any disease other than the rat-based bubonic plague': *The Black Death Transformed: Disease and Culture in Early Renaissance Europe* (London, 2002), 1. Susan Scott and Christopher J. Duncan, *Biology of Plagues: Evidence from Historical*

Populations (Cambridge, 2001) suggest haemorrhagic plague as an alternative diagnosis, probably a virus similar to Ebola or Marburg disease. However, John Hatcher, in his review of Cohn, argues there is 'a strong possibility that the problems we have in tying plague and the Black Death firmly together lie in mutations over the centuries in the plague bacilli, and/or changes in the relations between these microbes and their insect and animal hosts': *EHR*, 118 (2003), 989–91. The mutation theory would seem to have validity since the plague genome has now been sequenced and shown to be 'unusually fluid': J. Parkhill *et al.*, 'Genome sequence of *Yersinia pestis*, the causative agent of plague', *Nature*, 413 (2001), 523. For a similar conclusion see John Aberth, *From the Brink of the Apocalypse* (New York and London, 2001), 113.

4. Rosemary Horrox, 'Purgatory, Prayer and Plague, 1150–1380', *Death in England: An Illustrated History*, eds Peter C. Jupp and Clare Gittings (Manchester, 1999), 114–15; *idem, Black Death*, 73, 98–100, 154–5. Louis Heyligen (d. 1348), a musician in the service of Giovanni Colonna at the papal court of Avignon, wrote a letter describing the plague that appeared in a Flemish chronicle. Gabriel de Mussis (d. 1356), a lawyer from Piacenza, wrote *Historia de Morbo* (*History of the Death*). John Clynn, an Irishman, recorded the events of the plague 'in case anyone should be left alive in the future'. Aberth, *From the Brink of the Apocalypse*, 2–6, 114–15, 121–2.

5. Curtis V. Bostick, *The Antichrist and the Lollards: Apocalypticism in Late Medieval and Reformation England* (Leiden, 1998), 30–4.

6. Muriel A. Whitaker, '"Pearl" and Some Illustrated Apocalypse Manuscripts', *Viator*, 12 (1981), 183–96; Aberth, *From the Brink*, 185–6.

7. The plague encouraged the production of a wide range of chiliastic, visionary and 'prophetic' texts. These included the works of John of Bassigny, Brother William of Blofield (writing in the diocese of Norwich) and the Cedar of Lebanon vision. One of the most productive millenarian authors was John of Rupescissa, a Franciscan visionary whose work was known to Jean le Bel. His writings, not all associated with the plague, were highly politicised and included the *Liber secretorum eventum* (1349). Despite the apocalyptic connotations, such works were meant to inspire faith, hope and penance. Lerner, 'Western Eschatological Mentalities', 534–6, 541, 550–2.

8. Bernard McGinn, *Visions of the End: Apocalyptic Traditions in the Middle Ages* (New York, 1998), 230–3.

9. William Naphy and Andrew Spicer, *The Black Death and the History of Plagues, 1345–1730* (Stroud, 2000), 28.

10. Dyer, *Making a Living*, 228–9, 232–3.

11. Buchanan Sharp, 'The Food Riots of 1347 and the Medieval Moral Economy', *Moral Economy and Popular Protest: Crowds, Conflict and Authority*, eds Adrian Randall and Andrew Charlesworth (Houndsmill, 2000), 37.

12. Naphy and Spicer, *The Black Death and the History of Plagues*, 31–4.

13. William Rees, 'The Black Death in Wales', *Essays in Medieval History*, ed. R.W. Southern (London and New York, 1968), 185.

14. Naphy and Spicer, *The Black Death and the History of Plagues*, 37.

15. James Masschaele, 'The Public Space of the Marketplace in Medieval England', *Speculum*, 77 (2002), 386.

16. *CPR 1354–8*, 255. According to E.B. Fryde the sum was £1,000: 'The English Farmers of the Customs, 1343–51', *TRHS*, 5th ser. ix (1959), 15.

17. John Bell Henneman, 'The Black Death and Royal Taxation in France, 1347–1351', *Speculum*, 43 (1968), 413; R. Cazelles, 'La peste de 1348–1349 en langue d'oil, épidémie prolétarienne et enfantine', *Bulletin philologique et historique* (1962), 298–9, 303–6.

18. A.D. Carr, *Medieval Wales* (Basingstoke, 1995), 100. The traditional impression of France as a country wracked by a series of crises predating and resulting from the Black Death is challenged by James L. Goldsmith, 'The Crisis of the Late Middle Ages: The Case of France', *French History*, 9 (1995), 417–48. There is, however, little doubt that famine necessitated a number of grants and remissions from taxation in Bordeaux, the Angoumois and Poitou. See Pierre Capra, 'L'administration anglo-gasconne au temps de la lieutenance du Prince Noir, 1354–62', unpub. thesis (University of Paris, 1972), 884, 888–9 n. 4.

19. Paul V. Hargreaves, 'Seigniorial Reaction and Peasant Responses: Worcester Priory and its Peasants after the Black Death', *Midland History*, xxiv (1999), 53–5.

20. Preamble to the Ordinance of Labourers, 1349: Horrox, ed., *Black Death*, 287.

21. Chris Given-Wilson, 'The Problem of Labour in the Context of English Government, c.1350–1450', *The Problem of Labour in Fourteenth-Century England*, eds James Bothwell, P.J.P. Goldberg and W.M. Ormrod (York, 2000), 85, 88–9.

22. Statute of Labourers, *Statutes of the Realm*, eds A Luders *et al.*, 11 vols (London, 1810–28), I, 311; *English Historical Documents*, IV, 993; *BPR*, III, 415–16. For a discussion of the legal responses to the Black Death see R.C. Palmer, *English Law in the Age of the Black Death, 1348–1381: A Transformation of Governance and Law* (Chapel Hill, 1993); and, for a contrasting opinion, Anthony Musson, 'New Labour Laws, New Remedies? Legal Reaction to the Black Death "Crisis"', *Fourteenth Century England I*, ed. Nigel Saul (Woodbridge, 2000), 73–88.

23. Aberth, *From the Brink*, 138–9.

24. Dyer, *Making a Living*, 232; Musson, 'New Labour Laws', 75–9 who also notes that the regulations contained in the Ordinance and Statute of Labourers had been prefigured in earlier legislation.

25. A.R. Bridbury, 'The Black Death', *EcHR*, 2nd ser. xxvi (1973), 577–92; John Hatcher, 'England in the Aftermath of the Black Death', *Past and Present*, 144 (1994), 3–35; Musson, 'New Labour Laws', 86–8.

26. Chris Given-Wilson, 'Service, Serfdom and English Labour Legislation, 1350–1500', *Concepts and Patterns of Service in the Later Middle Ages*, eds Anne Curry and Elizabeth Matthew (Woodbridge, 2000), 21–37.

27. Hargreaves, 'Seignorial Reaction and Peasant Responses', 57–8; Aberth, *From the Brink*, 132–3, 136.

28. William Langland, *Piers the Ploughman*, trans. J.F. Goodridge (Harmondsworth, rev. ed. 1982), 89–90.

29. Evans, 'Some Notes on the History of the Principality, 79; A.D. Carr, 'The Black Death in Caernarfonshire', *Transactions of the Caernarvonshire Historical Society*, 61 (2000), 11.

30. *BPR*, III; 78, 328, 368, 377, 381, 391; P.H.W. Booth and A.D. Carr, eds, *Account of Master John de Burnham the younger, Chamberlain of Chester, of the*

Revenues of the Counties of Chester and Flint, Michaelmas 1361 to Michaelmas 1362 [Record Society of Lancashire and Cheshire, 125] (Manchester, 1991), 190–1.

31. R.A. Griffiths, *Conquerors and Conquered* (Far Thrupp, 1994), 140.
32. P.H.W. Booth, *The Financial Administration of the Lordship and County of Cheshire, 1272–1377* (Chetham Society, 3rd ser. xviii, 1981), 108.
33. *BPR*, IV, 194.
34. H.P.R. Finberg, *Tavistock Abbey* (Newton Abbot, 1969), 162–3. Stacy leased lands near Calstock, *BPR*, II, 54, 58, 61, 71.
35. John Hatcher, *Rural Economy and Society in the Duchy of Cornwall, 1300–1500* (Cambridge, 1970), 116–21.
36. H.S.A. Fox, 'Devon and Cornwall', *The Agrarian History of England and Wales, III, 1348–1500*, ed. Edward Miller (Cambridge, 1991), 171.
37. *BPR*, II, 183–4 and n. 1; Carr, 'Black Death in Caernarfonshire', 18; Evans, 'Notes on the History of the Principality', 83; Rees, 'Black Death in Wales', 186.
38. R.R. Davies, *Conquest, Coexistence and Change: Wales, 1063–1415* (Oxford, 1987), 399–400; Carr, *Medieval Wales*, 100–2; Dyer, *Making a Living*, 236.
39. Carr, 'Black Death in Caernarfonshire', 20.
40. Dyer, *Making a Living*, 242; J.A. Raftis, 'Changes in an English Village after the Black Death', *Mediaeval Studies*, 29 (1967), 174.
41. In Flintshire, between 1350 and 1364, three Welshmen held the office of sheriff: Ithel ap Cynwric Sais; Rhys ap Robert ap Gruffydd, and Kenwric ap Robert: C.R. Williams, ed., *The History of Flintshire from Earliest Times to the Act of Union* (Denbigh, 1961), 101.
42. Rees, 'Black Death in Wales', 196–7 and n. 1.
43. C47/9/57; SC12/22/97; Booth, *Financial Administration*, 173–5.
44. Dyer, *Making a Living*, 231.
45. Aberth, *From the Brink*, 131. He states this on the basis that the death rate in England could have been as high as 60 per cent, *ibid.*, 128.
46. In order of frequency the crimes recorded at these sessions were: assault, robbery, rape, abduction, extortion and homicide. Raiding and poaching in neighbouring counties were also common. This was the occasion for a major overhaul of the administration to increase revenue and establish law and order. P.H.W. Booth, 'Taxation and Public Order: Cheshire in 1353', *Northern History*, 12 (1976) 20–2, 25–8. See also CHES/17/4; *Knighton's Chronicle*, 120–2.
47. Raftis, 'English Village after the Black Death', 163–5.
48. Among the members of the prince's household and administration who died in 1349 were: Hugh Despenser; Richard FitzSimon, the prince's standard-bearer at Crécy; John of Castle Goodrich, controller of Cardiganshire and collector of customs in South Wales; Robert, one of the Swinnerton family from Staffordshire, several of whose members fought with the prince. In 1361 the victims were: Reginald Cobham; John Wingfield, the prince's business manager; William Kerdeston, who served in Norfolk, and had fought in 1346; William Diseworth, bailiff of Drakelowe manor, and John Hynton, bailiff of manor of Newport. Green, 'Household and Military Retinue', II, 30, 38–41, 58, 143, 153–4.

49. The episcopal mortality rate was 18 per cent. Ole J. Benedictow, *The Black Death, 1346–1353: The Complete History* (Woodbridge, 2004), 343; Gordon Leff, 'Bradwardine, Thomas (*c.*1300–1349)', *ODNB*, VII, 256–70; F.R. Lewis 'The Rectors of Llanbadarn Fawr, Cardiganshire, from 1246 to 1360', *Archaeologia Cambrensis*, 92 (1937), 243.

50. S.J. Payling, 'Social Mobility, Demographic Change and Landed Society in Late Medieval England', *EcHR*, 45 (1992), 54–6, 70.

51. Aberth, *From the Brink*, 153–4.

52. John Hatcher, *Plague, Population and the English Economy, 1348–1530* (Houndsmill, 1977), 13–14, 22, 68.

53. I. Bishop, '*Solacia* in *Pearl* and in Letters of Edward III Concerning the Death of his Daughter Joan', *Notes and Queries*, 229 (1984), 454–6.

54. On 'good and bad deaths' see Horrox, 'Purgatory, Plague and Prayer', 95–8.

55. The literature on Chaucer is so extensive that a single note could not begin to do it justice. For an introduction to pilgrimage see Jonathan Sumption, *Pilgrimage: An Image of Medieval Religion* (Totowa, NJ, 1975).

56. Colin Platt, *King Death: The Black Death and its Aftermath in Late-Medieval England* (Toronto, 1996), 138–41. See infra 170.

57. For a consideration of the debate regarding the importance of the plague on the development of macabre artistic images begun by Millard Meiss, *Painting in Florence and Sienna After the Black Death* (Princeton, 1951), see Paul Binski, *Medieval Death: Ritual and Representations* (London, 1996), 126–34; Phillip Lindley, 'The Black Death and English Art. A Debate and Some Assumptions', *The Black Death in England*, eds W.M. Ormrod and Philip Lindley (Stamford, 1996), 125–46. Huizinga saw the all-consuming thought of death in the later middle ages as a basic characteristic of the period not necessarily associated with the plague: *Waning of the Middle Ages*, 140–52.

58. See infra 165–7.

59. B. Windeatt ed., *English Mystics of the Later Middle Ages* (Cambridge, 1994), 1–13.

60. Aberth, *From the Brink*, 155–8.

61. *BPR*, I, 5; R.A. Griffiths, *The Principality of Wales in the Later Middle Ages. The Structure and Personnel of Government: 1, South Wales, 1277–1536* (Cardiff, 1972), 211.

62. GEC, XII, pt. 1, 587. Thirty-nine per cent of parish incumbents in the diocese of York died in the winter of 1348–9. In the years 1344–6, 132 priests had been ordained annually, in the period 1349–51 this rose to 402. D.M. Hadley, *Death in Medieval England: An Archaeology* (Stroud, 2001), 87.

63. John Gower, *Mirour de l'Omme*, trans. William Burton Wilson, rev. Nancy Wilson van Baak (East Lansing (MI), 1992), 268–77, ll. 20089–785; Langland, *Piers the Ploughman*, 27.

64. Aberth, *From the Brink*, 161–4.

65. *The Register of William Bateman, Bishop of Norwich, 1344–55*, I, ed. Phyllis E. Pobst (Woodbridge, 1996), xxx–xxxi.

66. This figure excludes 23 deaths, those of third or fourth holders of the benefice during the plague period. R.A. Davies, 'The Effect of the Black Death on the

Parish Priests of the Medieval Diocese of Coventry and Lichfield', *Historical Research*, 62 (1989), 86–9.

67. Douglas Jones, ed., *The Church in Chester, 1300–1540* [Chetham Society, 3rd ser. 7] (Manchester, 1957), 139. For further discussion of benefice exchange see Benedictow, *Black Death*, 343–5.

68. *Fasti Ecclesiae Anglicanae 1300–1541*, IX (Exeter Diocese), ed. Joyce M. Horn (London, 1964), 15, 33. Other benefice presentations/transfers in the 1360–2 outbreak among the clerks in the prince's retinue included:

William Clobho	All Saints, Wallingford	*BPR*, IV, 292, 406.
Andrew Gerard	Great Henny	*BPR*, IV, 407.
John Houndeswell	South Wooton, Norfolk	*BPR*, IV, 407.
William Burgeis	Croughton Church, Northants. He was presented subsequently to Farndon, Northants, at John Henxteworth's request	*BPR*, IV, 391, 393.
John Boyton	Received letters of presentation to the bishop of Norwich	*BPR*, IV, 391.
John Bondeby	Chilton church	*BPR*, IV, 411.

69. Philip Morgan, 'Of Worms and War: 1380–1558', *Death in England: An Illustrated History*, eds Peter Jupp and Clare Gittings (Manchester, 1999), 120.

Chapter Three

1. Froissart, *Chronicles*, ed. Brereton, 144.
2. Henri Denifle, *La guerre de cent ans et la desolation des églises, monastères et hôpitaux en France* (Paris, 1902), II, 86–95; Françoise Lehoux, *Jean de France, duc de Berri. Sa vie. Son action politique, 1340–1416* (Paris, 1966), I, 57. See also Nicholas Wright, *Knights and Peasants: The Hundred Years War in the French Countryside* (Woodbridge, 1998), 33–4 on differing attitudes to the 1355 campaign. He also notes Alain Chartier's comment that war being fought in France in the early fifteenth century was nothing more than brigandage and public violence.
3. Barber, *Life and Campaigns*, 52.
4. Richard Kaeuper, 'The Societal Role of Chivalry in Romance: Northwestern Europe', *Cambridge Companion to Medieval Romance*, ed. Roberta L. Krueger (Cambridge, 2000), 99.
5. Jean Juvenal des Ursins, cited by John Gillingham, 'Richard I and the Science of War in the Middle Ages', *War and Government in the Middle Ages: Essays in Honour of J.O. Prestwich*, eds John Gillingham and J.C. Holt (Cambridge, 1984), 85.
6. As suggested by Michael Stroud, 'Chivalric Terminology in Late Medieval Literature', *Journal of the History of Ideas*, 37 (1976), 323.
7. Novak, 'Battle-Related Trauma', 90.
8. Maurice Keen, *Chivalry* (New Haven and London, 1984), 221.

9. For a recent historical and historiographical survey see David Crouch, *The Birth of Nobility: Constructing Aristocracy in England and France, 900–1300* (Harlow, 2005), 222–52.

10. See above, Introduction n. 2.

11. Such understanding of the chivalric ethic as I have is dependent to a great extent on their scholarship even if specific references to their works are sparse among the following references. See in particular Richard Barber, *The Knight and Chivalry* (rev. ed. Woodbridge, 1995); Richard Kaeuper, *Chivalry and Violence in Medieval Europe* (Oxford, 1999); Keen, *Chivalry*; M.G.A. Vale, *Chivalry and Warfare: Warfare and Aristocratic Culture in England, France and Burgundy at the End of the Middle Ages* (Athens (Geo), 1981), 1–12.

12. For which see Johan Huizinga, *Homo Ludens: A Study of the Play Element in Culture* (London, 1970), 17–18, which modified some of his earlier arguments and saw chivalry as a restraining and civilising force.

13. For an illuminating discussion of these issues see Crouch, *Birth of Nobility*, 7–28.

14. Anne F. Sutton and Livia Visser-Fuchs, ' "Chevalerie . . . in som partie is worthi forto be commendid, and in some part to ben ammendid": Chivalry and the Yorkist Kings', *St George's Chapel, Windsor, in the Late Middle Ages*, eds Colin Richmond and Eileen Scarff (Windsor, 2001), 108.

15. For example, it is stated in a recent translation note, '*ritterlich*, we render literally as "knightly" rather than "chivalrous", since it most fundamentally connotes a rather violent way of life'. Norbert Elias, *The Civilizing Process: Sociogenic and Psychogenetic Investigations*, ed. and trans. Eric Dunning, Johan Goudsblom and Stephen Mennel (rev. ed., Oxford, 2000), xvii–xviii. Elias' work has been a subject of renewed interest in the fields of chivalry and courtesy over the last several years. See for example Vale, *Princely Court*, 17; Richard Kaeuper, 'Chivalry and the Civilizing Process', *Violence in Medieval Society*, ed. Richard Kaeuper (Woodbridge, 2000), 21–3, 33–4, where he questions Elias' assertions concerning the ability of medieval people to restrain their actions and emotions. Kaeuper argues they showed great concern with formal, ritual behaviour patterns although chivalry itself and the honour culture underpinning it were predicated on demonstrations of prowess and were defended with acts of violence.

16. Kaeuper, 'Societal Role of Chivalry', 99–100.

17. Kaeuper, 'Societal Role of Chivalry', 99.

18. In part because the faith of the knightly order 'had a markedly different tenor and tone' from that of the clerical class, 'it did not hinder them from killing and plundering.' Elias, *Civilizing Process*, 166.

19. G.C. Macauley, ed., *The Works of John Gower, 1330–1408* (Oxford, 1901): *Confessio Amantis*, ll. 3007–10.

20. As observed by Marc Bloch, *La société féodale* (Paris, 1939), *Feudal Society* (2 vols), trans. L.A. Manyon, 2nd ed. (London, 1971); Georges Duby, *A Chivalrous Society*, trans. Cynthia Postan (London, 1977); *idem, Les Trois Ordres ou l'Imaginaire du féodalisme* (Paris, 1978); *idem, The Three Orders: Feudal Society Imagined*, trans. Arthur Goldhammer (Chicago, 1980); Jean Flori, *L'essor de la chevalerie: XIᵉ–XIIᵉ siècles* (Geneva, 1986); *idem, Chevaliers et chevalerie au Moyen Age* (Paris, 1998).

21. Howard Kaminsky, 'Estate, Nobility and the Exhibition of Estate in the Later Middle Ages', *Speculum*, 68 (1993), 701. For further discussion of this incident see Hillay Zmora, *Monarchy, Aristocracy and State in Europe, 1300–1800* (London, 2000), 22–3; Jacques Mourier, 'Nobilitas quid est? Un procès à Tain-l'Hermitage en 1408', *Bibliothèque de l'École des Chartes*, 142 (1984), 255–69. The prohibition against manual labour provides an interesting comment on the character and disposition of Edward II who was famed for engaging in 'unsuitable pastimes'.
22. John Russell Major, *From Renaissance Monarchy to Absolute Monarchy: French Kings, Nobles and Estates* (Baltimore and London, 1994), 58–9. See also Gareth Prosser, '"Decayed Feudalism" and "Royal Clienteles": Royal Office and Magnate Service in the Fifteenth Century', *War, Government and Power in Late Medieval France*, ed. C.T. Allmand (Liverpool, 2000), 180, who argues that even those members of the nobility who made their livings as lawyers and royal officials remained part of a highly militarised group.
23. Kaeuper, *Chivalry and Violence*, 30–3.
24. Tyson, 'Some Thoughts on Four Old French Soldiers' *Lives*', 105–20.
25. Chandos Herald, *Life of the Black Prince*, eds. Pope and Lodge, 135.
26. Guillaume de Lorris et Jean de Meun, *Le Roman de la Rose*, ed. Félix Lecoy (Paris, 1968), I, 251, ll. 8205–8.
27. *BPR*, II, 105; H.J. Hewitt, *The Black Prince's Expedition of 1355–57* (repr., Barnsley, 2004), 192–3; Andrew Galloway, 'The Making of a Social Ethic in Late Medieval England: From Gratitudo to "Kyndenesse"', *Journal of the History of Ideas*, 55 (1994), 366, 368; Keen, *Chivalry*, 171.
28. Nigel Saul, 'A Farewell to Arms? Criticism of Warfare in Late Fourteenth-Century England', *Fourteenth Century England II*, 132–7.
29. See P.R. Coss, 'Cultural Diffusion and Robin Hood', *Past and Present*, 108 (1985); Richmond, 'An Outlaw and Some Peasants', 96–7. The first reference to Robin appears in 1377 but the first surviving ballad, *Robin Hood and the Monk*, dates from about 1450, and the *Gest of Robyn Hode*, appears about 50 years later. Internal evidence however, suggests that, at the latest, it was put together by 1400 and 'there are good reasons for thinking . . . the *Gest* is . . . a product of the first half of the fourteenth century'. Maddicott, 'Birth and Setting of the Ballads of Robin Hood', 276. Ayton suggests a date in or before the 1330s: 'Military Service and the Development of the Robin Hood Legend', 129–30.
30. Richmond, 'An Outlaw and Some Peasants', 92.
31. Kaeuper, 'Societal Role of Chivalry', 97.
32. Christine de Pizan, *Book of the Body Politic*, 59. See also Kaminsky, 'Estate, Nobility and the Exhibition of Estate', 699–700.
33. Nigel Saul, 'Chaucer and Gentility', *Chaucer's England: Literature in Historical Context*, ed. Barbara A. Hanawalt (Minnesota, 1992), 42; Crouch, *Birth of Nobility*, 127; Keen, *Chivalry*, 157–61.
34. Chandos Herald, *Life of the Black Prince*, eds Pope and Lodge, 2, ll. 57–62.
35. Saul, 'Chaucer and Gentility', 41–2; Kaeuper, 'Societal Role of Chivalry', 107.
36. This was predicated on 'adherence to a code of controlled violence in the service of furthering the political ends of a monarch'. David Laguardia, 'On

the Ethos of the Noble Warrior: Blaise de Monluc's Commentaries', *Medievalia et Humanistica*, 26 (1999), 45–61.

37. Saul, 'Chaucer and Gentility', 50–1.
38. Christine de Pizan, *Book of the Body Politic*, 28–9, 95–6.
39. Philippe Contamine concurred – in the thirteenth century at the latest, the French provinces saw a unification of the diverse strata of lay aristocracy which merged into a single group: 'Points de vue sur la chevalerie en France à la fin du moyen âge', *Francia* 4 (1976), 256.
40. Duby, *Chivalrous Society*, 75.
41. For a recent discussion of Duby's contribution see F.L. Cheyette, 'Georges Duby's Mâconnais after Fifty Years: Reading it Then and Now', *Journal of Medieval History*, 28 (2002), 291–317; *idem*, 'Some Reflections on Violence, Reconciliation and the "Feudal Revolution"', *Conflict in Medieval Europe: Changing Perspectives on Society and Culture*, eds Warren C. Brown and Piotr Gorecki (Aldershot, 2003), 243–64.
42. P.R. Coss, *The Lady in Medieval England, 1000–1500* (Stroud, 1998), 37; *idem*, *The Knight in Medieval England, 1000–1400* (Stroud, 1993), 50–2; *idem*, *The Origins of the English Gentry* (Cambridge, 2003), 18, where he questions why England failed to 'develop a caste nobility around the phenomenon of knighthood', cf David Crouch, *The Image of the Aristocracy in Britain, 1100–1300* (London, 1992), 153, who suggests a higher breed of knighthood developed for the upper nobility.
43. Coss, *Origins of the English Gentry*, 239.
44. Christine de Pizan, *Book of the Body Politic*, 50.
45. Christine de Pizan, *Book of Deeds of Arms* is first and foremost a military guide. While there is consideration of just wars (*ibid.*, 14–15), the perils of war and the consideration that a prince should give to the matter prior to setting out on a campaign (18–23), the bulk of the work is concerned with the appointment of military officers (e.g. 23–6), the qualities that they should possess (37–9), the lodging of troops, procedures for marching, crossing natural obstacles, preparations for battle, the arrangement of troops on the battlefield, provisions, advice on storming and defending a fortress, soldiers' pay (153–5), the distribution of booty and similar matters. A section is devoted to the proper use of tricks and subtlety in combat (163–4). A consideration of ransoms, judicial combats and coats-of-arms provides a more 'chivalric' aspect.
46. *The Riverside Chaucer*, ed. Larry D. Benson, 3rd ed. (Oxford, 1988): 'General Prologue', ll. 43–78.
47. Terry Jones, *Chaucer's Knight. A Portrait of a Medieval Mercenary*, rev. ed. (London, 1994); Maurice Keen, 'Chaucer and Chivalry Revisited', *Armies, Chivalry and Warfare*, ed. Strickland, 1–12; *idem*, 'Chaucer's Knight, the English Aristocracy and the Crusade', *English Court Culture in the Later Middle Ages*, eds V.J. Scattergood and J.W. Sherborne (London, 1983), 45–61.
48. K. Fowler, *Medieval Mercenaries. Volume One: The Great Companies* (Oxford, 2001), 44–53, 146ff.
49. Keen, *Chivalry*, 230–1.
50. Cited by Kaeuper, 'Societal Role of Chivalry', 102.
51. Christine de Pizan, *Book of the Body Politic*, 59, 63.

52. In the foreword to his translation of Frontinus' *Stratagems* for Charles VII, Jean de Rouvroy, dean of the faculty of theology in the University of Paris noted, 'more battles ... have been won by ruses and subtleties ... than by greater numbers'. M.G.A. Vale, *Charles VII* (London, 1974), 195.

53. *Life and Campaigns*, ed. Barber, 87.

54. *Froissart: Chronicles*, ed. Brereton, 179.

55. The earl of Pembroke, captured in 1372 at the battle of La Rochelle, was treated very badly by the Spanish. By comparison Thomas Gray was able to compose his *Scalacronica* while in captivity in Scotland. Despite his chivalric reputation Edward III had 100 Scottish prisoners beheaded on the morning after Halidon Hill and his intentions for the burghers of Calais is well known. A. King, ' "According to the custom used in French and Scottish wars": Prisoners and Casualties on the Scottish Marches in the Fourteenth Century', *Journal of Medieval History*, 28 (2002), 271, 276–7, 279–81, 283–4.

56. Barber, *Knight and Chivalry*, 242.

57. Froissart, *Chronicles*, ed. Brereton, 141.

58. For examples of the mantra 'qui plus fait, mieux vault' see Geoffroi de Charny, *The Book of Chivalry*, ed. and trans. R.W. Kaeuper and Elspeth Kennedy (Philadelphia, 1996), 87, 93, 95, 97, 99. Similarly, Chaucer and Dante judged individuals according to their worth although they were not as restrictive in their fields of judgement. Saul, 'Chaucer and Gentility', 49.

59. R. Cazelles, 'La règlementation royale de la guerre privée de St Louis à Charles V et la précarité des ordonnances', *Revue historique de droit français et étranger*, 38 (1960), 530–48.

60. 'In south-west France, the right to declare and wage private war was claimed by the nobility as an inalienable birthright.' M.G.A. Vale, 'Aristocratic Violence: Trial by Battle in the Later Middle Ages', *Violence in Medieval Society*, ed. Kaeuper, 167.

61. Kaeuper, 'Societal Role of Chivalry', 110. Note also Elias, *Civilizing Process*, 169: 'if ... the power of a central authority grows ... the people are forced to live in peace with each other ... Once the monopoly of physical power has passed to central authorities, not every strong man can afford the pleasure of physical attack. This is now reserved to those few legitimized by the central authority.'

62. *The Comedy of Dante Alighieri the Florentine. Cantica I, Hell*, trans. Dorothy L. Sayers (Harmondsworth, 1949), Canto xxxiv, 285–9.

63. *Froissart: Chronicles*, ed. Brereton, 178.

64. Paul Ducourtieux, *Histoire de Limoges* (Limoges, 1925, repr. Marseille, 1975), 53, 59; Barber, *Edward*, 226 and references in n. 23; *idem, Knight and Chivalry*, 240.

65. Bradbury, *Medieval Siege*, 161; Barber, *Edward*, 224–6.

66. Maurice Keen, *The Laws of War in the Late Middle Ages* (London, 1965), 120–1, 124. Keen provides numerous examples of legitimate savagery in siege warfare perpetrated by both English and French commanders in the Hundred Years War.

67. Simon Walker, 'Letters to the Dukes of Lancaster in 1381 and 1399', *EHR*, 106 (1991), 73. Cited by Galloway, 'Making of a Social Ethic', 374, who also

notes the incident of Gaunt being turned away by Henry Percy during the Peasants' Revolt. Gaunt was outraged and forced Percy to make a full apology in parliament. Percy was indebted to Gaunt for various political offices and they were distantly related. Percy later apologised for his 'disnaturesse'.

68. *Froissart: Chronicles*, ed. Brereton, 178.

69. John Gower, *Confessio Amantis*, ed. and trans. Terrence Tiller (Harmondsworth, 1963), 244–5, 248.

70. Mathew Strickland, 'A Law of Arms or a Law of Treason? Conduct in War in Edward I's Campaigns in Scotland, 1296–1307', *Violence in Medieval Society*, ed. Kaeuper, 40. See also *ibid.*, 64–8 for a comparison of Limoges with the 1296 campaign, especially the massacre at Berwick. Interesting parallels can be drawn between the actions of Edward III after the capture of Calais in 1347 with those of his grandfather at Stirling, *ibid.*, 73–5 and Strickland sees the fall of Harfleur to Henry V in 1415 in a similar light. For comments on battle-field mutilation of the aristocracy and the slaying of knights without holding them for ransom see *ibid.*, 43 and n. 21 and for similar consideration of the Hundred Years War, Rogers, 'Military Revolutions', 256–7.

71. Childs, 'Treason in the *Vita Edwardi Secundi*', 180–1, who notes that there are problems with the concept that the increasing harshness with which treason was treated was due to the influence of Roman law since such ideas were known as early as the twelfth century. See also D.A. Carpenter, 'From King John to the First English Duke, 1215–1337', *The House of Lords: A Thousand Years of British Tradition* (London, 1994), 29–35. For a contrary argument see J.G. Bellamy, *The Law of Treason in the Late Middle Ages* (Cambridge, 1970), 1–58; J. Dunbabin, 'Government', *The Cambridge History of Medieval Political Thought c.350–c.1450* (Cambridge, 1988), 492.

72. Cuttler, *Law of Treason*, 15.

73. Julian Pitt-Rivers, 'Honour and Social Status', *Honour and Shame: The Values of Mediterranean Society*, ed. J.G. Peristiany (London, 1965), 37; Knecht, *Valois*, 8.

74. The concept of the *diffidatio* had become increasingly uneasy even by 'Bracton's' time (d. 1268) – he was not the author of the work commonly ascribed to him. A comparison can be made with late twelfth-century tale of Raoul de Cambrai, in which a knight is forced to rebel against his lord, albeit some-what uneasily. 'Bracton' could not accept even the semi-legality of resistance to the king. However, 'Bracton' did not deny that kings were, in some ways, restricted by law and custom. S.J.T. Miller, 'The Position of the King in Bracton and Beaumanoir', *Speculum*, 31 (1956), 293; John Morrow, *History of Political Thought: A Thematic Introduction* (Basingstoke, 1998), 279; Cuttler, *Law of Treason*, 5, 21, 31.

75. *Statutes of the Realm*, I, 319; *English Historical Documents*, IV, 403. For further discussion see Bellamy, *Law of Treason*, 59–101.

76. Sutton and Visser-Fuchs, 'Chivalry and the Yorkist Kings', 122.

77. *Statutes of the Realm*, II, 98–9; *English Historical Documents*, IV, 406; C.D. Ross, 'Forfeiture for Treason in the Reign of Richard II', *EHR*, 71 (1956), 574.

78. Contamine, 'De la puissance aux privileges', 235 n. 2. According to Max Weber, membership of an estate was determined by a specific social estimation of honour on the basis of some quality common to many members and with

the expectation of a specific sort of way of life: *Wirtschaft und Gesellschaft*, 5th ed. (Tübingen, 1976), 534; H.H. Gerth and C. Wright Mills, *From Max Weber: Essays in Sociology* (New York, 1958), 186ff.

79. Chris Given-Wilson, *Chronicles: The Writing of History in Medieval England* (London, 2004), 99–102.

80. Cited by Kaminsky, 'Estate, Nobility and the Exhibition of Estate', 684–709, 695–6.

81. Christine de Pizan, *Book of the Body Politic*, 99, 104–5, 108.

82. Despite the reordering of political society, the concept of the three orders continued to hold sway. John Stafford, bishop of Bath and Wells, in an address to parliament in 1433, used as his text Psalms 71: 3 (*Be thou my strong habitation, whereunto I may continually resort: thou hast given commandment to save me; for thou [art] my rock and my fortress*) to consider the roll of the three estates in the maintenance of peace and justice in the realm. However, he divided them into the lords temporal and spiritual; the gentry; and the people. C.M.D. Crowder, 'Peace and Justice and 1400: A Sketch', *Aspects of Late Medieval Government and Society: Essays Presented to J.R. Lander*, ed. J.G. Rowe (Toronto and London, 1986), 53.

83. Kaminsky, 'Estate, Nobility and the Exhibition of Estate', 689, 691.

84. P.R. Coss, 'The Formation of the English Gentry', *Past and Present*, 147 (1995), 40–1, 53–4.

85. Richmond, 'An Outlaw and Some Peasants', 94–5. See also R.B. Dobson, Review of J.C. Holt, *Robin Hood* (1982), *Northern History*, 19 (1983), 219.

86. Richmond, 'An Outlaw and Some Peasants', 93.

87. Coss, *Origins of the English Gentry*, 240.

88. Coss, *Origins of the English Gentry*, 180, 239.

89. Kaminsky, 'Estate, Nobility and the Exhibition of Estate', 694 n. 49.

90. R. Cazelles, *Société politique, noblesse et couronne sous les règnes de Jean II et Charles V* (Paris, 1982), 60, notes: 'La noblesse des années 1350 est passablement différent de celle des années 1320–1330. Elles s'affirme davantage en tant qu''Etat'. Elles s'est durcie.'

91. Christine de Pizan, *Book of the Body Politic*, 78. Edouard Perroy stated, 'This social group lacked economic homogeneity': 'Social Mobility Among the French Noblesse', *Past and Present*, 21 (1962), 27. He also noted that at least in Forez in the late thirteenth and early fourteenth centuries, 'the bulk of the nobility was, comparatively speaking, very poor'. In a number of cases the mode of life of a lesser noble was 'not very different from that of his tenants', *ibid.*, 29.

92. Maurice Keen, 'Heraldry and Hierarchy, *Orders and Hierarchies in Late Medieval and Renaissance Europe*, ed. Jeffrey Denton (Toronto, 1999), 100.

93. K.B. McFarlane, *The Nobility of Late Medieval England* (Oxford, 1973), 9; Coss, *Origins of the English Gentry*, 239–40.

94. P.R. Coss, 'Identity and the Gentry c.1200–c.1340', *Thirteenth Century England VI*, 49. Coss argues, contrary to a number of other studies, that the formation of the gentry was dependent on the county (and county 'community'). This developed with the growing interaction between the shires and parliament, a process strengthened as a consequence of the baronial movement of the 1250s and 1260s, *ibid.*, 55ff. See also J.R. Maddicott, 'Parliament and the

Constituencies, 1272–1377', *The English Parliament in the Middle Ages*, eds R.G. Davies and J.H. Denton (Manchester, 1981), 61–87; *idem*, 'Edward I and the Lessons of Baronial Reform: Local Government, 1258–80', *Thirteenth Century England I*, eds P.R. Coss and S.D. Lloyd (Woodbridge, 1986), 1–30.

95. See Philip Morgan, 'Making the English Gentry', *Thirteenth Century England V*, eds P.R. Coss and S.D. Lloyd (Woodbridge, 1995), 21–8; C. Carpenter, 'Gentry and Community in Medieval England', *Journal of British Studies*, xxxiii (1994), 340–80.
96. Froissart, *Oeuvres*, ed. Lettenhove VII, 195–6. See Keen, *Chivalry*, 168 for further discussion of this incident. Knighton described Chandos as such with regard to his exploits in 1359: *Knighton's Chronicle*, 171.
97. Coss, 'Formation of the English Gentry', 50.
98. The title 'franklin' became subsumed by those of gentleman and yeoman. Holt, *Robin Hood*, 118–20.
99. Jean Batany, 'Le vocabulaire des catègories sociales chez quelques moralistes français vers 1200', *Ordres et classes*, eds Daniel Roche and Camille Labrousse (Paris, 1973), 62.
100. Hugh Collins, *The Order of the Garter, 1348–1461: Chivalry and Politics in Late Medieval England* (Oxford, 2000), 1.
101. Such organisations may indicate the weakness of feudal ties so that kings and great nobles used chivalry and membership of chivalric orders to tie their vassals more closely to their sides. Major, *Renaissance Monarchy*, 68.
102. Coss, *Knight in Medieval England*, 91, 100.
103. Collins, *Order of the Garter*, 41.
104. They included Richard FitzSimon, who carried his standard, James Audely, Walter Paveley, Henry Eam, Nigel Loryng, Mohun and Wale, the captal de Buch, Bartholomew Burghersh, the younger, John Lord Grey of Rotherfield and Roger Mortimer. The whereabouts of d'Aubrechicourt and Henry Eam are uncertain. The captal de Buch and Grosmont were involved in subsidiary action elsewhere. D'A.J.D. Boulton, *The Knights of the Crown. The Monarchical Orders of Knighthood in Later Medieval Europe, 1325–1520* (Woodbridge, 1987), 127–8.
105. They included John Burley, Lewis Clifford, Thomas Felton, Nicholas Sarnesfield, John Devereux, Peter Courtenay and John Bourchier. J.L. Gillespie, 'Richard II's Knights: Chivalry and Patronage', *Journal of Medieval History*, 13 (1987), 154; Collins, *Order of the Garter*, 44–5, 48–51.
106. Saul, 'Chaucer and Gentility', 44–5.
107. *Urbanus Magnus Danielis Becclesiensis*, ed. J.G. Smyly (Dublin, 1939); A.G. Elliott, 'The Faectus: Or The Art of Courtly Living', *Allegorica*, 2 (1977), 27–57; Robert Bartlett, *England under the Norman and Angevin Kings, 1075–1225* (Oxford, 2000), 579, 582–8; John Gillingham, 'From *Civilitas* to Civility: Codes of Manners in Medieval and Early Modern England', *TRHS*, 6th ser. xii (2002), 272–4.
108. Jonathan Nicholls, *The Matter of Courtesy: Medieval Courtesy Books and the Gawain-Poet* (Woodbridge, 1985), 18–21, 85–102.
109. Elias, *Civilizing Process*, 109–61; Gillingham, 'From *Civilitas* to Civility', 273–4, 276–7; Nicholls, *Matter of Courtesy*, 1, 7, 124.

110. Kaeuper, 'Chivalry and the Civilizing Process', 29.

111. Pitt-Rivers, 'Honour and Social Status', 21. See also *ibid.*, 29: 'The ultimate vindication of honour lies in physical violence.'

112. Froissart, *Oeuvres*, ed. Lettenhove, I, 78; Durant W. Robinson Jr, *A Preface to Chaucer: Studies in Medieval Perspectives* (Princeton, 1962), 456; Nicholls, *Matter of Courtesy*, 48, 155–6 and n. 28. The only extant copy of the *Edwardum*, Bodley MS 425, was made in the first half of the fourteenth century but it is likely to have been in existence for some time prior to this.

113. Gillingham, 'From *Civilitas* to Civility', 275.

114. Kaeuper, 'Chivalry and the Civilizing Process', 30–1.

115. Keen, Chivalry, 117 citing *Chronique de quatre premiers Valois*, 123–5.

116. David Burnley, *Courtliness and Literature in Medieval England* (London, 1998), 46.

117. Charny, *Book of Chivalry*, 191–5.

118. Odile Blanc, 'From Battlefield to Court: The Invention of Fashion in the Fourteenth Century', *Encountering Medieval Textiles and Dress: Objects, Texts, Images*, eds Désirée G. Koslin and Janet E. Snyder (Houndsmill, 2002), 158–9, 163. The author of the *Grandes Chroniques de France* said that the knights wore 'such short clothing that their rumps were barely covered, and so tight they needed help to undress. Others wore garments like women's, gathered at the small of the back, with coudière sleeves and capes with slashed edges'.

119. See for example, Froissart's description of the ladies rescued during the Jacquerie by Gaston Fébus and the captal de Buch at Meaux, and the complaint of Elizabeth de Burgh against Hugh Despenser, the younger, in 1326: *Chroniques*, III, ed. Diller, 144–5; Jennifer Ward, ed. and trans., *Women of the English Nobility and Gentry, 1066–1500* (Manchester, 1995), 116–19; G.A. Holmes, 'A Protest against the Despensers, 1326', *Speculum*, 30 (1955), 207–12.

120. *The Book of the Knight of the Tower*, trans. William Caxton, ed. M.Y. Offord [EETS] (London, 1971), 29, 38–40, 45–6.

121. Werner L. Gundersheimer, 'Renaissance Concepts of Shame and Pocaterra's Dialoghi Della Vergogna', *Renaissance Quarterly*, 47 (1994), 34–56, esp. 35–8, 42–3.

122. *The Book of the Knight of the Tower*, 168–9.

123. H.S. Offler, 'Thomas Bradwardine's "Victory Sermon" in 1346', *Church and Crown in the Fourteenth Century: Studies in European and Political Thought*, ed. A.I. Doyle (Aldershot, 2000), xiii, 13–14 and n. 34.

124. Christine de Pizan, *Treasure of the City of Ladies or, The Book of the Three Virtues*, trans. S. Lawson (Harmondsworth, 1985), 47, 55–6.

125. Kaeuper, *Chivalry and Violence*, 193.

Chapter Four

1. Chandos Herald, *Life of the Black Prince*, eds Pope and Lodge, 48.

2. Mark Girouard, *Life in the English Country House* (New Haven and London, 1978), 30.

3. Linda Paterson, *World of the Troubadours: Medieval Occitan Society, c.1100–c.1300* (Cambridge, 1993), 100, 103–4, 114–19.

4. Froissart, *Chroniques*, ed. Luce, VI, 93, 285; 'A Fourteenth Century Chronicle of the Grey Friars of Lynn', ed. Antonia Gransden, *EHR*, 72 (1957), 271.

5. Charny, *Book of Chivalry*, 87. See Juliet Vale, 'Violence and the Tournament', *Violence in Medieval Society*, ed. Kaeuper, 145–8 for a range of examples of injuries and fatalities incurred in later medieval tournaments. Nonetheless, the lifting of the papal injunction in 1316 may indicate their greater safety.

6. J. Cuvelier, *Chronique de Bertrand Du Guesclin*, ed. E. Charrière (Paris, 1839), I, ll. 11070ff; Barber, *Knight and Chivalry*, 225; Green, *Black Prince*, 45–6.

7. Steven Muhlberger, *Jousts and Tournaments: Charny and the Rules for Chivalric Sport in Fourteenth-Century France* (Union City (Ca.), 2002), 107.

8. Juliet Vale, *Edward III and Chivalry: Chivalrous Society and its Context, 1270–1350* (Woodbridge, 1982), 88–91.

9. *BPR*, IV, 73.

10. *BPR*, IV, 123.

11. In 1334, Edward III fought incognito as *Mons Lionel*, under the banner of Stephen Cosington and Thomas Bradeston at the Dunstable tournament, and at Dartford he competed under William Clinton's banner. Vale, *Edward III and Chivalry*, 68; Richard Barber and J. Barker, *Tournaments, Jousts, Chivalry and Pageants in the Middle Ages* (Woodbridge, 1989), 32; Barker, *Tournament in England*, 95–6, 130.

12. Barber, *Edward*, 154–5.

13. Green, *Black Prince*, 89.

14. Pierre Tucoo-Chala, *Gaston Fébus: un grand prince d'Occident au XIVᵉ siècle* (Pau, 1976), 150; Wulf Arlt, 'Machaut, Guillaume de', *The New Grove Dictionary of Music and Musicians*, ed. S. Sadie (London, 1980), xi, 428–36.

15. *BPR*, IV, 67, 72, 87, 167, 251, 283, 388–9; Nigel Wilkins, 'Music and Poetry at Court: England and France in the Late Middle Ages', *English Court Culture*, eds Scattergood and Sherborne, 195; Barber, *Edward*, 22, 30, 37.

16. John Southworth, *The English Medieval Minstrel* (Woodbridge, 1980), 106–7.

17. Tucoo-Chala, *Gaston Fébus*, 164–93 esp. 164–5, 167–8, 184.

18. *Sir Gawain and the Green Knight*, trans. Brian Stone, 2nd ed. (Harmondsworth, 1975), 64–5, 71–2, 74–6, 79–81, 92; Green, *Black Prince*, 89. See also Orme, *Childhood to Chivalry*, 191–8; Michael Thompson, 'Castles', *A Companion to the Gawain-Poet*, eds Derek Brewer and Jonathan Gibson (Cambridge, 1997), 122–4.

19. Tucoo-Chala, *Gaston Fébus*, 163; John Cummins, *The Hound and the Hawk: The Art of Medieval Hunting* (London, 2001), 4–5, 77, 102, 124, 220.

20. D. Huw Owen, 'Wales and the Marches', *Agrarian History of England and Wales, III*, 103; Davies, *Conquest, Coexistence and Change*, 399–400.

21. The principal stud was at Princes Risborough and others were located at Woking, Byfleet, Wisley (Surrey); Cippenham (Bucks); Somersham (Lincs) – thanks to Michael Jones for pointing out Jean's association with the area; Cottingham (Yorks); Macclesfield (Cheshire); Denbigh (Wales); Beckley (Oxon). Ann Hyland, *The Horse in the Middle Ages* (Stroud, 1999), 71–2.

22. Green, *Battle of Poitiers*, 103–4. The destriers for whom Botetourt had rsponsibility are named in the prince's register. For further discussion of the

importance of horses in a chivalric and military context see Kaeuper, *Chivalry and Violence*, 174.

23. Cummins, *Hound and Hawk*, 86; Green, *Battle of Poitiers*, 123.
24. Hyland, *Horse in the Middle Ages*, 92–4.
25. *BPR*, IV, 111–12.
26. *Knighton's Chronicle*, ed. Martin, 202; Nicholas Orme, 'Medieval Hunting: Fact and Fancy', *Chaucer's England*, ed. Hanawalt, 135.
27. *BPR*, III, 110–11, 115. He retained a vague interest in the estate and between 1369 and 1371 over £100 of repairs were carried out. SC6/772/5-7; R.A. Brown, H.M. Colvin, and A.J. Taylor, *The History of the King's Works: The Middle Ages* (London, 1963), II, 834.
28. Cummins, *Hound and Hawk*, 188–90, 247.
29. 'Bracton' classified thirteenth-century English society as follows: earls, barons, vavasours/magnates, knights, freemen and bondsmen: *Bracton de legibus et consuetudinibus Angliae: Bracton on the Laws and Customs of England*, ed. George E. Woodbine, 4 vols (Oxford, 1968–77), II, 32–3.
30. Grosseteste, *Statuta Familia*, BL Sloane MS 1986 f.193, published, in part by F.J. Furnivall, *The Babees Book: Medieval Manners for the Young etc*, ed. Edith Rickert [EETS] (London, 1908), 328–31; BL Harleian MS 6815 (Orders of service due to a duke, marquis and earl), cited by Girouard, *Life in the English Country House*, 46; C.M. Woolgar, *The Great Household in Late Medieval England* (New Haven and London, 1999), 19; Vale, *Princely Court*, 202–3; Bernard Guenée, *States and Rulers in Later Medieval Europe* (Oxford, 1985), 79.
31. John Russell, 'Boke of Nurture', ed. Furnivall, *The Babees Book*, 192, ll. 1130–2. See also 185–6, ll. 1002–5.
32. Pitt-Rivers, 'Honour and Social Status', 38.
33. See *infra* 30–1; Wright, *Political Poems and Songs*, I, 1ff.; Vale, *Princely Court*, 213–17.
34. Ward, ed., *Women of the English Nobility and Gentry*, 180–1.
35. Frances A. Underhill, 'Elizabeth de Burgh: Connoisseur and Patron', *The Cultural Patronage of Medieval Women*, ed. June Hall McCosh (Athens (Geo), 1996), 271; Jennifer Ward, 'Elizabeth de Burgh, Lady of Clare (d. 1360)', *Medieval London Widows, 1300–1500*, eds Caroline Barron and Anne Sutton (London and Rio Grande, 1994), 29–45.
36. *BPR*, III, 348–9, 393; IV, 16, 49, 51, 504.
37. Woolgar, *Great Household*, 132–3.
38. Elizabeth M. Biebel, 'Pilgrims to Table: Food Consumption in Chaucer's Canterbury Tales', *Food and Eating*, eds Carlin and Rosenthal, 17. Robert le Fisher (1351); and Nicholas Eton (1355) were among several of the keepers of the prince's swans on the Thames and elsewhere. *BPR*, IV, 33, 132.
39. On 18 May 1357 the prince ordered the purchase and swift delivery of royal sweetmeats, white sweetmeats, aniseed, sugar and other items. A horse was to be hired specially to deliver the items which appear to have been part of a recipe. *BPR*, IV, 204.
40. See for example *BPR*, IV, 601, 679.
41. Gower, *Confessio Amantis*, 242.

42. Christopher Dyer, 'English Diet in the Later Middle Ages', *Social Relations and Ideas. Essays in Honour of R.H. Hilton*, eds T.H. Aston, P.R. Coss, Christopher Dyer and Joan Thursk (Cambridge, 1983), 191–6.
43. Constance B. Hieatt and Robin F. Jones, 'Two Anglo-Norman Culinary Collections Edited from British Library Manuscripts Additional 32085 and Royal 12.C.xii', *Speculum*, 61 (1986), 859–60.
44 Green, 'Household and Military Retinue', II, 222; Woolgar, *Great Household*, 130–1, 137.
45. *BPR*, I, 49, 64, 72, 74, 117, 129.
46. Woolgar, *Great Household*, 140–2.
47. P.W. Hammond, *Food and Feast in Medieval England* (Stroud, 1996), 143–9.
48. Thereafter, no meal was to have more than two courses and no course to have more than two sorts of food (served without sauce), except on feast days when there might be three courses. N.B. Harte, 'State Control of Dress and Social Change in Pre-Industrial England', *Trade, Government and Economy in Pre-Industrial England: Essays Presented to F.J. Fisher*, eds D.C. Coleman and A.H. John (London, 1976), 134.
49. Hammond, *Food and Feast*, 126; A.S. Weber, 'Queu du Roi, Roi des Quex: Taillevent and the Profession of Medieval Cooking', *Food and Eating*, eds Carlin and Rosenthal, 145, 151–4.
50. Woolgar, *Great Household*, 175.
51. *Statutes of the Realm*, I, 280–1. The first western European sumptuary legislation was passed in France in 1294 and 'throughout the fourteenth century . . . the control of dress [became] an object of state and city policy throughout European society'. Harte, 'State Control of Dress', 133.
52. Frédérique Lachaud, 'Dress and Social Status in England Before the Sumptuary Laws', *Heraldry, Pageantry, and Social Display in Medieval Europe*, eds P.R. Coss and Maurice Keen (Woodbridge, 2002), 106.
53. *Statutes of the Realm*, I, 380; *Rotuli Parliamentorum*, II, 281–2.
54. Lachaud, 'Dress and Social Status in England Before the Sumptuary Laws', 119.
55. *Riverside Chaucer*, 24–5.
56. V.J. Scattergood, 'Fashion and Morality in the Late Middle Ages', *England in the Fifteenth Century*, ed. Daniel Williams (Woodbridge, 1987), 258. For a summary of the 'vestimentary transformations' of the first half of the fourteenth century in Italy, France, England, Germany and Bohemia see Blanc, 'From Battlefield to Court', 157–9.
57. Charny, *Book of Chivalry*, 189, 191.
58. Harte, 'State Control of Dress', 139–40; Scattergood, 'Fashion and Morality', 270.
59. Horrox, *Black Death*, 133.
60. Cited by Scattergood, 'Fashion and Morality', 265–6.
61. 1 Sept. 1362, *BPR*, IV, 467; Margaret Wade Labarge, *Gascony: England's First Colony, 1204–1453* (London, 1980), 149.
62. Green, *Black Prince*, 89; Emerson, *Black Prince*, 171. For the nature of garments worn and other related comments see Stella M. Newton, *Fashion in the Age of the Black Prince: A Study of the Years 1340–1365* (Woodbridge, 1988);

J.W. Sherborne, 'Aspects of English Court Culture in the Later Fourteenth Century', *English Court Culture*, eds Scattergood and Sherborne, 14–16.

63. Micheline Dupuy, *Le Prince Noir: Edouard seigneur d'Aquitaine* (Paris, 1970), 200.

64. Sekules, 'Philippa of Hainault and her Image', 167; P. Stafford, *Queens, Concubines and Dowagers. The King's Wife in the Early Middle Ages* (Leicester, 1998), 108–9.

65. W.M. Ormrod, '"In Bed with Joan of Kent": The King's Mother and the Peasants' Revolt', *Medieval Women: Texts and Contexts in Late Medieval Britain*, eds J. Wogan Browne *et al.* (Turnhout, 2000), 277–92; Richard Barber, 'Joan, suo jure countess of Kent, and princess of Wales and of Aquitaine [*called* the Fair Maid of Kent] (*c.*1328–1385)', *ODNB*, XXX, 137–9.

66. E.A.R. Brown, 'The Tyranny of a Construct: Feudalism and Historians of Medieval Europe', *American Historical Review*, 79 (1974), 1063–88; Susan Reynolds, *Fiefs and Vassals: The Medieval Evidence Reinterpreted* (Oxford, 1994). See also Edouard Perroy, 'Feudalism or Principalities in Fifteenth-Century France', *BIHR*, 20 (1945), 181–5, who stated over 50 years ago, 'I come to wonder if the word "feudalism" ought not to be discarded once and for all'.

67. Colin Richmond, 'An English Mafia?', *Nottingham Medieval Studies*, xxxvi (1992), 240.

68. This was recognised by William Huse Dunham, Jr, 'The Feudality of Retaining', *Lordship and Community in Medieval Europe*, ed. Frederic L. Cheyette (New York, 1968), 222–39, who believed bastard feudalism was 'a refinement, not a degeneration, of an earlier feudal custom'. *Ibid.*, 222. J.M.W. Bean noted bastard feudalism makes better sense in the light of a history of household lordship: *From Lord to Patron* (Manchester, 1989), 127. The fief-rente was used as early as Henry I's reign and Henry II adopted the method to obtain military service from continental nobles. Various feudal contracts made in the reigns of John and Henry III provide antecedents, if not models, for the indenture system. The change therefore was in the form but not the substance of the contractual principle.

69. Crouch, *Birth of Nobility*, 261–78.

70. Thomas Bisson, 'Medieval Lordship', *Speculum*, 70 (1995), 743–4.

71. D.A. Carpenter, 'The Second Century of English Feudalism', *Past and Present*, 168 (2000), 37–71.

72. J.H. Burns, *Lordship, Kingship and Empire: The Idea of Monarchy, 1400–1525* (Oxford, 1992), 17–19.

73. Chris Given-Wilson, *The Royal Household and the King's Affinity: Service, Politics and Finance in England, 1360–1413* (New Haven and London, 1986), 28. It had included about 150 members under Henry I and grew to a minimum of 363 servants during Edward II's reign.

74. Woolgar, *Great Household*, 10, 14–15.

75. Woolgar, *Great Household*, 46–7. It should be noted, however, that Charles L.H. Coulson, through a number of articles and in his *Castles in Medieval Society: Fortresses in England, France and Ireland in the Central Middle Ages* (Oxford, 2003) has emphasised the residential and decorative elements at the

expense of military features in earlier fortifications and remarks that the homes of nobility and royalty had always been 'public' places.

76. John M. Steane, *The Archaeology of Power: England and Northern Europe AD 800–1600* (Stroud, 2001), 42–3.

77. Shelagh Bond, 'The Medieval Constables of Windsor Castle', *EHR*, 82 (1967), 225–49, esp. 226–8, 234–6, 239, 248.

78. Given-Wilson, *Royal Household*, 34; Mary Whitely, 'The Courts of Edward III and Charles V', *Fourteenth Century England I*, 154–8.

79. Gawain approved of the combination of military strength and domestic comfort at Hautdesert. *Sir Gawain and the Green Knight*, ll. 793–99, cited by Nicholls, *Matter of Courtesy*, 46.

80. Woolgar, *Great Household*, 20.

81. Steane, *Archaeology of Power*, 108–9; Simon Thurley, *Royal Palaces of Tudor England* (New Haven and London, 1993), 8.

82. Woolgar, *Great Household*, 48, 61, 68.

83. Given-Wilson, *Royal Household*, 30–3.

84. Sekules, 'Philippa of Hainault and her Images', 167. See also John Cherry and Neil Stratford, *Westminster Kings and the Medieval Palace of Westminster* [British Museum Occasional Paper 115] (London, 1995), 28–49.

85. John of Joinville, *The Life of St. Louis*, trans. Rene Hague, ed. Natalis De Wailly (New York, 1955), 37–8. The king continued, in theory, to administer justice to his people, although in practice it tended to be delegated to the *maîtres des requêtes de l'hôtel*. Knecht, *Valois*, 15.

86. *The Treatise of Walter de Milemete De nobilitatibus, sapientiis, et prudentiis regum*, ed. M.R. James (Oxford, 1913), 159–86; Fréderique Lachaud, 'Un miroir au prince méconnu: le *De nobilitatibus, sapienciis et prudenciis regum* de Walter Milemete (vers 1326–1327)', *Guerre, pouvoir et noblesse au Moyen Âge: Mélanges en l'honneur de Philippe Contamine*, eds Jacques Paviots et Jacques Verger (Paris, 2000), 401–13.

87. Blanc, 'From Battlefield to Court', 161.

88. *Riverside Chaucer*, 25, ll. 95–100.

89. 'Vineyards were specialist gardens and redolent of status.' Woolgar, *Great Household*, 131.

90. Teresa McLean, *Medieval English Gardens* (London, 1989), 114–16, 267.

91. *BPR*, IV, 36, 91, 237, 363.

92. *BPR*, IV, 51.

93. Survey of Wales conducted by William Emeldon, E163/4/42. The survey of Cornwall showed castles in the duchy had been badly neglected since Earl Edmund's death in 1300: E120/1; P.L. Hull ed., *The Caption of Seisin of the Duchy of Cornwall, 1337* (Devon and Cornwall Record Society, 1971).

94. Launceston's curtain wall was repaired, the great hall was completely re-roofed and a new chamber built. *BPR*, II, 2, 48, 185; Colvin, *History of the King's Works*, II, 693–4. The prince also had Launceston church tower rebuilt: D. Mountfield, *Castles and Castle Towns of Great Britain* (London, 1993), 86. A great deal was spent at Restormel by the prince on repairs following the survey. E120/1/8, 29; E101/461/11; *BPR*, II, 168, 185; Colvin, *History of the King's Works*, II, 805. Tintagel had its roofs re-leaded, stables repaired

and great hall rebuilt with a buttery, pantry and stone-roofed kitchen. Colvin, *History of the King's Works*, II, 846; Andrew Saunders, 'Administrative Buildings and Prisons in the Earldom of Cornwall', *Warriors and Churchmen in the Middle Ages: Essays Presented to Karl Leyser*, ed. Timothy Reuter (London and Rio Grande, 1992), 199–204.

95. Colvin, *History of the King's Works*, II, 562–3. Additional properties included: Lydford castle (Devon) – used mainly as a prison; Mere Castle (Wilts); Cheylesmore manor house (War.); Beckley hunting lodge (Oxon).

96. The prince's wardrobe in London, located between the Old Jewry and Ironmonger Lane, included a great hall, great chamber, chapel, kitchen and storehouse. Between 1355 and 1359 a new chamber and chapel were built, and a roof and porch added to the hall. *BPR*, IV, 150, 236, 285; H.M. Colvin, ed., *The History of the King's Works* (London, 1963), I, 470–1; II, 981–2.

97. E101/470/7; 471/6; Colvin, *History of the King's Works*, I, 537–8.

98. Girouard, *Life in the English Country House*, 33.

99. Given-Wilson, *Royal Household*, 29.

100. Dabernon served at various times also as keeper of the fees, sheriff and constable of Trematon and Tintagel castles and keeper of game on Dartmoor. Skirbek served as havenor, feodary, and constable of Launceston. Green, 'Household and Military Retinue', II, 49–50, 130–1.

101. N.J.G. Pounds, 'The Duchy Palace at Lostwithiel, Cornwall', *Archaeological Journal*, 136 (1979), 205–7.

102. *BPR*, I, 151; IV, 41–2, 48, 62–3, 299, 302, 387, 426, 449, 502, 542, 562.

103. E101/490/3; Colvin, *History of the King's Works*, II, 851.

104. Dawson, *Black Prince's Palace at Kennington*, 10–13.

105. *BPR*, III, 137; IV, 150.

106. *BPR*, III, 247, 250, 311ff., 476; IV, 150, 236, 247–8, 313; Colvin, *History of the King's Works*, II, 967–8; H.E.J. Le Patourel, 'Rural Building in England and Wales', *Agrarian History of England and Wales, III*, 834.

107. Pierre Capra, 'Le séjour du Prince Noir, lieutenant du Roi; à l'archevêché de Bordeaux', *Revue Historique Bordeaux et département de la Gironde*, ns 7 (1958), 241–52. On Burghersh see Green, *Battle of Poitiers*, 104–5; *idem*, *Black Prince*, 53.

108. Pierre Capra, 'L'apogée politique au temps du Prince Noir (1355–1372)', *Bordeaux sous les Rois d'Angleterre*, ed. Yves Renouard (Bordeaux, 1965), 387; Hewitt, *Black Prince's Expedition*, 140; Russell, *English Intervention*, 59.

109. Woolgar, *Great Household*, 15.

110. Given-Wilson, *Royal Household*, 133. I am grateful to Professor Given-Wilson for providing me with the notes on which his calculations were based.

111. BL Cotton Julius C IV ff. 288–91 lists 128 named individuals plus more than 130 further companions, esquires and others. See also David Green, 'The Later Retinue of Edward the Black Prince', *Nottingham Medieval Studies*, xliv (2000), 141–51.

112. Green, 'Household and Military Retinue', 162–70, Table 2 – Annuities for Military Service. See also Philip Morgan, 'Cheshire and the Defence of the Principality of Aquitaine', *Transactions of the Historical Society of Lancashire and Cheshire*, 128 (1978), 144.

113. Sumption, *Trial by Battle*, 540–2. See also J. Delpit, *Collection générale des documents français qui se trouvent en Angleterre* (Paris, 1847), 136–7 (no. 48), 175 (nos. 19, 22), 134–68 (nos. 4, 9, 12, 14, 19, etc.), 176 (nos. 53, 55, 56).

114. E101/38/15, 17–18; Delpit, *Documents Français*, 176; Green, *Black Prince*, 106.

115. Green, 'Household and Military Retinue', II, 15–16.

116. Green, *Battle of Poitiers*, 99–100.

117. Green, 'Household and Military Retinue', II, 32–5; *idem, Battle of Poitiers*, 106–7.

118. David Green, 'Politics and Service with Edward the Black Prince', *Age of Edward III*, 54–5; *idem, Battle of Poitiers*, 126–8.

119. For a more detailed list of officers in the Black Prince's Household see Tout, *Chapters*, V, 431–40.

120. Philip Morgan, 'Felton, Sir Thomas (d. 1381)', *ODNB*, XIX, 286–7; G.F. Beltz, *Memorials of the Most Noble Order of the Garter* (London, 1841), 274–9; Green, *Battle of Poitiers*, 113–14.

121. Green, 'Household and Military Retinue', II, 133–7.

122. Green, 'Household and Military Retinue', II, 95–9.

123. Given-Wilson, *Royal Household*, 211. For differing interpretations of the costruction of the prince's retinue see Bean, *From Lord to Patron*, 14, 17, 58–62; Green, 'Politics and Service', 57–61. For the key military figures among the prince's household bachelors see David Green, 'The Military Personnel of Edward the Black Prince' *Medieval Prosopography*, 21 (2000), 138–9, 151–2.

124. Simon Walker, *The Lancastrian Affinity, 1361–1399* (Oxford, 1990), 18–19; David Green, 'Edward the Black Prince and East Anglia: An Unlikely Association', *Fourteenth Century England III*, 84 n. 9; *idem*, 'Military Personnel', 149–50.

125. Michael Jones and Simon Walker, 'Private Indentures for Life Service in Peace and War', *Camden Miscellany*, xxxii (1994), 80. Warburton was retained for life with two esquires on 6 June 1365 for £40 a year.

126. See Michael Hicks, *Bastard Feudalism* (London, 1995), 43–68; Dunham, 'Feudality of Retaining', 224.

127. Many aspects of the household were not functional but concerned 'religion, display, extravagance, courtesy, gesture and movement, indeed anything that underpinned status and magnificence'. Woolgar, *Great Household*, 16.

128. Vale, *Princely Court*, 220.

129. Woolgar, *Great Household*, 84.

130. John of Salisbury's *Policraticus* was extremely influential and read widely throughout Europe – Denis Foulechat translated it for Charles V. It was not a 'democratic' image: John used Pauline concepts to project an idealised social view in which a prince cared for his subjects and took note of their wishes and suggestions but there was no hint of a right to rebel against him. Guenée, *States and Rulers*, 39; Walter Ullmann, *Medieval Political Thought* (Harmondsworth, 1975), 123–4.

131. The image of the king as *gubernator* of the 'ship of state' is a classical (probably Horatian) idea and can be traced through the medieval period. For the eleventh

century see Wippo, *Gesta Chuonradi II Imperatoris*, ed. H. Bresslau, *MGH Scriptories Rerum Germanicarum* (Hanover, 1915). For the Church described as a ship (*navis*), see I.S. Robinson, 'Church and Papacy', *Cambridge History of Medieval Political Thought*, 255–7. My thanks to Patrick Healy for these references. See also Norma Thompson, *The Ship of State: Statecraft and Politics from Ancient Greece to Democratic America* (New Haven and London, 2001), 167.

132. Harding, *Medieval Law*, 257–9, 265, 271–8.

133. Major, *Renaissance Monarchy*, 65–6; '"Bastard Feudalism" and the Kiss: Changing Social Mores in Late Medieval and Early Modern France', *Journal of Interdisciplinary History*, xvii (1987), 509–35, esp. 515–16.

134. Tucoo-Chala, *Gaston Fébus*, 53–4. Comparisons can also be made with the Montfort dukes of Brittany who, after 1364, were conducting their own experiment in late medieval state building. Jones, 'Late Medieval State', 191.

135. Will Fisher, 'The Renaissance Beard: Masculinity in Early Modern England', *Renaissance Quarterly*, 54 (2001), 155–9. See also Robert Bartlett, 'Hair in the Middle Ages', *TRHS*, 6th ser. iv (1994), 43–60; Herbert Moller, 'The Accelerated Development of Youth: Beard Growth as a Biological Marker', *Comparative Studies in Society and History*, 29 (1987), 752–3.

136. J. Alexander and P. Binski, eds, *Age of Chivalry: Art in Plantagenet England, 1200–1400* (London, 1987), 477–8.

137. Sarah Hanley, *The Lit de Justice of the Kings of France: Constitutional Ideology in Legend, Ritual and Discourse* (Princeton, 1983), 24–5, 17. See also Froissart, *Oeuvres*, ed. Lettenhove, XIV, 10–11, 35–7. For further discussion see E.A.R. Brown and Richard C. Famiglietti, *The Lit de Justice: Semantics, Ceremonial and the Parlement of Paris, 1300–1600* (Sigmaringen, 1993).

138. *Anonimalle Chronicle*, 56: 'Et si fuist il si hauteyn et de si graunt port qil ne mettast de nully et si voldroit soeffrere diverses grauntz seignours del pais qe vendrayent au luy parler, demurrer quartre iours ou cynk avaunt qil dedeigna od eux parlere; et quant ils veindrent en sa presence ils les soeffreit genulere et chaunger les genules une quarter de iour avaunt qil comaunda estere.'

139. See, for comparison with later Valois practice, Vale, *Charles VII*, 194–228.

140. John Taylor, 'Richard II in the Chronicles', *Richard II: The Art of Kingship*, eds A. Goodman and J. Gillespie (Oxford, 1999), 21–2.

141. For a recent treatment of this see Arnd Retemeier, 'Born to be a Tyrant? The Childhood and Education of Richard II', *Fourteenth Century England II*, 147–58, esp. 156–7 on the influence or lack of it of *De Regimine Principum*.

142. Giles wrote, *On Ecclesiastical Power (De ecclesiastica Potestate)* in 1302 during the Franco-papal conflict to prove Boniface VIII's ultimate sovereignty. According to this all sacerdotal and regal powers were located in the pope. Such ideas could, however, be extended for the purposes of secular rulers through Giles' opinions on *dominium* – the right to exercise lordship, the subjection of one man to another. This was obtained through divine grace; it could not be inherited or acquired by conquest but only through baptism and receiving the other sacraments. If conferred properly on a sovereign, lordship had divine sanction. Morrow, *History of Political Thought*, 130–2; Ullmann, *Medieval Political*

Thought, 124–5; Antony Black, *Political Thought in Europe 1250–1450* (Cambridge, 1992), 49–51.

143. Now BN fr. 571.

144. Cambridge University Library MS Ee.2.17 contains a fragment of a French translation of Giles of Rome – *Le livre du gouvernement dez Roys et dex princes* – bound along with Vegetius, *Le livre de chevalerie*. This may have been a gift to Humphrey, duke of Gloucester, from one Robert Roos. It is possible though unlikely that this was a descendant of one of the Black Prince's life retainers and mayor of Bordeaux. If so it would provide another Gascon association with Giles of Rome. William Thorp owned another copy of Giles' work (Oxford, Bodleian Library, MS Bodley 234). A man of the same name was a member of the prince's household in Aquitaine and fought with him in the 1355–6 campaigns. Coincidentally he had links to Robert Roos. A further fourteenth-century copy was in the possession of the house of Bonhommes at Ashridge at the time of the Dissolution. Green, 'Household and Military Retinue', II, 183; C.F. Briggs, *Giles of Rome's De Regimine Principum* (Cambridge, 1999), 55–6, 61–2, 153–4, 166, 170.

145. Michael Bennett, 'Richard II and the Wider Realm', *Richard II*, eds Goodman and Gillespie, 189–90.

146. Walter Ullmann, 'This Realm of England is an Empire', *Journal of Ecclesiastical History*, 30 (1979), 175–203.

147. J.M. Wallace-Hadrill, *The Barbarian West: The Early Middle Ages A.D. 400–1000* (London, 1962), 128. Thanks to Patrick Healy for this reference.

148. For a summary of the significance of the Vulgate, the Church Fathers and Aristotle on the evolution of medieval political thought see Guenée, *States and Rulers*, 37–9; M.S. Kempshall, *The Common Good in Late Medieval Political Thought* (Oxford, 1999), 130–56 (on the influence of Aristotle on Giles of Rome); Black, *Political Thought*, 9–12, 20–1, 77–8; Ullmann, *Medieval Political Thought*, 159–73; Morrow, *History of Political Thought*, 133. It is important to note that rather than introducing new theories into political discourse it is likely that Aristotle was used to bolster existing positions.

149. Offler, 'Bradwardine's "Victory Sermon"', 2–4. It was an argument used by Aquinas and developed by Dante in *De monarchia*: 'What can be done by one man is better done by one man than by several.' Guenée, *States and Rulers*, 67; Morrow, *History of Political Thought*, 132.

150. Arthur Stephen McGrade, 'Somersaulting Sovereignty: A Note on Reciprocal lordship in Wyclif', *Church and Sovereignty*, ed. Wood, 261–8; Harding, *Medieval Law*, 266. According to Bellamy, English kings turned to Roman law rather than Germanic feudal law of mutual fidelity to bolster their positions: *Law of Treason*, 9–14.

151. Burns, *Lordship, Kingship and Empire*, 57.

152. C.M. Barron, 'The Deposition of Richard II', *Politics and Crisis*, eds Taylor and Childs, 145.

153. Nigel Saul, 'The Kingship of Richard II', *Richard II*, eds Goodman and Gillespie, 40.

154. 'The English development from the early thirteenth century onwards showed the preponderance of the feudal function of the king at the expense of his

theocratic function.' Ullmann, *Medieval Political Thought*, 149. Monarchical power to ennoble was particularly evident in France and helped to bolster royal authority. Perroy, *Social Mobility*, 33 and n. 1.

155. Guenée, *States and Rulers*, 39.

156. Jean de Terrevermeille, born *c*.1370 at Nîmes wrote, in about 1418, the *Tractatus*, a work divided into three parts, one being *Contra rebelles suorum regum*. Written in the context of civil war it denounces rebellion, and yet supports the dauphin's action of trying to seize the post of regent. In order to do this Terrevermeille advanced the concept of quasi-hereditary succession. It was essentially a divine right to succeed, yet allowed for the forfeiture of royal authority in the case of a *rex inutilis* such as Charles VI: his power should be transferred to another although he should not be removed from the throne. Burns, *Lordship, Kingship and Empire*, 40–5.

157. In England the feudal contract created a legal bond between lord and vassal. The king therefore was part of the feudal community and this necessitated an element of consent in the governing process. At its most extreme there was the possibility of the *diffidatio*, the repudiation of the contract. This was not applicable to a theocratic kingship because no such contract existed. Ullmann, *Medieval Political Thought*, 147.

158. *Anonimalle Chronicle*, 56; Paterson, *World of the Troubadours*, 68–71, 88, 101–4, 108–10. In England and northern France, beneath the formal contracts of retainer or other ties there was a code of social conduct to govern retaining in practice consisting of traditions, attitudes and convictions. 'The values which governed this politico-military system were hono[u]r and integrity, good faith and the keeping of contracts' supported by mutual advantages to lord and retainer. Such codes and opinions did not necessarily hold sway in the Occitan. Dunham, 'Feudality of Retaining', 227.

159. J. Moisant, *Le Prince Noir en Aquitaine* (Paris, 1894), 112 n. 1; Barber, *Edward*, 181–2, 185.

160. Eleanor C. Lodge, *Gascony Under English Rule* (London, 1926), 101. For details of the concessions made by the prince in return for the tax see *Livre des Bouillons* (Bordeaux, 1867), 172–7; *Le Livre Noir et les Établissements de Dax* (Bordeaux, 1902) [Archives historiques du Département de la Gironde, 37], 369–76 no. xlix.

161. Arlette Higounet-Nadal, *Périgeux au xive et xve siècles* (Bordeaux, 1978), 148.

162. Rymer, III, i, 548; Robert Favreau, 'Comptes de la sénéchausée de Saintonge', *Bibliothèque de l'École des Chartes*, 117 (1959), 76; Pierre Chaplais, 'Some Documents Regarding the Fulfilment and Interpretation of the Treaty of Brétigny', *Camden* 3rd ser. xix (1952), 52–3 and nn. 1, 2. William Seris, for example, became president of the sovereign court and governor of Benon. He returned to the French fold in 1369 and Charles V rewarded him with the office of president of the Parlement of Paris.

163. *Histoire générale de Languedoc*, eds C. Devic et J. Vaissete *et al.* 16 vols (Osnabruck, 1973), X, 1404–6.

164. Childs, 'Treason in the *Vita Edwardi Secundi*', 179; Prestwich, 'Ordinances of 1311', 12.

165. For a discussion of 'political languages' divided into Roman law, feudal customary law, theology, and those influenced by Aristotle and Cicero see Black, 'Political Languages in Late Medieval Europe', 313–28. Many of these were adopted by the author of the *Vita Edwardi Secundi* and employed in his discussion of treason (*lesa magestatis* and *proditio*), kingship (*magestas*) and the 'State' (*res publica*), Childs, 'Treason in the *Vita Edwardi Secundi*', 179–91.

166. Nicholas Perkins, '*Hoccleve's* Regiment of Princes', *Counsel and Constraint* (Cambridge, 2001), 137.

167. Ralph V. Turner, 'The Meaning of Magna Carta since 1215', *History Today*, 53 (2003), 29–35.

168. Dunham and Wood, 'Right to Rule', 744–6; Guenée, *States and Rulers*, 81.

169. Arjo Vanderjagt, '*Qui sa vertu anoblist*'. *The Concepts of noblesse and chose publiques in Burgundian Political Thought* (Groningen, 1981), 48–9, 64, 66; Morrow, *History of Political Thought*, 153.

170. Cecil H. Clough, 'Late Fifteenth-Century English Monarchs Subject to Italian Renaissance Influence', *England and the Continent*, ed. Mitchell, 301–2.

171. Christine de Pizan, *Book of the Body Politic*, 38–9.

172. Froissart, *Chroniques*, X, pt 2, ed. Raynaud, 213. For further discussion see Peter Ainsworth, 'Froissardian Perspectives on Late-Fourteenth-Century Society', *Orders and Hierarchies*, ed. Denton, 56–73.

173. Edouard Perroy, 'Feudalism or Principalities in Fifteenth-Century France', *BIHR*, 20 (1945), 181.

Chapter Five

1. Peter de la Mare, first Speaker of the Commons, at the Good Parliament, 1376, according to Thomas Walsingham, *Chronicon Angliae*.

2. Harding, *Medieval Law*, 252.

3. G.L. Harriss, 'The Formation of Parliament, 1272–1377', *The English Parliament in the Middle Ages*, eds R.G. Davies and J.H. Denton (Manchester, 1981), 42; Gwilym Dodd, 'The Lords, Taxation and the Community of Parliament in the 1370s and Early 1380s', *Parliamentary History*, 20 (2001), 303.

4. Saul, 'A Farewell to Arms?', 131.

5. Valente, 'The Deposition and Abdication of Edward II', 852–81.

6. H.G. Richardson and G.O. Sayles, 'The Earliest Known Official Use of the Term Parliament', *EHR*, 82 (1967), 747–50.

7. Coss, *Origins of the English Gentry*, 125–6; Maddicott, 'Edward I and the Lessons of Baronial Reform', *Thirteenth Century England I*, 30.

8. Harriss, *King, Parliament and Public Finance*, 81, 84. The *Modus* can be found in a number of medieval manuscripts. There were two versions completed in the 1320s, one possibly in or around 1321 (perhaps for the July parliament) and a revision was carried out before 1330. Interest in the *Modus* revived in Richard II's reign and a further copy was made using both earlier versions. John Taylor, 'The Manuscripts of the *Modus Tenendi Parliamentum*', *EHR*, 83 (1968), 676–8, 682.

9. Walter Burley was almost certainly not, as asserted by Harding, the Black Prince's tutor and his relationship to Simon Burley is uncertain: *Medieval Law*, 262–3. Copies of Burley's *Politics* were bound in with Giles of Rome's *De Regimine Principum* in Cambridge University Library, MS Ii.2.8; Pembroke College, MS 158; Oxford, Balliol College, MS 282: Briggs, *Giles of Rome's De Regimine Principum*, 154, 156–7, 165.
10. The legislative activities of Edward I's reign are of particular importance in this regard. See Prestwich, *Edward I*, ch. 10.
11. Pamela Nightingale, 'Knights and Merchants: Trade, Politics and the Gentry in Late Medieval England', *Past and Present*, 169 (2000), 36–7.
12. In a recent study of certain late medieval parliaments S.J. Payling defined a 'lawyer' as 'any MP who was regularly named to the quorum of the peace or served as a clerk of the peace or county coroner; who acted as filacer or attorney in the central courts; who served as a town recorder or clerk; or who is known to have attended an inn or court of chancery'. Using these criteria, in 1395, ten knights of the shire and 29 burgesses can be classified as men of law – some 15 per cent of the Commons: 'The Rise of Lawyers in the Lower House, 1395–1536', *Parchment and People: Parliament in the Middle Ages*, ed. Linda Clark [Parliamentary History, Special Issue, 2004], 104. Thanks to Gwilym Dodd for bringing this to my attention.
13. Coss, *Origins of the English Gentry*, 184.
14. G.L. Harriss, 'Political Society and the Growth of Government in Late Medieval England', *Past and Present*, 138 (1993), 28–57.
15. The methods were (1) A payment to cancel an eyre or a fine to excuse a county from an obligation. This was used most regularly, for example in 1340–1 when there were enquiries into county maladministration. Essex and Norfolk agreed to pay 4,000 marks, and Herefordshire, 3,000 marks. In all instances the fines proved difficult to collect; (2) commissioners were sent to exhort the county community to make a grant; (3) a subsidy was demanded from regional assemblies. W.N. Bryant, 'The Financial Dealings of Edward III with the County Communities, 1330–60', *EHR*, 83 (1968), 760–3. The methods are comparable to those used by the Black Prince to raise money in Cheshire where parliamentary taxation did not pertain.
16. Dodd, 'Lords, Taxation and the Community of Parliament', 289, 292.
17. Michael Prestwich, 'Parliament and the Community of the Realm in Fourteenth-Century England', *Parliament and Community*, eds Art Cosgrove and J.I. McGuire (Belfast, 1983), 14–15.
18. It should be noted there is a major discrepancy between these demands and the statutes enacted in 1341, which has raised suspicion about the authenticity of the 1340 petitions. G.L. Harriss, 'The Commons' Petition of 1340', *EHR*, 78 (1963), 628–9.
19. *Rotuli Parliamentorum*, II, 164–5; *English Historical Documents*, IV, 443.
20. For a strong argument asserting the continuing authority of the monarch in the late medieval parliament see Gwilym Dodd, 'Crown, Magnates and Gentry: The English Parliament, 1369–1421', unpub. D.Phil. thesis (University of York, 1998), esp. 21ff.

21. Cazelles, *Société politique*, 213–29; Henneman, 'Black Death and Royal Taxation',
408–9, 416.

22. W.M. Ormrod, 'The Personal Religion of Edward III', *Speculum*, 64 (1989),
876. While in Low Countries from the later months of 1338 Edward blessed
885 people, touching for the king's evil: Bryce Lyon, 'What were Edward III's
Priorities: the Pleasures of Sports or Charity?', *Revue d'Histoire Ecclésiastique*,
xcii (1997), 130–1.

23. Harding, *Medieval Law*, 255–6, 271–2. French kings consistently demanded
that representatives were sent with sufficient authority to make financial grants.
The king could control the Estates by choosing the date and place of the meetings although he could become dependent upon it in times of crisis. The letters
summoning members to the Estates, although varied in form, explained, if not
explicitly, the issues to be discussed. Claude Soule, *Les Etats Généraux de France
(1302–1789). Etude historique, comparative et doctrinale* (Heule, 1968), 31–2.

24. Henneman, 'Black Death and Royal Taxation', 406.

25. Dodd, 'Lords, Taxation and the Community of Parliament', 287 and n. 5.

26. J.S. Bothwell, *Edward III and the English Peerage: Royal Patronage, Social
Mobility and Political Control in Fourteenth-Century England* (Woodbridge,
2004), 15–27.

27. J.S. Roskell, 'The Problem of the Attendance of the Lords in Medieval
Parliaments', *BIHR*, xxix (1956), 155, 168; J.S. Bothwell, 'Edward III and the
"New Nobility": *Largesse* and Limitation in Fourteenth-Century England', *EHR*,
112 (1997), 1112. The new members of the peerage included such members
of the prince's retinue as: Ralph Stafford (1351); Michael de la Pole (1366);
Richard Stafford (1371); and Guichard d'Angle, earl of Huntingdon (1377).
J. Enoch Powell and Keith Wallis, *The House of Lords in the Later Middle Ages:
A History of the English House of Lords to 1540* (London, 1968), 355, 365, 369,
381. Others with close links to the prince who were regularly summoned to
parliament included members of families such as the Audleys of Helegh, Greys
of Ruthin, Ufford earls of Suffolk, FitzAlans of Arundel and representatives of
the Bohun, Beauchamp, Courtenay, Clinton and Montague families.

28. Scott L. Waugh, *England in the Reign of Edward III* (Cambridge, 1991), 194.

29. *Rotuli Parliamentorum*, III, 347; *English Historical Documents*, IV, 405–6.

30. Coss, 'Identity and the Gentry', 60.

31. Coss, *Origins of the English Gentry*, 184; Black, *Political Thought*, 163–4.

32. Robert Steele, ed., *Three Prose Versions of the Secretum Secretorum* [EETS]
(London, 1898).

33. Perkins, *Hoccleve's Regiment of Princes*, 87.

34. J.R. Maddicott, 'The County Community and the Making of Public Opinion in
Fourteenth-Century England', *TRHS*, 5th ser. xxviii (1978), 27–43.

35. Black, *Political Thought*, 166.

36. Judith Ferster, *Fictions of Advice: The Literature and Politics of Counsel in Late
Medieval England* (Philadelphia, 1996), 19–23.

37. Walsingham, whose account was based on the Lancastrian deposition articles,
recorded that in 1398 Richard II tried to usurp some of parliament's powers
and rewrote the parliamentary rolls to disguise this. The deposition articles pay
much attention to the king's rejection of counsel. Both Lydgate and the author of

Richard the Redeless attributed Richard's fall to evil or cursed counsel. Perkins, *Hoccleve's Regiment of Princes*, 62–3, 65.

38. *Rotuli Parliamentorum*, III, 415; *English Historical Documents*, IV, 415.
39. W.M. Ormrod, *Political Life in Medieval England, 1300–1450* (Basingstoke, 1995), 33; J.P. Genet, 'Political Theory and Local Communities in Later Medieval France and England', *The Crown and Local Communities in France and England in the Fifteenth Century*, eds J.R.L. Highfield and Robin Jeffs (Gloucester, 1981), 19.
40. I made this claim before, rather baldly and badly, and was rightly taken to task for it. It was pointed out 'it would have been difficult for the heir to the throne *not* to be a political animal' and reference was made to the prince's insensitive actions in the Welsh marches and attempts to make the Church contribute more to the war effort in the 1370s. Chris Given-Wilson and Michael Prestwich, 'Introduction', *Age of Edward III*, 2.
41. *BPR*, IV, 44; H.G. Richardson and G.O. Sayles, 'The Parliaments of Edward III', *BIHR*, viii (1930), 65–7; Delachenal, *Charles V*, II, 54.
42. *Eulogium Historiarum*, ed. F.S. Haydon (London, 1858–63), III, 337–9. It is unlikely that the events happened as described or that they happened in 1374. Archbishop Whittelsey's participation would not have been possible due to a terminal illness. J.I. Catto redates the council to 1373, soon after Pentecost: 'An Alleged Great Council of 1374', *EHR*, 82 (1967), 764–71; Diana Wood, 'Rule from Europe? Four English Views of Papal Authority in the Fourteenth Century', *England and the Continent*, ed. Mitchell, 107.
43. Harriss, 'Formation of Parliament, 1272–1377', 58.
44. Thomas Walsingham, *The St Albans Chronicle. The Chronicle Maiora of Thomas Walsingham, I, 1376–1394*, ed. and trans. John Taylor, Wendy Childs and Leslie Watkiss (Oxford, 2003), 12; G.A. Holmes, *The Good Parliament* (Oxford, 1975), 134–5, 137–8.
45. *Rotuli Parliamentorum*, II, 321. Walsingham suggests Lyons failed with his attempt to bribe the prince to offset the threat of execution: Walsingham; *St Albans Chronicle*, 19.
46. B. Wilkinson, *The Chancery under Edward III* (Manchester, 1929), 125.
47. The brothers exchanged gifts after the end of the principality on 23 Nov. 1372, 24 Dec. 1372, 13 Apr. 1373 and on 8 Jan. 1375 the prince was given 'le couvercle ove un pomel esnamillez de noir ove plume d'esterych'. S. Armitage-Smith, *John of Gaunt's Register, I* (Camden Society, 3rd ser. xx, 1911), 96, 112–13, 191–3, 278.
48. J. Dahmus, *William Courtenay, Archbisop of Canterbury, 1381–1396* (Philadelphia, 1966), 23.
49. See, for example, Packe, *Edward III*, 291–2.
50. Walsingham, *St Albans Chronicle*, 13. This is supported by Malvern's continuation of the Polychronicon: *Polychronicon Ranulphi Higden monachi Cestrensis; together with the English translations of John Trevisa and of an unknown writer of the fifteenth century*, ed. J.R. Lumby (London, 1882), VIII, 386.
51. By contrast with the Lancastrian Affinity, MPs who served in the prince's retinue were drawn from a wide geographical area and represented at least 21 of the 36 counties who returned members. Green, 'Politics and Service', 63–4; W.M. Ormrod, *The Reign of Edward III* (New Haven and London, 1990), 208–9.

52. Maddicott, 'Parliament and the Constituencies', 74. On the independence or otherwise of the Commons in parliament see K.B. McFarlane, 'Parliament and Bastard Feudalism' *TRHS* 4th ser. xxvi (1944), 53–79; *idem, Nobility*, 279–97; H.G. Richardson, 'The Commons and Medieval Politics', *TRHS*, 4th ser. xxviii (1946), 21–45; and with particular regard to the 1376 assembly, Holmes, *Good Parliament*, 134–9.

53. *Rotuli Parliamentorum*, II, 136, 238, 257, 277, 286, 333.

54. Gaunt had as few as three and as many as 13 MPs in every parliament from 1372 to 1397 (five or six in the 1370s, seven or eight in the 1380s and between ten and 13 in the 1390s): Walker, *Lancastrian Affinity*, 148–9, 196, 237–40.

55. *Anonimalle Chronicle*, 79–80.

56. Doris Rayner, 'The Forms and Machinery of the "Commune Petition" in the Fourteenth Century Part 1', *EHR*, 56 (1941), 198–233; 'Part 2', 549–70; Harriss, 'Formation of Parliament', 50–1. See also Maddicott, 'Parliament and the Constituencies', 76–7; H.G. Richardson and G.O. Sayles, 'The Parliaments of Edward III', pt. 2, *BIHR*, ix (1931), 3–4; W.R. Jones, 'The English Church and Royal Propaganda During the Hundred Years War', *Journal of British Studies*, 19 (1979), 24–5 and n. 35.

57. The prince retained or had had close associations with, among others, the following royal justices: William Shareshull, chief justice of the King's Bench; John Stonor, chief justice of the Common Bench; Henry Green, king's justice. Some of these men, along with others such as the prince's servants, John Wingfield and Robert Eleford, also undertook *oyer* and *terminer* commissions instigated at the prince's request. The prince's *register* provides numerous examples of pardons given following military service with him, particularly after the Poitiers expedition.

58. They included: William Shareshull, the chief lawyer on the prince's council; his junior, Richard Willoughby; Roger Hillary, another legal advisor to the council and chief justice of Common Pleas; Richard Talbot, who fought at Poitiers and was deputy-justice of South Wales; Thomas Bradeston, another military companion who fought at Poitiers and served as justice of South Wales and constable of Carmarthen; Ralph, earl of Stafford, brother of Richard, one of the prince's closest military and administrative servants; and Henry Green, a member of the prince's council. For further discussion see Green, 'Politics and Service', 62–5; *idem*, 'Black Prince and East Anglia', 94–5, nn. 60–2.

59. *Rotuli Parliamentorum*, II, 269–70; Chris Given-Wilson, 'Purveyance for the Royal Household, 1362–1413', *BIHR*, 56 (1983), 145; *idem, Royal Household*, 111–13; Leonard E. Boyle, 'William of Pagula and the Speculum Regis Edwardi III', *Mediaeval Studies*, 32 (1970), 329–36.

60. Nigel Saul, *Richard II* (New Haven and London, 1997), 20–1.

61. It was described in the *Anonimalle Chronicle*, the Brut and the Continuation of the Polychronicon. There is also Langland's story of the rat parliament in B text of Piers Plowman. John Taylor, 'The Good Parliament and its Sources', *Politics and Crisis*, eds Taylor and Childs, 81–4; Gwilym Dodd, 'A Parliament Full of Rats? Piers Plowman and the Good Parliament of 1376', *Historical Research*, 79 (2006), 21–49. My thanks to the author for showing me a copy of this in advance of publication. A sermon preached by Bishop Brinton in the course of

the parliament was also recorded. *Sermons of Thomas Brinton, Bishop of Rochester (1373–1389)*, ed. Sister Mary Aquinas Devlin, 2 vols (Camden Soc. 3rd ser, 1954), I, xxiv–xxvi; II, 315–21.

62. Arvanigian, 'A Lancastrian Polity?', 138; Taylor, 'Good Parliament and its Sources', 82–4.

63. According to Walsingham these were the bishops of Norwich, Rochester, Carlisle and London – William Courtenay (1375–81), who became archbishop of Canterbury (1381–96). The prince assisted Courtenay in his early career and the link between the two men was such that Richard II had him buried near Edward in Canterbury. According to the *Anonimalle Chronicle*, John Harewell, the bishop of Bath and Wells, and an executor of the prince's will, was part of the committee. According to the parliament roll, Adam Hoghton, another close associate of the Black Prince and bishop of St Davids (1361–89) was involved.

   The barons (forming an inter-communing committee) were Henry Percy, Richard Stafford (who was a key member of the prince's household), Guy Brian (who had very close links to the royal family), and Roger Beauchamp (Henry Scrope, according to parliament roll).

   The peers were Edmund Mortimer, earl of March; Thomas Beauchamp, earl of Warwick; William Ufford, earl of Suffolk; and Hugh, earl of Stafford. Many of these had family links to the prince and Stafford was closely associated with him. Walsingham, *St Albans Chronicle*, 3–5.

64. *Anonimalle Chronicle*, 80–1, 84; Dodd, 'Lords, Taxation and the Community of Parliament', 305–6 and n. 110.

65. Michael Bennett, 'Edward III's Entail and the Succession to the Crown, 1376–1471', *EHR*, 113 (1998), 580–607; Walsingham, *St Albans Chronicle*, lxi–iii, 38–40, 54, 68–70; Froissart, *Chroniques*, ed. Diller, IV, 355.

66. Dodd, 'Crown, Magnates and Gentry', 21ff. provides an important corrrective to any exaggeration of the development of the power of the Commmons.

67. Michael Clanchy, 'Does Writing Construct the State?', *Journal of Historical Sociology*, 15 (2002), 68–9; Rees Davies, 'The State: the Tyranny of a Concept?', *ibid.*, 71–4; Colin Richmond, 'When/What was the English State: the Latter Midddle Ages', *ibid.*, 75–6, 79, 80, 84–85 – 'the expulsion of the Jews in 1290 is certain proof of the existence of the English state'. Susan Reynolds, 'There were States in Medieval Europe: A Response to Rees Davies', *Journal of Historical Sociology*, 16 (2003), 550–2.

Chapter Six

1. 'Mais je sui ore poeuvres et cheitifs. Parfond en la terre gis. Ma grande beauté est tut alee. Ma char est tut gasté.' Diana Tyson, 'The Epitaph of the Black Prince', *Medium Aevum*, 46 (1977), 98–104. The earliest known version of the text is the *Disciplina Clericalis* of Petrus Alphonsi, d. 1110. It is a variant of the *Siste viator* theme.

2. Colin Richmond, 'Religion', *Fifteenth-Century Attitudes*, ed. Rosemary Horrox (Cambridge, 1994), 195; R.N. Swanson, *Church and Society in Late Medieval England* (Oxford, 1989), 267. As Paul Binski says, the prince's effigy is that of a warrior, youthful and vigorous but the epitaph tells a truer story, not only of

the inevitability of death but of the slow decline that marked his last years: *Medieval Death*, 77, 97, 147. For a translation of the text of the will see Harvey, *Black Prince and his Age*, 160–5.

3. Sophie Oosterwijk, 'Of Corpses, Constables and Kings: The *Danse Macabre* in Late Medieval and Renaissance Culture', *Journal of the British Archaeological Association*, 157 (2004), 62–7.
4. Horrox, 'Purgatory, Plague and Prayer', 93–4; Platt, *King Death*, 151; Binski, *Medieval Death*, 135.
5. Andrew Martindale, 'The Knights and the Bed of Stones: A Learned Confusion of the Fourteenth Century', *Journal of the British Archaeological Association*, cxlii (1989), 66–74.
6. Some of the best examples are the Cobham memorials at Cobham (Kent) and Lingfield (Surrey) for which see Nigel Saul, *Death, Art, and Memory in Medieval England: The Cobham Family and their Monuments, 1300–1500* (Oxford, 2001).
7. The emaciated *transi* was popular in England, the worm motif was common in France, and snakes and frogs were most notable on *transi* from Germany and Austria. Kathleen Cohen, *Metamorphosis of a Death Symbol: The Transi Tomb in the Late Middle Ages and the Renaissance* (Berkeley, 1973), 2.
8. See infra 67.
9. The lower epitaph reads: 'I was a pauper born, then to primate here raised, now I am cut down and served up for worms . . . behold my grave. Whoever you may be who will pass by, I ask for your remembrance, you who will be like me after you die: horrible in all things, dust, worms, vile flesh.' Binski, *Medieval Death*, 143. See also R.B. Dobson, 'Two Ecclesiastical Patrons: Archbishop Henry Chichele of Canterbury (1414–43) and Bishop Richard Fox of Winchester (1501–28)', *Gothic: Art for England 1400–1547*, eds Richard Marks and Paul Williamson (London, 2003), 234–6; Cohen, *Metamorphosis of a Death Symbol*, 4, 15–16.
10. Marjorie M. Malvern, 'An Earnest "monyscyon" and "thinge delectabyll" Realized Verbally and Visually in "A Disputacion betwyx the body and wormes", a Middle English Poem Inspired by Tomb Art and Northern Spirituality', *Viator*, 13 (1982), 417, 419–21.
11. John Lydgate, *The Daunce of Death*, ed. Florence Warren [EETS] (London, 1931), 74.
12. Malvern, 'An earnest "monyscyon"', 436.
13. Green, *Black Prince*, 12.
14. Samantha Riches, *St George: Hero, Martyr and Myth* (Stroud, 2000), 104–7, 117–18; C.T. Allmand, 'Les Saints Anglais et la Monarchie Anglaise au bas Moyen Âge', *Saint-Denis et la royauté: Études offertes à Bernard Guenée*, eds Françoise Autrand, Claude Gauvartd et Jean-Marie Moeglin (Paris, 1999), 751–6.
15. *Life and Campaigns*, 128.
16. Barber, *Edward*, 240.
17. Margaret Aston, 'Popular Religious Movements in the Middle Ages', *Faith and Fire* (London, 1993), 2.
18. For example, 900 masses were ordered by Edward III to be said for his brother, John of Eltham. See Ormrod, *Edward III*, 60, 153 who states this was not the result of guilty conscience for an alleged murder as alleged by the Scottish

writer John Fordun. See also Tom Beaumont-James, 'John of Eltham, History and Story: Abusive International Discourse in Late Medieval England, France and Scotland', *Fourteenth Century England II*, 67–9.

19. 'Whether or not the chantry chapel related to the *locus classicus* of ideas of late medieval anxiety, the Black Death of 1347–51, is very much a matter of opinion.' Binski, *Medieval Death*, 121. He notes that the chantry provided a range of responses to dealing with the afterlife that evolved well before the plague but the need for their construction may have been encouraged by a wish to reinforce social boundaries in the context of the post-plague redistribution of wealth.

20. Eamon Duffy, 'Late Medieval Religion', *Gothic: Art for England, 1400–1547*, 56–67.

21. Swanson, *Church and Society*, 255; Hamilton, *Religion in the Medieval West*, 122.

22. Finberg, *Tavistock Abbey*, 18; M. Webster, 'John Dabernon and his Will', *Devon and Cornwall Notes and Queries*, 36 (1989), 178.

23. *BPR*, III, 344, 361–3; *Knighton's Chronicle*, 122; Booth and Carr, *Account of Master John de Brunham*, 149; John Harvey, *The Black Prince and his Age* (London, 1976), 76.

24. See infra 66.

25. 3 Mar. 1362, 19 Feb. 1363, *BPR*, IV, 423, 462, 488.

26. BL Eg.Ch 2130.

27. Robert W. Dunning, 'The West-Country Carthusians', *Religious Belief and Ecclesiastical Careers in Late Medieval England*, ed. Christopher Harper-Bill (Woodbridge, 1991), 37.

28. Walter Mauny's interest in the order may have been prompted by his association with Grosmont and Gaunt who both had dealings with Beauvale priory (Notts) and he was assisted with the foundation costs by the bishop of London, Michael Northburgh, who left £2,000 to the London Carthusians in his will of 1361. See J.I. Catto, 'Religion and the English Nobility in the Later Fourteenth Century', *History and Imagination: Essays in honour of H.R. Trevor-*Roper, eds Hugh Lloyd-Jones, Valerie Pearl and Blair Worden (London, 1981), 52; David Knowles and W.F. Grimes, *Charterhouse: The Foundation in the Light of Recent Discoveries* (London, 1954), 6, 27; Jonathan Sumption, 'Mauny, Sir Walter (*c.*1310–1372)', *ODNB*, XXXVII, 445–8; William F. Taylor, *The Charterhouse of London* (London, 1912), 3, 17; W. Hope St John, *History of the London Charterhouse* (London, 1925), 6. William Lord Latimer and Peter Veel were others among the prince's acquaintances who were patrons of the Carthusian order or who requested their prayers. Saul, *Richard II*, 298 n. 13.

29. Catto, 'Religion and the English Nobility', 46–7; Michael Jones, 'Knolles, Sir Robert (d. 1407)', *ODNB*, XXXI, 952–7.

30. F.H. Crossley, 'Chronological Data of Churches of Cheshire', *Transactions of the Lancashire and Cheshire Antiquarian Society*, lvii (1943–4), 88; Kenneth Fowler, 'Calveley, Sir Hugh (d. 1394)', *ODNB*, IX, 565–8.

31. Colin Richmond, 'Religion and the Fifteenth-Century Gentleman', *Church, Politics and Patronage*, ed. R.B. Dobson (Gloucester, 1984), 198–203.

32. James G. Clarke, 'Selling the Holy Places: Monastic Efforts to Win Back the People in Fifteenth-Century England', *Social Attitudes and Political Structures in the Fifteenth Century*, ed. Tim Thornton (Stroud, 2000), 15–17, 22,

24–5, 28; *idem*, 'Mare, Thomas de la (*c*.1309–1396)', *ODNB*, XXXVI, 620–2. For membership of the St Albans confraternity see BL Cotton Nero D VII, ff. 129ra–130rb.

33. The struggle between Philippe IV and Boniface VIII drew England into its orbit through the 1296 papal bull, *Clericos Laicos*, that forbade clerics from contributing to secular taxation. This was revised by *Esti de Statu* in 1297, which allowed for such taxation during periods of emergency, and certainly established the primacy of royal authority over the English church. Later, the Franco-papal rivalry may have ameliorated relations between Edward I and Boniface VIII, who had been critical of English activities in Scotland.

34. Francesco Petrarcha, 'Against a Detractor of Italy', *Invectives*, ed. and trans. David Marsh (Cambridge, (Mass.), 2003), 445. See also *Petrarch's Lyric Poems: The Rime Sparse and Other Lyrics*, ed. and trans. Robert M. Dunning (Cambridge, (Mass.), 1976), poems 136–8; Morris Bishop, *Petrarch and his World* (London, 1964), 311ff.

35. Wood, 'Rule from Europe?', 97.

36. Giles of Rome ascribed the origin of all lordship to God and in turn to his representative the pope who held *plenitudo potestatis*. Wyclif linked *dominum* and grace but saw the king as the only divinely appointed medium through which God's power was communicated. Burns, *Lordship, Kingship and Empire*, 25–6.

37. Cary J. Nederman, *Community and Consent: The Secular Political Theory of Marsiglio of Padua's Defensor Pacis* (London, 1995); Harding, *Medieval Law*, 262; Ullmann, *Medieval Political Thought*, 200–14; Wood, 'Rule from Europe?', 98–102.

38. Stephen E. Lahey, *Philosophy and Politics in the Thought of John Wyclif* (Cambridge, 2003), 26; On FitzRalph see Katherine Walsh, *A Fourteenth Century Scholar and Primate: Richard FitzRalph in Oxford, Armagh and Avignon* (Oxford, 1981); *idem*, 'Fitzralph , Richard (b. before 1300, d. 1360)', *ODNB*, IXX, 917–22; Aubrey Gwynn, 'The Sermon Diary of Richard FitzRalph', *Proceedings of the Royal Irish Academy*, xliv (1937), section c, 1–59. My thanks to Niav Gallagher for sharing her thoughts on this matter with me.

39. Lahey, *Philosophy and Politics*, 108. On *De civili domino* and Wyclif's other works on lordship see *ibid.*, 110–38.

40. Wood, 'Rule from Europe?', 102–10, 112.

41. Emmanuel Le Roy Ladurie, *Montaillou: Cathars and Catholics in a French Village, 1294–1324*, trans. Barbara Bray (Harmondsworth, 1978), 231, 234–5, 239.

42. Swanson, *Church and Society*, 330–1, 333–5.

43. Michael Wilks, 'Wyclif and Hus as Leaders of Religious Protest Movements', *Schism, Heresy and Protest* [SCH, 9] ed. Derek Baker (Cambridge, 1972), 115–16, 118–19, 124.

44. The names of the Lollard Knights were crudely erased from Woodstock's copy of Walsingham's Short Chronicle (MS Bodley 316), possibly by Thomas himself. He was closely acquainted with those named and owned a Wycliffite Bible. A vernacular Lollard dialogue between a friar and a secular clerk is also dedicated to him (Trinity College Dublin MS 244). *Knighton's Chronicle*, 294 and n. 1; Jill C. Havens, 'A Curious Erasure in Walsingham's Short Chronicle and the Politics

of Heresy', *Fourteenth Century England II*, 97, 100, 103–5; J.A.F. Thomson, *The Transformation of Medieval England, 1370–1529* (Harlow, 1983), 356–7.

45. Geoffrey Martin, 'Knighton's Lollards', *Lollardy and Gentry in the Later Middle Ages*, eds Margaret Aston and Colin Richmond (Stroud, 1997), 36.

46. Margaret Aston and Colin Richmond, 'Introduction', *Lollardy and Gentry*, 2, 7.

47. Michael Wilks, 'Royal Priesthood: The Origins of Lollardy', *Wyclif: Political Ideas and Practice. Papers by Michael Wilks* (Exeter, 2000), 110.

48. Wilks, 'Wyclif and Hus', 110.

49. Wilks, 'Wyclif and Hus', 125–7; Margaret Aston, 'Wycliffe and the Vernacular', *Faith and Fire*, 36–49.

50. Alistair Dunn, *The Great Rising of 1381* (Stroud, 2002), 62; *Knighton's Chronicle*, 243; R.B. Dobson, *The Peasants' Revolt of 1381* (London, 1970), 373.

51. J.I. Catto, 'The Religious Identity of the Followers of Wyclif', *The Medieval Church: Universities, Heresy and the Religious Life* [SCH Subsidia 11], eds Peter Biller and R.B. Dobson (Woodbridge, 1999), 145–7; K.B. McFarlane, *Lancastrian Kings and Lollard Knights* (Oxford, 1972), 148–9.

52. Saul, *Richard II*, 9, 297–8 and n. 13.

53. Havens, 'A Curious Erasure', 95–6; Peter Fleming, 'Clifford, Sir Lewis (*c*.1330–1404)', *ODNB*, XII, 101–2.

54. McFarlane, *Lancastrian Kings*, 165, 207–26; J.I. Catto, 'Sir William Beauchamp between Chivalry and Lollardy', *The Ideals and Practices of Medieval Knighthood III*, eds C. Harper-Bill and R. Harvey (Woodbridge, 1990), 39–48; W.T. Waugh, 'The Lollard Knights', *Scottish Historical Review*, xi (1913–14), 58, 64, 75–6.

55. N.H. Nicolas, ed., *Testamenta Vetusta*, 2 vols (London, 1826), I, 14–15. Braybroke was related to Joan and in 1363 she had petitioned the pope on his behalf for a canonry and prebendary of York: *Calendar of Papal Letters, Petitions, I*, 397.

56. See V.J. Scattergood, ed., *The Works of Sir John Clanvowe* (Cambridge, 1975). He also wrote *The Boke of Cupide, God of Loue*, a romantic, lyrical piece, 'a courtier's frippery'. Swanson, *Church and Society*, 33; John M. Bowers, 'Three Readings of *The Knight's Tale*: Sir John Clanvowe, Geoffrey Chaucer, and James I of Scotland', *Journal of Medieval and Early Modern Studies*, 34 (2004), 279–87.

57. Binski, *Medieval Death*, 133. On problems in using wills to identify Lollards see Catto, 'Fellows and Helpers', 156–9; J.A.F. Thomson, 'Knightly Piety and the Margins of Lollardy', *Lollardy and Gentry*, 95–6.

58. Wilks, 'Royal Priesthood', 106. See also Siegrid Düll, Anthony Luttrell, and Maurice Keen, 'Faithful unto Death: The Tomb Slab of Sir William Neville and Sir John Clanvowe, Constantinople 1391', *Antiquaries Journal* 71 (1991), 174–90; McFarlane, *Lancastrian Kings*, 162, 164–5; Waugh, 'Lollard Knights', 58–63; Charles Kightly, 'Lollard Knights (*act. c*.1380–*c*.1414)', *ODNB*, XXXIV, 333–4.

59. Green, 'Household and Military Retinue', II, 232.

60. Green, 'Household and Military Retinue', II, 241–4.

61. *CPR, 1377–81*, 234.

62. J.A.F. Thomson, 'Orthodox Religion and the Origins of Lollardy', *History*, 74 (1989), 44–8.

63. McFarlane, *Lancastrian Kings*, 166; *GEC*, I, 24–6.

64. E403/551; *Annales Ricardi Secundi et Henrici Quarti*, ed. J. de Trokelowe, *Chronica et Annales* [Rolls Ser.], ed. H.T. Riley (London, 1866), 183; Anne Hudson, *The Premature Reformation: Wycliffite Texts and Lollard History* (Oxford, 1988), 89–90. On Clifford see *ibid.*, 291–2; Margaret Aston, *Lollards and Reformers: Images and Literacy in Late Medieval Religion* (London, 1984), 98 n. 117.

65. Wilks, 'Royal Priesthood', 110.

66. Maurice Keen, 'The Influence of Wyclif', *Wyclif in his Times*, ed. Anthony Kenny (Oxford, 1986), 129.

67. A. Tuck, 'Carthusian Monks and Lollard Knights: Religious Attitudes at the Court of Richard II', *Studies in the Age of Chaucer, Proceedings I: Reconstructing Chaucer*, eds Paul Strohm and T.J. Heffernan (Knoxville (TN), 1984), 153.

68. Catto, 'Fellows and Helpers', 145, 154ff. and n. 35.

69. *CCR, 1381–5*, 553.

70. BL Cotton Caligula D III f. 102; C61/79/12; 81/6; 83/10; *GEC*, IV, 144–50.

71. Havens, 'A Curious Erasure', 105.

72. 13 Sept. 1372, *Calendar of Papal Registers, Letters IV*, 182.

73. 30 Jan. 1380, *CPR, 1377–81*, 590.

74. *Calendar of Papal Letters, Petitions, I*, 521–2. Joan also made a personal petition for plenary remission of sins at the hour of her own death, 3 Apr. 1366, *ibid.*, 525. On 17 June 1373 she was granted permission to choose her own confessor with authority to commute her vows, with the exception of those of continence and pilgrimage, *Calendar of Papal Registers, Letters IV*, 185.

75. *Calendar of Papal Letters, Petitions, I*, 456.

76. BL Sloane 282 ff. 5–17b.

77. Michael F. Bailey, 'From Sorcery to Witchcraft: Clerical Conceptions of Magic in the Later Middle Ages', *Speculum*, 76 (2001), 964–9, 971–2, 986–7.

Conclusion

1. Shakespeare, *Richard II*, 2:3 l. 103.

2. Walsingham, *St Albans Chronicle*, 37–8.

3. Walsingham, *St Albans Chronicle*, 37.

4. In 1386 Richard was reminded of his father and grandfather who 'laboured all their lives, with endless exertions in heat, in cold, in tireless endeavour to conquer the kingdom of France.' *Knighton's Chronicle*, 359.

5. Given-Wilson, *Chronicles*, 99–111.

6. Ramon Lull, *The Book of the Order of Chyvalry*, trans. William Caxton, ed. A.T.P. Byles (London, 1926), 84.

7. Barber, *Knight and Chivalry*, 149.

8. George Huppert, *After the Black Death: A Social History of Early Modern Europe* (Indianapolis, 1986), 57, 65. In just the same way that the chivalric romances had glamorised violence and brutality so too did the Robin ballads composed for yeomen. On violence in the Robin ballads see A.J. Pollard, 'Idealising Criminality: Robin Hood in the Fifteenth Century', *Pragmatic Utopias: Ideas and Communities, 1200–1630*, eds Rosemary Horrox and Sarah Rees Jones (Cambridge, 2001), 158–61.

9. Barker, *Tournament in England*, 184; Huizinga, *Waning of the Middle Ages*, 272.
10. Cummins, *Hound and Hawk*, 104–7, 135. Early commentaries on Psalm 80 construe the boar as a devil or his agent or make an association with the Gaderene swine.
11. Chandos Herald, *Life of the Black Prince*, eds Pope and Lodge, 7, ll. 236–9. See Kaeuper, *Chivalry and Violence*, 181–2 for further discussion of chivalric destruction and violation of people and property.
12. Le Baker, *Chronicon*, 152; Lesley A. Coote, *Prophecy and Public Affairs in Later Medieval England* (York, 2000), 130–3, 143.
13. Coote, *Prophecy and Public Affairs*, 30–1, 124, 127–8, 141, 144.
14. Devlin, 'Sermons of Thomas Brinton', I, 74–9; II, 354–7.
15. Walsingham, *St Albans Chronicle*, 33.
16. Walsingham, *St Albans Chronicle*, 35–6. Gilbert, as the prince's candidate, served as bishop of Bangor and later became bishop of St David's: *Fasti Ecclesiae Anglicanae 1300–1541*, II (Hereford Diocese), ed. Joyce M. Horn (London, 1962), 2; Davies, *Conquest, Coexistence and Change*, 398. Such a process fits within fairly conventional rituals. During the *Ordo Visitandi* a priest would hold a crucifix before the dying person, to comfort and drive away evil sprits that lay in wait for the soul. He would then ask seven questions – the questioning was intended to ensure the Devil could not take advantage of any sins or incorrect beliefs and also because any unconfessed sins would be made public at the Last Judgement: Christopher Daniell, *Death and Burial in Medieval England, 1066–1550* (London, 1997), 36.
17. *History of William Marshal*, II, ed. A.J. Holden, trans. S. Gregory and David Crouch (London, 2004), ll. 17885ff.
18. Horrox, 'Purgatory, Plague and Prayer', 96.
19. A.G. Rigg, 'Propaganda of the Hundred Years War: Poems on the Battles of Crécy and Durham (1346): A Critical Edition', *Traditio*, 54 (1999), 174–5; Offler, 'Bradwardine's Victory Sermon', 6, 11–12, 16. The sermon attributed the triumphs of 1346 in France and Scotland as well as elsewhere throughout Edward's reign directly to divine intervention and support for England. The flower of Scottish knighthood was said to have been defeated by a very ordinary group of Englishmen – a statement which, no doubt, would not have sat too happily with the members of the de la Zouche, Percy, Mowbray and Neville families who fought at Neville's Cross.

20.
> *Francia, feminea, pharisea, vigoris ydea,*
> *Linxea, viperea, vulpine, lupina, Medea,*
> *Callida, sirena, crudelis, acerba, superba,*
> *Es fellis plena, mel dans; latet anguis in herba.*
> *Sub duce Philippo Valeys, cognomina lippo*

. . . by comparison with . . .

> *Tercius Edwardus, aper Anglicus et leopardus,*
> *Rex tuus est verus, veniens tibi dente severus:*
>   Rigg, 'Propaganda', 177.

21. Wood, 'Rule from Europe', 112.
22. Norman Housley, '*Pro deo et patria mori*: Sanctified Patriotism in Europe, 1400–1600', *War and Competition Between States*, ed. Philippe Contamine (Oxford, 2000), 221–8, esp. 221–2.
23. *English Historical Documents*, IV, 1194–5, 1212–13.
24. Jones, 'Late Medieval State', 119.
25. Dyer, *Making a Living in the Middle Ages*, 228.
26. Jones, 'Late Medieval State', 123.
27. Davies, *Conquest, Coexistence and Change*, 403.
28. Hatcher, *Rural Economy*, 116–19.
29. *Knighton's Chronicle*, 199.

BIBLIOGRAPHY

Manuscript Sources

British Library
Cotton Caligula D III
Cotton Galba E III
Cotton Julius C IV
Cotton Nero D VII
Egerton Charters 2130
Harleian MS 6815
Sloane MS 1986

National Archives, Public Record Office (Kew, London)
C47	Chancery Miscellanea
C61	Gascon Rolls
CHES	Palatinate of Chester
E30	Exchequer: Diplomatic
E101	Exchequer: Accounts Various
E120	Exchequer: King's Remembrancer: The Caption of Seisin of the Duchy of Cornwall
E163	Exchequer: King's Remembrancer: Miscellanea
E371	Exchequer: Lord Treasurer's Remembrancer: Originalia Rolls
E403	Exchequer: Issue Rolls
SC1	Ancient Correspondence
SC6	Ministers' and Receivers' Accounts
SC7	Special Collections: Papal Bulls
SC12	Special Collections: Rentals and Surveys, Portfolios

Printed Sources

'A Fourteenth-Century Chronicle of the Grey Friars of Lynn', ed. Antonia Gransden, *EHR*, 72 (1957), 270–78.
'A Letter of Edward the Black Prince Describing the Battle of Nájera in 1367', ed. A.E. Prince, *EHR*, 41 (1926), 415–18.
Annales Ricardi Secundi et Henrici Quarti, ed. J. de Trokelowe, *Chronica et Annales*, ed. H.T. Riley [Rolls Ser.] (London, 1866).
Anonimalle Chronicle, 1333–1381, ed. V.H. Galbraith (Manchester, 1927).
Archives administratives de la ville de Reims, ed. Pierre Varin (Paris, 1848).

Armitage-Smith, S., ed., *John of Gaunt's Register, I* (Camden Society, 3rd ser. xx, 1911).

Avesbury, Robert of, *De gestis mirabilibus regis Edwardi Tertii*, ed. E.M. Thompson. [Rolls Ser.] (London, 1889).

Barber, Richard, ed. and trans., *The Life and Campaigns of the Black Prince* (London, 1979).

Bel, Jean Le, *Chronique*, ed., J. Viard et E. Déprez, 2 vols (Paris, 1904).

Bernard of Clairvaux, 'In Praise of the New Knighthood', trans. Conrad Greenia, *Treatises III, The Works of Bernard of Clairvaux*, vol. 7, Cistercian Fathers Series 19 (Kalamazoo (MI), 1977), 127–67.

Bonet, Honoré, *The Tree of Battles of Honoré Bonet*, trans. G.W. Coopland (Liverpool, 1949).

Book of the Knight of the Tower, trans. William Caxton, ed. M.Y. Offord [EETS] (London, 1971).

Booth, P.H.W. and Carr, A.D., eds, *Account of Master John de Burnham the younger, Chamberlain of Chester, of the Revenues of the Counties of Chester and Flint, Michaelmas 1361 to Michaelmas 1362* [Record Society of Lancashire and Cheshire, 125] (Manchester, 1991).

Bracton de legibus et consuetudinibus Angliae: Bracton on the Laws and Customs of England, ed. George E. Woodbine, 4 vols (Oxford, 1968–77).

Brinton, Thomas, *The Sermons of Thomas Brinton, Bishop of Rochester (1373–1389)*, ed. Sister Mary Aquinas Devlin, 2 vols, Camden Society (3rd ser. viii, 1954).

Calendar of Papal Letters, Petitions.

Calendar of Papal Registers.

Chandos Herald, *La Vie du Prince Noir by Chandos Herald*, ed. Diana Tyson (Tübingen, 1975).

Chandos Herald, *The Life of the Black Prince*, ed. and trans. E. Lodge and M.K. Pope (Oxford, 1910).

Charny, Geoffroi de, *Jousts and Tournaments: Charny and the Rules for Chivalric Sport in Fourteenth-Century France*, ed. and trans. Steven Muhlberger (Union City (Ca.), 2002).

Charny, Geoffroi de, *The Book of Chivalry*, ed. and trans. R.W. Kaeuper and Elspeth Kennedy (Philadelphia, 1996).

Chartularies of St. Mary's Abbey. Dublin and the Register of its House at Dunbrody; and Annals of Ireland, ed. J.T. Gilbert, 2 vols (London, 1884–6).

Chaucer, Geoffrey, *The Riverside Chaucer*, ed. Larry D. Benson, 3rd ed. (Oxford, 1988).

Chronicon Galfridi le Baker de Swynebroke, ed. E.M. Thompson (Oxford, 1889).

Chronique des quatre premiers Valois, 1327–1393, ed. S. Luce (Paris, 1862).

Clanvowe, John, *The Works of Sir John Clanvowe*, ed. V.J. Scattergood (Cambridge, 1975).

Cuvelier, *Chronique de Bertrand du Guesclin*, ed. E. Charrière (Paris, 1839).

De Eucharistica Tractatus Maior: Accedit Tractatus de Eucharistica et Poenitentia sive De Confessione, ed. J. Loserth (London, 1892, repr. 1966).

De Veritate Sacre Scripturae, ed. Rudolf Buddenseig, 3 vols (London, 1905).

Delpit, J., *Collection générale des documents français qui se trouvent en Angleterre* (Paris, 1847).

English Historical Documents, III, ed. Harry Rothwell (London, 1975).

English Historical Documents, IV, 1327–1485, ed. A.R. Myers (London, 1969).

Eulogium Historiarum, ed. F.S. Haydon (London, 1858–63).

Froissart, Jean, *Chroniques*, eds S. Luce, G. Raynaud et L. Mirot, 15 vols (Paris, 1869–1975).

Froissart, Jean, *Chroniques. Le Manuscript d'Amiens*, 5 vols, ed. Georges T. Diller (Geneva, 1991–8).

Froissart, Jean, *Froissart: Chronicles*, ed. and trans. Geoffrey Brereton (Harmondsworth, 1978).

Froissart, Jean, *Oeuvres*, ed. Kervyn de Lettenhove, 26 vols (Brussels, 1867–77).

Furnivall, Frederick J., ed., *The Babees Book, The Bokes of Nurture of Hugh Rhodes and John Russell, etc.* [EETS] (London, 1868; repr. New York, 1969).

Furnivall, F.J., ed., *The Babees Book: Medieval Manners for the Young etc*, ed. Edith Rickert [EETS] (London, 1908).

Gower, John, *Confessio Amantis*, ed. and trans. Terrence Tiller (Harmondsworth, 1963).

Gower, John, *Mirour de l'Omme*, trans. William Burton Wilson, rev. Nancy Wilson van Baak (East Lansing (MI), 1992).

Gower, John, *The Works of John Gower, 1330–1408*, ed. G.C. Macauley (Oxford, 1901).

Henry of Grosmont, Duke of Lancaster, *Le Livre de Seyntz Medicines (1354)*, ed. E.J. Arnould (Oxford, 1940).

Higden, Ranulf, *Polychronicon Ranulphi Higden monachi Cestrensis; together with the English translations of John Trevisa and of an unknown writer of the fifteenth century*, ed. J.R. Lumby (London, 1882).

Histoire générale de Languedoc, eds C. Devic and J. Vaissete *et al.* 16 vols (Osnabruck, 1973).

Hull, P.L., ed., *The Caption of Seisin of the Duchy of Cornwall, 1337* (Devon and Cornwall Record Society, 1971).

Joinville, John of, *The Life of St. Louis*, trans. Rene Hague, ed. Natalis De Wailly (New York, 1955).

Jones, Michael and Simon Walker, eds, 'Private Indentures for Life Service in Peace and War', *Camden Miscellany*, xxxii (1994), 1–190.

King Arthur's Death: The Alliterative Morte Arthure *and Stanzaic* Le Morte Arthur, trans. Brian Stone (Harmondsworth, 1988).

Knighton, Henry, *Knighton's Chronicle 1337–1396*, ed. G. Martin (Oxford, 1995).

'La bataille de Nájera: le communiqué du Prince Noir', ed. Eugene Déprez, '*Revue Historique*, cxxxvi (1921), 37–52.

'Lanercost Chronicle', ed. and trans. H. Maxwell, *Scottish Historical Review*, 6–10 (1909–13).

Langland, William, *Piers the Ploughman*, trans. J.F. Goodridge (Harmondsworth, rev. ed. 1982), 27.

Le livre de chasse de Gaston Phébus, trad. fr. Robert et A. Bossuat (Paris, 1931).

Le Livre Noir et les Établissements de Dax [Archives historiques du Département de la Gironde, 37] (Bordeaux, 1902).

Livre des Bouillons (Bordeaux, 1867).

Lorris, Guillaume de, et Meun, Jean de, *Le Roman de la Rose*, ed. Félix Lecoy (Paris, 1968).

Lull, Ramon, *The Book of the Order of Chyvalry*, trans. William Caxton, ed. A.T.P. Byles (London, 1926).

Lydgate, John, *The Daunce of Death*, ed. Florence Warren [EETS] (London, 1931).

Machaut, Guillaume de, *La prise d'Alixandre (The Taking of Alexandria)* ed. and trans. R. Barton Palmer (New York and London, 2002).

Machiavelli, Niccolò, *The Prince*, trans. George Bull (Harmondsworth, 2003), Ch. xvii.

Marsilius of Padua, *Writings on the Empire: Defensor Minor and De Translatione Imperii*, ed. C.J. Nederman (Cambridge, 1993).

Milemete, Walter de, *The Treatise of Walter de Milemete. De nobilitatibus, sapientiis, et prudentiis regum*, ed. M.R. James (Oxford, 1913).

Monahan, A.P., *John of Paris, On Royal and Papal Power, A Translation with Introduction of the De Potestate Regia et Papali of John of Paris* (New York, 1974).

Murimuth, Adam, *Continuatio Chronicarum*, ed. E.M. Thompson (London, 1889).

Petrarcha, Francesco, *Invectives*, ed. and trans. David Marsh (Cambridge (Mass.), 2003).

Petrarcha, Francesco, *Petrarch's Lyric Poems: The Rime Sparse and Other Lyrics*, ed. and trans. Robert M. Dunning (Cambridge, (Mass.), 1976).

Phébus, Gaston, *Le livre de la chasse. Ms. fr. 616 de la Bibliothèque Nationale de Paris*, eds Marcel Thomas et François Avril, 1986 (Graz, 1976).

Pichon, Jérôme and Vicaire, Georges, *Le viander de Guillaume Tirel dit Taillevent* (Paris, 1892).

Pizan, Christine de, *The Book of Deeds of Arms and of Chivalry*, trans. Sumner Willard, ed. Charity Cannon Willard (Pennsylvania, 1999).

Pizan, Christine de, *The Book of the Body Politic*, ed. and trans. Kate L. Forhan (Cambridge, 1994).

Pizan, Christine de, *Treasure of the City of Ladies or, The Book of the Three Virtues*, trans. S. Lawson (Harmondsworth, 1985).

Pizan, Christine de, *Le livre des fais et bonnes meurs du sage roy Charles V*, 2 vols, ed. S. Solente (Paris, 1936–1940).

Pobst, Phyllis E., ed., *The Register of William Bateman, Bishop of Norwich, 1344–55* (Woodbridge, 1996).

Rotuli Parliamentorum II, ed. J Strachey *et al.* (London, 1783).

Sir Gawain and the Green Knight, trans. Brian Stone, 2nd ed. (Harmondsworth, 1975).

'Song of the Husbandmen' and 'Song against the King's Taxes', *Thomas Wright's Political Songs of England: From the Reign of John to that of Edward II*, ed. Peter Coss (Cambridge, 1996), 149–52, 182–6.

Statutes of the Realm, ed. A Luders *et al.* 11 vols (London, 1810–28).

Steele, Robert, ed., *Three Prose Versions of the Secretum Secretorum* [EETS] (London, 1898).

Testamenta Vetusta, ed. N.H. Nicolas, 2 vols (London, 1826).

Usk, Adam, *Chronicle of Adam Usk, 1377–1421*, ed. and trans. Chris Given-Wilson (Oxford, 1997).

Villani, Giovanni, *Historia Universalis*, ed. L.A. Muratori (*Rerum Italicarum Scriptores*, xiii, 1728).

Vita Edwardi Secundi, ed. N. Denholm-Young (London, 1957).

Walsingham, Thomas, *The St Albans Chronicle. The Chronica Maiora of Thomas Walsingham, I, 1376–1394*, ed. and trans. John Taylor, Wendy Childs and Leslie Watkiss (Oxford, 2003).

Westminster Chronicle, 1381–1394, ed. and trans. L.C. Hector and B. Harvey (Oxford, 1982).

Wippo, *Gesta Chuonradi II Imperatoris*, ed. H. Bresslau, *MGH Scriptores Rerum Germanicarum* (Hanover, 1915).

Wright, T., ed., *Political Poems and Songs Relating to English History*, 2 vols (London, 1859–61).

Wrottesley, G., ed., *Crécy and Calais from the Public Records* (Collections for a History of Staffordshire edited by the William Salt Archaeological Society, xviii).

Wyclif, John, *De Civili Domino*, eds R.L. Poole and J. Loserth, 4 vols (London, 1885–1904).

Wyclif, John, *De Officio Regis*, eds Alfred W. Pollard and Charles Sayle (London, 1887).

Wynnere and Wastoure, ed. Stephanie Trigg [EETS] (Oxford, 1990).

Secondary Sources

Aberth, John *From the Brink of the Apocalypse* (New York and London, 2001).

Ainsworth, Peter, 'Froissardian Perspectives on Late-Fourteenth-Century Society', *Orders and Hierarchies in Late Medieval and Renaissance Europe*, ed. Jeffrey Denton (Toronto, 1999), 56–73.

Alexander, J. and Binski, P., eds, *Age of Chivalry: Art in Plantagenet England, 1200–1400* (London, 1987).

Allmand, C.T., 'Fifteenth-Century Versions of Vegetius', *De Re Militari*', *Armies, Chivalry and Warfare* in Medieval Britain and France, ed. Mathew Strickland (Stamford, 1988), 30–45.

Allmand, C.T., *The Hundred Years War: England and France at War, c.1300–c.1450* (Cambridge, 1988).

Allmand, C.T., 'Les Saints Anglais et la Monarchie Anglaise au bas Moyen Âge', *Saint-Denis et la royauté: Études offertes à Bernard Guenée*, ed. Françoise Autrand, Claude Gauvartd et Jean-Marie Moeglin (Paris, 1999), 751–6.

Arvanigian, Mark, 'A Lancastrian Polity? John of Gaunt, John Neville and the War with France, 1368–88', *Fourteenth Century England III*, ed. W.M. Ormrod (Woodbridge, 2004), 121–42.

Aston, Margaret, 'Huizinga's Harvest: England and the *Waning of the Middle Ages*', *Medievalia et Humanistica*, 9 (1979), 1–24.

Aston, Margaret, *Faith and Fire* (London, 1993).

Aston, Margaret, *Lollards and Reformers: Images and Literacy in Late Medieval Religion* (London, 1984).

Aubrey Gwynn, 'The Sermon Diary of Richard FitzRalph', *Proceedings of the Royal Irish Academy*, xliv (1937), section c, 1–59.

Autrand, Françoise, 'La déconfiture. La bataille de Poitiers (1356) à travers quelques texts française des XIVe et XVe siècles', *Guerre et société en France, en Angleterre et en Bourgogne XIVe–XVe siècles*, eds Philippe Contamine, Charles Giry-Deloison et Maurice Keen (Lille, 1991), 93–121.

Ayton, Andrew, 'Military Service and the Development of the Robin Hood Legend in the Fourteenth Century', *Nottingham Medieval Studies*, xxxvi (1992), 126–47.

Ayton, Andrew, 'English Armies in the Fourteenth Century', *Arms, Armies and Fortifications in the Hundred Years War*, eds Anne Curry and M. Hughes (Woodbridge, 1994), 21–38.

Ayton, Andrew, 'The English Army and the Normandy Campaign of 1346', *England and Normandy in the Middle Ages*, ed. David Bates and Anne Curry (London, 1994), 253–68.

Ayton, Andrew, *Knights and Warhorses: Military Service and the English Aristocracy under Edward III* (Woodbridge, 1994).

Ayton, Andrew, 'Arms, Armour and Horses, *Medieval Warfare: A History*, ed. Maurice Keen (Oxford, 1999), 186–208.

Ayton, Andrew, 'Sir Thomas Ughtred and the Edwardian Military Revolution', *The Age of Edward III* , ed. J.S. Bothwell (York, 2001), 107–32.

Ayton, Andrew and Preston, Philip, eds, *The Battle of Crécy, 1346* (Woodbridge, 2005).

Ayton, Andrew and Price, J.L., 'Introduction: The Military Revolution from a Medieval Perspective', *The Medieval Military Revolution: State, Society and Military Change in Medieval and Early Modern Europe*, eds Andrew Ayton and J.L. Price (London, 1995), 1–22.

Bailey, Michael F., 'From Sorcery to Witchcraft: Clerical Conceptions of Magic in the Later Middle Ages', *Speculum*, 76 (2001), 960–90.

Barber, Richard, *Edward Prince of Wales and Aquitaine* (Woodbridge, 1978).

Barber, Richard, *The Knight and Chivalry*, rev. ed. (Woodbridge, 1995).

Barber, Richard and Barker, J., *Tournaments, Jousts, Chivalry and Pageants in the Middle Ages* (Woodbridge, 1989).

Barker, Juliet, *The Tournament in England, 1100–1400* (Woodbridge, 1986).

Barron, C.M., 'The Deposition of Richard II', *Politics and Crisis in Fourteenth-Century England*, eds W.R. Childs and J. Taylor (Gloucester, 1990), 132–49.

Bartlett, Robert, 'Hair in the Middle Ages', *TRHS*, 6th ser. iv (1994), 43–60.

Bartlett, Robert, *England under the Norman and Angevin Kings, 1075–1225* (Oxford, 2000).

Bates, David and Curry, Anne, eds, *England and Normandy in the Middle Ages* (London, 1994).

Bean, J.M.W., *From Lord to Patron* (Manchester, 1989).

Beaumont-James, Tom, 'John of Eltham, History and Story: Abusive International Discourse in Late Medieval England, France and Scotland', *Fourteenth Century England II*, ed. Chris Given-Wilson (Woodbridge, 2002), 63–80.

Bellamy, J.G., *The Law of Treason in the Late Middle Ages* (Cambridge, 1970).

Beltz, G.F., *Memorials of the Most Noble Order of the Garter* (London, 1841).

Benedictow, Ole J., *The Black Death, 1346–1353: The Complete History* (Woodbridge, 2004).

Bennett, Mathew, 'The Development of Battle Tactics in the Hundred Years War', *Arms, Armies and Fortifications in the Hundred Years War*, eds Anne Curry and M. Hughes (Woodbridge, 1994), 1–20.

Bennett, Mathew, 'The Medieval Warhorse Reconsidered', *Medieval Knighthood V*, eds Stephen Church and Ruth Harvey (Woodbridge, 1995), 19–40.

Bennett, Mathew, 'The Myth of Military Supremacy of Knightly Cavalry', *Armies, Chivalry and Warfare in Medieval Britain and France: Proceedings of the 1995 Harlaxton Symposium*, ed. Matthew Strickland (Stamford, 1998), 304–16.

Bennett, Michael, 'Edward III's Entail and the Succession to the Crown, 1376–1471', *EHR*, 113 (1998), 580–607.

Bennett, Michael, 'Richard II and the Wider Realm', *Richard II: The Art of Kingship*, eds A. Goodman and J. Gillespie (Oxford, 1999), 187–204.

Beriac-Lainé, Françoise and Given-Wilson, Chris, 'Edward III's Prisoners of War: The Battle of Poitiers and its Context', *EHR*, 116 (2001), 802–33.

Beriac-Lainé, Françoise and Given-Wilson, Chris, *Les prisonniers de la bataille de Poitiers* (Paris, 2002).

Biebel, Elizabeth M., 'Pilgrims to Table: Food Consumption in Chaucer's Canterbury Tales', *Food and Eating in Medieval Europe*, eds Martha Carlin and Joel T. Rosenthal (London and Rio Grande, 1998), 15–26.

Binski, Paul, *Medieval Death: Ritual and Representations* (London, 1996).

Bishop, I., '*Solacia* in *Pearl* and in Letters of Edward III Concerning the Death of his Daughter Joan', *Notes and Queries*, 229 (1984), 454–6.

Bishop, Morris, *Petrarch and his World* (London, 1964).

Bisson, Thomas, 'Medieval Lordship', *Speculum*, 70 (1995), 743–59.

Black, Anthony, 'Political Languages in Late Medieval Europe', *The Church and Sovereignty, c.590–1918* [SCH Subsidia 9], ed. Diana Wood (Oxford, 1991), 313–28.

Black, Anthony, *Political Thought in Europe, 1250–1450* (Cambridge, 1992).

Black, Jeremy, *A Military Revolution? Military Change and European Society, 1550–1800* (Basingstoke, 1991).

Blanc, Odile, 'From Battlefield to Court: The Invention of Fashion in the Fourteenth Century', *Encountering Medieval Textiles and Dress: Objects,*

Texts, Images, eds Désirée G. Koslin and Janet E. Snyder (Houndsmill, 2002), 157–72.

Bond, Shelagh, 'The Medieval Constables of Windsor Castle', *EHR*, 82 (1967), 225–49.

Booth, P.H.W., 'Taxation and Public Order: Cheshire in 1353', *Northern History*, 12 (1976), 16–31.

Booth, P.H.W., *The Financial Administration of the Lordship and County of Cheshire, 1272–1377* (Chetham Society, 3rd ser. xviii, 1981).

Bostick, Curtis V., *The Antichrist and the Lollards: Apocalypticism in Late Medieval and Reformation England* (Leiden, 1998).

Bothwell, J.S., 'Edward III and the "New Nobility": *Largesse* and Limitation in Fourteenth-Century England', *EHR*, 112 (1997), 1111–40.

Bothwell, J.S., ed., *The Age of Edward III* (York, 2001).

Bothwell, J.S., *Edward III and the English Peerage: Royal Patronage, Social Mobility and Political Control in Fourteenth-Century England* (Woodbridge, 2004).

Boulton, D'A.J.D., *The Knights of the Crown. The Monarchical Orders of Knighthood in Later Medieval Europe, 1325–1520* (Woodbridge, 1987).

Bowers, John M., 'Three Readings of *The Knight's Tale*: Sir John Clanvowe, Geoffrey Chaucer, and James I of Scotland', *Journal of Medieval and Early Modern Studies*, 34 (2004), 279–87.

Boyle, Leonard E., 'William of Pagula and the Speculum Regis Edwardi III', *Mediaeval Studies*, 32 (1970), 329–36.

Bradbury, Jim, *The Medieval Archer* (New York, 1985).

Bradbury, Jim, *The Medieval Siege* (Woodbridge, 1992).

Brewer, Derek and Gibson, Jonathan, eds, *A Companion to the Gawain-Poet* (Cambridge, 1997).

Bridbury, A.R., 'The Black Death', *EcHR*, 2nd ser. xxvi (1973), 577–92.

Briggs, C.F., *Giles of Rome's De Regimine Principum* (Cambridge, 1999).

Brown, E.A.R., 'The Tyranny of a Construct: Feudalism and Historians of Medieval Europe', *American Historical Review*, 79 (1974), 1063–88.

Brown, E.A.R. and Famiglietti, Richard C., *The Lit de Justice: Semantics, Ceremonial and the Parlement of Paris, 1300–1600* (Sigmaringen, 1993).

Brown, Michael, *The Black Douglases: War and Lordship in Late Medieval Scotland, 1300–1455* (East Linton, 1998).

Bryant, W.N., 'The Financial Dealings of Edward III with the County Communities, 1330–60', *EHR*, 83 (1968), 760–71.

Burnley, David, *Courtliness and Literature in Medieval England* (London, 1998).

Burns, J.H., ed., *The Cambridge History of Medieval Political Thought, c.350–c.1450* (Cambridge, 1988).

Burns, J.H., *Lordship, Kingship and Empire: The Idea of Monarchy, 1400–1525* (Oxford, 1992).

Burrows, Montagu, *The Family of Brocas of Beaurepaire and Roche Court* (London, 1886).

Capra, Pierre, 'Le séjour du Prince Noir, lieutenant du Roi; a l'archevêché de Bordeaux', *Revue Historique Bordeaux et département de la Gironde*, ns 7 (1958), 241–52.

Capra, Pierre, 'L'apogée politique au temps du Prince Noir (1355–1372)'; *Bordeaux sous les Rois d'Angleterre*, ed. Yves Renouard (Bordeaux, 1965), 369–404.

Capra, Pierre, 'L'administration anglo-gasconne au temps de la lieutenance du Prince Noir, 1354–62', unpub. thesis (University of Paris, 1972).

Carpenter, C., 'Gentry and Community in Medieval England', *Journal of British Studies*, xxxiii (1994), 340–80.

Carpenter, D.A., 'From King John to the First English Duke, 1215–1337', *The House of Lords: A Thousand Years of British Tradition* (London, 1994).

Carr, A.D., *Medieval Wales* (Basingstoke, 1995).

Carr, A.D., 'The Black Death in Caernarfonshire', *Transactions of the Caernarvonshire Historical Society*, 61 (2000), 7–22.

Catto, J.I., 'An Alleged Great Council of 1374', *EHR*, 82 (1967), 764–71.

Catto, J.I., 'Religion and the English Nobility in the Later Fourteenth Century', *History and Imagination: Essays in Honour of H.R. Trevor-Roper*, ed. Hugh Lloyd-Jones, Valerie Pearl and Blair Worden (London, 1981), 43–55.

Catto, J.I., 'Sir William Beauchamp between Chivalry and Lollardy', *The Ideals and Practices of Medieval Knighthood III*, eds C. Harper-Bill and R. Harvey (Woodbridge, 1990), 39–48.

Catto, J.I., 'Fellows and Helpers: The Religious Identity of the Followers of Wyclif', *The Medieval Church: Universities, Heresy, and the Religious Life. Essays in Honour of Gordon Leff* [SCH Subsidia, 11], eds Peter Biller and R.B. Dobson (Woodbridge, 1999), 141–61.

Cazelles, R., 'La règlementation royale de la guerre privée de St Louis à Charles V et la précarité des ordonnances', *Revue historique de droit français et étranger*, 38 (1960), 530–48.

Cazelles, R., 'La peste de 1348–1349 en langue d'oil, epidémie proletarienne et enfantine', *Bulletin philologique et historique* (1962), 293–305.

Cazelles, R., *Société politique, noblesse et couronne sous les règnes de Jean II et Charles V* (Paris, 1982).

Chaplais, Pierre, 'Some Documents Regarding the Fulfilment and Interpretation of the Treaty of Brétigny', *Camden* 3rd ser. xix (1952).

Chaplais, Pierre, 'The Making of the Treaty of Paris (1259) and the Royal Style', *EHR*, 67 (1952), 235–53.

Chaplais, Pierre, *Piers Gaveston: Edward II's Adoptive Brother* (Oxford, 1994).

Cherry, John and Stratford, Neil, *Westminster Kings and the Medieval Palace of Westminster* [British Museum Occasional Paper 115] (London, 1995).

Cheyette, F.L., 'Georges Duby's Mâconnais after Fifty Years: Reading it Then and Now', *Journal of Medieval History*, 28 (2002), 291–317.

Childs, Wendy, 'Treason in the *Vita Edwardi Secundi*', *Thirteenth Century England VI*, ed. Richard Britnell, Robin Frame and Michael Prestwich (Woodbridge, 1997), 177–91.

Clarke, James G., 'Selling the Holy Places: Monastic Efforts to Win Back the People in Fifteenth-Century England', *Social Attitudes and Political Structures in the Fifteenth Century*, ed. Tim Thornton (Stroud, 2000), 13–32.

Clough, Cecil H., 'Late Fifteenth-Century English Monarchs Subject to Italian Renaissance Influence', *England and the Continent in the Middle ages: Studies in Memory of Andrew Martindale*, ed. John Mitchell (Stamford, 2000), 28–34.

Cohen, Kathleen, *Metamorphosis of a Death Symbol: The Transi Tomb in the Late Middle Ages and the Renaissance* (Berkeley, 1973).

Cohn, Samuel K. Jr, *The Black Death Transformed: Disease and Culture in Early Renaissance Europe* (London, 2002).

Collins, Hugh, *The Order of the Garter, 1348–1461: Chivalry and Politics in Late Medieval England* (Oxford, 2000).

Colvin, H.M. *et al.*, *The History of the King's Works*, 2 vols (London, 1963).

Contamine, Philippe, *Guerre, état et société a la fin du Moyen Âge. Etudes sur les armies des rois de France, 1337–1494* (Paris, 1972).

Contamine, Philippe, 'La guerre de cent ans en France: Une approche économique', *BIHR*, 47 (1974), 125–49.

Contamine, Philippe, *L'oriflamme de Saint-Denis aux xive et xve siècles* (Nancy, 1975).

Contamine, Philippe, 'De la puissance aux privilèges: doléances de la noblesse française envers la monarchie aux XIVe et XVe siècles', *La noblesse au moyen âge, XIe–XVe siècles. Essais à la mémoire de Robert Boutruche*, ed. Philippe Contamine (Paris, 1976), 235–57.

Contamine, Philippe, 'Points de vue sur la chevalerie en France à la fin du moyen âge, *Francia* 4 (1976), 255–86.

Contamine, Philippe, *War in the Middle Ages*, trans. M. Jones (Oxford, 1984).

Coote, Lesley A., *Prophecy and Public Affairs in Later Medieval England* (York, 2000).

Coss, P.R., 'Cultural Diffusion and Robin Hood', *Past and Present*, 108 (1985), 35–79.

Coss, P.R., *The Knight in Medieval England, 1000–1400* (Stroud, 1993).

Coss, P.R., 'The Formation of the English Gentry', *Past and Present*, 147 (1995), 38–64.

Coss, P.R., 'Identity and the Gentry *c*.1200–*c*.1340', *Thirteenth Century England VI*, eds Richard Britnell, Robin Frame and Michael Prestwich (Woodbridge, 1997), 49–60.

Coss, P.R., *The Lady in Medieval England, 1000–1500* (Stroud, 1998).

Coss, P.R., *The Origins of the English Gentry* (Cambridge, 2003).

Coulson, Charles L.H., *Castles in Medieval Society: Fortresses in England, France and Ireland in the Central Middle Ages* (Oxford, 2003).

Crossley, F.H., 'Chronological Data of Churches of Cheshire', *Transactions of the Lancashire and Cheshire Antiquarian Society*, lvii (1943–4), 71–137.

Crouch, David, *The Image of the Aristocracy in Britain, 1100–1300* (London, 1992).

Crouch, David, *The Birth of Nobility: Constructing Aristocracy in England and France, 900–1300* (Harlow, 2005).

Crowder, C.M.D., 'Peace and Justice and 1400: A Sketch', *Aspects of Late Medieval Government and Society: Essays Presented to J.R. Lander*, ed. J.G. Rowe (Toronto and London, 1986), 53–81.

Cummins, John, *The Hound and the Hawk: The Art of Medieval Hunting* (London, 2001).

Curry, Anne, *The Hundred Years War* (Houndsmill, 1993).

Curry, Anne and Hughes, Michael, eds, *Arms, Armies and Fortifications in the Hundred Years War* (Woodbridge, 1994).

Cuttler, S.H., *The Law of Treason and Treason Trials in Later Medieval France* (Cambridge, 1981).

d'Avray, David L., 'Papal Authority and Religious Sentiment in the Late Middle Ages', *The Church and Sovereignty, c.590–1918* [SCH Subsidia 9], ed. Diana Wood (Oxford, 1991), 393–408.

Daniell, Christopher, *Death and Burial in Medieval England, 1066–1550* (London, 1997).

Davies, R.A., 'The Effect of the Black Death on the Parish Priests of the Medieval Diocese of Coventry and Lichfield', *Historical Research*, 62 (1989), 85–90.

Davies, R.R., *Lordship and Society in the March of Wales, 1282–1400* (Oxford, 1978).

Davies, R.R., *Conquest, Coexistence and Change: Wales, 1063–1415* (Oxford, 1987).

Dawson, Graham J., 'The Black Prince's Palace at Kennington, Surrey', *British Archaeological Reports*, 26 (1976).

Delachenal, Roland, *Histoire de Charles V*, 5 vols (Paris, 1909–31).

Delisle, Leopold, *Histoire du château et de sires de Saint-Saveur-le-Vicomte* (Valognes, 1867).

Denifle, Henri, *La guerre de cent ans et la desolation des églises, monastères et hôpitaux en France* (Paris, 1902).

Desportes, Pierre, *Reims et les Remois aux xiiie et xive siècles* (Paris, 1979).

DeVries, Kelly, 'Hunger, Flemish Participation and the Flight of Philip VI: Contemporary Accounts of the Siege of Calais, 1346–47', *Studies in Medieval and Renaissance History*, 12 (1991), 131–81.

DeVries, Kelly, 'The Impact of Gunpowder Weaponry on Siege Warfare in the Hundred Years War', *The Medieval City under Siege*, eds Ivy A. Corfis and Michael Wolfe (Woodbridge, 1995), 227–44.

DeVries, Kelly, *Infantry Warfare in the Early Fourteenth Century: Discipline, Tactics and Technology* (Woodbridge, 1996).

DeVries, Kelly, 'Teenagers at War during the Middle Ages', *The Premodern Teenager: Youth in Society, 1150–1650*, ed. Konrad Eisenbichler (Toronto, 2002), 207–23.

Dobson, R.B., *The Peasants' Revolt of 1381* (London, 1970).

Dobson, R.B., Review of J.C. Holt, *Robin Hood* (1982) in *Northern History*, 19 (1983), 219.

Dobson, R.B., 'Two Ecclesiastical Patrons: Archbishop Henry Chichele of Canterbury (1414–43) and Bishop Richard Fox of Winchester (1501–28)', *Gothic: Art for England 1400–1547*, eds Richard Marks and Paul Williamson (London, 2003), 234–6.

Dodd, Gwilym, 'Crown, Magnates and Gentry: The English Parliament, 1369–1421', unpub. DPhil. thesis (University of York, 1998).

Dodd, Gwilym, 'The Lords, Taxation and the Community of Parliament in the 1370s and Early 1380s', *Parliamentary History*, 20 (2001), 287–310.

Duby, G., *A Chivalrous Society*, trans. Cynthia Postan (London, 1977).

Ducourtieux, Paul, *Histoire de Limoges* (Limoges, 1925, repr. Marseille, 1975).

Düll, Siegrid, Luttrell, Anthony and Keen, Maurice, 'Faithful unto Death: The Tomb Slab of Sir William Neville and Sir John Clanvowe, Constantinople 1391', *Antiquaries Journal* 71 (1991), 174–90.

Dunham, William Huse Jr, 'The Feudality of Retaining', *Lordship and Community in Medieval Europe*, ed. Frederic L. Cheyette (New York, 1968), 222–39.

Dunham, William Huse Jr and Wood, Charles T., 'The Right to Rule in England: Depositions and the Kingdom's Authority, 1327–1485', *American Historical Review*, 81 (1976), 738–61.

Dunn, Alistair, *The Great Rising of 1381* (Stroud, 2002).

Dunning, Robert W., 'The West-Country Carthusians', *Religious Belief and Ecclesiastical Careers in Late Medieval England*, ed. Christopher Harper-Bill (Woodbridge, 1991), 33–42.

Dupuy, Micheline, *Le Prince Noir: Edouard seigneur d'Aquitaine* (Paris, 1970).

Dyer, Christopher, 'English Diet in the Later Middle Ages', *Social Relations and Ideas. Essays in Honour of R.H. Hilton*, eds T.H. Aston, P.R. Coss, Christopher Dyer and Joan Thursk (Cambridge, 1983), 191–216.

Dyer, Christopher, *Making a Living in the Middle Ages: The People of Britain, 850–1520* (New Haven and London, 2002).

Elias, Norbert, *The Civilizing Process: Sociogenic and Psychogenetic Investigations*, ed. and trans. Eric Dunning, Johan Goudsblom and Stephen Mennel (rev. ed. Oxford, 2000).

Emerson, Barbara, *The Black Prince* (London, 1976).

Evans, D.L., 'Some Notes on the History of the Principality of Wales in the Time of the Black Prince, 1343–1376', *Transactions of the Honourable Society of Cymrodorion* (1925–6), 25–107.

Evans, Michael, *The Death of Kings: Royal Deaths in Medieval England* (London, 2003).

Fasti Ecclesiae Anglicanae 1300–1541, II (Hereford Diocese), ed. Joyce M. Horn (London, 1962).

Fasti Ecclesiae Anglicanae 1300–1541, IX (Exeter Diocese), ed. Joyce M. Horn (London, 1964).

Favier, Jean, *La Guerre de Cent Ans* (Paris, 1980).

Favreau, Robert, 'Comptes de la sénéchausée de Saintonge', *Bibliothèque de l'École des Chartes*, 117 (1959), 73–88.

Federico, Sylvia, 'The Imaginary Society: Women in 1381', *Journal of British Studies*, 40 (2001), 159–83.

Ferster, Judith, *Fictions of Advice: The Literature and Politics of Counsel in Late Medieval England* (Philadelphia, 1996).

Finberg, H.P.R., *Tavistock Abbey* (Newton Abbot, 1969).

Fiorato, Veronica, Boylston, Anthea and Knüsel, Christopher, ed., *Blood Red Roses. The Archaeology of a Mass Grave From the Battle of Towton AD 1461* (Oxford, 2000).

Fisher, Will, 'The Renaissance Beard: Masculinity in Early Modern England', *Renaissance Quarterly*, 54 (2001), 155–87.

Foster, Harold D., 'Assessing Disaster Magnitude', *Professional Geographer*, 28 (1976), 241–7.

Fowler, K., ' "News from the Front": Letters and Dispatches of the Fourteenth Century', *Guerre et société en France en Angleterre et en Bourgogne XIVe–XVe siècles*, eds Philippe Contamine, Charles Giry-Deloison, and Maurice Keen (Lille, 1991), 63–92.

Fowler, K., *Medieval Mercenaries. Volume One: The Great Companies* (Oxford, 2001).

Fox, H.S.A., 'Devon and Cornwall', *The Agrarian History of England and Wales, III, 1348–1500*, ed. Edward Miller (Cambridge, 1991), 152–7, 303–23, 722–43.

Fryde, E.B., 'The Dismissal of Robert de Wodehouse from the Office of Treasurer, December 1338', *EHR*, 67 (1952), 74–8.

Fryde, E.B., 'The English Farmers of the Customs, 1343–51', *TRHS*, 5th ser. ix (1959), 1–17.

Fryde, E.B., 'Financial Resources of Edward III in the Netherlands, 1337–40, Pt. 2', *Revue Belge de Philologie et d'Histoire*, 45 (1967), 1142–216.

Gaier, Claude, 'L'invincibilité anglaise et le grande arc après la guerre de cent ans: un mythe tenace', *Tijdschrift voor gescheidenis*, 91 (1978), 378–85.

Galloway, Andrew, 'The Making of a Social Ethic in Late Medieval England: From Gratitudo to "Kyndenesse" ', *Journal of the History of Ideas*, 55 (1994), 365–83.

Genet, J.P., 'Political Theory and the Relationship in England and France between the Crown and Local Communities', *The Crown and Local Communities in France and England in the Fifteenth Century*, eds J.R.L. Highfield and Robin Jeffs (Gloucester, 1981), 19–32.

Gerth, H.H. and Mills, C. Wright, *From Max Weber: Essays in Sociology* (New York, 1958).

Gillespie, J.L., 'Richard II's Knights: Chivalry and Patronage', *Journal of Medieval History*, 13 (1987), 143–59.

Gillingham, John, 'Richard I and the Science of War in the Middle Ages', *War and Government in the Middle Ages: Essays in Honour of J.O. Prestwich*, eds John Gillingham and J.C. Holt (Cambridge, 1984), 78–91.

Gillingham, John, 'From *Civilitas* to Civility: Codes of Manners in Medieval and Early Modern England', *TRHS*, 6th ser. xii (2002), 267–89.

Gillingham, John, '"Up with Orthodoxy!": In Defense of Vegetian Warfare', *Journal of Medieval Military History II*, eds Bernard S. Bachrach, Kelly DeVries and Clifford J. Rogers (Woodbridge, 2004), 149–58.

Girouard, Mark, *Life in the English Country House* (New Haven and London, 1978).

Given-Wilson, Chris, 'Purveyance for the Royal Household, 1362–1413', *BIHR*, 56 (1983), 145–63.

Given-Wilson, Chris, *The Royal Household and the King's Affinity: Service, Politics and Finance in England, 1360–1413* (New Haven and London, 1986).

Given-Wilson, Chris, 'Service, Serfdom and English Labour Legislation, 1350–1500', *Concepts and Patterns of Service in the Later Middle Ages*, eds Anne Curry and Elizabeth Matthew (Woodbridge, 2000), 21–37.

Given-Wilson, Chris, 'The Problem of Labour in the Context of English Government, *c.*1350–1450', *The Problem of Labour in Fourteenth-Century England*, eds James Bothwell, P.J.P. Goldberg and W.M. Ormrod (York, 2000), 85–100.

Given-Wilson, Chris, *Chronicles: The Writing of History in Medieval England* (London, 2004).

Goldsmith, James L., 'The Crisis of the Late Middle Ages: The Case of France', *French History*, 9 (1995), 417–48.

Green, David, 'The Household and Military Retinue of Edward the Black Prince', unpub. PhD, 2 vols (University of Nottingham, 1999).

Green, David, 'The Later Retinue of Edward the Black Prince', *Nottingham Medieval Studies*, xliv (2000), 141–51.

Green, David, 'The Military Personnel of Edward the Black Prince' *Medieval Prosopography*, 21 (2000), 133–52.

Green, David, *The Black Prince* (Stroud, 2001).

Green, David, 'Politics and Service with Edward the Black Prince', *The Age of Edward III*, ed. J.S. Bothwell (York, 2001), 53–68.

Green, David, *The Battle of Poitiers, 1356* (Stroud, 2002).

Green, David, 'Edward the Black Prince and East Anglia: An Unlikely Association', *Fourteenth Century England III*, ed. W.M. Ormrod (Woodbridge, 2004), 83–98.

Griffiths, R.A., *The Principality of Wales in the Later Middle Ages. The Structure and Personnel of Government: 1, South Wales, 1277–1536* (Cardiff, 1972).

Griffiths, R.A., 'The Crown and the Royal Family in Later Medieval England', *King and Country: England and Wales in the Fifteenth Century* (London, 1991), 15–26.

Griffiths, R.A., *Conquerors and Conquered* (Far Thrupp, 1994).

Guenée, Bernard, *States and Rulers in Later Medieval Europe* (Oxford, 1985).

Gundersheimer, Werner L., 'Renaissance Concepts of Shame and Pocaterra's Dialoghi Della Vergogna', *Renaissance Quarterly*, 47 (1994), 34–56.

Hadley, D.M., *Death in Medieval England: An Archaeology* (Stroud, 2001).

Haines, Roy M., *Death of a King* (Scotforth, 2002).

Haines, Roy M., *King Edward II: Edward of Caernarfon, His Life Reign and its Aftermath, 1284–1330* (Montreal, 2003).

Hamilton, J.S., *Piers Gaveston, Earl of Cornwall 1307–1312: Politics and Patronage in the Reign of Edward II* (Detroit, 1988).

Hamilton, J.S., 'Charter Witness Lists for the Reign of Edward II', *Fourteenth Century England I*, ed. Nigel Saul (Woodbridge, 2000), 1–20.

Hammond, P.W., *Food and Feast in Medieval England* (Stroud, 1996).

Hanley, Sarah, *The Lit de Justice of the Kings of France: Constitutional Ideology in Legend, Ritual and Discourse* (Princeton, 1983).

Harari, Yuval Noah, 'Strategy and Supply in Fourteenth-Century Western European Invasion Campaigns', *Journal of Military History*, 64 (2000), 297–334.

Harding, Alan, *Medieval Law and the Foundations of the State* (Oxford, 2002).

Hardy, Robert, 'Longbow', *Arms, Armies and Fortifications in the Hundred Years War*, eds Anne Curry and M. Hughes (Woodbridge, 1994), 161–81.

Hargreaves, Paul V., 'Seigniorial Reaction and Peasant Responses: Worcester Priory and its Peasants after the Black Death', *Midland History*, xxiv (1999), 53–78.

Harris, P. Valentine, 'Archery in the First Half of the Fourteenth Century', *Journal of the Society of Archer-Antiquaries*, 13 (1970), 19–21.

Harriss, G.L., 'The Commons' Petition of 1340', *EHR*, 78 (1963), 625–54.

Harriss, G.L., *King, Parliament and Public Finance in Medieval England to 1369* (Oxford, 1975).

Harriss, G.L., 'The Formation of Parliament, 1272–1377', *The English Parliament in the Middle Ages*, eds R.G. Davies and J.H. Denton (Manchester, 1981), 29–60.

Harriss, G.L., 'Political Society and the Growth of Government in Late Medieval England', *Past and Present*, 138 (1993), 28–57.

Harte, N.B., 'State Control of Dress and Social Change in Pre-Industrial England', *Trade, Government and Economy in Pre-Industrial England: Essays Presented to F.J. Fisher*, ed. D.C. Coleman and A.H. John (London, 1976), 132–65.

Harvey, John, *The Black Prince and his Age* (London, 1976).

Hatcher, John, *Rural Economy and Society in the Duchy of Cornwall, 1300–1500* (Cambridge, 1970).

Hatcher, John *Plague, Population and the English Economy, 1348–1530* (Houndsmill, 1977).

Hatcher, John, 'England in the Aftermath of the Black Death', *Past and Present*, 144 (1994), 3–35.

Hatcher, John, Review of S.K. Cohn Jr, *The Black Death Transformed: Disease and Culture in Early Renaissance Europe* (London, 2002) in *EHR*, 118 (2003), 989–91.

Havens, Jill C., 'A Curious Erasure in Walsingham's Short Chronicle and the Politics of Heresy', *Fourteenth Century England II*, ed. Chris Given-Wilson (Woodbridge, 2002), 95–106.

Henneman, John Bell, 'The Black Death and Royal Taxation in France, 1347–1351', *Speculum*, 43 (1968), 405–28.

Hewitt, H.J., *The Black Prince's Expedition of 1355–57* (repr. Barnsley, 2004).

Hicks, Michael, *Bastard Feudalism* (London, 1995).

Hieatt, Constance B. and Butler, Sharon, eds, *Curye on Inglish: English Culinary Manuscripts of the Fourteenth Century (Including the Forme of Cury)* [EETS] (London, 1985).

Hieatt, Constance B. and Jones, Robin F., 'Two Anglo-Norman Culinary Collections Edited from British Library Manuscripts Additional 32085 and Royal 12.C.xii', *Speculum*, 61 (1986), 859–82.

Higounet-Nadal, Arlette, *Périgeux au xiv* et xv* siècles* (Bordeaux, 1978).

Holmes, G.A., 'A Protest against the Despensers, 1326', *Speculum*, 30 (1955), 207–12.

Holmes, G.A., 'Judgement on the Younger Despenser, 1326', *EHR*, 70 (1955), 261–7.

Holmes, G.A., *The Good Parliament* (Oxford, 1975).

Holt, J.C., *Robin Hood*, 2nd ed. (London, 1989).

Horrox, Rosemary, *The Black Death* (Manchester, 1994).

Horrox, Rosemary, 'Purgatory, Prayer and Plague, 1150–1380', *Death in England: An Illustrated History*, eds Peter C. Jupp and Clare Gittings (Manchester, 1999), 90–118.

Housley, Norman, '*Pro deo et patria mori*: Sanctified Patriotism in Europe, 1400–1600', *War and Competition Between States*, ed. Philippe Contamine (Oxford, 2000), 221–8.

Hoyt, Robert S., 'The Coronation Oath of 1308: The Background of "les leys et les custumes"', *Traditio*, 11 (1955), 235–57.

Hoyt, Robert S., 'The Coronation Oath of 1308', *EHR*, 71 (1956), 353–83.

Hudson, Anne, *The Premature Reformation: Wycliffite Texts and Lollard History* (Oxford, 1988).

Huizinga, Johan, *Herfsttij der Middeleeuwen* (Haarlem, 1919); *The Waning of the Middle Ages: A Study of the Forms of Life, Thought and Art in France and the Netherlands in the XIV*th* and XV*th* Centuries*, trans. F. Hopman (London, 1924); *The Autumn of the Middle Ages*, trans. Rodney J. Payton and Ulrich Mammitzsch (Chicago, 1996).

Huizinga, Johan, *Homo Ludens: A Study of the Play Element in Culture* (London, 1970).

Hunt, Edwin S., 'A New Look at the Dealings of the Bardi and Peruzzi with Edward III', *Journal of Economic History*, 50 (1990), 149–62.

Huppert, George, *After the Black Death: A Social History of Early Modern Europe* (Indianapolis, 1986).

Hyland, Ann, *The Horse in the Middle Ages* (Stroud, 1999).

Jones, Douglas, ed., *The Church in Chester, 1300–1540* (Chetham Society, 3rd ser. vii, 1957).

Jones, Michael, *Ducal Brittany, 1364–1399: Relations with England and France During the Reign of Duke John IV* (Oxford, 1970).

Jones, Michael, 'Sir Thomas Dagworth et la guerre civile en Bretagne au xiv* siècle: quelques documents inédits', *Annales de Bretagne*, lxxxviii (1980), 621–39.

Jones, Michael, 'Edward III's Captains in Brittany', *England in the Fourteenth Century. Proceedings of 1985 Harlaxton Symposium*, ed. W.M. Ormrod (Woodbridge, 1986), 99–118.

Jones, Michael, 'The Late Medieval State and Social Change: A View from the Duchy of Brittany', *L'État ou le Roi: Les foundations de la modernité monarchique en France (xive–xviie siècles)*, eds Neithard Bulst, Robert Descimon et Alain Guerreau (Paris, 1996), 117–44.

Jones, Michael, ed. *New Cambridge Medieval History*, VI (Cambridge, 2000).

Jones, Richard L.C., 'Fortifications and Sieges in Western Europe *c*.800–1450', *Medieval Warfare*, ed. Maurice Keen (Oxford, 1999), 163–85.

Jones, Terry, *Chaucer's Knight. A Portrait of a Medieval Mercenary*, rev. ed. (London, 1994).

Jones, W.R., 'The English Church and Royal Propaganda During the Hundred Years War', *Journal of British Studies*, 19 (1979), 18–30.

Kaeuper, Richard, *Chivalry and Violence in Medieval Europe* (Oxford, 1999).

Kaeuper, Richard, 'Chivalry and the Civilizing Process', *Violence in Medieval Society*, ed. Richard Kaeuper (Woodbridge, 2000), 21–38.

Kaeuper, Richard, 'The Societal Role of Chivalry in Romance: Northwestern Europe', *Cambridge Companion to Medieval Romance*, ed. Roberta L. Krueger (Cambridge, 2000), 97–114.

Kaminsky, Howard, 'Estate, Nobility and the Exhibition of Estate in the Later Middle Ages', *Speculum*, 68 (1993), 684–709.

Keegan, John, *Face of Battle: A Study of Agincourt, Waterloo and the Somme* (Harmondsworth, 1978).

Keen, Maurice, *The Laws of War in the Late Middle Ages* (London, 1965).

Keen, Maurice, 'Huizinga, Kilgour and the Decline of Chivalry', *Medievalia et Humanistica*, 8 (1977), 1–20.

Keen, Maurice, 'Chaucer's Knight, the English Aristocracy and the Crusade', *English Court Culture in the Later Middle Ages*, eds V.J. Scattergood and J.W. Sherborne (London, 1983), 45–61.

Keen, Maurice, *Chivalry* (New Haven and London, 1984).

Keen, Maurice, 'The Influence of Wyclif', *Wyclif in his Times*, ed. Anthony Kenny (Oxford, 1986), 100–9.

Keen, Maurice, 'Chaucer and Chivalry Revisited', *Armies, Chivalry and Warfare in Medieval Britain and France*, ed. Matthew Strickland (Stamford, 1998), 1–12.

Keen, Maurice, 'Heraldry and Hierarchy', *Orders and Hierarchies in Late Medieval and Renaissance Europe*, ed. Jeffrey Denton (Toronto, 1999), 94–108.

Keen, Maurice, ed., *Medieval Warfare* (Oxford, 1999).

Kempshall, M.S., *The Common Good in Late Medieval Political Thought* (Oxford, 1999).

Kilgour, Raymond, *The Decline of Chivalry as Shown in the French Literature of the Late Middle Ages* (Cambridge, 1937).

King, A., ' "According to the custom used in French and Scottish wars": Prisoners and Casualties on the Scottish Marches in the Fourteenth Century', *Journal of Medieval History*, 28 (2002), 263–90.

Knecht, Robert J., *The Valois: Kings of France, 1328–1589* (London and New York, 2004).

Knowles, David and Grimes, W.F., *Charterhouse: The Foundation in the Light of Recent Discoveries* (London, 1954).

Labarge, Margaret Wade, *Gascony: England's First Colony, 1204–1453* (London, 1980).

Lachaud, Frédérique, 'Un miroir au prince méconnu: le *De nobilitatibus, sapienciis et prudenciis regum* de Walter Milemete (vers 1326–1327)', *Guerre, pouvoir et noblesse au Moyen Âge: Mélanges en l'honneur de Philippe Contamine*, eds Jacques Paviots et Jacques Verger (Paris, 2000), 401–13.

Lachaud, Frédérique, 'Dress and Social Status in England Before the Sumptuary Laws', *Heraldry, Pageantry, and Social Display in Medieval Europe*, ed. P.R. Coss and Maurice Keen (Woodbridge, 2002), 105–23.

Laguardia, David, 'On the Ethos of the Noble Warrior: Blaise de Monluc's Commentaries', *Medievalia et Humanistica*, 26 (1999), 45–61.

Lahey, Stephen E., *Philosophy and Politics in the Thought of John Wyclif* (Cambridge, 2003).

Le Patourel, H.E.J., 'Rural Building in England and Wales', *The Agrarian History of England and Wales, 3: 1348–1500*, ed. Edward Miller (Cambridge, 1991), 820–90.

Le Patourel, John, 'Edward III and the Kingdom of France', *History*, 43 (1958), 173–89.

Le Roy Ladurie, Emmanuel, *Montaillou: Cathars and Catholics in a French Village, 1294–1324*, trans. Barbara Bray (Harmondsworth, 1978).

Lehoux, Françoise, *Jean de France, duc de Berri. Sa vie. Son action politique, 1340–1416* (Paris, 1966).

Lerner, Robert E., 'The Black Death and Western Eschatological Mentalities', *American Historical Review*, 86 (1981), 533–52.

Lewis, F.R., 'The Rectors of Llanbadarn Fawr, Cardiganshire, from 1246 to 1360', *Archaeologia Cambrensis*, 92 (1937), 233–46.

Lindley, Phillip, 'The Black Death and English Art. A Debate and Some Assumptions', *The Black Death in England*, ed. W.M. Ormrod and Philip Lindley (Stamford, 1996), 125–46.

Lloyd, John E., *A History of Carmarthenshire* (Cardiff, 1935).

Lodge, Eleanor C., *Gascony Under English Rule* (London, 1926).

Lord, Carla, 'Queen Isabella at the Court of France', *Fourteenth Century England II*, ed. Chris Given-Wilson (Woodbridge, 2002), 45–52.

Lydon, James, 'The Impact of the Bruce Invasion, 1315–27', *A New History of Ireland II: Medieval Ireland 1169–1534*, ed. Art Cosgrove (Oxford, 1976), 275–302.

Lyon, Bryce, 'What were Edward III's Priorities: the Pleasures of Sports or Charity?', *Revue d'Histoire Ecclésiastique*, xcii (1997), 126–34.

Maddicott, J.R., *Thomas of Lancaster, 1307–22* (Oxford, 1970).

Maddicott, J.R., 'The Birth and Setting of the Ballad of Robin Hood', *EHR*, 93 (1978), 276–99.

Maddicott, J.R., 'The County Community and the Making of Public Opinion in Fourteenth-Century England', *TRHS*, 5th ser. xxviii (1978), 27–43.

Maddicott, J.R., 'Parliament and the Constituencies, 1272–1377', *The English Parliament in the Middle Ages*, eds R.G. Davies and J.H. Denton (Manchester, 1981), 61–87.

Maddicott, J.R., 'Edward I and the Lessons of Baronial Reform: Local Government, 1258–80', *Thirteenth Century England I*, eds P.R. Coss and S.D. Lloyd (Woodbridge, 1986), 1–30.

Major, John Russell, 'Bastard Feudalism and the Kiss: Changing Social Mores in Late Medieval and Early Modern France', *Journal of Interdisciplinary History*, xvii (1987), 509–35.

Major, John Russell, *From Renaissance Monarchy to Absolute Monarchy: French Kings, Nobles and Estates* (Baltimore and London, 1994).

Malvern, Marjorie M., 'An Earnest "monyscyon" and "thinge delectabyll" Realized Verbally and Visually in "A Disputacion betwyx the body and wormes", a Middle English Poem Inspired by Tomb Art and Northern Spirituality', *Viator*, 13 (1982), 415–43.

Marsden, Peter, *Sealed by Time: The Loss and Recovery of the Mary Rose* (Portsmouth, 2003).

Martindale, Andrew, 'The Knights and the Bed of Stones: A Learned Confusion of the Fourteenth Century', *Journal of the British Archaeological Association*, cxlii (1989), 66–74.

Marvin, Julia, 'Cannibalism as an Aspect of Famine in Two English Chronicles', *Food and Eating in Medieval Europe*, eds Martha Carlin and Joel T. Rosenthal (London and Rio Grande, 1998), 73–87.

Masschaele, James, 'The Public Space of the Marketplace in Medieval England', *Speculum*, 77 (2002), 383–421.

McFarlane, K.B., 'Parliament and Bastard Feudalism' *TRHS* 4th ser. xxvi (1944), 53–79.

McFarlane, K.B., *Lancastrian Kings and Lollard Knights* (Oxford, 1972).

McFarlane, K.B., *The Nobility of Late Medieval England* (Oxford, 1973).

McGinn, Bernard, *Visions of the End: Apocalyptic Traditions in the Middle Ages* (New York, 1998).

McGlynn, Sean, 'The Myths of Medieval Warfare', *History Today*, 44 (1994), 28–34.

McGrade, Arthur Stephen, 'Somersaulting Sovereignty: A Note on Reciprocal Lordship in Wyclif', *The Church and Sovereignty, c.590–1918* [SCH Subsidia 9], ed. Diana Wood (Oxford, 1991), 261–8.

McKisack, May, *The Fourteenth Century: 1307–1399* (Oxford, 1959).

McLean, Teresa, *Medieval English Gardens* (London, 1989).

Meiss, Millard, *Painting in Florence and Sienna After the Black Death* (Princeton, 1951).

Menache, S., 'Isabelle of France, Queen of England: A Reconsideration', *Journal of Medieval History*, x (1984), 107–24.

Miller, S.J.T., 'The Position of the King in Bracton and Beaumanoir', *Speculum*, 31 (1956), 263–96.

Moisant J., *Le Prince Noir en Aquitaine* (Paris, 1894).

Morgan, Philip, 'Cheshire and the Defence of the Principality of Aquitaine', *Transactions of the Historical Society of Lancashire and Cheshire*, 128 (1978), 139–60.

Morgan, Philip, *War and Society in Medieval Cheshire, 1277–1403* (Manchester, 1987).

Morgan, Philip, 'Making the English Gentry', *Thirteenth Century England V*, eds P.R. Coss and S.D. Lloyd (Woodbridge, 1995), 21–8.

Morgan, Philip, 'Of Worms and War: 1380–1558', *Death in England: An Illustrated History*, eds Peter Jupp and Clare Gittings (Manchester, 1999), 119–46.

Morillo, Stephen, 'Battle-Seeking: The Contexts and Limits of Vegetian Strategy', *Journal of Medieval Military History I*, ed. Bernard S. Bachrach (Woodbridge, 2002), 21–41.

Morrow, John, *History of Political Thought: A Thematic Introduction* (Basingstoke, 1998).

Mountfield, D., *Castles and Castle Towns of Great Britain* (London, 1993).

Mourier, Jacques, '*Nobilitas quid est?* Un procès à Tain-l'Hermitage en 1408', *Bibliothèque de l'École des Chartes*, 142 (1984), 255–69.

Musson, Anthony, 'New Anthony Labour Laws, New Remedies? Legal Reaction to the Black Death "Crisis"', *Fourteenth Century England I*, ed. Nigel Saul (Woodbridge, 2000), 73–88.

Naphy, William and Spicer, Andrew, *The Black Death and the History of Plagues, 1345–1730* (Stroud, 2000).

Nederman, C.J., *Community and Consent: The Secular Political Theory of Marsiglio of Padua's Defensor Pacis* (London, 1995).

Nederman, C.J., ed., *Political Thought in Early Fourteenth-Century England: Treatises by Walter of Milemete, William of Pagula, and William of Ockham* (Turnhout, 2003).

Newton, Stella M., *Fashion in the Age of the Black Prince: A Study of the Years 1340–1365* (Woodbridge, 1988).

Nicholas, David, *Medieval Flanders* (London, 1992).

Nicholls, Jonathan, *The Matter of Courtesy: Medieval Courtesy Books and the Gawain-Poet* (Woodbridge, 1985).

Nicholson, Helen, *Medieval Warfare: Theory and Practice of War in Europe 300–1500* (Houndsmill, 2004).

Nightingale, Pamela, 'Knights and Merchants: Trade, Politics and the Gentry in Late Medieval England', *Past and Present*, 169 (2000), 36–62.

Offler, H.S., 'England and Germany at the Beginning of the Hundred Years War', *EHR*, 54 (1939), 608–31.

Offler, H.S., 'Thomas Bradwardine's "Victory Sermon" in 1346', *Church and Crown in the Fourteenth Century: Studies in European and Political Thought*, ed. A.I. Doyle (Aldershot, 2000), XIII, 1–40.

Oosterwijk, Sophie, 'Of Corpses, Constables and Kings: The *Danse Macabre* in Late Medieval and Renaissance Culture', *Journal of the British Archaeological Association*, 157 (2004), 61–90.

Orme, Nicholas, *From Childhood to Chivalry: The Education of the English Kings and Aristocracy, 1066–1530* (London, 1984).

Orme, Nicholas, 'Medieval Hunting: Fact and Fancy', *Chaucer's England: Literature in Historical Context*, ed. Barbara A. Hanawalt (Minnesota, 1992), 133–53.

Orme, Nicholas, *Medieval Children* (New Haven and London, 2001).

Ormrod, W.M., 'The Personal Religion of Edward III', *Speculum*, 64 (1989), 849–77.

Ormrod, W.M., *The Reign of Edward III* (New Haven and London, 1990).

Ormrod, W.M., 'England, Normandy and the Beginnings of the Hundred Years War, 1259–1360', *England and Normandy in the Middle Ages*, eds David Bates and Anne Curry (London, 1994), 197–213.

Ormrod, W.M., *Political Life in Medieval England, 1300–1450* (Basingstoke, 1995).

Ormrod, W.M., '"In Bed with Joan of Kent": The King's Mother and the Peasants' Revolt', *Medieval Women: Texts and Contexts in Late Medieval Britain*, ed. J. Wogan Browne *et al.* (Turnhout, 2000), 277–92.

Packe, M., *King Edward III*, ed. L.C.B. Seaman (London, 1983).

Palmer, R.C., *English Law in the Age of the Black Death, 1348–1381: A Transformation of Governance and Law* (Chapel Hill, 1993).

Parker, Geoffrey, *The Military Revolution: Military Innovation and the Rise of the West, 1500–1800*, 2nd ed. (Cambridge, 1996).

Parsons, John Carmi, 'The Intercessory Patronage of Queens Margaret and Isabella of France', *Thirteenth Century England VI*, eds Richard Britnell, Robin Frame and Michael Prestwich (Woodbridge, 1997), 145–56.

Paterson, Linda, *World of the Troubadours: Medieval Occitan Society, c.1100–c.1300* (Cambridge, 1993).

Payling, S.J., 'Social Mobility, Demographic Change and Landed Society in Late Medieval England', *EcHR*, 45 (1992), 51–73.

Payling, S.J., 'The Rise of Lawyers in the Lower House, 1395–1536', *Parchment and People: Parliament in the Middle Ages*, ed. Linda Clark [Parliamentary History, Special Issue, 2004], 103–20.

Perkins, Nicholas, *Hoccleve's Regiment of Princes: Counsel and Constraint* (Cambridge, 2001).

Perroy, Edouard, 'Feudalism or Principalities in Fifteenth-Century France', *BIHR*, 20 (1945), 181–5.

Perroy, Edouard, *The Hundred Years War*, trans. W.B. Wells (London, 1951).

Perroy, Edouard, 'Social Mobility Among the French *Noblesse*', *Past and Present*, 21 (1962), 25–38.

Pitt-Rivers, Julian, 'Honour and Social Status', *Honour and Shame: The Values of Mediterranean Society*, ed. J.G. Peristiany (London, 1965), 21–77.

Plaisse, A., *À travers le Cotentin: la grande chevauchée guerrière d'Edouard III en 1346* (Cherbourg, 1994).

Platt, Colin, *King Death: The Black Death and its Aftermath in Late-Medieval England* (Toronto, 1996).

Pollard, A.J., 'Idealising Criminality: Robin Hood in the Fifteenth Century', *Pragmatic Utopias: Ideas and Communities, 1200–1630*, eds Rosemary Horrox and Sarah Rees Jones (Cambridge, 2001), 156–73.

Porter, E., 'Chaucer's Knight, the Alliterative *Morte Arthure* and the Medieval Laws of War: A Reconsideration', *Nottingham Medieval Studies*, xxvii (1983), 56–78.

Pounds, N.J.G., 'The Duchy Palace at Lostwithiel, Cornwall', *Archaeological Journal*, 136 (1979), 203–17.

Powell, J. Enoch and Wallis, Keith, *The House of Lords in the Later Middle Ages: A History of the English House of Lords to 1540* (London, 1968).

Prestwich, Michael, 'Victualing Estimates for English Garrisons in Scotland During the Early Fourteenth Century', *EHR*, 82 (1967), 536–43.

Prestwich, Michael, 'Parliament and the Community of the Realm in Fourteenth-Century England', *Parliament and Community*, eds Art Cosgrove and J.I. McGuire (Belfast, 1983), 5–24.

Prestwich, Michael, 'The Charges against the Despensers, 1321', *BIHR*, lviii (1985), 95–100.

Prestwich, Michael, 'The Ordinances of 1311 and the Politics of the Early Fourteenth Century', *Politics and Crisis in Fourteenth-Century England*, ed. W.R. Childs and J. Taylor (Gloucester, 1990), 1–18.

Prestwich, Michael, 'Why did Englishmen Fight in the Hundred Years War?', *Medieval History*, 2 (1992), 58–65.

Prestwich, Michael, 'Was There a Military Revolution in Medieval England?', *Recognitions: Essays Presented to Edmund Fryde*, eds Colin Richmond and Isobel M.W. Harvey (Aberystwyth, 1996), 19–38.

Prestwich, Michael, *Armies and Warfare in the Middle Ages: The English Experience* (New Haven and London, 1996).

Prestwich, Michael, *Edward I* (New Haven and London, 1997).

Prestwich, Michael, *The Three Edwards: War and State in England, 1272–1377*, 2nd ed. (London, 2003).

Prince, A.E., 'The Strength of English Armies in the Reign of Edward III', *EHR*, 46 (1931), 364–5.

Prosser, Gareth, '"Decayed Feudalism" and "Royal Clienteles": Royal Office and Magnate Service in the Fifteenth Century', *War, Government and Power in Late Medieval France*, ed. C.T. Allmand (Liverpool, 2000), 175–89.

Raftis, J.A., 'Changes in an English Village after the Black Death', *Mediaeval Studies*, 29 (1967), 158–77.

Rayner, Doris, 'The Forms and Machinery of the "Commune Petition" in the Fourteenth Century Part 1', *EHR*, 56 (1941), 198–233; 'Part 2', 549–70.

Rees, William, 'The Black Death in Wales', *TRHS* 4th ser. iii (1920), 115–35; repr. in R.W. Southern, ed., *Essays in Medieval History* (London, 1968).

Retemeier, Arnd, 'Born to be a Tyrant? The Childhood and Education of Richard II', *Fourteenth Century England II*, ed. Chris Given-Wilson (Woodbridge, 2002), 147–58.

Reynolds, Susan, *Fiefs and Vassals: The Medieval Evidence Reinterpreted* (Oxford, 1994).

Richardson, H.G., 'The Commons and Medieval Politics', *TRHS*, 4th ser. xxviii (1946), 21–45.

Richardson, H.G., 'The English Coronation Oath', *Speculum*, 24 (1949), 44–75.

Richardson, H.G. and Sayles, G.O., 'The Parliaments of Edward III', *BIHR*, viii (1930), 65–82.

Richardson, H.G. and Sayles, G.O., 'The Parliaments of Edward III', pt. 2, *BIHR*, ix (1931), 1–18.

Richardson, H.G. and Sayles, G.O., 'The Earliest Known Official Use of the Term "Parliament"', *EHR*, 82 (1967), 474–50.

Riches, Samantha, *St George: Hero, Martyr and Myth* (Stroud, 2000).

Richmond, Colin, 'Religion and the Fifteenth-Century Gentleman', *Church, Politics and Patronage*, ed. R.B. Dobson (Gloucester, 1984), 193–208.

Richmond, Colin, 'An English Mafia?', *Nottingham Medieval Studies*, xxxvi (1992), 235–43.

Richmond, Colin, 'An Outlaw and Some Peasants: The Possible Significance of Robin Hood', *Nottingham Medieval Studies*, xxxvii (1993), 90–101.

Richmond, Colin, 'Religion', *Fifteenth-Century Attitudes*, ed. Rosemary Horrox (Cambridge, 1994), 183–201.

Rigg, A.G., 'Propaganda of the Hundred Years War: Poems on the Battles of Crécy and Durham (1346): A Critical Edition', *Traditio*, 54 (1999), 169–211.

Roberts, Michael, *The Military Revolution, 1560–1660: An Inaugural Lecture Delivered Before the Queen's University of Belfast* (Belfast, 1956).

Robinson, Durant W. Jr, *A Preface to Chaucer: Studies in Medieval Perspectives* (Princeton, 1962).

Rodger, N.A.M., *The Safeguard of the Sea: A Naval History of Britain, I, 660–1649* (London, 2004).

Rogers, Clifford J., 'The Military Revolutions of the Hundred Years War', *Journal of Military History*, 57 (1993), 241–78.

Rogers, Clifford J., 'Edward III and the Dialectics of Strategy', *TRHS*, 6th ser. iv (1994), 83–102.

Rogers, Clifford J., ed., *The Military Revolution Debate: Readings on the Military Transformation of Early Modern Europe* (Boulder, 1995).

Rogers, Clifford J., 'The Efficacy of the English Longbow: A Reply to Kelly DeVries, *War in History*, 5 (1998), 233–42.

Rogers, Clifford J., ed., *The Wars of Edward III: Sources and Interpretations* (Woodbridge, 1999).

Rogers, Clifford J., *War Cruel and Sharp: English Strategy Under Edward III, 1327–1360* (Woodbridge, 2000).

Rogers, Clifford J., 'The Vegetian "Science of Warfare"', *Journal of Medieval Military History I*, ed. Bernard S. Bachrach (Woodbridge, 2002), 1–19.

Roney, Lois, 'Winner and Waster's "Wyse Wordes": Teaching Economics and Nationalism in Fourteenth-Century England', *Speculum*, 69 (1994), 1070–1100.

Roskell, J.S., 'The Problem of the Attendance of the Lords in Medieval Parliaments', *BIHR*, xxix (1956), 153–204.

Roskell, J.S., Clarke, L. and Rawcliffe, C., eds, *History of Parliament, 1386–1421* (Stroud, 1993).

Ross, C.D., 'Forfeiture for Treason in the Reign of Richard II', *EHR*, 71 (1956), 560–75.

Russell, P., *The English Intervention in Spain and Portugal in the Reigns of Edward III and Richard II* (Oxford, 1955).

Sadie, S., ed., *The New Grove Dictionary of Music and Musicians* (London, 1980).

Salter, Elizabeth, 'The Timeliness of Wynnere and Wastoure', *Medium Aevum*, 47 (1978), 40–65.

Saul, Nigel, 'Chaucer and Gentility', *Chaucer's England: Literature in Historical Context*, ed. Barbara A. Hanawalt (Minnesota, 1992), 41–55.

Saul, Nigel, *Richard II* (New Haven and London, 1997).

Saul, Nigel, 'The Kingship of Richard II', *Richard II: The Art of Kingship*, ed. A. Goodman and J. Gillespie (Oxford, 1999), 37–58.

Saul, Nigel, *Death, Art, and Memory in Medieval England: The Cobham Family and their Monuments, 1300–1500* (Oxford, 2001).

Saul, Nigel, 'A Farewell to Arms? Criticism of Warfare in Late Fourteenth-Century England', *Fourteenth Century England II*, ed. Chris Given-Wilson (Woodbridge, 2002), 132–7.

Saunders, Andrew, 'Administrative Buildings and Prisons in the Earldom of Cornwall', *Warriors and Churchmen in the Middle Ages: Essays Presented to Karl Leyser*, ed. Timothy Reuter (London and Rio Grande, 1992), 199–204.

Scattergood, V.J. and Sherborne, J.W., eds, *English Court Culture in the Later Middle Ages* (London, 1983).

Scattergood, V.J., 'Fashion and Morality in the Late Middle Ages', *England in the Fifteenth Century*, ed. Daniel Williams (Woodbridge, 1987), 255–72.

Schrader, Charles R., 'A Handlist of the Extant Manuscripts containing the *De re militari* of Flavius Vegetius Renatus', *Scriptorium*, 33 (1979), 280–305.

Schrader, Charles R., 'The Influence of Vegetius' *De re militari*', *Military Affairs*, 45 (1981), 167–72.

Scott, Susan and Duncan, Christopher J., *Biology of Plagues: Evidence from Historical Populations* (Cambridge, 2001).

Sekules, Veronica, 'Dynasty and Patrimony in the Self-Construction of an English Queen: Philippa of Hainault and her Images', *England and the Continent in the Middle Ages. Studies in Memory of Andrew Martindale*, ed. John Mitchell (Stamford, 2000), 157–74.

Sharp, Buchanan, 'The Food Riots of 1347 and the Medieval Moral Economy', *Moral Economy and Popular Protest: Crowds, Conflict and Authority*, eds Adrian Randall and Andrew Charlesworth (Houndsmill, 2000), 33–54.

Sharpe, Margaret, 'The Administrative Chancery of the Black Prince Before 1362', *Essays in Medieval History Presented to T.F. Tout*, eds A.G. Little and F.M. Powicke (Manchester, 1925), 321–33.

Sherborne, J.W., 'Aspects of English Court Culture in the Later Fourteenth Century', *English Court Culture in the Later Middle Ages*, eds V.J. Scattergood and J.W. Sherborne (London, 1983), 1–27.

Showalter, Dennis E., 'Caste, Skill and Training: The Evolution of Cohesion in European Armies from the Middle Ages to the Sixteenth Century', *Journal of Military History*, 57 (1993), 407–30.

Smith, Robert D., 'Artillery and the Hundred Years War: Myth and Interpretation', *Arms, Armies and Fortifications in the Hundred Years War*, eds Anne Curry and M. Hughes (Woodbridge, 1994), 151–60.

Soule, Claude, *Les Etats Généraux de France (1302–1789). Etude historique, comparative et doctrinale* (Heule, 1968).

Southworth, John, *The English Medieval Minstrel* (Woodbridge, 1980).

St John, W. Hope, *History of the London Charterhouse* (London, 1925).

Steane, John M., *The Archaeology of Power: England and Northern Europe AD 800–1600* (Stroud, 2001).

Stirland, Ann, *Raising the Dead: The Skeleton Crew of Henry VIII's Great Ship, the Mary Rose* (Chichester, 2000).

Storey-Challenger, S., *L'administration anglaise du Ponthieu après le traité de Brétigny, 1361–1369* (Abbeville, 1975).

Strickland, Mathew, 'A Law of Arms or a Law of Treason? Conduct in War in Edward I's Campaigns in Scotland, 1296–1307', *Violence in Medieval Society*, ed. Richard Kaeuper (Woodbridge, 2000), 39–78.

Stroud, Michael, 'Chivalric Terminology in Late Medieval Literature', *Journal of the History of Ideas*, 37 (1976), 323–34.

Sumption, Jonathan, *The Hundred Years War, I: Trial by Battle* (London, 1990).

Sumption, Jonathan, *The Hundred Years War, II: Trial by Fire* (London, 1999).

Sutton, Anne F. and Visser-Fuchs, Livia, ' "Chevalerie . . . in som partie is worthi forto be commendid, and in some part to ben ammendid": Chivalry and the Yorkist Kings', *St George's Chapel, Windsor, in the Late Middle Ages*, eds Colin Richmond and Eileen Scarff (Windsor, 2001), 107–33.

Swanson, R.N., *Church and Society in Late Medieval England* (Oxford, 1989).

Taylor, Craig, 'Edward III and the Plantagenet Claim to the French Throne', *The Age of Edward III*, ed. J.S. Bothwell (York, 2001), 155–69.

Taylor, Craig, 'The Salic Law and the Valois Succession to the French Crown', *French History*, 15 (2001), 358–77.

Taylor, John, 'The Manuscripts of the *Modus Tenendi Parliamentum*', *EHR*, 83 (1968), 673–88.

Taylor, John, 'The Good Parliament and its Sources', *Politics and Crisis in Fourteenth-Century England*, eds W.R. Childs and J. Taylor (Gloucester, 1990), 81–96.

Taylor, John, 'Richard II in the Chronicles', *Richard II: The Art of Kingship*, ed. A. Goodman and J. Gillespie (Oxford, 1999), 15–36.

Taylor, William F., *The Charterhouse of London* (London, 1912).

Thompson, Norma, *The Ship of State: Statecraft and Politics from Ancient Greece to Democratic America* (New Haven and London, 2001).

Thomson, J.A.F., *The Transformation of Medieval England, 1370–1529* (Harlow, 1983).

Thomson, J.A.F., 'Orthodox Religion and the Origins of Lollardy', *History*, 74 (1989), 39–55.

Thomson, J.A.F., 'Knightly Piety and the Margins of Lollardy', *Lollardy and Gentry in the Later Middle Ages*, ed. Margaret Aston and Colin Richmond (Stroud, 1997), 95–111.

Thurley, Simon, *Royal Palaces of Tudor England* (New Haven and London, 1993).

Tout, T.F., 'The Tactics of the Battles of Boroughbridge and Morlaix', *EHR*, 19 (1904), 711–15.

Tout, T.F., 'Firearms in England in the Fourteenth Century', *EHR*, 26 (1911), 666–702.

Tout, T.F., *Chapters in the Administrative History of Mediaeval England: The Wardrobe, the Chamber and the Small Seal*, 6 vols (Manchester, 1920–33).

Tuck, A., 'Carthusian Monks and Lollard Knights: Religious Attitudes at the Court of Richard II', *Studies in the Age of Chaucer, Proceedings I: Reconstructing Chaucer*, eds Paul Strohm and T.J. Heffernan (Knoxville (TN), 1984), 149–61.

Tucoo-Chala, Pierre, *Gaston Fébus: un grand prince d'Occident au XIVe siècle* (Pau, 1976).

Turner, Ralph V., 'The Meaning of Magna Carta since 1215', *History Today*, 53 (2003), 29–35.

Tyson, Diana, 'The Epitaph of the Black Prince', *Medium Aevum*, 46 (1977), 98–104.

Tyson, Diana, 'Authors, Patrons and Soldiers – Some Thoughts on Some Old French Soldiers' *Lives*', *Nottingham Medieval Studies*, xlii (1998), 105–20.

Ullmann, Walter, *Medieval Political Thought* (Harmondsworth, 1975).

Ullmann, Walter, 'This Realm of England is an Empire', *Journal of Ecclesiastical History*, 30 (1979), 175–203.

Underhill, Frances A., 'Elizabeth de Burgh: Connoisseur and Patron', *The Cultural Patronage of Medieval Women*, ed. June Hall McCosh (Athens (Geo.), 1996), 266–87.

Vale, Juliet, *Edward III and Chivalry: Chivalrous Society and its Context, 1270–1350* (Woodbridge, 1982).

Vale, Juliet, 'Violence and the Tournament', *Violence in Medieval Society*, ed. Richard Kaeuper (Woodbridge, 2000), 143–58.

Vale, M.G.A., *Charles VII* (London, 1974).

Vale, M.G.A., *Chivalry and Warfare: Warfare and Aristocratic Culture in England, France and Burgundy at the End of the Middle Ages* (Athens (Geo.), 1981), 1–12.

Vale, M.G.A., *The Angevin Legacy and the Hundred Years War, 1250–1340* (Oxford, 1990).

Vale, M.G.A., 'Aristocratic Violence: Trial by Battle in the Later Middle Ages', *Violence in Medieval Society*, ed. Richard Kaeuper (Woodbridge, 2000), 159–81.

Vale, M.G.A., *The Princely Court: Medieval Courts and Culture in North-West Europe* (Oxford, 2001).

Valente, Claire, 'The Deposition and Abdication of Edward II', *EHR*, 113 (1998), 852–81.

Valente, Claire, 'The *Lament of Edward II*: Religious Lyric, Political Propaganda', *Speculum*, 77 (2002), 422–39.

Vanderjagt, Arjo, 'Qui sa vertu anoblist'. *The Concepts of noblesse and chose publiques in Burgundian Political Thought* (Groningen, 1981).

Verbruggen, J.F., *The Art of Warfare in Western Europe During the Middle Ages: From the Eighth Century to 1340*, trans. Sumner Willard and Mrs R.W. Southern, 2nd ed. (Woodbridge, 1997).

Verbruggen, J.F., 'Flemish Urban Militias Against the French Cavalry Armies in the Fourteenth and Fifteenth Centuries', trans. Kelly DeVries, *Journal of Medieval Military History I*, ed. Bernard S. Bachrach (Woodbridge, 2002), 145–69.

Verbruggen, J.F., *The Battle of the Golden Spurs: Courtrai, 11 July 1302*, ed. Kelly DeVries, trans. David Richard Ferguson (Woodbridge, 2002).

Viard, J., 'La campagne de juillet-août et la bataille de Crécy', *Le Moyen Age*, 2nd ser. xxvii (1926), 1–84.

Walker, Simon, *The Lancastrian Affinity, 1361–1399* (Oxford, 1990).

Walker, Simon, 'Letters to the Dukes of Lancaster in 1381 and 1399', *EHR*, 106 (1991), 75–9.

Walsh, Katherine, *A Fourteenth Century Scholar and Primate: Richard FitzRalph in Oxford, Armagh and Avignon* (Oxford, 1981).

Ward, Jennifer, 'Elizabeth de Burgh, Lady of Clare (d. 1360)', *Medieval London Widows, 1300–1500*, ed. Caroline Barron and Anne Sutton (London and Rio Grande, 1994), 29–45.

Ward, Jennifer, ed. and trans., *Women of the English Nobility and Gentry, 1066–1500* (Manchester, 1995).

Watson, Fiona, 'Settling the Stalemate: Edward I's Peace in Scotland, 1303–1305', *Thirteenth Century England VI*, eds Michael Prestwich, Richard Britnell and Robin Frame (Woodbridge, 1997), 127–44.

Waugh, Scott L., *England in the Reign of Edward III* (Cambridge, 1991).

Waugh, W.T., 'The Lollard Knights', *Scottish Historical Review*, xi (1913–14), 55–92.

Weber, A.S., 'Queu du Roi, Roi des Quex: Taillevent and the Profession of Medieval Cooking', *Food and Eating in Medieval Europe*, eds Martha Carlin and Joel T. Rosenthal (London and Rio Grande, 1998), 145–58.

Weber, Max, 'Politics as a Vocation', *From Max Weber*, ed. and trans. H.H. Gerth and C.W. Mills (Oxford, 1946), 77–128.

Weber, Max, *Wirtschaft und Gesellschaft*, 5th ed. (Tübingen, 1976).

Webster, M., 'John Dabernon and his Will', *Devon and Cornwall Notes and Queries*, 36 (1989), 176–84.

Wentersdorf, Karl P., 'The Clandestine Marriages of the Fair Maid of Kent', *Journal of Medieval History*, 5 (1979), 203–31.

Whitaker, Muriel A., '"Pearl" and Some Illustrated Apocalypse Manuscripts', *Viator*, 12 (1981), 183–96.

Whitely, Mary, 'The Courts of Edward III and Charles V', *Fourteenth Century England I*, ed. Nigel Saul (Woodbridge, 2000), 153–66.

Wilkins, Nigel, 'Music and Poetry at Court: England and France in the Late Middle Ages', *English Court Culture in the Later Middle Ages*, eds V.J. Scattergood and J.W. Sherborne (London, 1983), 183–204.

Wilkinson, B., *The Chancery under Edward III* (Manchester, 1929).

Wilkinson, B., *Constitutional History of Medieval England, 1216–1399, II: Politics and the Constitution, 1307–1399* (London, 1952).

Wilks, Michael, *The Problem of Sovereignty in the Later Middle Ages* (Cambridge, 1963).

Wilks, Michael, 'Wyclif and Hus as Leaders of Religious Protest Movements', *Schism, Heresy and Protest* [SCH, 9], ed. Derek Baker (Cambridge, 1972), 109–30.

Wilks, Michael, *Wyclif: Political Ideas and Practice. Papers by Michael Wilks* (Exeter, 2000).

Williams, C.R., ed., *The History of Flintshire from Earliest Times to the Act of Union* (Denbigh, 1961).

Windeatt, B., ed., *English Mystics of the Later Middle Ages* (Cambridge, 1994).

Wood, Diana, ed., *The Church and Sovereignty, c.590–1918* [SCH Subsidia 9], (Oxford, 1991).

Wood, Diana, 'Rule from Europe? Four English Views of Papal Authority in the Fourteenth Century', *England and the Continent in the Middle Ages: Studies in Memory of Andrew Martindale: Proceedings of the 1996 Harlaxton Symposium*, ed. John Mitchell (Stamford, 2000), 97–112.

Woolgar, C.M., *The Great Household in Late Medieval England* (New Haven and London, 1999).

Wright, Nicholas, *Knights and Peasants: The Hundred Years War in the French Countryside* (Woodbridge, 1998).

Ziegler, J.E., 'Edward III and Low Country Finances: 1338–1340, with Particular Emphasis on the Dominant Position of Brabant', *Revue Belge de Philologie et d'Histoire*, 61 (1983), 802–17.

Zmora, Hillay, *Monarchy, Aristocracy and State in Europe, 1300–1800* (London, 2000).

INDEX

Salisbury, John of, author of *Policraticus*
 (*c*.1115–80) 133, 137
Saône, River 55
Sarum, Use of 66
Saxoferrano, Bartolus de, Italian jurist
 (d. 1357) 84
Scotland 1, 4–8, 12, 16–17, 19, 28–30,
 34, 39, 41, 48, 93, 104, 136, 142,
 146, 149, 155, 160, 187
Secretum Secretorum 126, 151
Seine, River 55
Selwood (Somer.) 170
shame 79, 91, 103–4, 172
Sheen (Surrey) 125–6
Shenley (Herts.) 179
Shotwick (Ches.) 112
Shropshire 68, 157
Sicily 112
sieges 10, 12, 15, 36, 47–9, 90, 92–3
Shareshull, William, justice (1289/
 90–1370) 158 nn. 57–8
Sir Gawain and the Green Knight 1, 81,
 102, 111
Skirbeck, John, steward of Cornwall 11, 128
Sluys, battle of (1340) 12, 32
Smithfield (London) 110, 112, 171
Somerset 62
Somersham (Hunts.) 112
Somme, River 36, 46
Song against the King's Taxes (*c*.1340) 143
Song of the Husbandman (*c*.1340) 143
sovereignty 13–14, 17–19, 21–2, 27–8,
 108, 120, 125, 132–3, 173
Spain/Spanish 14, 22, 90, 112, 155–6,
 170, 179
Speaker of the House 158
 see also Peter de la Mare
Spiritual Franciscans 175
Stacy, William, Tavistock burgess 60
Stafford, Ralph, 1st earl of Stafford
 (1301–72) 29
Stafford, Richard, Lord Stafford of Clifton
 (*c*.1305–80) 131
Staffordshire 68
Stakford, Gilbert, minstrel 111
Stamford (Lincs.) 112
State, *see also* Max Weber 8, 91, 93, 114,
 121–2, 138 n. 165, 142, 152, 153,
 160, 182, 188–9
Statutes
 Statute of Additions (1413) 97
 Statute of Labourers (1351) 58, 62

Statute of Praemunire (1353) 173
Statute of Provisors (1351) 173
Statute of Purveyors (1352) 158
Statute of Quia Emptores (1290) 75
Statute of Treasons (1352) 94
Stratton, William, the prince's tailor 11
Stury, Richard, 'Lollard knight' (*c*.1327–95)
 178, 181
Sully, John (d. *c*.1388) 29, 112
sumptuary laws 59, 64, 96–7, 99, 113,
 117–18
Suso, Heinrich, German mystic
 (1295–1366) 66
Swinderby, William, Lollard preacher 176
Swynford, Katherine, née Katherine Roelt,
 duchess of Lancaster (*c*.1350–1403)
 15
Swynnerton, Robert, dean of St Mary's,
 Stafford and rector of Barrow (Ches.)
 67

Taillebourg, battle of (1351) 43
Tauler, Johannes, German Dominican and
 mystic (*c*.1300–61) 66
Tavistock (Devon) 60, 170
taxation 32, 46, 63, 137, 142–8, 151, 153,
 155–7, 183, 186, 189
 attacks on tax revenue 46, 73, 74, 90
 church 174
 exemption 80
 France 73–4, 149
 papal 154
 see also fouage, poll tax
Tello, Don, brother of Enrique of
 Trastamara 95
Thames Valley 123
Thomas of Lancaster, 2nd earl of Lancaster,
 2nd earl of Leicester, earl of Lincoln
 (*c*.1278–1322) 4, 93
Thomists 173
Three Living and the Three Dead 66
Three Orders 77, 90, 96 and n. 82
Tintagel (Corn.) 127
Tirel, Guillaume de (Taillevent), author of
 Le viander (*c*.1310–95) 116
Toledo cathedral 170
Totesham, Richard, governor of La
 Rochelle, seneschal of Saintonge,
 Angoumois, steward of Bigorre
 34
Touraine 26
Tournai 10, 46